Issues in Eucharistic Praying
in East and West

Issues in Eucharistic Praying in East and West

Essays in Liturgical and Theological Analysis

Edited by
Maxwell E. Johnson

A PUEBLO BOOK

Liturgical Press   Collegeville, Minnesota
www.litpress.org

A Pueblo Book published by Liturgical Press

Cover design by David Manahan, OSB. Illustration by Frank Kacmarcik, OblSB

Library of Congress Cataloging-in-Publication Data

Issues in Eucharistic praying in East and West : essays in liturgical and theological analysis / edited by Maxwell E. Johnson.
        p.   cm.
Includes index.
"A Pueblo Book."
ISBN 978-0-8146-6227-4 — ISBN 978-0-8146-6248-9 (e-book)
1. Eucharistic prayers—Catholic Church—History and criticism.
2. Catholic Church—Liturgy—Texts—History and criticism.   3. Eucharistic prayers—Eastern churches—History and criticism.   4. Eastern churches—Liturgy—Texts—History and criticism. I. Johnson, Maxwell E., 1952–

BX2015.6.I77   2011
264'.02036—dc22   2010032156

Contents

Maxwell E. Johnson

Introduction

In 1997 my former dissertation director and now Notre Dame colleague Paul F. Bradshaw edited an important volume titled *Essays on Early Eastern Eucharistic Prayers*,[1] a collection containing several essays by then-graduate students from a Notre Dame doctoral seminar in liturgical studies that Bradshaw had offered on the development of Eucharistic prayers in the Christian East, together with the inclusion of essays by other colleagues. Since Bradshaw has referred to me on occasion as his "alter ego,"[2] it should come as no surprise that this collection of essays has a similar genesis. That is, several of the essays in this collection also stem from various Notre Dame doctoral seminars I have been privileged to lead over the last five years or so on liturgical topics like the anaphora, the Sanctus, the Eucharistic prayer, and, most recently, liturgy in ancient Jerusalem. And, also similar to the earlier volume, to which this could easily be viewed as a companion, essays by colleagues in the field of liturgiology, both from the United States and abroad, including Bradshaw himself, are also included.

How this volume differs from the earlier *Essays on Early Eastern Eucharistic Prayers* is that not only are Western Eucharistic prayers also included (e.g., essays that deal directly or indirectly with the Roman *canon missae*) but that contemporary issues are included as well (e.g., the sources of the Eucharistic prefaces in the *Missale Romanum* of Paul VI [1969] as well as attention to the use of the anaphora of *Addai and Mari* by the Assyrian Church of the East and the Assyro-Chaldean Catholic Church). In so doing it is intended that a wider audience may be reached by focusing on some theological-liturgical issues beyond specific Eucharistic prayers.

---

1. Paul F. Bradshaw, ed., *Essays on Early Eastern Eucharistic Prayer* (Collegeville: Liturgical Press, 1997).

2. Paul F. Bradshaw, "Is Liturgical History a Thing of the Past?" Berakah Response, *Proceedings* (2008): 32.

This is not to say, however, that the Eucharistic prayers of the Christian East do not receive a major focus in this collection. Indeed, there is probably no Eastern Christian tradition, except the Georgian, that is not dealt with to some extent herein. These essays address liturgical issues related to the anaphora of *Addai and Mari*, the reservation of what is called the *Malka* in East Syrian Christianity, various views of Eucharistic "consecration" in the Byzantine liturgy, essays on classic Eastern texts like the Strasbourg Papyrus and the Barcelona Papyrus, possible Egyptian influence on Jerusalem Eucharistic praying, the Armenian anaphora of St. Athanasius, the Basilian anaphoras, the entrance of the Sanctus into the Eucharistic prayer, and, certainly not least, the quite probably Eastern (West Syrian) origins of the anaphora of the so-called *Apostolic Tradition*—traditionally ascribed to Hippolytus of Rome in the early third century (ca. 217) but most likely neither Hippolytan nor Roman nor third century.[3]

This collection is organized thematically rather than chronologically, especially because the various anaphoras and other issues dealt with often come from within the same historical periods but from differing churches and/or geographical areas. The collection begins with a New Testament essay, Paul Bradshaw's "Did Jesus Institute the Eucharist at the Last Supper?" which challenges traditional assumptions not only about the Last Supper narratives in the synoptic Gospels and Paul but of the very use and theology of that narrative in early Christian prayer. Bradshaw juxtaposes the "body and blood" language of the synoptic and Pauline narratives to the "flesh" language of the Johannine tradition and the influence of both on early Christianity, arguing for different Eucharistic theologies as the result, one focused more on Christ's sacrifice and the other more on communion with him.

Since it is widely accepted that the classic East Syrian anaphora called *Addai and Mari* originally contained no such institution narrative, and still does not in the liturgical practice of the Assyrian Church of the East, the next essay, Nick Russo's "The Validity of the Anaphora of *Addai and Mari*: Critique of the Critiques," fits logically here after Bradshaw's piece. In this essay, however, Russo is less concerned with the historical issues surrounding *Addai and Mari*, although he does treat those in detail, and much more with contemporary reactions to the July 2001 Pontifical Council for Promoting Christian Unity

---

3. On this see P. Bradshaw, M. Johnson, and L.E. Phillips, *The Apostolic Tradition: A Commentary*, Hermeneia (Minneapolis: Fortress Press, 2002).

document *Guidelines for Admission to the Eucharist between the Chaldean Church and the Assyrian Church of the East*, which actually permits officially Chaldean Catholics to commune at liturgies of the Assyrian Church of the East using the *Anaphora of Addai and Mari* without an institution narrative recited in it. Not surprisingly, these guidelines have been both highly praised by several major liturgical scholars, including Robert Taft and Enrico Mazza, and severely criticized by others. Russo leads us through these reactions and into a deeper awareness of the theological issues involved.

Staying within East Syria for the present, Bryan Spinks's essay, "The Mystery of the Holy Leaven (*Malka*) in the East Syrian Tradition," introduces us to another way of providing continuity between the current Eucharistic celebration of the Assyrian Church of the East and the Last Supper. That is, a powdery substance called the Holy Leaven or *Malka* is reserved and a portion is mixed with the bread made for every Eucharistic celebration. This *Malka*, renewed every year at the Holy Thursday *Qurbana* (Divine Liturgy), is believed to have come from the loaves used at the Last Supper itself. As Spinks writes:

> the *Malka* serves to relate and link what the Church is doing now with what was done then in the upper room. It is the Holy Leaven rather than a spoken narrative that provides continuity with what was done at the Last Supper. Symbol takes the place of words. Canon law in requiring the use of the *Malka* for a valid Eucharist expresses the sacramentality of the *Malka*. Just as the omission of the Words of Institution in the Roman rite would render the Mass invalid, so without the *Malka*, the Church of the East celebration would not be a legitimate and valid Eucharist, because the continuity with the Last Supper would be lost.[4]

The next two essays both deal with relationships between the Christian East and Roman Eucharistic praying. Matthieu Smyth in "The Anaphora of the So-called 'Apostolic Tradition' and the Roman Eucharistic Prayer,"[5] based on the developing scholarly consensus regarding the origins, authenticity, and provenance of the *Apostolic Tradition*, demonstrates that the influential anaphora of chapter 4, which makes

4. Spinks, 67 below.

5. This essay originally appeared in French as "L'anaphore de la prétendue 'Tradition Apostolique' et la prière eucharistique Romaine," *Revue des sciences religieuses* 81, no. 1 (2007): 95–118. It appears here in English translation by my Notre Dame colleague Michael Driscoll, associate professor of theology.

it into almost all contemporary Western liturgical rites in some version, displays what only can be called a "West Syrian" or "Antiochene" anaphoral pattern. That is, in spite of what both scholars and liturgical reformers argued in the early twentieth century, the so-called "Eucharistic prayer of Hippolytus of Rome," the foundation for Eucharistic Prayer II in the Roman Rite today, was not and is not Roman, and, in fact, as Smyth demonstrates, much of the Roman Canon is actually older than this prayer!

A correlation between Roman Eucharistic praying, that is, the Roman *canon missae*, and Eastern Eucharistic praying, in this case, the Alexandrian Strasbourg Papyrus, is argued by Walter Ray in "Rome and Alexandria: Two Cities, One Anaphoral Tradition." Although it has often been asserted by scholars that the Roman *canon missae* and the Alexandrian anaphora known as St. Mark had a common origin, Ray's approach builds on the work of Enrico Mazza and Geoffrey Cuming on the Strasbourg Papyrus and argues that what is common both to the canon and to St. Mark is Strasbourg's tripartite anaphoral structure, which both prayers expanded in similar ways, perhaps even as derived from each other or by both from a common source. This common source, he suggests, however tentatively, may have been in use at Jerusalem before Cyril (John) in the fourth century.

Paul Bradshaw's essay "The Barcelona Papyrus and the Development of Early Eucharistic Prayers" continues the Egyptian theme of Eucharistic praying since the fourth-century Barcelona Papyrus is usually identified as the earlier Greek version of the seventh-century Louvain Coptic Papyrus, both of which take their place in the evolution of Alexandrian anaphoral development. Responding gratefully and critically to the recent edition and commentary on the Barcelona Papyrus by Michael Zheltov, "The Anaphora and the Thanksgiving Prayer from the Barcelona Papyrus: An Underestimated Testimony to the Anaphoral History in the Fourth Century,"[6] Bradshaw suggests that, in addition to the Egyptian elements that are clearly present in the prayer (e.g., pre-Sanctus and Sanctus), other elements more characteristic of a West Syrian anaphoral pattern akin to the anaphora in chapter 4 of the so-called *Apostolic Tradition* may point to an Antiochene origin for the core of the prayer, which would have then been expanded into its final form at the time the papyrus itself was produced. He says, "both [prayers, the cores of Barcelona and *Apostolic Tradition*] originate out of

6. *Vigiliae Christianae* 62 (2008): 467–504.

a shared tradition of anaphoral construction, and one that seems more likely to have been in West Syria than in Egypt, although the existence of such a variant tradition in Egypt cannot be entirely ruled out."[7]

An Egyptian relationship to Syro-Palestine Eucharistic praying in the third and fourth centuries, which the two previous essays by Ray and Bradshaw have touched upon, is analyzed more directly by John Paul Abdelsayed in "Liturgical Exodus in Reverse: A Reevaluation of the Egyptian Elements in the Jerusalem Liturgy." Basing his approach on the earlier well-known essays by Geoffrey Cuming[8] and Bryan Spinks,[9] Abdelsayed brings the topic up to date by attention to more recent scholarship and by attention to the how and why of Egyptian influence in early Christian liturgy.

My own contribution, "Recent Research on the Anaphoral Sanctus: An Update and Hypothesis," offers a summary of the *status questionis* on the interpolation of the Sanctus into Eucharistic praying. After summarizing the work of Robert Taft, Bryan Spinks, and Gabriele Winkler, the latter of which will take us into the Ethiopian liturgical tradition, I offer a tentative hypothesis on the *theological* reasons why the Sanctus would have entered the anaphora in the first place. That is, based on suggestions by both Spinks and Winkler, I argue that, while scholarship has rightly been concerned with the what, when, and how of the anaphoral interpolation of the Sanctus, the theological why of its inclusion also needs attention and may provide one underestimated key to the puzzle of its anaphoral use.

Based on his doctoral dissertation, written at the University of Tübingen under the direction of Gabriele Winkler, Hans-Jürgen Feulner's essay, "The Armenian Anaphora of St. Athanasius," introduces readers, many here for the first time I suspect, to the Eucharistic prayer in the *Badarag* (Divine Liturgy) of the Armenian Apostolic and Armenian Catholic Churches. In this model essay of comparative liturgiology, Feulner provides an English translation of the entire Eucharistic prayer as well as a detailed commentary on its historical and theological development, together with underscoring the Syrian, Byzantine, and even Roman influences on this ancient Christian tradition.

---

7. Bradshaw, p. 137 below.

8. G.J. Cuming, "Egyptian Elements in the Jerusalem Liturgy," *Journal of Theology Studies* 25 (1974): 117–24.

9. Bryan Spinks, "The Jerusalem Liturgy of the *Catecheses Mystagogicae*: Syrian or Egyptian?" *Studia Patristica* 18.2 (1989): 391–96.

In an appendix to this essay, the complete text of this anaphora in English translation is also provided.

Apart from the anaphora in *Apostolic Tradition* 4, probably no other Eucharistic prayer has generated so much modern ecumenical interest and use as the anaphora known as St. Basil, a prayer existing in multiple Eastern versions—Egyptian, Syriac, Armenian, and, of course, Byzantine—and used today as the basis for Eucharistic Prayer IV in the *Missale Romanum* of Pope Paul VI and for Prayer D in the American *Book of Common Prayer*, the latter of which, originally composed as an ecumenical Eucharistic prayer by Marion Hatchett (Episcopal), Eugene Brand (Lutheran), Don Saliers (Methodist), Aidan Kavanagh (Roman Catholic), and several others,[10] was subsequently copied in other contemporary Protestant worship books. Anne Vorhes McGowan's essay, "The Basilian Anaphoras: Rethinking the Question," offers a detailed and critical summary of the *status questionis*, based primarily on current German scholarship, most especially an appreciative analysis of the work of Gabriele Winkler from her recent monograph, *Das Basilius-Anaphora*.[11]

With his essay "The Moment of Eucharistic Consecration in Byzantine Thought," Russian scholar Michael Zheltov, whose work on the Barcelona Papyrus has been noted already above, brings us into the Byzantine world of Eastern Orthodoxy. He offers here an important and necessary corrective to the widespread misunderstanding, especially, but not only, in the West, that Byzantine Christianity understands the "consecration" of the Eucharist as the "epiclesis" of the Holy Spirit in distinction to the recital of the narrative of institution, which, since Ambrose of Milan, has tended to characterize Western practice and theology. Rather, Zheltov notes that in spite of official positions, in the Byzantine liturgical tradition "consecration" is attributed to the anaphora itself, to intinction or commixture, and even to elevation, the major focus of his study. In so doing he also introduces English readers to a variety of Russian liturgical scholarship.

10. Marion Hatchett, *A Common Eucharistic Prayer* (New York: Church Publishing Co., 1975).

11. G. Winkler, *Das Basilius-Anaphora: Edition der beiden armenischen Redaktionen und der relevanten Fragmente, Übersetzung und Zusammenschau aller Versionen im Licht der orientalischen Überlieferungen*, Anaphorae Orientales 2: Anaphorae Armeniacae 2 (Rome: Pontificio Istituto Orientale, 2005).

The issue of consecration is also addressed, though in a very different context, by Albertus G.A. Horsting in "Transfiguration of Flesh: Literary and Theological Connections between Martyrdom Accounts and Eucharistic Prayers." Horsting not only shows the overall Eucharistic context of and themes present in various martyrdom accounts but also notes that the connection is so strong between the martyrs and the Eucharist that their bodies—or other remains (relics)—would become viewed and venerated as "eucharistized," consecrated, or holy (bones "more valuable than gold," according to the account of the *Martyrdom of Polycarp*), with which and with whom some form of communion at their tombs would be sought.

Due perhaps to the contemporary dominance and presumed normativeness of the Syro-Byzantine or Antiochene patterns of Eucharistic praying, or because it was believed that the anaphora in *Apostolic Tradition* 4 was the *original* Roman prayer, liturgical scholars and practitioners alike have tended to ignore the Roman *canon missae*. In "The Mother of God, the Forerunner, and the Saints of the Roman Canon: A Euchological *Deësis*," Neil J. Roy provides not only a summary of the development of the *canon missae* but also opens a window to view the artistry of the final form of the text. Here he concerns himself especially with the parallel listings of the saints before and after the narrative of institution, both in the *Communicantes* (beginning with Mary) and the *Nobis quoque peccatoribus* (beginning with John the Baptist), forming, as it were, a euchological *deësis*, similar to the common iconographic depictions of the same, especially in the Christian East, where the *Theotokos* and John the Baptist flank Christ in worship and intercession.

Finally, Nathaniel Marx's essay, "The Revision of the Prefaces in the Missal of Paul VI," offers a clear and detailed analysis of the sources used in the compilation of the current Roman Eucharistic prefaces. Marx demonstrates, against those who would denigrate the *Missale Romanum* of Paul VI as being something only "new" or "cavalier" created by experts reflecting only the contemporary age, that the prefaces themselves are the product of serious engagement with the very sources of the Roman euchological tradition as that tradition is known through the available liturgical sources used in their composition. Marx suggests the following as a way to guide our thoughts on liturgical revision:

> Perhaps the work of revising liturgical texts is more like tending a garden than preserving a city's architectural monuments. In addition to

caring for the best plants, it is necessary to weed out unhealthy ones, transplant some to more appropriate locations, prune back undesirable growth, graft new vines onto older stock, and plant new seeds. None of these activities need change the fundamental "character" of the garden as one grown "over the course of centuries."[12]

As we have seen already, among the essays in this collection are several that deal with the origins and early development of Eucharistic praying, part of a wider scholarship in recent years that has exposed just how much more diverse were the earliest forms than has been traditionally assumed and how much more slowly what are thought of as the classical patterns of Eucharistic prayers were in taking shape. It is sometimes imagined that the motivating force behind this research may be a desire to re-create that primitive diversity in modern practice and to remove from today's Eucharistic prayers elements, such as the narrative of institution, that are now recognized as having been somewhat later additions to ancient prayers rather than part of their primordial core.[13]

Such suspicions are, however, misplaced. Let me be perfectly clear: *Addai and Mari*, like *Didache* 9–10 and the Strasbourg Papyrus, may not have had an institution narrative originally, a practice continued by the Church of the East even today. The anaphora in chapter 4 of the so-called *Apostolic Tradition* may be neither Roman nor Hippolytan nor early third century. The Sanctus may not have been a primitive component in Eucharistic praying. But no one is suggesting that Eucharistic prayers today should be composed without narratives of institution. No one is suggesting that the multiple versions of the anaphora from *Apostolic Tradition* 4 in various liturgical traditions should not be used anymore since the prayer might not be what scholars thought it was some forty or fifty years ago. And no one is suggesting that we compose Eucharistic prayers without the inclusion of the Sanctus. Anyone who thinks that this is somehow the contemporary agenda behind historical liturgical scholarship today is simply wrong, though it is clear

12. Marx, p. 381 below.

13. This appears to be the case, for example, in Gordon Lathrop's recent article, "The Reforming Gospels: A Liturgical Theologian Looks again at Eucharistic Origins," *Worship* 82 (2009): 194–212. See in particular his comment in n. 11 about Paul Bradshaw's alleged failure to articulate his own presuppositions and agendas.

that not that long ago history was considered not only instructive but also normative, that somehow the earlier a text might be, the more authoritative it was for contemporary liturgical practice. But liturgical historians do not work that way anymore. Archaeologists do not dig beneath the surface of sites where very many generations of peoples have lived and expose the different layers of habitation in order to persuade modern humans to return to the conditions of prehistoric dwellings, nor are liturgical historians bent on excavating the various strata of the past in order to restore some sort of imaginary primitive purity! The gradual development of liturgical practice involved the positive refinement and enrichment of earlier ways of thinking, speaking, and acting, even if it also tended to bring along with it elements of impoverishment and distortion.[14] But it is only when we have a clearer picture of the stages of that evolution that we are in a position to make any judgments about which of these trends were of genuine lasting value and which represented a loss of something significant from earlier times. Indeed, it is not up to liturgical historians to reform liturgy; all the historian can do is to unpack as carefully and clearly as possible the richness and diversity of the liturgical traditions as they actually appear in history. What legitimate liturgical authorities in the various churches do with the results of liturgical history in service to liturgical reform and renewal is something altogether distinct.

We hope this collection of essays will be of service to those who wish a supplementary textbook for courses in the Eucharistic liturgy, especially at the master's level, and for those involved in various ministries as a way to continue building their knowledge and understanding of various developments in Eucharistic praying today. Clearly, one of the primary goals of this volume has been to offer an update on the state of the question on various Eucharistic prayers today and, as such, it is hoped that these essays will become required reading for students of liturgy.

I want to acknowledge those people who have made this collection possible. Thanks go to the contributors themselves for trusting me to include their previously unpublished work here for the first time. Similarly, I wish to acknowledge my colleague Michael Driscoll for his translation of Matthieu Smyth's "The Anaphora of the So-called

14. See both the essay by Lathrop referred to in the preceding note and Paul F. Bradshaw, "The Homogenization of Christian Liturgy—Ancient and Modern: Presidential Address," *Studia Liturgica* 26 (1996): 1–15.

'Apostolic Tradition' and the Roman Eucharistic Prayer."[15] My thanks go as well to two scholars not represented directly in this volume but who have served as consultants for some of the essays, namely, M. Daniel Findikyan of St. Nersess Armenian Seminary, New Rochelle, New York, and Sr. Vassa Larin at the University of Vienna. My thanks go also to my graduate assistants Nathaniel Marx for his assistance in the preparation and proofing of the manuscript, and Cody Unterseher for proofreading the entire book and assisting with the index. Finally, I wish to thank both Peter Dwyer and Hans Christoffersen of Liturgical Press, Collegeville, Minnesota, for their willingness to take on this project and see it through to publication under the Pueblo imprint.

Maxwell E. Johnson
University of Notre Dame
March 25, 2010
The Annunciation of Our Lord

15. See above, note 5.

Paul F. Bradshaw

I. Did Jesus Institute the Eucharist at the Last Supper?

The answer to the question posed in my title might seem obvious: "Of course he did; we have the evidence of the Synoptic Gospels to prove it." But as you may well have guessed already, I do not think it is as simple as that. Otherwise, this would turn out to be a very short essay indeed.[1]

THE FOURTH GOSPEL

Let us start with St. John's Gospel, where there is no account of the institution of the Eucharist within the narrative of the Last Supper. Commentators usually say that John has deliberately left it out and replaced it with the account of Jesus washing the disciples' feet for his own reasons. But that is to assume that the Evangelist—and every Christian of the time—knew that the account of the institution of the Eucharist really did belong with the Last Supper, and he chose not to put it there. But that is precisely to beg the question. We do not actually know whether anyone in the first century other than the writers of the Synoptic Gospels and St. Paul thought it took place on the night before Jesus died—and even St. Paul does not say that occasion was a Passover meal as the others do. So if we suppose for the sake of argument that the writer of the Fourth Gospel did not know of a tradition that Jesus said that bread and wine were his body and blood at the

---

1. This was first given as a public lecture at the University of Notre Dame on July 12, 2006, and subsequently revised. I am grateful to my colleagues present at the lecture who offered valuable suggestions for its improvement. Some of the material in it had already appeared in a different form in my book, *Eucharistic Origins* (London: SPCK/New York: Oxford University Press, 2004), to which the reader is referred for further details on a number of points. All translations of primary sources, including Scripture texts, in this essay are by the author.

1

Last Supper, is there anywhere else in that Gospel that might look like an institution narrative?

What about chapter 6? Here we have the account of the feeding of the five thousand by Jesus, in which twelve baskets are filled with the leftovers from five barley loaves. And then, referring back to it on the following day, Jesus says that it was not Moses who gave them the bread from heaven; "my Father gives you the true bread from heaven. For the bread of God is that which comes down from heaven and gives life to the world" (John 6:32-33). And he goes on to say, "I am the bread of life. . . . I am the living bread that came down from heaven . . . and the bread that I shall give for the life of the world is my flesh" (John 6:48, 51). Several scholars have already suggested that this latter statement is John's version of the saying over the bread at the Last Supper,[2] and some have claimed that this form could in one way at least be closer to the original, as neither Hebrew nor Aramaic have a word for "body" as we understand the term, and so what Jesus would have said at the Last Supper would have been the Aramaic equivalent of "This is my flesh."[3]

There is, however, a difference of opinion among scholars as to whether what follows (and some would say even verse 51c itself) is an integral part of the material or a subsequent interpolation, either by the original author or by a later redactor.[4] This section includes the saying, "Truly, truly, I say to you unless you eat the flesh of the Son of Man and drink his blood, you do not have life in you" (John 6:53). Many who would excise these verses would do so on the grounds that the earlier sayings are sapiential in nature, while the later verses have a more decidedly sacramental character. But there is another reason why at least part of this later material may be an addition to the original core. While the concept of eating flesh might have been difficult for a Jew to comprehend, the concept of drinking blood would

---

2. The earliest to suggest this seems to have been J. H. Bernard, *A Critical and Exegetical Commentary on the Gospel according to John*, International Critical Commentary 29 (Edinburgh: T & T Clark, 1928), [clxxf.]; see also Raymond E. Brown, *The Gospel According to John, i-xii*, Anchor Bible Commentary (Garden City, NY: Doubleday, 1966), 285: "it is possible that we have preserved in vi 51 the Johannine form of the words of institution."

3. See, for example, Brown, *Gospel According to John, i-xii*, ibid.

4. For a summary of the debate, see Francis J. Moloney, *The Johannine Son of Man*, 2nd ed. (Rome: Libreria Ateneo Salesiano, 1978), 93ff.

have been an abomination. Thus it seems more likely that this part of the discourse would have been appended later, in a Gentile environment, and would not have formed part of the earlier Jewish stratum.

It seems possible, therefore, that the writer of the Fourth Gospel knew of a primitive tradition in which Jesus associated bread with his flesh, and this in the context of a feeding miracle rather than the Last Supper. But did any other early Christians know of such a tradition, or is it a peculiarity of this Gospel? Let us take a look.

EARLY CHRISTIAN DOCUMENTS

The Didache

The *Didache* or "Teaching of the Twelve Apostles" is commonly thought to be a very early Christian text, perhaps as old as the canonical Gospels themselves. Chapters 9 and 10 contain what appear to be prayers for use at a Eucharistic meal accompanied by brief directions.[5] This meal includes a cup (apparently of wine rather than water,[6] as the accompanying prayer refers to "the holy vine of David") as well as bread. The bread and wine are not described here as being either the body and blood of Christ or the flesh and blood of Christ but simply as spiritual food and drink, and so offer us little help in this regard. It is to be noted, however, that this material does not associate the meal with the Last Supper or with Jesus' death in any way. Instead, the prayers speak of Jesus as bringing life, knowledge, and eternal life— themes that are also characteristic of the Fourth Gospel.[7] And to this we may add that chapter 9 also uses the word "fragment" when speaking of the bread rather than the normal Greek word for a loaf—and fragments are explicitly mentioned in the various feeding stories in the Gospels but not in the Last Supper narratives. Could it be that behind the text in the *Didache* is a remembrance of spiritual food

5. For the Greek text and an English translation, see Kurt Niederwimmer, *The Didache: A Commentary* (Minneapolis: Fortress Press, 1998), 139–67. For the debate about the nature of the meal described in these particular chapters, see Bradshaw, *Eucharistic Origins*, chap. 2; and also idem, "Yet Another Explanation of *Didache* 9–10," *Studia Liturgica* 36 (2006): 124–28.

6. On early Eucharistic practices where water was used rather than wine, see Bradshaw, *Eucharistic Origins*, 51–55.

7. See Johannes Betz, "The Eucharist in the Didache," in *The Didache in Modern Research*, ed. Jonathan A. Draper, 244–75 (Leiden/New York: Brill, 1996).

and drink being associated with one of those stories? That suggestion may not be very convincing on its own, but let us go on to other early Christian writers.

Ignatius of Antioch

When Ignatius of Antioch mentions the Eucharist, writing in the early second century, it is Christ's flesh that he speaks of and not his body. He says, "Take care, therefore, to have one Eucharist, for there is one flesh of our Lord Jesus Christ and one cup for union in his blood" (*Philadelphians* 4). Notice that, while he includes a cup along with the reference to flesh, he does not describe the contents (which may have been wine or water—he is not explicit about this) directly as blood. In another letter he also criticizes some because "they abstain from Eucharist and prayer, because they do not confess the Eucharist to be flesh of our Saviour Jesus Christ, which suffered for our sins, which the Father by his goodness raised up" (*Smyrnaeans* 7.1). His choice of the word "flesh" rather than "body" suggests an affinity with the Eucharistic tradition behind the Fourth Gospel rather than that of the Synoptics or Paul, which he shows no sign of knowing.

Justin Martyr

Similar language is also used by Justin Martyr in the middle of the second century: "not as common bread or common drink do we receive these things; but just as our Saviour Jesus Christ, being incarnate through (the) word of God, took both flesh and blood for our salvation, so too we have been taught that the food over which thanks have been given through (a) word of prayer which is from him, from which our blood and flesh are fed by transformation, is both the flesh and blood of that incarnate Jesus" (*First Apology* 66.2). Here Justin is more explicit in his association of the contents of the cup with the blood of Jesus than was Ignatius, but shares the same tradition, reflected in the Fourth Gospel, that remembered Jesus speaking about his flesh rather than his body.

Justin, however, is the first writer outside the New Testament to reveal knowledge of another tradition that did speak about body and blood. For, in addition to the words I have just cited, he goes on to say: "the apostles in the memoirs composed by them, which are called Gospels, have handed down what was commanded them: that Jesus having taken bread, having given thanks, said, 'Do this in my remembrance; this is my body'; and similarly having taken the cup and having given thanks, said, 'This is my blood'; and gave to them alone" (*First Apology* 66.3). Justin here claims to be quoting from "the Gospels," by which it might seem that he was familiar with the Synoptic texts themselves. But none of them record as the words of Jesus, "Do this in my remembrance; this is my body"—at least not in that order. The only one of them to contain the words "Do this in my remembrance" at all is the Gospel of Luke, and then only in the manuscripts that contain the longer version of the Last Supper narrative, and they do not record Jesus' words over the cup as "This is my blood" but as "This cup is the new covenant in my blood . . ." Yet in the one place in his writings where it is certain that Justin is quoting Luke's Gospel, it is the so-called Western text that he knows, the manuscript tradition that contains the shorter version of the institution narrative lacking the command to "do this in my remembrance."[8] So it is almost certainly not from the Gospels as known to us that Justin has actually drawn this saying, but from some other source, most likely a collection of sayings of Jesus that had these words in a somewhat different form. This would help explain why so many of the other features of the Synoptic Last Supper narrative fail to make an appearance in Justin's writings. There is, for example, no mention of the words having been said on the night before he died or of any of the interpretative phrases that form part of the sayings in the New Testament versions, such as "body *given for you*" or "blood *poured out for you.*"

Perhaps even more significant than these omissions is that there is no reference to the action of the breaking of the bread, which is recorded in all of the Synoptic texts and in Paul's account of the Last Supper in 1 Corinthians 11. Not only is this missing from Justin's recollection of Jesus here but it is also not explicitly mentioned in Justin's two accounts of actual Christian Eucharistic practice in this same section of his work, although it can be said to be implied there (*First Apology* 65, 67). Now the one place in the New Testament where breaking bread is not mentioned in relation to Jesus giving thanks over bread is in the account of the miraculous feeding of the multitude with loaves and fishes in John 6. Could it be that the tradition that Justin knows links Jesus' saying with a version of that story rather than the Last Supper? There is also another similarity between that story and Justin's vocabulary. When Justin recalls that Jesus "similarly" took the cup,

8. See Helmut Koester, *Ancient Christian Gospels: Their History and Development* (London: SCM Press, 1990), 360–402, esp. 365.

the Greek word that he uses is not *homoios*, found in the Last Supper accounts of Luke and Paul, but *hosautos*, used in John 6:11 of Jesus "similarly" taking the fish.[9] Admittedly, this variation could be just a coincidence, but the omission of a reference to breaking the bread looks more significant, especially when we add to it the fact that Irenaeus, writing later in the second century, appears to have been familiar with a similar tradition.

Irenaeus

Like Justin, Irenaeus makes no mention of the context of the Eucharistic sayings when he quotes them, neither of the Last Supper nor of the impending passion. He simply says, "He took that created thing, bread, and gave thanks, saying, 'This is my body.' And the cup likewise, which is part of that creation to which we belong, he declared his blood . . ." (*Adversus haereses* 4.17.5). Not only, like Justin, does his version of the sayings lack any of the interpretative phrases attached to them in the New Testament accounts, but there is again no mention of the breaking of the bread. True, Irenaeus shows no knowledge of the use of "flesh" rather than "body," but the close parallels between his account of Jesus' words and Justin's suggest that both are drawing on a catechetical tradition as to the origin of the Eucharist that has come down independently of the Gospel texts themselves and that did not link it with the narrative of the Last Supper.

Unlike Justin, however, Irenaeus is definitely also familiar with at least one of the Gospel accounts of the Last Supper themselves, as he quotes part of the Matthean version elsewhere in the same work.[10] Nevertheless, it is upon its eschatological statement about drinking in the kingdom that he comments, passing over in silence the reference

---

9. Justin also uses this same link word in reference to the bread and cup of the Eucharist in his *Dialogue with Trypho* 41.3.

10. "When he had given thanks over the cup, and had drunk of it, and given it to the disciples, he said to them: 'Drink of it, all (of you): this is my blood of the new covenant, which will be poured out for many for forgiveness of sins. But I tell you, I will not drink henceforth of the fruit of this vine until that day when I will drink it new with you in my Father's kingdom'" (*Adversus haereses* 5.33.1). We may note the use of the future tense here, "which will be poured out," a reading that recurs in a number of other renderings of the Matthean narrative, but also the description of Jesus drinking before giving the cup to the disciples or saying the words, something not otherwise found in Matthew.

to the "blood of the new covenant, which will be poured out for many for forgiveness of sins" and not making any explicit connection to the Eucharist. Indeed, although at one point in his writing Irenaeus does move from mention of redemption with the blood of the Lord to the cup of the Eucharist as being communion in his blood,[11] he does not develop the link further. Like Justin, he sees the Eucharistic body and blood of Jesus primarily in terms of nourishment for human flesh, and so giving it the hope of resurrection to eternal life, rather than as that which was sacrificed for human salvation. Thus he says, "as the bread, which is produced from the earth, when it receives the invocation of God, is no longer common bread but the Eucharist, consisting of two realities, earthly and heavenly; so also our bodies, when they receive the Eucharist, are no longer corruptible, having the hope of the resurrection to eternity" (*Adversus haereses* 4.18.5). And later he goes on to speak of our flesh being "nourished from the body and blood of the Lord" and "nourished by the cup which is his blood, and receives increase from the bread which is his body" (ibid. 5.2.3).

North Africa: Tertullian and Cyprian

It is therefore not until we get to Tertullian in North Africa at the end of the second century that we find a Christian writer outside the New Testament who locates Jesus' words in their paschal context and refers to the covenant, even if Tertullian does not mention either giving thanks or breaking the bread. He says, "Having taken bread and given it to the disciples, he made it his body by saying, 'This is my body' . . . Similarly, when mentioning the cup and making the covenant to be sealed by his blood, he affirms the reality of his body" (*Adversus Marcionem* 4.40.3).

His fellow countryman Cyprian in the middle of the third century goes further and quotes two of the New Testament accounts of the Last Supper in one of his letters. He first cites part of the Matthean version: "For, on the eve of his passion, taking the cup, he blessed, and gave (it) to his disciples, saying, 'Drink of this, all (of you); for this is the blood of the covenant, which will be poured out for many for forgiveness of sins. I tell you, I shall not drink again of this fruit of the vine until that day when I shall drink new wine with you in my

---

11. "Now if this flesh is not saved, neither did the Lord redeem us with his blood, nor is the cup of the Eucharist communion in his blood, nor is the bread which we break communion in his body" (*Adversus haereses* 5.2.2).

Father's kingdom.'"[12] A little later in the same letter, Cyprian quotes Paul's account of the Last Supper in 1 Corinthians 11. "The Lord Jesus, on the night he was betrayed, took bread, and gave thanks, and broke it, and said, 'This is my body, which shall be given for you: do this in my remembrance.' In the same way also after supper, he took the cup, saying, 'This cup is the new covenant in my blood: do this, as often as you drink it, in my remembrance.' For as often as you eat this bread and drink the cup, you proclaim the Lord's death until he comes."[13]

Not only does Cyprian quote these texts in full, but the whole basis of the argument in the letter in which they are cited is that Christians are obliged to imitate Jesus when they celebrate the Eucharist and do exactly what he did at the Last Supper. This includes using wine and water mixed together and not just water alone, as some of his contemporaries were doing. Naturally this argument runs into some difficulties when it comes to the hour of celebration, for Cyprian's church clearly has the Eucharist in the morning and not the evening, but he does his best: "It was fitting for Christ to offer about the evening of the day, so that the very hour of sacrifice might show the setting and evening of the world, as it is written in Exodus, 'And all the people of the synagogue of the children of Israel shall kill it in the evening'; and again in the Psalms, 'the lifting up of my hands (as) an evening sacrifice.' But we celebrate the resurrection of the Lord in the morning" (*Epistula* 63.16).

There appear to be two main reasons why Cyprian drew on the New Testament texts in this way when his predecessors had not. First, those texts were now coming to be regarded not merely as apostolic writings but as authoritative Scripture, which therefore tended to override whatever might be contained in other written or oral traditions. Second, Cyprian's church faced a period of persecution, when some of its members might be required to offer the sacrifice of their

12. *Epistula* 63.9. There are two interesting variants here from the text of the Gospel as it is generally known to us. He uses the verb "bless" over the cup instead of "give thanks," a variant that also turns up in the Roman Canon of the Mass, and also the future tense "which will be poured out for you," instead of the present tense. This second variant also occurs in Irenaeus's citation of this passage and in what is known as the Old Latin translation of the Gospel.

13. Ibid. 63.10. Here Cyprian has another variant, using the future tense in connection with the bread, "which will be given up (*tradetur*) for you," against the usual text that has simply "which is for you."

lives. In this pastoral context, therefore, it was more important than ever to link the celebration of the Eucharistic rite with Jesus' own sacrificial oblation of his body and blood: "For if Jesus Christ, our Lord and God, is himself the high priest of God the Father and first offered himself as a sacrifice to the Father, and commanded this to be done in his remembrance, then that priest truly functions in the place of Christ who imitates what Christ did and then offers a true and full sacrifice in the church to God the Father, if he thus proceeds to offer according to what he sees Christ himself to have offered."[14]

CONTINUING INDEPENDENT TRADITIONS?

On the basis of this admittedly limited evidence, it would appear that it was not until the third century that the New Testament texts came to dominate what was thought and said by Christians about the institution of the Eucharist. Yet even after that, liturgical formulae did not always conform their wording of the narrative of the Last Supper precisely to what was recorded in those venerable documents, but variants continued to flourish.

Thus, the institution narrative in the Eucharistic prayer of the so-called *Apostolic Tradition* of Hippolytus[15] begins by paralleling the form in Justin Martyr ("taking bread, giving thanks to you, he said"), with its omission of the conjunction "and" and with its lack of any explicit reference to the supper or to breaking the bread. But then, when it cites the words of Jesus himself, it has "Take, eat, this is my body that will be broken for you"—a mixture of those found in Matthew ("Take, eat, this is my body") and those in some manuscripts of 1 Corinthians ("This is my body that is broken for you"), but without the latter's command to repeat the action. The use of the future tense, "will be broken," is unusual in early Christian citations of the words of Jesus, although we have noted that "will be given up for you" is found in Cyprian's quotation of 1 Corinthians 11:24, and "will be broken" also appears again in the institution narrative of the Eucharistic prayer quoted by Ambrose of Milan in the fourth century (*De sacramentis* 4.21). The words over the cup ("This is my blood that is shed for you. When you do this, you do my remembrance") offer no precise parallel with any one of the canonical accounts, although "that is shed for you"

14. *Epistula* 63.14. See further Bradshaw, *Eucharistic Origins*, 110–12.
15. See Paul F. Bradshaw, Maxwell E. Johnson and L. Edward Phillips, *The Apostolic Tradition: A Commentary* (Minneapolis: Fortress Press, 2002), 37–48.

corresponds to what is found in the longer text of Luke, and the final command echoes 1 Corinthians 11:25. It should also be noted that the account lacks any statement that Jesus then distributed the bread and wine to his disciples.

On the other hand, the Eucharistic prayer in the mid-fourth-century *Sacramentary of Sarapion*[16] does mention the night when Jesus was betrayed, the supper, and also the breaking of the bread, although strangely omits any reference to Jesus "blessing" or "giving thanks." The narrative appears to be chiefly a combination of components from 1 Corinthians 11 and Matthew's version, with words and phrases from the bread unit copied into the cup unit, and vice versa, so as to increase the parallelism of the two. However, as one construction that does not appear verbatim in any of the New Testament versions also turns up in some other earlier Christian writings, this suggests that at least part of it may again be drawn from an older independent tradition rather than having simply been manufactured out of the New Testament material. The words over the cup, "Take, drink . . . ," a form that is found in none of the New Testament versions, might be thought to be simply an attempt to parallel the Matthean version of the words over the bread, "Take, eat, this is my body." But because the same words are also found in the anonymous treatise *In Sanctum Pascha*, previously regarded as the work of Hippolytus but now thought to date from the second century[17]; in writings of Origen in the third century before he went to Caesarea (*Commentarius in Evangelium Ioannis* 32.24; *Homiliae in Jeremiam* 12); in Eusebius of Caesarea in the fourth century (*Demonstratio evangelica* 8.1.28); and in the *Mystagogical Catecheses* attributed to Cyril of Jerusalem (4.1)—sources that are both geographically and temporally so disparate—this may well be yet another form of an independent sayings tradition.

Everything that we have examined so far would seem to point toward the conclusion that it was not the New Testament accounts of the Last Supper that originally shaped what Christians thought and said about Jesus' words concerning his flesh and blood or body and blood, nor even an oral tradition that paralleled those written

---

16. See Maxwell E. Johnson, *The Prayers of Sarapion of Thmuis: A Literary, Liturgical, and Theological Analysis*, Orientalia Christiana Analecta 249 (Rome: Pontifico Istituto Orientale, 1995), 219–33.

17. Text in Pierre Nautin, ed., *Homélies pascales I*, Sources chrétiennes 27 (Paris: Éditions du Cerf, 1950), no. 49.

accounts, but a quite independent tradition or traditions. This strand did not at first link Jesus' sayings specifically with the night before he died or the Last Supper, nor did it include the sort of interpretative phrases that we find in the New Testament versions, such as "body *given for you*" or "blood *poured out for you*," that relate them to his sacrificial death. And even when the New Testament did begin to be regarded as authoritative Scripture, it did not manage completely to efface some elements in these earlier independent catechetical versions from liturgical usage, but they continue to find a place in a number of Eucharistic prayers.

This claim, however, may still sound improbable. Granted that other traditions may have existed prior to the books that came to make up the New Testament being written, nevertheless those books were widely known to Christians long before the third century. Not every one of them may have been current in every region of the ancient Christian world, but one or other of the written accounts of the Last Supper would surely have been known and would have affected how the story was told, would it not? An independent tradition of Eucharistic sayings could surely not have survived and ignored the association of the words over bread and cup with Christ's sacrificial death that is made both in the Synoptic Gospels and in 1 Corinthians as soon as these writings began to be disseminated.

That may seem a likely scenario, but is not perhaps exactly how things were in early Christianity. For instance, Paul's letter to the Romans was obviously widely circulated and well known to Christians in many places, and so one might expect that the baptismal theology of chapter 6, of dying and rising with Christ, would have played a significant part in shaping the language and thought about the meaning of baptism in the early centuries. But that is not the case, and a baptismal theology of new birth, generally related to what we find in John 3, appears to have dominated the scene instead, as much in the West as in the East.[18] In the light of this, it perhaps appears less

---

18. See Maxwell E. Johnson, "Baptism as 'New Birth *Ex Aqua et Spiritu*': A Preliminary Investigation of Western Liturgical Sources," in *Comparative Liturgy Fifty Years after Anton Baumstark*, ed. Robert F. Taft and Gabriele Winkler, 787–807, Orientalia Christiana Analecta 265 (Rome: Pontifico Istituto Orientale, 2001). Reprinted in Johnson, *Worship: Rites, Feasts, and Reflections* (Portland, OR: Pastoral Press, 2004), 37–62; Dominic Serra, "Baptism: Birth in the Spirit or Dying with Christ," *Ecclesia Orans* 22 (2005): 295–314.

remarkable that much Christian thinking about Eucharistic presence in the first and second centuries also continued to follow what might be described as Johannine rather than Synoptic or Pauline paths. In this regard we may also note that pictorial representations of the Eucharist found in the Roman catacombs allude to the feeding miracles of Jesus and not to the Last Supper.[19]

THE NEW TESTAMENT ACCOUNTS

In any case, the Last Supper version of the Eucharistic sayings of Jesus may not have been as widespread or dominant even in first-century Christianity as the existence of four accounts of it in the New Testament books may lead us to suppose. Obviously the tradition that Jesus spoke these words on the night that he was betrayed was known to Paul when he wrote his first letter to the Corinthian Christians some twenty years after the death of Jesus, as he quotes them in the letter, with the interpretative phrases that relate them to that death and with the command to repeat the action in remembrance of Jesus (11:23-26). He does not, however, state specifically that the supper was a Passover meal. The narrative, he claims, he "received from the Lord." New Testament scholars debate just what Paul means on the occasions when he says that certain traditions come from the Lord.[20] He cannot mean directly from the earthly Jesus, as he never knew him. The only possibilities, therefore, seem to be either from a Christian source that he believes to have preserved a trustworthy version of what Jesus actually said and did, or alternatively by some sort of direct revelation. But in either case, we have no reason to jump to the conclusion that it was a universal or well-known tradition within early Christianity. Indeed, his Corinthian correspondents do not seem to be very familiar with it and need reminding, even though Paul says he had already told them it previously.

But what about the Synoptic Gospel accounts? Does not the fact that Jesus' words are recorded in all three Gospels as having been uttered at the Last Supper show that this tradition was widespread in the first century? Let us take a closer look. New Testament scholars have long

19. See the examples described in Geoffrey Wainwright, *Eucharist and Eschatology* (London: Epworth Press, 1971), 42–43.
20. Cf. Galatians 1:12; 1 Corinthians 7:10; and for a discussion of the question, see, for example, C. K. Barrett, *A Commentary on the First Epistle to the Corinthians* (London: A & C Black, 1968), 264–66.

recognized that there is what has been called a "double strand" within these Last Supper narratives: on the one hand, an eschatological focus, represented chiefly by the statement "I shall not drink of the fruit of the vine . . . ," in the three Gospel texts, and on the other hand, the words over the bread and cup relating them to Jesus' body and blood. While these scholars might disagree as to whether or not these words go back to the historical Last Supper, they generally share a consensus that they would already have been combined with the eschatological theme in the Eucharistic practice of the Palestinian Christian communities prior to Pauline influence.[21] However, over twenty years ago the French scholar Xavier Léon-Dufour, in a book to which too little attention has been paid, proposed that the two strands were transmitted through two distinct literary genres and he implied that their combination was actually the work of the evangelists themselves, although he did not develop the consequences of this latter thesis.[22] He was not the first to suggest that the Eucharistic sayings of Jesus had been interpolated into an earlier narrative of Jesus' last Passover meal with his disciples,[23] but was the first to offer a plausible explanation for this phenomenon.

If we examine the Synoptic texts themselves, we can easily see some signs of the division to which Léon-Dufour and others have pointed. In Mark's account, in chapter 14, there is the repetition of the phrase "as they were eating" in verses 18 and 22, which might be thought to suggest a combination of two separate beginnings of a narrative. Equally odd in this text is the fact that the disciples are said to have drunk from the cup before Jesus says the words that interpret its meaning (14:23-24). And if we turn to Luke's narrative, we find another oddity, at least if we accept the longer version of the text as authentic: not only are two cups mentioned, one before and one after

21. See, for example, R. H. Fuller, "The Double Origin of the Eucharist," *Biblical Research* 8 (1963): 60–72; A. J. B. Higgins, *The Lord's Supper in the New Testament* (London: SCM Press, 1952), 56–63; Eduard Schweizer, *The Lord's Supper according to the New Testament* (Philadelphia: Fortress Press, 1967), 25.

22. *Le Partage du pain Eucharistique selon le Nouveau Testament* (Paris: Éditions du Seuil, 1982); English translation, *Sharing the Eucharistic Bread* (New York: Paulist Press, 1987), 82ff.

23. See, for example, Rudolf Bultmann, *The History of the Synoptic Tradition* (Oxford: Blackwell, 1963), 265; S. Dockx, "Le récit du repas pascal. Marc 14, 17-26," *Biblica* 46 (1965): 445–53.

supper (22:17, 20), but also there is the apparently contradictory situation of Jesus declaring in verse 18 that he will no longer drink of the fruit of the vine and then in verse 20 of his doing so.

So, then, let us follow the lead suggested by Léon-Dufour and attempt to untangle the two strands. If we separate the Eucharistic sayings and the material in which they are embedded from the rest of the Last Supper narratives, what we have left are accounts of a Passover meal containing eschatological statements by Jesus that are complete in themselves, with no signs of dislocation, as follows (the Eucharistic sayings strand being indicated by the use of italics and the longer version of Luke by brackets):

MARK 14	LUKE 22
[17]And when it was evening, he came with the twelve. [18]And as they were at table eating, Jesus said, "Truly, I say to you that one of you will betray me, one eating with me." [19]They began to be sorrowful and to say to him one by one, "Is it I?" [20]He said to them, "(It is) one of the twelve, one dipping with me in the dish. [21]For the Son of man goes as it is written concerning him, but woe to that man by whom the Son of man is betrayed. (It would have been) good for him if that man had not been born." [22]*And as they were eating, having taken bread, having blessed (it), he broke (it) and gave (it) to them and said, "Take; this is my body."* [23]And having taken a cup, having given thanks, he gave (it) to them, and they all drank from it. [24]And he said to them, *"This is my blood of the [new] covenant, which (is) poured out for many.* [25]Truly, I say to you, I shall not drink again of the fruit of the vine until that day when I drink it new in the kingdom of God."	[14]And when the hour came, he sat at table, and the apostles with him. [15]And he said to them, "With desire I have desired to eat this Passover with you before I suffer, [16]for I say to you, I shall not/never again eat it until it is fulfilled in the kingdom of God." [17]And having accepted a cup, having given thanks, he said, "Take this, and share it among you; [18]for I say to you, I shall not drink from now on from the fruit of the vine until the kingdom of God comes." [19]*And having taken bread, having given thanks, he broke (it) and gave (it) to them, saying, "This is my body [which (is) given for you. Do this in my remembrance." [20]And the cup likewise after the supper, saying, "This cup (is) the new covenant in my blood, which (is) poured out for you].* [21]But behold the hand of the one betraying me (is) with me on the table. For the Son of man goes according to what has been determined, but woe to that man by whom he is betrayed." [22]And they began to question one another, which of them. . . .

14

Mark and Luke may have variations in the order in which the various sayings are arranged, but they are telling basically the same story. Mark has the conversation about betrayal first, while Luke begins with a statement by Jesus about not eating of the Passover again. Both then follow with Jesus taking a cup and saying he will also not drink of the cup again, and Luke has the conversation about betrayal afterwards. Thus the focus of these Last Supper narratives is on eschatology and upon impending betrayal. They make total sense without the body and blood sayings, and those sayings therefore look like secondary insertions.

In the case of Mark's version, what seems to have happened is that the Evangelist has worked the Eucharistic sayings material into this preexistent narrative where he could best fit it. He thus inserted the bread saying unit immediately after the discussion on betrayal, and the blood saying after the existing reference to the cup. This has resulted, as I said earlier, in the repetition of a beginning, "as they were eating," and of the cup being shared before the interpretative words are spoken. Matthew has tried to solve this difficulty in his version by applying an editorial hand to Mark's text and converting the narrative statement, "they all drank of it," into the command, "Drink of it, all" (26:27-28).

Luke appears to have done something slightly different from Mark in combining the two sets of material. But here, things get somewhat complicated because of the existence of two quite different manuscript traditions of Luke's narrative, a shorter one and a longer one.[24] Since either of these might be the original one, we need to be able to account for the combination in both cases. If we assume first that the longer one is the original, then Luke appears to have acquired a separate version of the sayings narrative from Mark, as there are several differences between the two: Luke has "given thanks" where Mark has "blessed"; Luke does not have "Take" but does add "which is given for you. Do this in my remembrance" to the saying "This is my body"; and while Mark has "This is my blood of the new covenant which is poured out for many" as the words over the cup, Luke has the variant "This cup is the new covenant in my blood which is poured out for you." Luke also treats the material differently, and appears simply to have dropped the sayings narrative into the eschatological Last

24. For details, see Joachim Jeremias, *The Eucharistic Words of Jesus* (London: SCM Press, 1966), 139–52.

Supper as a single block, and it is this that has produced the two cups and the apparently contradictory situation of Jesus declaring in verse 18 that he will no longer drink of the fruit of the vine and then in verse 20 of his doing so.

On the other hand, the shorter version of Luke's text may be the original, with the longer being an expansion by a later hand. This has a shorter saying over the bread, and lacks entirely the Eucharistic saying over the cup. Although in the course of the twentieth century the weight of scholarly opinion has swung in favor of regarding the longer form as authentic, chiefly because of the strong manuscript support for it, it seems to me more likely that the shorter is what the Evangelist wrote, because otherwise there appears to be no good reason for the shorter ever to have existed at all. Who would have wanted to curtail the longer account? Moreover, while it was once commonly thought that it would have been anomalous for anyone to have composed a Last Supper account that placed cup first and bread second, because that would have contradicted the order followed in early Christian liturgical practice, there is now a growing body of opinion that believes that just such an order was not unknown among the earliest Christian practices.[25] If this were so, then it is easy to see how the Evangelist, with his eschatological narrative already containing a mention of the paschal meal and its cup with a saying over it, might have read Mark's version and thought that he also ought to include the saying over the bread in his account, and so simply slipped in the saying copied from Mark, changing the verb "bless" to the more familiar "give thanks" as he did so.[26]

Incidentally, this explanation also provides a solution to two perceived problems with the received text. First, some scholars have claimed that the Last Supper cannot have been a Passover meal because unleavened bread (*azuma*) would have been used on that occasion and not ordinary bread (*artos*). Against this, Joachim Jeremias argued strongly that the latter word could also be used for unleavened

25. See Bradshaw, *Eucharistic Origins*, chap. 3.

26. The suggestion that Luke simply added Mark's saying over the bread to his Passover material has already been made by others: see Henry Chadwick, "The Shorter Text of Luke xxii 15-20," *Harvard Theological Review* 50 (1957): 249–58; B. P. Robinson, "The Place of the Emmaus Story in Luke-Acts," *New Testament Studies* 30 (1984): 481–97, esp. 488–90.

bread.[27] However, if the sayings were in truth a later interpolation into the narrative, no doubts can be cast on the Last Supper having been a Passover meal on the grounds of the choice of word. Second, there is the unusual "mixed" usage of "bless" over the bread but "give thanks" over the cup that we find in Mark and Matthew. In spite of a persisting misconception among many New Testament scholars that these verbs are merely synonyms that might be employed interchangeably, they actually refer to two quite different Jewish liturgical constructions.[28] One might well have expected that a tradition that employed "bless" over the bread would have done the same over the cup, just as the Lukan and Pauline versions use "thank" for both. However, if Mark were grafting his sayings material on to a source where "thank" was already in use for the eschatological saying over the cup, it would account for his retaining that verb in relation to the new cup saying that he added, while at the same time inserting the full unit concerning the bread from a source that had used the verb "bless" for both.

In other words, according to this scenario, we do not really have four independent witnesses in the New Testament to the Last Supper tradition as containing the sayings of Jesus about body and blood. We have one witness, Paul, to a tradition that Mark also hears about, though it is not in his core narrative of the passion, and so he adds it rather clumsily, and it is then copied, to varying degrees, by Matthew and Luke. This suggests that, far from the two strands of the tradition having been integrated at a very early stage, there were Christian communities in the second half of the first century that still did not connect the tradition of the sayings of Jesus about his body and blood over bread and cup directly with a Passover meal at which he made an eschatological statement, nor even with the night before he died.

THE EMERGENCE OF THE EUCHARIST

How, then, do I think that the Eucharistic sayings of Jesus developed and the early Christian Eucharistic practices emerged? I believe that the regular sharing of meals was fundamental to the common life

27. Jeremias, *Eucharistic Words of Jesus*, 62–66.

28. See further Paul F. Bradshaw, *Daily Prayer in the Early Church* (London: SPCK, 1981/New York: Oxford University Press, 1982; reprinted Eugene, OR: Wipf & Stock, 2008), 11–16; idem, *The Search for the Origins of Christian Worship*, 2nd ed. (London: SPCK/New York: Oxford University Press, 2002), 43–44.

of the first Christian communities, as it apparently had been to Jesus' own mission. At these meals they would have experienced an eschatological anticipation of God's kingdom, one of the primary marks of which was that the hungry are fed and many come from East and West to feast (Matt 8:11; Luke 13:29), and they would have responded by calling upon Jesus to return, crying *Marana tha* (1 Cor 16:22; *Didache* 10.6; Rev 22:20). They would have recalled stories of Jesus eating—not just with his disciples but scandalously with tax collectors and sinners. They would have recollected that he had miraculously fed large multitudes with small quantities of food. And they would have remembered that he had once, perhaps in relation to one of these feeding miracles, associated his own flesh with bread. At least some communities of impoverished Christians, whose staple food would have been bread and little else and whose meals generally did not include wine, came to associate what they called the breaking of bread[29] with feeding on the flesh of Jesus. In other cases, where wealthy members of the local congregation would entertain their brothers and sisters in the faith to a more substantial supper in their homes each week, either on the eve of the Sabbath or at its conclusion, the bread and wine of the meal might have been thought of as simply "spiritual food and drink" (as in the *Didache*), or as the flesh and blood of Jesus, although in some Greek-speaking circles the expression "body and blood" came to be preferred. In neither case, because they did not associate what they were doing specifically with the Last Supper or with the annual Passover meal, did they apparently experience any qualms about doing it much more often than once a year or feel the necessity to adhere strictly to the order of that meal in their own practices.

Someone, however, possibly St. Paul himself, did begin to associate the sayings of Jesus with the supper that took place on the night before he died, and interpreted them as referring to the sacrifice of his body and blood and to the new covenant that would be made through his death. This interpretation had some influence within the churches founded by Paul and possibly beyond. It certainly reached the author of Mark's Gospel, who inserted a version of the sayings into his already existing supper narrative, perhaps because he was compiling his account of Jesus in Rome, where the Christians were particularly subject to sporadic persecution and so the association of their own spiritual meals with the sacrificed body and blood of their Savior would

29. For a discussion of this term, see Bradshaw, *Eucharistic Origins*, 55–59.

have been especially encouraging to believers facing possible martyrdom themselves, however novel to them was this juxtaposition of the two traditions. But this combination does not otherwise seem to have been widely known in early Christianity. It was only much later, as the New Testament books gained currency and authority, that it began to shape both the catechesis and the liturgy of the churches, and to shift the focus of Eucharistic thought from feeding to sacrifice.

Does any of this matter? Is it important whether the ultimate roots of Jesus' sayings may lie in the life-giving feeding of those who were hungry rather than in primary association with his imminent death? Did not that sacrificial death also come to be viewed by Christians as life-giving, and therefore to an equal degree as spiritually nourishing? Was anything really lost? I think so. While I believe it was, and is, perfectly legitimate for Christians to interpret Jesus' sayings in relation to his death, whenever and wherever they may have first been uttered, yet I believe a valuable balanced insight was lost by an excessive focus on the power of his sacrificed body and blood and a consequent diminishing of the value of his living and nourishing flesh and blood. In particular, it led in the course of time to a decline in the reception of communion, as that came to be seen as less important for believers than the offering of the Eucharistic sacrifice—to a disproportionate emphasis, if you like, on altar rather than on table.

Nicholas V. Russo

II. The Validity of the Anaphora of
Addai and Mari: Critique of the Critiques

INTRODUCTION

"The Christians in Iraq are one of the oldest surviving communities of Christians on the planet. Yet because of endless oppression, their numbers have dwindled by nearly a million since 2003." So laments Robert Marcarelli, filmmaker of the recent documentary *Facing Extinction: Christians of Iraq*.[1] The Christian presence in the Middle East, especially in Iraq, is fading to the point of extinction. Over the past decade especially, the instability wrought by warfare and religious fundamentalism has killed, or forcibly driven into diaspora throughout the world, the majority (roughly 3.5 million) of Iraqi Christians. The few that remain are caught in the crossfire between military operations that take little account of their safety, insurgent combatants who consider Christian lives expendable, and terrorists who actively target those lives.

The once-vibrant church life of these Christians has been brought to the brink of collapse. With the patriarchate of the Assyrian Church of the East in asylum in Chicago, Illinois,[2] and that of its Catholic counterpart, the Chaldean Catholic Church, under duress in Baghdad, the maintenance of liturgical ministry to serve the remaining faithful has been virtually impossible. Adding to the difficulty is what can only be described as a terrorist campaign against Christian clergy. On June 3, 2007, a Chaldean priest and three subdeacons were murdered in Mosul outside the Church of the Holy Spirit just after the Sunday celebration of the Eucharist. The following year, Paulos Faraj Rahho,

---

1. Robert Marcarelli, *Facing Extinction: The Christians of Iraq*, filmed on location in Iraq, Jordan, and Washington, DC, 2008.

2. A rival Catholicos resides in Baghdad over the so-called Ancient Church of the East; disputes over liturgical practices and the hereditary succession of patriarchs led to a formal schism with the Church of the East in 1968. For an accessible account see Christoph Baumer, *The Church of the East: An Illustrated History of Assyrian Christianity* (London: I. B. Tauris, 2006).

archbishop of Mosul, was abducted and three of his companions were killed on February 29. Archbishop Rahho was murdered some days later and buried in a shallow grave.[3] These are but two recent manifestations of anti-Christian violence that has gone unchecked for over a decade.* As a result, several of these Christian communities bereft of ordained ministers have crossed ecclesial lines to celebrate the sacraments with communities of their Sister Church who still have serving clergy. The attacks are not limited to personnel alone but are aimed often at churches and church-owned property. Since 2001, at least forty churches and monasteries have been destroyed and dozens more forcibly abandoned.[4]

Nor is this crisis limited to Iraq. The widespread nature of the Assyrian and Chaldean diasporas (throughout the Middle East, Western Europe, Scandinavia, Australia, and North America) has made it impossible to provide for the pastoral care of every enclave. And though several Middle Eastern countries have offered Iraqi Christians safe haven (most notably Jordan), they eke out a marginalized existence and are often prevented from entering the workforce. Thus, even if ministers were available, the lack of resources and the uncertainty surrounding their immigrant status make sustaining church life well nigh impossible.

Cognizant of these dire circumstances, the Holy See approved on July 20, 2001,[5] what eminent liturgiologist Robert Taft has called "the most remarkable magisterial document since Vatican II."[6] In this decree, the Supreme Magisterium of the Roman Catholic Church

* See page 62.

3. Carol Glatz, "Kidnappers take Iraqi archbishop, kill his three companions," February 29, 2008, *Catholic News Service*. Sadly, Archbishop Rahho had presided over the funerals of Father Ganni and subdeacons Daoud, Hanna, and Wid—the four victims of the 2007 attack.

4. For an account up to 2004, see "ChaldoAssyrian Churches in Iraq," Position Paper II, *Assyrian Academic Society* (May 2004), available online at http://www.hrwf.net/reports/ext/ChaldoAssyrian_Churches_in_Iraq.pdf (accessed March 23, 2010). The paper also notes another lamentable chapter in recent Iraqi history: in the 1940s and 50s, an indigenous Jewish population of 120,000 was removed from the country.

5. Promulgated October 26, 2001.

6. Robert F. Taft, SJ, "Mass Without the Consecration? The Historic Agreement on the Eucharist between the Catholic Church and the Assyrian Church of the East Promulgated 26 October 2001," *Worship* 77.6 (2003): 483. For a treatment of Eucharistic consecration in the Byzantine Rite, see Michael Zheltov, "The Moment of Eucharistic Consecration in Byzantine Thought," pp. 263–306 below.

recognizes the validity of the Assyrian form[7] of the anaphora of *Addai and Mari*[8]—a Eucharistic prayer without the Words of Institution ("This is my body . . . This is my blood . . .") in continuous use since its redaction in the third century among the faithful of the Church of the East. In addition, the decree also permits Chaldean Catholics, members of its Sister Church, to receive, in cases of necessity, the Eucharist at a liturgy in which this anaphora is used.

The decision was indeed remarkable. In consultation with leading liturgical scholars and theologians, and bringing to bear over a half century of research, the Holy See offered a solution that was at once pastorally practical, ecumenically sensitive, and historically grounded. Not since the Second Vatican Council has *Liturgiewissenschaft* (scientific liturgical scholarship) had such a direct and profound effect on the lives of worshiping Christians. Most Roman Catholics, however, would share the reaction of reporter John Allen, who referred to this document as "an obscure Assyrian liturgical agreement."[9] Few have ever heard of the Church of the East or of Chaldean Catholics, and still fewer of the anaphora of *Addai and Mari*. Yet, since its promulgation, an increasing number of Roman Catholic theologians have come out strongly against the decision, with some urging that it be revoked. Why has a document affecting a tiny minority of Eastern Christians become such a cause célèbre?

THE EUCHARISTIC AGREEMENT

Guidelines

To understand the backlash, we need to look first at the decree and the developments leading to it. In order to provide for the celebration

---

7. I use this term, as opposed to "original" or "more ancient," deliberately; on why, see below.

8. In the earliest manuscripts, it is simply *Qûdāšâ dašlîḥê*, lit. "The Sanctification of the Apostles." East Syrian tradition ascribes the anaphora to Addai (Thaddeus) and Mari, the apostle of Edessa and his disciple. Gelston notes that "it is sometimes suggested that the original reference was to the twelve apostles, the identification with Addai and Mari being secondary." In either case, the claim is that the prayer is of apostolic origin. See Anthony Gelston, *The Eucharistic Prayer of Addai and Mari* (Oxford: Clarendon Press, 1992), 22–23, 47.

9. John J. Allen Jr., "The Word From Rome," *National Catholic Reporter* 2.32 (April 4, 2003), online archive at http://www.nationalcatholicreporter.org/word/word0404.htm.

of the *Qurbana* (i.e., the Divine Liturgy, the Mass) in the absence of ordained ministers, a preliminary document titled Pastoral Disposition for Eucharistic Hospitality between the Assyrian Church and the Catholic Church (dated May 23, 1998) proposed that Chaldean Catholics be permitted to receive the Eucharist confected at an Assyrian liturgy using the Assyrian form of the anaphora of *Addai and Mari*. The issue was not one of practical difficulty—Chaldean Catholics and the faithful of the Church of the East use the same liturgical languages (Syriac and Arabic) and share the same apostolic heritage—but of theological implication. Given the importance of the Institution Narrative in traditional Roman Catholic sacramental theology, how could the Supreme Magisterium tacitly recognize for Catholics under its jurisdiction the validity of a Eucharistic prayer lacking that formula?

To address this "dogmatic question," the preparatory document adduced five arguments to support its recommendation and to square it soundly with Catholic Eucharistic doctrine. First, it underscored the Catholic Church's respect and veneration for the traditional practices of the Churches of the Christian East. Second, it acknowledged the great antiquity of the anaphora of *Addai and Mari*; it is the oldest Eucharistic prayer still in use today. Third, in response to some who have alleged that the Institution Narrative must have dropped out of *Addai and Mari* at some point in the manuscript tradition, it referenced the scholarly consensus that the original form of the anaphora never contained the Words of Institution and that it is not unique in that respect; several other early Eucharistic prayers similarly lack the dominical words. Fourth, through its references to the Mystical Supper, to the example provided by Christ, to his sacrifice, and to the oblation of the Church, *Addai and Mari* explicitly and consciously grounds its celebration in Christ's institution of the Eucharist. And fifth, that connection with the institution is further supported by the other East Syrian anaphoras (those of *Theodore the Interpreter* and *Nestorius*), by East Syrian liturgical commentators, and by the tradition of the *Malka* in which a piece of Holy Leaven (believed to have been given by Jesus to St. John) is added to the Eucharistic bread before the celebration of the *Qurbana*, thereby linking the present celebration with all previous ones back to the Mystical Supper itself.[10]

---

10. Since the preparatory document is not publically available for general consumption, we rely here on the summary provided by Robert Taft in his "Mass Without the Consecration?" 482–509; here at 484–85. Taft was one of

Three years later, the Pontifical Council for Promoting Christian Unity officially promulgated the decision in Guidelines for Admission to the Eucharist between the Chaldean Church and the Assyrian Church of the East.[11] To the points made above, Guidelines added three further supporting arguments. First, it highlighted the "ecumenical rapprochement" between the Catholic and Assyrian Churches throughout the 1990s and the initiatives undertaken by Patriarch Raphaël Bidawid (Chaldean) and Patriarch Mar Dinkha IV (Church of the East) to pave the way for full ecclesial unity.[12] Second, it affirmed the doctrinal and liturgical orthodoxy of the Church of the East, declaring that in her "are to be found 'true sacraments, and above all, by apostolic succession, the priesthood and the Eucharist.'"[13] And third, it reiterated that *Addai and Mari* "was composed and used with the clear intention of celebrating the Eucharist in full continuity with the Last Supper and according to the intention of the Church," noting that its validity was "never officially contested" in the Christian East nor in the West.[14] While the Words of Institution are not found "in a coherent narrative way . . . *ad litteram*," they are nonetheless present "in a dispersed euchological way . . . integrated in successive prayers of thanksgiving, praise and intercession."[15]

On the basis of these theological positions, the official decree set forth the following guidelines for Eucharistic hospitality. First, in cases of necessity the Assyrian faithful are permitted to receive the Eucharist at a Chaldean *Qurbana*, and Chaldeans, at an Assyrian. Second, in such cases, it is understood that the Assyrian and Chaldean *Qurbane* are celebrated according to the proper *ordines* of their respective liturgical traditions. Third, when Chaldean faithful participate in an Assyrian *Qurbana*, the Assyrian minister is "warmly invited to insert the words of the Institution in the Anaphora of *Addai and Mari*, as allowed

---

twenty-six scholars to whom this document was sent for feedback. On the *Malka*, see the following essay by Bryan Spinks, pp. 63–70.

11. An English translation can be found on the official web site of the Vatican at the following stable link: http://www.vatican .va/roman_curia/pontifical_councils/chrstuni/documents/ rc_pc_chrstuni_doc_20011025_chiesa-caldea-assira_en.html.

12. Guidelines, § 2.1.

13. Ibid., § 3.3; quoting *Unitatis Redintegratio*, § 15.3.

14. Ibid., § 3.2.

15. Ibid., § 3.4.

by the Holy Synod of the Assyrian Church of the East."[16] And fourth, the provisions made apply exclusively to members of the Chaldean Church and the Assyrian Church of the East and only in relation to the celebration of the Eucharist.

Provision

Some months later, a supplementary document crafted in agreement with the Congregation for the Doctrine of the Faith and the Congregation for the Oriental Churches elaborated the Guidelines further. In greater detail, the supplement insists that "the words of Institution are not absent . . . , but explicitly mentioned in a dispersed way, from the beginning to the end, in the most important passages of the Anaphora."[17] As such, on January 17, 2001, the Congregation for the Doctrine of the Faith concluded that the Assyrian form of *Addai and Mari* can be considered valid; Pope John Paul II affirmed the Congregation's findings. For pastoral implementation, the supplement suggested again that Assyrian ministers are "warmly invited to insert the words of Institution" when Chaldean faithful are present as a sign of "fraternal respect" and "to bring the present use of *Addai and Mari* into line with the general usage in every Eucharistic Prayer both in the Christian East and in the Christian West."[18] In support of this recommendation, Provision cites an Assyrian Synod assembled in 1978 that offered its ministers the option of adding the dominical words. Yet strangely, the following paragraph underscores the importance of respecting the integrity of the liturgical patrimony of each particular Church. "It would be liturgically improper," it insists, "to transfer particular elements of one liturgical tradition into another . . . without taking from the particularity of the first and harming the coherence of the second."[19] It would seem that the Words of Institution are precisely the sort of element whose interpolation would be discouraged and, while not explicitly mentioning the Institution Narrative in this context, one is left with the impression that that was indeed the intention and that the supplement veils an unsettled debate.

16. Ibid., § 4.3.
17. Provision Between the Chaldean Church and the Assyrian Church of the East, § 2.8.
18. Ibid., § 3.3.
19. Ibid., § 3.4.

Only the Words of Institution

Whatever the state of affairs among the contributors to the Provision, it quickly became evident that the matter was by no means settled. In short order, a flurry of opposition began to appear in print questioning the historical, ecumenical, and theological bases upon which the decree rested. Monsignor Brunero Gherardini, director of *Divinitas*, a theological journal published by the Vatican press, took a decidedly trenchant tone in his reaction to the matter. "Whosoever presumes to celebrate the Eucharist by silencing or altering the words used by Him [i.e., Christ] at the moment of the institution," he declared, "does not perform an act of homage to Christ, but rather its opposite."[20] Paraphrasing the Councils of Trent and Florence, he goes on to clarify that without the dominical words "the sacrament does not exist," and that "the celebrant consecrates the bread and the wine only with the words used by Christ and in no other way."[21] To support his uncompromising position, Gherardini presents Roman Catholic hylomorphic (matter and form) sacramental theology as the apex of a trajectory that he traces from the Bible, through the patristic sources and Thomas, to Trent, and as the touchstone against which the question of the anaphora's validity ought to be tested.

The claim that the Eucharist is consecrated by the recitation of the Institution Narrative alone, "and in no other way," runs afoul of critical liturgical history and theology. If Gherardini were correct, then the ineluctable conclusion would be that the Church, or at least many parts of it, did not celebrate the Eucharist for the first three hundred years of her existence. To be sure, precious few exemplars of pre-Nicene Eucharistic prayers have come down to us. But of those that have, none contains the dominical words. To explain this enigma, earlier scholarship tended to try to explain these prayers away as something other than celebrations of the Eucharist. Josef Jungmann,[22] to take but one example, considered the prayers of *Didache* 9 and 10 as constituting an *agape*, because they nowhere recounted the Narrative of Institution. Such assumptions and reasoning, however, are

20. Brunero Gherardini, "Le parole della Consecrazione eucaristica," *Divinitas* (Nova Series) Numero Speciale (2004): 141–70; here at 163.

21. Ibid.

22. Josef Andreas Jungmann, *The Early Liturgy: To the Time of Gregory the Great* (Notre Dame: University of Notre Dame Press, 1959), 35–36.

rightly rejected as "apriorisme"[23] and circular. Given the frequency of ἐυχαριστέω (ten times in twelve verses)[24] in the *Didache*, one wonders just what the community of second-century suburban Syrians thought they were doing when they uttered those prayers over *bread* (τό κλάσμα, "fragment, morsel") and *wine* (τό ποτήριον, "cup"), if not celebrating the Lord's Supper![25]

More generally erroneous, however, is the underlying assumption that there ever existed a clearly defined monolithic Eucharistic tradition from which only the most derelict of fringe groups diverged. One need look no further than the New Testament to find variety in the way the Eucharist was celebrated and understood. If one is inclined to view the Institution Narratives in the Synoptics and Paul as constituting a model liturgy to be emulated, which is not at all certain,[26] one would be shocked at the level of disagreement concerning the details and wording of so crucial a moment in Christ's ministry. In Luke (22:17-20), for example, the order of thanksgiving/blessing is not bread-cup as in Mark (14:22-26), Matthew (26:26-30), and 1 Corinthians (11:23-26), but cup-bread-cup. Similarly, Matthew and Mark alone refer to a hymn that concluded the meal (Matt 26:30; Mark 14:26), while Luke and Paul seem unaware of this tradition. Even over the words Christ used, the Synoptics and Paul do not concur with one another. Still more shocking may be the fact that some early Christian groups appear to have celebrated the Eucharist without wine, and some with the addition of milk and honey.[27]

Such pluriformity was not limited to the Eucharist. Research on Christian initiation has revealed a multitude of ritual processes, ges-

23. Taft, "Mass Without the Consecration?" 489, quoting Alfons Raes, "Le Récit de l'institution eucharistique dans l'anaphore chaldéenne et malabare des Apôtres," *Orientalia Christiana Periodica* 10 (1944): 216–26, here at 220.

24. Including nominal forms.

25. The section begins (9:1): περὶ δὲ τῆς εὐχαριστίας . . . , "concerning the Eucharist . . ."

26. See Paul F. Bradshaw, *Eucharistic Origins* (London: SPCK, 2004), 43–60; Andrew B. McGowan, "'Is There a Liturgical Text in This Gospel?': The Institution Narratives and Their Early Interpretive Communities," *Journal of Biblical Literature* 118.1 (1999): 73–87; Gelston, *Eucharistic Prayer of Addai and Mari*, 2–21.

27. See Andrew B. McGowan, *Ascetic Eucharists: Food and Drink in Early Christian Ritual Meals* (Oxford: Clarendon Press/New York: Oxford University Press, 1999).

tures, signs, and interpretations. Some communities baptized with a water bath followed by an anointing and hand laying. Others anointed first, then entered the font. Still others baptized through the pouring of oil alone, without any use of water. Some associated the gift of the Spirit with the bath, and others with the oil. Some ministers used an active formula—"I baptize you in the name . . ."—while others, a passive one—"N. is baptized in the name . . ." Roman and North African baptismal theology tended to be shaped by Romans 6, where the neophyte is conformed to the death and resurrection of Christ, whereas in the East, a John 3 theology of baptismal rebirth in the Spirit seems to have been more pronounced.

Not even the liturgy of Rome herself was uniform. We need look no further than the Quartodeciman controversy during the pontificate of Victor to find Roman Christians celebrating liturgy differently from one another. The liturgy, as well as many other aspects of early Christianity, even within one city, was characterized by great diversity. Uniformity emerged only slowly as Christian metropolises began exercising influence and authority over their surrounding regions and as regional and ecumenical councils and religious pilgrimage fostered liturgical cross-fertilization. All this is to give the lie, as Robert Wilken had almost a half century ago, to the belief that early Christianity was uniform and unchanging and that if it were otherwise, it would cease to be authentic.[28] As Taft has often stressed, "the past is always instructive, but never normative." Our liturgies are authentic/valid not because they are identical to the ones celebrated in the tenth century, or the third, or the first, or some other golden age, but because they are in continuity with what has been handed on "not as an inert treasure, but as a dynamic inner life."[29]

The Whole Anaphora as Consecratory?

Drawing on recent advances in research on the origins and evolution of Eucharistic praying, Robert Taft defended the decision on three bases. First, the consensus among liturgical historians is that the earliest anaphoras did not contain a recitation of the Institution Narrative.

28. Robert L. Wilken, *The Myth of Christian Beginnings: History's Impact on Belief* (Garden City, NY: Doubleday, 1971).
29. Robert F. Taft, "The Liturgical Year: Studies, Prospects, Reflections," *Worship* 55 (1981): 2–23, here at 2–3. Taft is describing tradition; I am applying what he says to liturgy.

In fact, *"there is not a single extant pre-Nicene eucharistic prayer that one can prove contained the Words of Institution."*[30] Second, quite unlike later scholastic sacramental theology, early patristic commentators, both Eastern and Western, considered the *whole* anaphora consecratory, and not simply one element (e.g., the Institution Narrative or *epiclesis*) within it. This view is supported also by the structure of the Roman Canon, which speaks in places before the *Qui pridie*/Institution Narrative (*Te igitur*,[31] *Quam oblationem*[32]) as if the gifts are already being consecrated, and in places after it (*Supra quae*,[33] *Supplices te rogamus*[34]), as if the consecration has yet to occur.[35] And third, many of the same commentators (Ambrose, John Chrysostom, John of Damascus) understand the consecratory efficacy of the Words of Institution as deriving from Christ's having spoken them once for all, as it were, and not from a priest's subsequent liturgical repetition.[36]

30. Taft, "Mass Without the Consecration?" 493; emphasis in the original. The only possible exception may be the anaphora of the so-called Barcelona Papyrus: a very early Eucharistic prayer containing both an epiclesis and the Words of Institution. Eminent Russian liturgiologist Michael Zheltov has argued that this anaphora may have been redacted as early as the third century; see his "The Anaphora and the Thanksgiving Prayer from the Barcelona Papyrus: An Underestimated Testimony to the Anaphoral History in the Fourth Century," *Vigiliae Christianae* 62.5 (2008): 467–504. Other scholars, most notably Paul F. Bradshaw, believe those elements were interpolated into a preexisting core during the latter half of the fourth century; see his "The Barcelona Papyrus and the Development of Early Eucharistic Prayers," 129–38 below.

31. "We therefore pray and beseech you, . . . to accept and bless these gifts"; ET in R. C. D. Jasper and G. J. Cuming, *Prayers of the Eucharist: Early and Reformed*, 3rd revised ed. (Collegeville: Liturgical Press, 1990), 164.

32. "Vouchsafe, we beseech you, O God, to make this offering wholly blessed, approved, ratified, reasonable, and acceptable; that it may become to us the body and blood of your dearly beloved Son Jesus Christ our Lord"; Jasper and Cuming, *Prayers of the Eucharist*, 164–65.

33. "Vouchsafe to look upon them with a favorable and kindly countenance, and accept them"; Jasper and Cuming, *Prayers of the Eucharist*, 165.

34. "We humbly beseech you, almighty God, bid these things be borne by the hands of your angel to your altar on high, in the sight of your divine majesty, that all of us who have received the most holy body and blood of your Son by partaking at this altar may be filled with all heavenly blessing and grace"; Jasper and Cuming, *Prayers of the Eucharist*, 165.

35. Taft, "Mass Without the Consecration?" 495–503.

36. Taft, "Mass Without the Consecration?" 503–6.

With each of these our next critic, Ansgar Santogrossi, disagreed.[37] Citing David Berger[38] and Edward Yarnold,[39] Santogrossi argued that the Eucharistic prayer(s) known to Justin Martyr (ca. 150) contained the Words of Institution and that they were considered to be consecratory. "So likewise have we been taught," Justin writes, that the "food eucharistized by *a word* of prayer *which is from him* . . . is the flesh and blood of that Jesus who was made flesh."[40] Given that Justin immediately goes on to paraphrase the dominical words, these scholars posit that the "word of prayer which is from him" is in fact the Institution Narrative invoked over the gifts. As such, Justin would constitute a pre-Nicene witness to its use in Eucharistic praying.[41]

While it is certainly possible that Justin is alluding to the liturgical recitation of the Words of Institution in this context, he describes Eucharistic praying elsewhere with no reference to them whatever. In chapter 65, he notes that the president (ὁ προεστώς) simply

> gives praise and glory (λαβὼν αἶνον καὶ δόξαν) to the Father of the universe, through the name of the Son and of the Holy Ghost, and offers thanks at considerable length for our being counted worthy to receive these things at His hands. And when he has concluded the prayers and thanksgivings (τὰς εὐχὰς καὶ τὴν εὐχαριστίαν), all the people present express their assent by saying Amen.[42]

And again in chapter 67, Justin says only that "the president in like manner offers prayers and thanksgivings (εὐχὰς ὁμοίως καὶ εὐχαριστίας), according to his ability (ὅση δύναμις αὐτῷ), and the people assent,

37. Ansgar Santogrossi, "Historical and Theological Argumentation in Favour of Anaphoras without Institution Narrative: a Critical Appraisal," in *Die Anaphora von Addai und Mari: Studien zu Eucharistie und Einsetzungsworten*, ed. Uwe Michael Lang (Bonn: Verlag Nova & Vetera, 2007), 175–210.

38. David Berger, "'Forma huius sacramenti sunt verba Salvatoris'—Die Form des Sakramentes der Eucharistie," *Divinitas* (Nova Series) Numero Speciale (2004): 171–99, here at 184–85.

39. E. J. Yarnold, "Anaphoras without Institution Narratives?" *Studia Patristica* 30 (1997): 395–410, here at 407.

40. οὕτως καὶ τὴν δι᾿ εὐχῆς λόγου τοῦ παρ᾿ αὐτοῦ εὐχαριστηθεῖσαν τροφήν . . . ἐκείνου τοῦ σαρκοποιηθέντος Ἰησοῦ καὶ σάρκα καὶ αἷμα ἐδιδάχθημεν εἶναι. *First Apology*, 66.2 (PG 6:428C–429A).

41. Santogrossi, "Historical and Theological Argumentation," 177.

42. *First Apology*, 65.2–3 (PG 6:428A–B); ET in *ANF* 1:185.

saying Amen."[43] Admittedly, it cannot be proven that the Institution Narrative was not part of the "prayers and thanksgiving," but neither can it be proven that it was. Moreover, most translators understand "according to his ability," to refer to *extempore* prayer. And though euchological freedom was probably guided by certain conventions and forms,[44] we need not conclude that the dominical words figured in every Eucharistic prayer. That said, even if they did, Justin would be the exception that proves the rule for the pre-Nicene period.

Likewise, Santogrossi argued that those patristic texts that Taft assembled to show that early commentators reckoned the entire anaphora as consecratory ought to be interpreted otherwise. According to his reading, Ambrose, Isidore of Seville, and even John of Damascus unanimously declare that "This is my body, etc." is the "instrumentally efficacious sacramental form," and that these words alone are "efficacious for *transubstantiation*."[45] Ambrose, for example, writes: "However as often as we receive the sacraments, *which are transfigured by the mystery of the holy prayer into the flesh and blood*, we proclaim the death of the Lord."[46] But, Santogrossi clarifies, since "'This is my body etc.' and the Narrative *are* also prayer addressed to God . . . it is illegitimate to conclude . . . that the Fathers in question would not have considered 'This is my body etc.' as in itself operative of the mystery, had it occurred to them to raise the question."[47]

There are clearly passages in which is highlighted the power of the dominical words to change the bread and wine. But it is surely anachronistic to suggest that Ambrose, Isidore, and John attributed *instrumental causality* to the Words of Institution, or anything else for that matter, since they wrote several centuries before these scholastic categories, and the philosophical system of which they were a part, were

---

43. *First Apology*, 67.2 (PG 6:429B); ET in *ANF* 1:186.

44. See Allan Bouley, *From Freedom to Formula: The Evolution of the Eucharistic Prayer from Oral Improvisation to Written Texts*, Studies in Christian Antiquity 21 (Washington, DC: Catholic University of America Press, 1981).

45. Santogrossi, "Historical and Theological Argumentation," 188; emphasis added.

46. Nos autem quotiescumque sacramenta sumimus, quae per sacrae orationis mysterium in carnem transfigurantur et sanguinem, mortem Domini annunciamus. *De fide*, 4.10.124 (CSEL 78.201); ET in Edward J. Kilmartin, *The Eucharist in the West: History and Theology* (Collegeville: Liturgical Press, 1998), 16; emphasis added.

47. Santogrossi, "Historical and Theological Argumentation," 176–77.

articulated. Santogrossi is quite right: it never occurred to Ambrose or Isidore to ask what effected transubstantiation, but not because they implicitly assumed the answer to be the Institution Narrative but because their sacramental theology was "more redolent of Bible and prayer than of school and thesis, . . . more impressionistic than systematic, more suggestive than probative."[48] Note that Ambrose says that the gifts are transfigured (*transfigurantur*)—a word more evocative of Tabor than Thomas; *transubstantio* does not enter theological parlance until the twelfth century.[49] The perceived need to dogmatize *the* moment at and means by which bread and wine become body and blood was fueled by the Eucharistic controversies that plagued the Western Church beginning with the speculations of Paschasius Radbertus (9th c.). Taft rightly describes this development as a "narrowing of the perspective,"[50] and one that is certainly not normative for the Church catholic.

Santogrossi also rejects appeals to the ambiguity of the Roman Canon to justify the validity of *Addai and Mari*. The fact that the Roman Canon speaks at points before the *Qui pridie* (Institution Narrative) as if the gifts are already consecrated, and at points after it, as if they have yet to be, does not betray any ambiguity in instrumental causality but simply reveals the constraints of language.

> The adoring priest praying the Canon, nearly overwhelmed by the reality of what occurs in the Narrative he recites to God and the words of Christ he invokes over the gifts, naturally prolongs the moment of the event by evoking various of its aspects, which of course speech cannot request at the same time as it pronounces Christ's words.[51]

So for Santogrossi, there is no ambiguity at all. The perceived inexactitude over the precise moment of consecration is due to the spiritual

---

48. Taft, "Mass Without the Consecration?" 495. Taft uses these dichotomies to characterize liturgical language, not patristic sacramental theology, but I believe they apply to both.

49. Frank L. Cross and Elizabeth A. Livingstone, eds., *The Oxford Dictionary of the Christian Church*, 3rd ed. (Oxford: Oxford University Press, 2005), articles on *Eucharist* and *Transubstantiation*; available by subscription at www.oxford-christianchurch.com.

50. Taft, "Mass Without the Consecration?" 498.

51. Santogrossi, "Historical and Theological Argumentation," 188.

ecstasy of the celebrant, his desire to prolong the experience, and the inability of language to operate synchronically and diachronically.

However, liturgical language does indeed operate in that way. What Taft calls "the proleptic and reflexive nature of liturgical discourse"[52] is amply demonstrated by the *anamnesis* of the Byzantine Divine Liturgy. Immediately following the Words of Institution, the anaphora of *John Chrysostom* reads:

> Remembering, therefore, this precept of salvation and everything *that was done* for our sake, the cross, the tomb, the resurrection on the third day, the ascension into Heaven, the enthronement at the right hand, *the second and glorious coming again*: We offer You Your own, from what is Your own, in all and for the sake of all.[53]

Notice how the prayer remembers (μεμνημένοι, perfect middle participle of μιμνήσκω/μιμνήσκομαι) "the second and glorious coming again," among "everything that *was done* (γεγενημένων—*perfect* passive participle of γίγνομαι) for our sake." That is the very essence of liturgical discourse: to make present to the faithful the already- and not-yet-accomplished mysteries of the economy of salvation, through the power of the Holy Spirit: "the foretaste of the future inheritance."[54]

Recent research on the origin and development of the Roman Canon further undermines Santogrossi's position. In his work on the early evolution of Eucharistic praying, Enrico Mazza suggested that the Words of Institution interrupt the flow of the Roman Canon by bisecting the commemorations of the living and the dead and, therefore, that the *verba domini* were likely not integral to the earliest stratum.[55] Unconvinced by his thematic-narrative analysis, Santogrossi points to the many linking clauses and words (e.g., *igitur*, "therefore"; *unde*,

---

52. Taft, "Mass Without the Consecration?" 495.

53. A. Hänggi and I. Pahl, *Prex eucharistica, Vol. 1: Textus e variis liturgiis antiquioribus selecti*, Spicilegium Friburgense 12, 3rd ed. (Freiburg: Schweiz, 1998), 226. ET in Melkite Greek-Catholic Eparchy of Newton, *The Divine and Holy Liturgy of Our Father among the Saints John Chrysostom, Archbishop of Constantinople* (2008), 64; emphasis added.

54. From the Presanctus of the Byzantine anaphora of St. Basil, paraphrasing Rom 8:23 and 2 Cor 1:22.

55. Enrico Mazza, *The Origins of the Eucharistic Prayer* (Collegeville: Liturgical Press, 1995), 280–85. See also, id., "Che cos'è l'anafora eucaristica?" *Divinitas* (Nova Series) Numero Speciale (2004): 37–56.

"for which reason") that bind the Canon into a coherent whole. "In the Roman Canon," he insists, "we clearly have organic unity at various points through conjunctions and relative pronouns."[56]

To be fair, G. G. Willis's short but highly illuminating analysis of the rhythmic endings (*clausulae*) that occur in the *Canon Missae* points, from the standpoint of philology, to the antiquity of the Institution Narrative.[57] From roughly the fourth through the seventh centuries, Roman liturgical compositions conformed to a system of stylized rhythmic endings known as *cursus*.[58] When compared to the collects of the ancient sacramentaries, the Roman Canon has relatively few of these endings—a sign of its antiquity. And of the twenty-two *clausulae* that are found from *Te igitur* through *Nobis quoque*, none appear in the sections containing the Institution Narrative (*Qui pridie* and *Simili modo*). This would seem to suggest that these constitute "the earliest part of the Canon."[59] Similarly, the quotations of the Canon (from *Quam oblationem* to *Supplices te rogamus*) in Ambrose's *De sacramentis* (ca. 390) contain only one rhythmic ending.[60] Yet, even the primitive form of the text known to Ambrose, Willis dates from the period 350–70.[61] Thus, while the Institution Narrative may have been integral to the Roman Canon and to Roman Eucharistic praying from the mid-fourth century on, it does not follow that that had been Roman practice since Peter.

As for the claim that Christ's *ephapax* utterance of the Institution Narrative is eternally consecratory, not a celebrant's repetition, Santogrossi believes again that proper interpretation of patristic texts leads to no such conclusion. Singling out a passage from Chrysostom's *Homily 2 on 2 Timothy* cited by Taft, Santogrossi shows that liturgical

---

56. Santogrossi, "Historical and Theological Argumentation," 187.

57. G. G. Willis, "*Cursus* in the Roman Canon," in id., *Essays in Early Roman Liturgy*, Alcuin Club Collections Nº XLVI (London: SPCK, 1964), 113–17.

58. Willis notes that "the *cursus* became the rule in the papal chancery from the time of Siricius (384–98), and disappeared after St. Gregory the Great (604), and in the case of liturgical composition it prevailed roughly from 350 or a little later till about 650"; "*Cursus* in the Roman Canon," 113.

59. Willis, "*Cursus* in the Roman Canon," 116.

60. The version of the Canon known to Ambrose is slightly different than the Gregorian form, which contains seven *clausulae* from *Quam oblationem* to *Supplices te rogamus*—an indication to Willis that Ambrose likely witnesses to an earlier form of the text; "*Cursus* in the Roman Canon," 116.

61. Willis, "*Cursus* in the Roman Canon," 117.

repetition is indeed required. "The latter [offering] is in no way inferior to the former," Chrysostom insists, "because the same one who sanctified the one, sanctifies the other too. For just as *the words that God spoke are the same as the ones the priest pronounces now*, so is the offering the same. . . ."[62] The "symbol is completed," that is, the Eucharist is confected, according to Santogrossi's reading, precisely because the priest repeats the same words Christ used at the Last Supper.[63]

But his interpretation ignores two facts. First, this passage comes from a homily and, as such, does not represent a systematic or exhaustive exposition of Chrysostom's sacramental theology. In another homily (*De coemeterio et de cruce*, 3),[64] for instance, Chrysostom clearly sees the consecration occurring at the *epiclesis*, whereas in his *Homily on the Betrayal of Judas*, 6,[65] we find him waxing eloquent on the transformative power of "This is my body . . ." again. Is he incapable of making up his mind? Certainly not. His reflections spring from and are shaped by the scriptural reading on which he is commenting. As such, they are occasional and contextual, not abstract and absolute. It is not surprising that Chrysostom focuses on the Words of Institution in a homily on the betrayal of Judas and on the *epiclesis* in a homily in which the Holy Spirit figures prominently. Second, Chrysostom's thrust in *Homily 2 on 2 Timothy* is not to attribute instrumental efficacy to the Words of Institution, but to show that the shortcomings of the priest do not render the offering made on the present altar inferior to the offering of Christ:

> Is it the good life or the virtue of the priest that confers so much on you? *The gifts which God bestows are not such as to be effects of the virtue of the priest.* All is of grace. His part is but to open his mouth, while God works all: the priest only performs a symbol.[66]

Chrysostom is exegeting 2 Timothy 1:8-10, where Paul begs Timothy not to be ashamed of him and which speaks of God who "saved us and called us to a holy life, *not according to our works* but according to

---

62. *In ep. 2 ad Tim.* 2.4 (PG 62:612); ET in Taft, "Mass Without the Consecration?" 506; emphasis added.

63. Santogrossi, "Historical and Theological Argumentation," 196.

64. PG 49:397–98.

65. PG 49:380, 389–90.

66. PG 62:612; ET adapted from NPNF 13:483; emphasis added.

his own design and the grace bestowed on us in Christ Jesus."[67] Quite naturally, Chrysostom capitalized on the reading to explain that the efficacy of the mysteries is not diminished by the unworthiness of the minister. Santogrossi's interpretation is *eisegetical* proof texting.

A Disciplina Arcani

One of the arguments used by The Pontifical Council for Promoting Christian Unity to support their decision is that the Roman Church has always respected the traditional practices of the Oriental Churches. Therefore, if *Addai and Mari* was traditionally celebrated without the Words of Institution, the Roman Church would have to accept it as valid *prima facie*. But, according to Santogrossi and Uwe Lang,[68] our final critic, the original form of *Addai and Mari* may not have lacked an Institution Narrative. If they are correct, then the Assyrian form would not in fact be traditional. They agree with those scholars who believe that the "anomalies in the grammatical and thematical flow"[69] of the anaphora point to a now-missing Institution Narrative. But given the unanimity of the manuscript tradition, how, why, and when did the Narrative fall out? Hearkening back to a suggestion made by Bernard Botte and echoed by Louis Bouyer,[70] both Santogrossi and Lang contend that the Narrative is missing "because it used to be committed to memory and recited secretly."[71] They believe that the Words of Institution would have fallen under the so-called *disciplina arcani*, or "discipline of secrecy." Santogrossi ventures:

> It is possible that the earliest manuscript of *Addai and Mari* lacked the Institution Narrative precisely for this reason [i.e., to prevent the sacred words from falling into the hands of persecutors and unbelievers], and that later copyists were simply being faithful to what they had

67. 2 Tim 1:9; ET in NAB; emphasis added.

68. Uwe Michael Lang, "Eucharist without Institution Narrative? The Anaphora of *Addai and Mari* Revisited," in id., ed., *Die Anaphora von Addai und Mari: Studien zu Eucharistie und Einsetzungsworten* (Bonn: Verlag Nova & Vetera, 2007), 31–65; here at 57–61.

69. Santogrossi, "Historical and Theological Argumentation," 197.

70. Bernard Botte, "Problèmes de l'anaphore syrienne des Apôtres Addaï et Mari," *L'Orient Syrien* 10 (1965): 89–106; here at 103–4; Louis Bouyer, *Eucharist: Theology and Spirituality of the Eucharistic Prayer*, trans. Charles U. Quinn (Notre Dame: University of Notre Dame Press, 1968), 151–52.

71. Lang, "Eucharist without Institution Narrative?" 57.

before them. And all along the Institution Narrative was being added in actual celebration.[72]

Lang adds that Tertullian, Origen, Cyril of Jerusalem, Ambrose, and Innocent all shared the conviction that certain doctrines and practices were not to be disclosed to the uninitiated.[73] And for East Syria in particular, he draws attention to two liturgical commentaries that indicate that certain parts of the anaphora were recited silently "so that the words, on being heard, should not be learnt by laymen, women and children, with the result that the divine words are held to be ordinary and (so) despised."[74]

Most scholars now rightly reject this line of reasoning.[75] First, the Church of the East seems to have had no such scruple concerning the Words of Institution. In the two other Assyrian anaphoras (those of *Theodore* of Mopsuestia and *Nestorius*), the Institution Narrative is recited and it appears in the manuscripts. To be sure, the anaphoras of *Theodore* and *Nestorius* were redacted in the post-Nicene era when one would assume that the *disciplina arcani* was no longer rigorously enforced. However, one might then ask why the dominical words were not added into later manuscripts of *Addai and Mari* once *Theodore* and *Nestorius* rendered the practice of doing so acceptable. If at some point after Nicea adding the dominical words was no longer considered taboo, why would the later manuscripts needlessly mimic a defunct tradition of secrecy?

Second, as Lang himself admits, there are countless works from the pre-Nicene period where we find the Words of Institution, and other texts that were allegedly guarded in like manner (e.g., the Lord's Prayer), freely quoted. To refer to the passage cited by Santogrossi, Justin quotes them in his *First Apology*: a work (1) intended, at least in theory, for widespread public consumption, and (2) written at a time

72. Santogrossi, "Historical and Theological Argumentation," 198.

73. Lang, "Eucharist without Institution Narrative?" 58–60.

74. Gabriel of Qatar, *Commentary on the Liturgy*, V.2:66, ET in Sebastian Brock, "Gabriel of Qatar's Commentary on the Liturgy," *Hugoye* 6.2 (2003): 18; reprinted in id., *Fire from Heaven: Studies in Syriac Theology and Liturgy* (Cornwall: Ashgate, 2006), XVII, 18.

75. Gelston, *The Eucharistic Prayer of Addai and Mari*, 74; Alfons Raes, "Le Récit de l'institution eucharistique dans l'anaphore chaldéene et malabare des Apôtres," *Orientalia Christiana Periodica* 10 (1944): 216–26, here at 225.

of heightened persecution when we would expect the *disciplina arcani* to have been more strictly observed. Recent work has argued that the discipline of secrecy was employed, especially in the fourth century, to instill a sense of awe in catechumens, and not necessarily to keep the most sacred mysteries from persecutors.[76]

Third, for the discipline of secrecy to have been practicable, we should expect to find some sort of indication in the manuscripts—a symbol, rubric, incipit, marginal note, etc.—showing the celebrant the point at which he was to recite the Narrative from memory. To my knowledge, there are no such symbols or rubrical indications anywhere in the manuscript tradition. To assume that the priest knew where they belonged is belied by the many places (at least four) where one finds the Narrative inserted according to the supplemental folia and printed missals. Surely the mere *location* of the dominical words would not have been under wraps too.

Finally, Lang misinterprets the commentaries indicating that certain sections of the anaphora were recited quietly. When Gabriel Qatraya (seventh c.) says that "the entire section" is said sotto voce, Lang understands him to be referring to "the first *gehanta* [prayer of inclination] after the Sanctus and before the diaconal admonition 'Pray in your hearts.'"[77] Gabriel says no such thing:

> 63. *That the herald cries out* and says *"Stand well and be attentive"* to what is being done: (this) is *an instruction of the priesthood* who prepare the entire [201b] people so that *everyone stands* with great attention *before God at that awesome* and dread *time.*

> 64. *The incense at this point: a symbol of the aromatic spices with which the body of our Saviour was embalmed.*

> 65. *That the priest inclines himself three times and recites the holy words* of the offering of the oblation: *a symbol of the three days during which the humanity of our Lord was under the authority of death.*

> 66. *The fact that he recites the entire section quietly, but at the end raises his voice so that the people can hear:* first, because it is *a Mystery that is being performed, and it is not appropriate that all the people should know of it;* and secondly, *so that the words, on being heard, should not be learnt by laymen,*

76. Juliette Day, "Adherence to the *Disciplina Arcani* in the Fourth Century," *Studia Patristica* 35 (Leuven: Peeters, 2001): 266–70.

77. Lang, "Eucharist without Institution Narrative?" 60.

women and children, with the result that the divine worlds [words] are held to be ordinary and (so) despised.

67. The fact that [202a] he raises his voice at the end (is) so that, along with the priest, the people should participate with the response "Amen."

68. The fact that, at the moment of the epiclesis [lit. hovering] *the herald cries out* and says *"In your minds* pray; *in stillness* and fear be standing": *in order to teach us that at this moment full of awe it is not appropriate that we should utter our prayers in an audible voice, but rather, in stillness, within the heart.*[78]

There is no indication that the "entire section" recited quietly refers to the post-Sanctus. Rather Gabriel seems to indicate that *much* of the anaphora is recited in a low voice. Note that the "herald" calls the congregation to greater attention at the *epiclesis* because at that moment petition is made that "the Holy Spirit should come and perfect and complete the Holy Mysteries." Presumably, a proclamation is required because the *epiclesis* is inaudible. So the concern for sacrality applies to the whole anaphora and not to one part. It cannot be argued, therefore, that the *gehanta* was executed inaudibly because it contained the dominical words. While *gehanta* (lit. "inclined, bowed, bent") refers to the posture, *gehanta* prayers are normally recited sotto voce and this is a hallmark of prayers of inclination from all liturgical traditions.[79] The silence means nothing. Moreover, since Gabriel's testimony is from the seventh century, it may not reflect the way in which the anaphora was originally prayed.

Evidence from the Missionaries

Lang attempts to set the suggestion on firmer ground with support from modern and pre-modern testimonies. A sixteenth-century manuscript (Vat. Syr. 66) containing the anaphora of *Addai and Mari* (fos. 104[v]–107[v]) has an Institution Narrative inserted on a supplementary folio (101[a]).[80] As Lang notes, the whole of the Eucharistic rite was prob-

---

78. Gabriel of Qatar, *Commentary on the Liturgy*, V.2:57–71, ET in Brock, "Gabriel of Qatar's Commentary on the Liturgy," 17–19; italics in Brock are to indicate the passages repeated in Abraham bar Lipeh's epitome.

79. See Robert Payne Smith, *A Compendious Syriac Dictionary* (Oxford: Clarendon Press, 1903), 62A. For the West and the Byzantine East, cf. *oratio secreta, mystikos.*

80. Gelston, *Eucharistic Prayer of Addai and Mari*, 31, 43.

ably added to a preexisting pontifical by Mar Joseph Sulaka, whose brother Mar John Simon was elected rival catholicos in opposition to the hereditary catholicosate. In 1553, Pope Julius III recognized his election and consecrated John Simon Patriarch. The upshot of this controversy was the creation of the Chaldean Catholic Church and the logical assumption would be that the addition of the Institution Narrative in this manuscript was a *sine qua non* for union with Rome. Lang hastens to cite the *Guidelines* document, which insists that "for the period of the Catholic Patriarchate under Patriarch Sulaka, no document exists to prove that the Church of Rome insisted on the insertion of an Institution narrative into the Anaphora of *Addai and Mari.*"[81]

As further proof that the Narrative was not added by coercion, Lang notes that canons 109–10 of the Synod of Diamper (1599), though clearly intended to Latinize the Malabar rite, imply that the Words of Institution were already integral to the Malabar version of *Addai and Mari.*[82] And describing the work of Aleixo de Menezes, the Portuguese archbishop of Goa who led the synod, Antonio de Gouvea

> notes that "Chaldean prelates" had been "sent from Babylon" and that they, out of ignorance, had words added to or removed from the "forma da Consagração" at will. However, an archbishop, whom Gouvea credits with more theological erudition, introduced a fixed formula of consecration.[83]

Lang takes Gouvea's observation as another indication "that the words of Institution were already part of the Malabar liturgy before Diamper and belonged to an oral tradition that had not yet been fixed."[84] And for the Chaldeans, Lang adduces the testimony of nineteenth-century

81. Guidelines, § 2.5.

82. Lang, "Eucharist without Institution Narrative?" 31–33. Two dissertations have challenged the validity of the synod: Jonas Thaliath, "The synod of Diamper," diss. (Rome: Pontifical Gregorian University, 1958); Joseph Kuzhinjalil, "The disciplinary Legislation of the Synod of Diamper," diss. (Rome: Pontifical Oriental Institute, 1975). See also Paul Pallath, "The Synod of Diamper: Valid or Invalid?" in *The Synod of Diamper Revisited*, ed. George Nedungatt, SJ, 199–226 (Rome: Pontifico Instituto Orientale, 2001).

83. A. de Gouvea, *Iornada do Arcebispo de Goa Dom Frey Aleixo de Menezes Primaz da India Oriental* (Coimbra, 1606), appendix, as summarized by Lang, "Eucharist without Institution Narrative?" 33.

84. Lang, "Eucharist without Institution Narrative?" 33.

Anglican missionaries to Urmia (northwestern Iran) who claim that the Institution Narrative was inserted from memory:

> It is especially to be noted that the holy words in which our Lord and God Jesus Christ instituted the most holy sacrament of the Eucharist, and which, as far as the Liturgy of the Blessed Apostles is concerned, *were never committed to writing by the Syrians, though the priest always pronounced them when celebrating the mysteries*, are inserted in their place, which is sufficiently certain from a comparison of other liturgies of the same people, and from inquiry into the custom of the priests; but they stand apart because they rest on the authority of no ancient codex. They are in the form in which the blessed Apostle Paul repeated them in his First Epistle to the Corinthians.[85]

Finally, for the Church of the East, Lang cites William Macomber, who reports that in the liturgies he had attended in which *Addai and Mari* was prayed, the dominical words were used.[86]

All of the evidence advanced, though important for understanding its modern development, tells us nothing about the original form and early evolution of *Addai and Mari*. For the Synod of Diamper, Lang admits that "we have no witnesses to the unrevised form of the Malabar rite before 1599."[87] The testimony of Gouvea is secondhand, and it is not at all clear that before Diamper the Malabrese version of *Addai and Mari* contained the Words of Institution. Gouvea reports that the "ignorant" Chaldean prelates added or removed words from the "form of consecration." Against Lang's interpretation, it seems more probable that the uncertainty of these Chaldean bishops is owing to the recent introduction of the dominical words in their own liturgy. The disarray of Malabar and Chaldean practice in this respect likely derives from the novelty of the interpolation in general than from a long-standing

---

85. Anonymous, *The Liturgy of the Holy Apostles Addai and Mari, together with Two additional liturgies to be said on certain feasts and other days: and the Order of Baptism* (Urmi: Archbishop of Canterbury's Mission, 1890; London: SPCK, 1893), ix; emphasis added.

86. William F. Macomber, "A History of the Chaldean Mass," *Worship* 51 (1977): 107–20; here at 119.

87. Lang, "Eucharist without Institution Narrative?" 33. The lack of liturgical texts from before Diamper is likely due to what Macomber called the "high-handed interference by the Portuguese"; see Macomber, "History of the Chaldean Mass," 115.

oral tradition "that had not yet been fixed."[88] At any rate, F. C. Burkitt warned that, because of the high-handed Portuguese reforms and the possibility that *Addai and Mari* was only recently introduced to India at that time, "we may not cite the so-called Malabar Liturgy, as ancient evidence, derived from a semi-independent source" of the East Syrian liturgical tradition.[89] For their part, the testimony of the Anglican missionaries and Macomber is far too recent to be of any value.[90] Yet Lang is responsible and sober in the weight he gives this data. He confesses "that the insertion of an Institution Narrative in the text of *Addai and Mari* in this [early modern] period is secondary and cannot prove its presence in the early form of the anaphora."[91]

Attempts at Reconstructing the Primitive Shape

Since there is no exemplar that includes the Words of Institution in the manuscript tradition, Lang surveys the theories on where the Narrative may have once belonged. These theories posit at least two possible places in the text where ambiguous antecedents and awkward grammatical constructions suggest missing words or phrases. The relevant sections are E, F, and G according to the divisions of Gelston's critical edition.

E

36 Do Thou, O my Lord, in thy manifold and ineffable mercies
37 make a good and gracious remembrance
38 for all the upright and just fathers who were pleasing before thee,
39 in the commemoration of the body and blood of thy Christ,

---

88. Ibid.

89. "But we cannot use the Malabar Rite as evidence for the Nestorian Rite in India earlier than the end of the 15th century, for there is nothing to suggest that the service books used by the new clergy were an old and unrevised form taken from surviving Malabari liturgical codices." F. C. Burkitt, "The Old Malabar Liturgy," *Journal of Theological Studies* 29 (1928): 155–57, here at 157; paraphrase from Edward Craddock Ratcliff, "The Original Form of the Anaphora of *Addai and Mari*: A Suggestion," *Journal of Theological Studies* 30 (1928–29): 23–32, here at 25.

90. Macomber himself testifies that even in the printed Assyrian missals, the Words of Institution are inserted into *Addai and Mari* on a separate slip of paper or are not found at all; Macomber, "A History of the Chaldean Mass," 119.

91. Lang, "Eucharist without Institution Narrative?" 36.

40 which we offer to thee upon the pure and holy altar, *as thou hast taught us,*

41 and make with us thy tranquility and thy peace all the days of the age,

42 (*Response*: Amen)

F

43 that all the inhabitants of the world may know thee,

44 that thou alone art God the true Father,

45 and thou didst send our Lord Jesus Christ thy Son and thy Beloved,

46 and he, our Lord and our God, taught us in his life-giving Gospel

47 all the purity and holiness of the prophets and apostles and martyrs and confessors

48 and bishops and priests and deacons,

49 and all the children of the holy catholic Church,

50 those who have been signed with the sign of holy Baptism.

G

51 *And we also*, O my Lord, thy unworthy, frail, and miserable servants, who are *gathered* [*in thy name*][92] and stand before thee,

52 *and have received by tradition the example which is from thee,*

53 rejoicing and glorifying and exalting and commemorating

54 and celebrating this great and awesome mystery

55 of the passion and death and resurrection of our Lord Jesus Christ.[93]

First, in lines 40 and 52, the anaphora makes clear that the present offering is modeled on Christ's example viz. "as thou hast taught us," and "the example which is from thee." Second, the words "and we also" in line 51 suggest that the present praying community is being compared or contrasted to a group already mentioned. Third, in the Syriac of section G there is no main verb, only a series of participles and a perfect ("and have received"), which governs the parenthetical clause in line 52.

To explain these peculiarities, Bernard Botte proposed that the "we also" of line 51 compares the participants of the present Eucharist with those at the Last Supper, and that the words "in thy name" found in some later manuscripts echo a form of Institution Narrative known

92. According to Botte's reconstruction, Bernard Botte, "L'Anaphore chaldéenne des Apôtres," *Orientalia Christiana Periodica* 15 (1949): 259–76.

93. Gelston, *Eucharistic Prayer of Addai and Mari*, 51–55; emphasis added.

to Aphrahat and Ephrem: "whenever you are gathered *in my name*." These, together with what he described as the anamnetical character of section G, led Botte to conclude that an Institution Narrative must have preceded this section.[94] Some years later, Bryan Spinks concurred with Botte's proposal and suggested further that the verb "receive" (*qbl*) connotes "receiving tradition" in rabbinic Hebrew and refers explicitly to the Institution Narrative in 1 Corinthians 11:23: "For I *received* (παρέλαβον / *qablet* in the Peshitta NT) from the Lord that which I handed on to you . . . ." Its use in *Addai and Mari*, Spinks argued, may well point to the presence of an Institution Narrative there too.[95] Lang also cites Gelston, who highlights that the words "tradition" (line 52, *yûbālâ*), "example" (line 52, *ṭûpsâ*),[96] "celebrating" (line 54, *ʿābdînan*), and "mystery" (line 54, *rāzâ*) all carry technical sacramental/liturgical overtones that connect the present celebration of the Eucharist to the example Christ commanded to be repeated.[97, 98]

William Macomber also believed the Words of Institution preceded section G. According to his reconstruction, the reference to the "upright and just fathers" in line 38 would have been joined to the list of venerables beginning in line 47 and the Institution Narrative, which he argued lay between the two, dropped out at some point.[99] In the corresponding section of the Maronite *Sharar*, a closely related anaphora thought to derive from the same core from which *Addai and Mari* evolved, this is precisely where the Words of Institution are found. Given these—the clear references to the Last Supper, the

94. Botte, "L'Anaphore chaldéenne des Apôtres," 273ff.

95. Bryan D. Spinks, *Addai and Mari—The Anaphora of the Apostles: A Text for Students*, Grove Liturgical Study 24 (Bramcote, Nottingham: AlcuinGROW, 1980), 28. Spinks argued, however, that the Institution Narrative was probably a later addition to both *Addai and Mari* and *Sharar*; the common core that lies beneath the two anaphoras had no Narrative; cf. Bryan D. Spinks, "The Original Form of the Anaphora of the Apostles: A Suggestion in Light of the Maronite Sharar," *Ephemerides Liturgicae* 91 (1977): 146–61.

96. Syriac transliteration of τύπος, i.e., "type" or "likeness."

97. Gelston, *Eucharistic Prayer of Addai and Mari*, 107–8.

98. I wish to thank Dr. Edward G. Mathews, Jr., for his guidance in transliterating the Syriac according to the generally accepted norms. I bear sold responsibility for any errors that remain.

99. William F. Macomber, "The Ancient Form of the Anaphora of the Apostles," in *East of Byzantium: Syria and Armenia in the Formative Period*, ed. Nina G. Garsoian, 73–88, here at 79–80 (Washington, DC: Dumbarton Oaks, 1982).

seemingly technical vocabulary, and the confused syntax of section G—Lang confidently asserts that "it is obvious that this would be a fitting place for the Institution Narrative."[100]

Recent studies have questioned these reconstructions and the arguments for an occult Institution Narrative. For his part, Anthony Gelston proposed at least three ways of resolving the grammatical problems of section G that do not assume the Words of Institution. The "we also" of line 51, understood by Botte to link the present praying community with that of the Last Supper, could be construed as adding or contrasting the present community (1) to the inhabitants of the earth of line 43, (2) the departed of line 47, or (3) to the ministers and other members of the Church of lines 48–50. "In each case," Gelston notes, "a satisfactory sense is obtained,"[101] without conjuring a missing Narrative.

The problem of identifying a main verb for section G, however, still remains. As the text stands, the only grammatically acceptable solution is that the verb "to know" (line 43) governs all of sections F and G: the sense being "that all the inhabitants of the world may know thee . . ." (line 43) "and [that] we also [may know thee]" (line 51). Gelston acknowledges that "it does mean that the whole of ll. 41–55 constitutes a single, rather straggling, sentence."[102] As a result, he proposes that an earlier form of *Addai and Mari* might have looked like this:

E – F

Do thou, O my Lord, in thy manifold mercies
make a good remembrance for all the upright and just fathers,
the prophets and apostles and martyrs and confessors,
in the commemoration of the body and blood of thy Christ,
which we offer to thee upon the pure and holy altar,
as thou hast taught us in his life-giving Gospel.
And make with us thy tranquility and thy peace all the days of the age,
that all the inhabitants of the world may know thee,
that thou alone art God the true Father,
and thou didst send our Lord Jesus Christ thy Son and thy Beloved.
And may they stand before thee in all purity and holiness,
the bishops and priests and deacons
and all the children of the holy Church,
signed with the sign of holy Baptism.

100. Lang, "Eucharist without Institution Narrative?" 46.
101. Gelston, *Eucharistic Prayer of Addai and Mari*, 105.
102. Ibid., 104.

G

And we also, O my Lord, thy servants, who are gathered *and stand
    before thee*,
and have received by tradition the example which is from thee,
rejoicing and glorifying and exalting and commemorating and
    celebrating this mystery
of the passion and death and resurrection of our Lord Jesus Christ.[103]

On the basis of a comparison with a sixth-century East Syrian
anaphora fragment published by R. H. Connolly,[104] Gelston suggests
that the verb linking the two sections was originally "to stand" viz.
"*may they stand before thee* in all purity and holiness, the bishops . . .
and all the children of the holy church . . . and we also . . . who
are gathered *and stand before thee*."[105] Notice also that the reference to
the "upright and just fathers" (line 38) is here joined directly to the
"prophets and apostles . . ." of line 47. However, against Macomber,
who supposed that this fusion accounts for the disappearance of an
intervening Institution Narrative, Gelston follows Engberding[106] and
argues that "the intervening material . . . [is] a secondary insertion."[107]
Yet, even if we reject this as another improvable reconstruction, the
text as it stands exhibits a clear sequence of thought:

(a) Statements that this is a eucharistic gathering for priestly service
(l. 51) and offering (l. 40) and cultic celebration (l. 54);

(b) an *anamnēsis* of the passion, death, and resurrection of Christ
(ll. 53–55) or variously of his body and blood (l. 39); and

(c) a deliberate reference of the present celebration to the institution of
the Eucharist at the Last Supper (ll. 40b and 52).[108]

103. Ibid., 121; emphasis added.
104. R. H. Connolly, "Sixth-Century Fragments of an East-Syrian
Anaphora," *Oriens Christianus* ns 12–14 (1925): 99–128.
105. Gelston, *Eucharistic Prayer of Addai and Mari*, 105; emphasis added.
106. Hieronymus Engberding, "Zum anaphorischen Fürbittgebet der ost-
syrischen Liturgie der Apostel Addaj und Mar(j)," *Oriens Christianus* 41 (1957):
102–24; here at 107ff. Engberding also sees a connection between "thou hast
taught us" (line 40) and "he . . . taught us" (line 46) and regards lines 41–45 as
a later elaboration. Gelston modifies Engberding's reconstruction somewhat
so that the "prophets and apostles . . ." (line 47) directly modify "the upright
and just fathers" (line 38).
107. Gelston, *Eucharistic Prayer of Addai and Mari*, 97–98.
108. Ibid., 108.

Even without an Institution Narrative, Gelston sees no deficiency in *Addai and Mari*'s articulation of the intent to fulfill the Lord's command to make memorial of his saving passion and resurrection:

> There may be no formal Institution Narrative and no independent *anamnēsis* as a separate section of the anaphora, but it cannot be denied that the substance of both such elements is clearly present in the anaphora in such a way as to suggest that it is of primary importance in determining the nature of what is being done.[109]

From a grammatical, thematic, and theological perspective, *Addai and Mari* constitutes a coherent and complete prayer both as it exists in the manuscript tradition and in Gelston's proposed earlier form.

Other scholars refuse to posit any hypothetical reconstructions of the primitive core behind *Addai and Mari* and *Sharar*. For Sarhad Jammo, *Addai and Mari* as it appears in the earliest manuscript, the tenth-century *Ḥudra* of the Church of Mar Esh'aya in Mosul, *is* the common core.[110] Since every paragraph of *Addai and Mari* is paralleled in the Maronite *Sharar*, while the reverse is not true, Jammo sees no "need for a phantom common core for both. A&M is the Urtext of Peter III (= *Sharar*)."[111] Nonetheless, through a comparison with the *Birkat ha-Mazon* (the Jewish meal blessing believed to be the model from which early Christian Eucharistic prayers developed), *Didache* 10, and *Apostolic Constitutions* VII, 25, Jammo believes that *Addai and Mari* evolved in at least three stages to its present form. Following Ratcliff,[112] he identifies the Sanctus and the *epiclesis* as later additions to the earliest stratum, and the references to the Last Supper (Gelston's lines 39–46), as yet a further expansion. The resulting grammatical confusion he attributes to the "hasty composition and

109. Ibid., 108–9.

110. Published in William F. Macomber, "The Oldest Known Text of the Anaphora of the Apostles *Addai and Mari*," *Orientalia Christiana Periodica* 32 (1966): 335–71.

111. Sarhad Jammo, "The Anaphora of the Apostles *Addai and Mari*: A Study of Structure and Historical Background," *Orientalia Christiana Periodica* 68 (2002): 5–35; here at 10.

112. Edward Craddock Ratcliff, "The Original Form of the Anaphora of *Addai and Mari*: A Suggestion," *Journal of Theological Studies* 30 (1928–29): 23–32; here at 32.

patchwork" of this final expansion.[113] While Jammo may have been too confident in the conclusions he draws from the verbal parallels with the *Birkat ha-Mazon*, he is convinced that "the Eucharistic Institution narrative could not belong to the original text of our Anaphora."[114]

The East Syrian Liturgical Commentaries

Despite the emerging consensus among liturgical historians, Lang turns to five East Syrian liturgical commentaries for confirmation that the Words of Institution were always part of *Addai and Mari*. In his fifteenth catechetical homily, Theodore of Mopsuestia († 428) comments on much of the anaphora, but makes no mention of the Institution Narrative. However, Lang is certain that the anaphora known to Theodore must have contained one since, in the preceding homily, he quotes a Narrative that fuses Matthew 26:26-28 and 1 Corinthians 11:24-25, "and hence is most likely a liturgical formula."[115] Similarly, in the *Homily on the Mysteries* attributed to Narsai († 502),[116] the author quotes a version of the dominical words that does not correspond directly to any of the biblical versions; Lang again assumes we are dealing with a liturgical formula.[117] More persuasive perhaps is the seventh-century *Commentary on the Liturgy* by Gabriel Qatraya referred to earlier. In the fifth *Memra* (i.e., metrical homily), Gabriel writes:

> Up to here the Church depicts, through her types, the Mystery/symbol of the death and burial of Christ. From now on the priest approaches to depict the

113. Jammo, "Anaphora of the Apostles *Addai and Mari*," 20–27.

114. Jammo, "Anaphora of the Apostles *Addai and Mari*," 5; id., "The Quddasha of the Apostles *Addai and Mari*," *Syriac Dialogue* 1 (Vienna: Pro Oriente Foundation, 1994): 168–82.

115. Lang, "Eucharist without Institution Narrative?" 51.

116. See Sebastian Brock, "Diachronic aspects of Syriac word formation: an Aid for Dating Anonymous Texts," in René Lavenant, ed., *V. Symposium Syriacum*, Katholieke Universiteit, Leuven, 29–31, August 1988, Orientalia Christiana Analecta 236 (Rome: Pontifical Oriental Institute, 1990): 321–30; according to Brock, this homily is to be dated somewhat later in the early sixth century.

117. Syriac text in Alphonse Mingana, *Selected Works of Narsai*, 2 vols. (Piscataway: Gorgias Press, 2009); ET in J. Armitage Robinson, ed., Richard Hugh Connolly, *The Liturgical Homilies of Narsai*, Texts and Studies 8.1 (Eugene, OR: Wipf & Stock Publishers, 2004), 16–17.

type of the Resurrection through the recital [199b] of the holy words from his mouth, and by the sign (*rushma*) of the cross which is in his hand. *For just as our Lord Jesus Christ, when he transmitted these Mysteries, blessed, gave thanks and said (these words), so the Church, in accordance with his bidding, separates out a single priest to be the one who blesses and gives thanks, in the likeness of Christ our Lord. Through the recital, he indicates that he is uttering the words of our Lord,* (saying) "This is my body which is broken for you for the forgiveness of sins" (1 Cor. 11:24). *After the priest's recital, blessing the bread and the wine, through the grace of the Holy Spirit which overshadows, they become henceforth the Body and Blood of Christ—not by nature, but by faith and effectiveness.*[118]

Here it seems unmistakable that we are dealing with a liturgical recitation of the Institution Narrative, at least over the bread, within the context of an anaphora. The question is which anaphora? A little later in the *Memra* (V.73:4), Gabriel writes that "through the suffering and death (of Christ) we have been held worthy of this entire gift, in order that we might have expectation of resurrection and delight with Christ in eternal life."[119] Lang sees here a "striking reference to 'the passion and death and resurrection of our Lord' [Gelston's line 55], which has an equivalent only in the anamnetical part of *Addai and Mari*, not in *Theodore* or *Nestorius*."[120] If he is correct, "this would mean that Gabriel of Qatar attests the presence of an Institution Narrative in *Addai and Mari*, at least for his time."[121]

Lang is on shakier ground when he adduces the anonymous commentary once attributed to George of Arbela († 987). Writing some time after Gabriel, the author comments on the post-Sanctus in these terms:

> When [the celebrant] comes to the end of the narrative about the sacrifice, that is, when the Lord delivered his body and blood, he completes

118. *Commentary on the Liturgy* V.2:56, ET in Sebastian Brock, "Gabriel of Qatar's Commentary on the Liturgy," *Hugoye* 6.2 (2003): 17; reprinted in id., *Fire from Heaven*, XVII, 17; emphases are Brock's; Syriac available at http://syrcom.cua.edu/hugoye/Vol6No2/HV6N2Brock.html#S3.

119. Brock, "Gabriel of Qatar's Commentary on the Liturgy," 20–21. Lang does not cite the passage from Gabriel's *Commentary*, so I am left to assume that this is the verbal correspondence he wishes to highlight.

120. Lang, "Eucharist without Institution Narrative?" 55.

121. Ibid.

the *gehanta* with the seal of the Trinity, and the people, because, being perfect, they know the secret (prayer) of the priest, answer "Amen."[122]

While it is possible that the author has the anaphora of *Theodore* in mind,[123] Lang proposes that, since *Addai and Mari* was used far more frequently, "the reference to the Institution Narrative . . . may well apply to *Addai and Mari* as well."[124]

And finally, in the *Book of the Pearl*, Abdisho bar Brika († 1318) quotes an Institution Narrative and writes that "the matter of this sacrament Christ ordained to be of wheat and wine, as being most fit to represent body and blood. *The form he conveys through his life-giving word,* and by the descent of the Holy Spirit."[125] Lang notes that Abdisho reveals an acquaintance with Aristotelian categories and that "it would seem inconceivable that in a more popular catechetical work like the *Book of the Pearl* such an emphasis could have been put on the Institution Narrative if it had not been part of *Addai and Mari,* the anaphora most frequently used in the Church of the East."[126]

Beginning with Abdisho, we can make several observations. First, we must question Lang's contention that an Institution Narrative that does not match one of the biblical iterations, or fuses two or more of them together, *must* be a liturgical formula. It is likely that Abdisho is quoting the words from memory so that the lack of a verbatim correspondence to the Synoptics or Paul springs from a rather free paraphrase or pastiche of all of them. Such inexactitude is a demonstrable hallmark of the patristic quotation of Scripture. Second, Abdisho refers to the Words of Institution as spoken by Christ at the Last Supper, not by the minister praying the anaphora. Third, his entire treatment of the Eucharist smacks of apologetic rancor. In the following section, Abdisho defends the practice of the *Malka* in these terms:

122. R. H. Connolly, ed., *Anonymi auctoris Expositio officiorum ecclesiae, Georgio Arbelensi vulgo adscripta,* Corpus Scriptorum Christianorum Orientalium, Scriptores Syri 91–92 (Paris: C. Poussielgue, 1911–15) CSCO 64, 71–72, 76 (Louvain: L. Durbecq, 1954); here at vol. 92, 55–59.

123. Lang notes the correspondence between this passage (IV.23:58-59) and the *Anaphora of Theodore* in the edition of Hänggi-Pahl, *Prex eucharistica,* 382–84.

124. Lang, "Eucharist without Institution Narrative?" 56.

125. *Marganitha* IV.5; ET modified by Lang from G. P. Badger, *The Nestorians and their Rituals,* 2 vols. (London, 1852), vol. 2, 409; emphasis added.

126. Lang, "Eucharist without Institution Narrative?" 57.

The holy and blessed Apostles, Thomas and Bartholomew of the Twelve, and Adi [sic] and Mari of the Seventy, who discipled the East, committed to all the Eastern Churches a Holy Leaven, to be kept for the perfecting of the administration of the Sacrament of our Lord's Body until His coming again. And should any Christians dispute the fact of the above-mentioned Apostles having committed to those of the East this Leaven, on the ground that Peter, the head of the Apostles, and his companions did not commit it to the Westerns, and should object to us on this wise: "If it be as you say, then one of these two consequences must result: either the Apostles did not agree in their mode of discipling, which is impossible, or this tradition of yours is false." We reply: The Easterns from the day of their discipleship up to this day have kept their faith as a sacred deposit, and have observed, without change, the Apostolical Canons; and notwithstanding all the persecutions which they have suffered from many kings, and their subjection to the severe yoke of a foreign power, they have never altered their creed nor changed their canons. Such as are well versed in such matters know full well the labour and care required on the part of Christians to observe these canons, and more especially to preserve this Leaven, in a difficult country, where there is no Christian sovereign to support them, nor any commander to back them, and where they are continually persecuted, vexed, and troubled. Had this Leaven not been of apostolical transmission they would not, most assuredly, have endured all these afflictions and trials to keep it together with the orthodox faith. Then, as to their argument drawn from Peter and the great Apostles who discipled the west, we have this to oppose to them,—that those Apostles did transmit the same to the Westerns, but that with their alteration of the faith, the canons also were corrupted, through the influence of heretical rulers. And, in proof of this statement, we urge that if they all held the traditions of the Apostles, the Franks would not offer an unleavened, and the Romans [Greeks] a leavened oblation; since the Apostles did not transmit it in two different ways. Therefore the Westerns have changed the faith and the canons, and not the Easterns.[127]

It seems that certain "westerners" have questioned East Syrian liturgical practice compelling Abdisho to defend his tradition. It may be for this reason also that Abdisho dwells almost exclusively on the Words of Institution in his treatment "Of the oblation." Considering the centrality of the Holy Spirit in all East Syrian liturgical commentaries and especially in its Eucharistic theology, it is odd that Abdisho makes no

---

127. *Marganitha* IV.6; ET in Badger, *Nestorians and their Rituals*, vol. 2, 409–10.

mention of the *epiclesis* in this section but concludes nonetheless that "the form he [Christ] conveys through his life-giving word, *and by the descent of the Holy Spirit.*" The emphasis placed on the dominical words is so lopsided that it appears that Abdisho is overcompensating in the face of Western critics. We might conjecture further that Abdisho may be coming to the defense of *Addai and Mari* itself. In the end, we can only speculate which anaphora Abdisho had in mind and whether it contained an Institution Narrative. What is certain, however, is that Abdisho's Nisibis had contacts with a West that found much to criticize in the East Syrian tradition. And, as we shall see below, it may have been through Western influence that the Words of Institution entered East Syrian anaphoral praying. Ultimately, since his witness comes from such a late date and from a time after significant contacts with the West, it tells us nothing of the unalloyed liturgical theology of East Syria and nothing of the original form of *Addai and Mari* in particular.

The commentary of Ps.-George of Arbela is equally inconclusive. First, it is by no means assured that the author is referring to a proper Institution Narrative when he speaks of "the narrative about the sacrifice . . . when the Lord delivered his body and blood." It is possible that the *gehanta* contained an account of the Last Supper without a verbatim repetition of the Words of Institution in the first person. Nevertheless, if we grant Lang's reading that this passage is referring to the dominical words, we may question whether the author was commenting on *Addai and Mari*. Note that Ps.-George indicates that this *gehanta* concluded "with the seal of the Trinity." The "seal of the Trinity" I take to be some kind of trinitarian doxology to which, as the author says, "the people . . . answer 'Amen.'" If that is the case, it would seem certain that the author does not have *Addai and Mari* in mind here since *none* of the *gehanta* prayers in that anaphora concludes with such a doxology. The corresponding *gehanta* prayers of the anaphoras of *Theodore*[128] and *Nestorius*,[129] on the other hand, contain Institution

---

128. ET in Bryan D. Spinks, *Mar Nestorius and Mar Theodore the Interpreter: The Forgotten Eucharistic Prayers of East Syria*, Alcuin GROW Liturgical Study 45 (Cambridge: Grove Books, 1999), 30, 35–36. For critical edition, see Jacob Vadakkel, *The East Syrian Anaphora of Mar Theodore of Mopsuestia: A Critical Edition*, Oriental Institute of Religious Studies Publications 129 (Vadavathoor: Kottayam, India, 1989).

129. Anthony Gelston, "The Origin of the Anaphora of *Nestorius*: Greek or Syriac?" in J. F. Coakley and K. Parry, eds., *The Church of the East: Life and*

Narratives *and* do indeed conclude with trinitarian doxologies. It is surely these anaphoras, and not *Addai and Mari*, that are providing the fodder for his commentary at this point.[130]

The same can be said for the *Commentary* of Gabriel of Qatar (ca. 615–25). In the *memra* where he treats the anaphora (*Brit. Mus. Or. 3336*: fos. 199ʳ–200ʳ), Gabriel quotes an Institution Narrative and stresses its significance, but, as Spinks observed, "the commentary is so general that it could serve for practically any anaphora."[131] In fact, the few verbal resonances that may exist in the commentary at this point are with the anaphora of *Theodore*. However, Spinks draws attention to two earlier passages (fos. 184ʳ and 196ʳ) that do not deal directly with the Eucharistic prayer but do quote the Words of Institution and add the peculiar admonition "Be doing thus whenever you gather together in my memory," which is not biblical in either the Greek or Peshitta NT and may be an East Syrian liturgical embolism. After the first of these, Gabriel continues: "But if the mysteries are performed in memory *of the passion, death, and resurrection of our Lord*, the holy apostles have correctly ordered us that everyday [sic] if possible we should not taste anything until we receive the holy mysteries."[132]

Thought, Bulletin of the John Rylands University Library of Manchester 78.3 (1996): 73–86. Gelston concludes, against earlier scholarship, that the anaphora was composed in Syriac and not translated from a Greek original. See also his related study, "The Biblical Citations in the Syriac Anaphoras of James and the Twelve Apostles," *Studia Patristica* 35 (Leuven: Peeters, 2001): 271–74.

130. Another possibility is that Ps.-George is referring to the commixture rite that takes place *after* the anaphora. In his *Homily* XXI, Narsai († 503) writes: "He breaks the Bread and casts [it] into the Wine, and he signs and says: '*In the name of the Father and the Son and the Spirit*, an equal nature.' With the name of the Divinity, three hypostases, he completes his words; and as one dead he raises the Mystery, as a symbol of the verity." ET in R. H. Connolly, *The Liturgical Homilies of Narsai* (Cambridge: Cambridge University Press, 1909), 59; emphasis added. However, since the congregation does not respond with "Amen," this is a less plausible referent than the *gehanta* prayers of *Theodore* and *Nestorius*. See also, Bryan D. Spinks, "A Note on the Anaphora Outlined in Narsai's Homily XXXII," *Journal of Theological Studies* 31 (1980): 82–93.

131. Bryan D. Spinks, "*Addai and Mari* and the Institution Narrative: The Tantalising Evidence of Gabriel Qatraya," *Ephemerides Liturgicae* 98 (1984): 60–67; here at 63.

132. Fos. 184ʳ–185ᵛ; ET in Spinks, "Tantalising Evidence of Gabriel Qatraya," 66; emphasis in Spinks.

This phrase—"memory of the passion, death, and resurrection of our Lord"—appears in the preanaphoral prayer of both *Theodore* and *Nestorius*. But Spinks notes that it also appears in the *"anamnesis"* of *Addai and Mari*: "and celebrating this great and awesome mystery of the passion and death and resurrection of our Lord Jesus Christ."[133] Since the Institution Narrative that Gabriel quotes is not biblical, Spinks concludes that it is a liturgical formula and that his whole discussion would logically be dictated by the narrative sequence of the anaphora. If so, then Gabriel would have to be following *Addai and Mari* here because the same phrase in *Theodore* and *Nestorius* occurs in their respective preanaphoras, not after their Institution Narratives. This suggested to Spinks that the form of *Addai and Mari* known to Gabriel may have contained the Words of Institution. Ultimately, he confesses that "the evidence . . . remains inconclusive."[134]

Though the argument is indeed "tantalizing," Spinks hastens to point out that even if Gabriel's *Addai and Mari* contained the dominical words, it does not mean that they belonged to the earliest stratum. In fact, as noted above, Spinks argued in an earlier piece that the Institution Narrative was added during the catholicosate of Mar Aba I (540–52) when the anaphoras of *Theodore* and *Nestorius* were introduced.[135] Moreover, since the argument relies on Botte's hypothetical reconstruction of the particular form of Institution Narrative posited for *Addai and Mari*, it rises and falls on the merits of that reconstruction. As we have seen, Gelston was unconvinced by Botte's hypothesis because it rested on an emendation of the text not supported by the earliest manuscripts.[136] In addition, even if Gabriel is referring to the liturgical Institution Narrative and *anamnesis* in folios 184–85, those two elements alone are not enough to prove that the sequence of *one* anaphora is guiding his comments. It is equally likely that Gabriel is drawing from memory freely from all three anaphoras. Thus, the Words of Institution he quotes may be those of *Theodore* or *Nestorius*, while the phrase "memory of the passion, death, and resurrection of our Lord" may be drawn from *Addai and Mari*. Alternatively, Gabriel

---

133. Gelston, *Eucharistic Prayer of Addai and Mari*, 54–55; lines 54–55.

134. Spinks, "Tantalising Evidence of Gabriel Qatraya," 67.

135. Bryan D. Spinks, "The Original Form of the Anaphora of the Apostles: A Suggestion in Light of Maronite Sharar," *Ephemerides Liturgicae* 91 (1977): 146–61.

136. Gelston, *Eucharistic Prayer of Addai and Mari*, 106–7.

may not be quoting *any* Eucharistic prayer. Spinks warns that "while the context invites reference to an anamnesis, Qatraya is not at this point discussing the anaphora, and so the context does not demand such a reference."[137]

Narsai's homily *On the Mysteries* brings us no closer to *Addai and Mari*'s phantom Institution Narrative. Though he quotes the Words of Institution,[138] Narsai claims the anaphora upon which he is commenting was composed by Theodore, an attribution that Macomber considered reliable.[139] Lang was aware that Narsai was not referring to *Addai and Mari* and so it is unclear why he adduces the homily, unless perhaps to demonstrate that Eucharistic prayers with Institution Narratives were known in East Syria by the early decades of the sixth century. That the East Syrian tradition prayed such anaphoras, however, has never been questioned. Narsai surely cannot be used to prove that the Words of Institution were to be found in *Addai and Mari* as well in spite of whatever euchological trend to which he is witness.

Finally, the homilies of Theodore of Mopsuestia do not reflect East Syrian liturgical practice. Though Theodore "The Interpreter," as he is revered, was clearly influential and determinative in the East Syrian theological tradition,[140] he was born in Antioch and served as bishop of Mopsuestia (modern: Yakapinar), a town on the Pyramus River in

---

137. Spinks, "Tantalising Evidence of Gabriel Qatraya," 67.

138. "*Homily XVII*: To this effect did the Son of the Most High make confession to His Father, and these words He spoke when He gave His Body and His Blood. 'This,' said He, 'is My Body, which I have given for the debts of the world; and this, again, is My Blood, the which I have willed should be shed for sins. Whoso eateth with love of My Body and drinketh of My Blood liveth for ever, and abideth in Me, and I in him. Thus be ye doing for My memorial in the midst of your Churches; and My Body and My Blood be ye receiving in faith. Be ye offering bread and wine, as I have taught you, and I will accomplish and make them the Body and Blood. Body and Blood do I make the bread and wine through the brooding and operation of the Holy Spirit'"; ET in Connolly, *Liturgical Homilies of Narsai*, 16–17.

139. William F. Macomber, "An Anaphora Prayer Composed by Theodore of Mopsuestia," *Parole de l'Orient* 6–7 (1975–76): 341–47; as cited by Lang, "Eucharist without Institution Narrative?" 52.

140. See Sebastian Brock, "The 'Nestorian' Church: A Lamentable Misnomer," in J. F. Coakley and K. Parry, eds., *The Church of the East: Life and Thought, Bulletin of the John Rylands University Library of Manchester* 78.3 (Manchester, 1996): 23–35; reprinted in Brock, *Fire From Heaven*, 1–14.

Cilicia south of Cappadocia and over two hundred miles west of the East Syrian metropolises of Edessa and Nisibis (and over five hundred miles northwest of Seleucia-Ctesiphon). It must also be remembered that Theodore wrote after the defeat of Julian the Apostate (363) and the westward expansion of the Persian Empire, which further isolated most of East Syria from the Greco-Roman West. As such, whatever can be gleaned from his homilies regarding the structure and content of the Eucharistic prayer(s) known to him cannot be applied to *Addai and Mari*.[141] Second, the objections to nonverbatim or biblically fused Institution Narratives being liturgical formulae apply here with equal force. However, given his proximity to Antioch and Cappadocia and his personal acquaintance with John Chrysostom, the anaphora(s) Theodore prayed likely contained the Words of Institution. So the most that can be said is that Theodore's liturgical theology may have been influential in the *subsequent* adoption of Eucharistic prayers with Institution Narratives in the East Syrian tradition. But since he never commented on *Addai and Mari*, and wrote over a century after its composition, Theodore's homilies shed no light on its original form and contents.

The Reform of Isho'yahb III

Yet even if we grant Lang's interpretation of the liturgical commentaries and ignore the unanimous silence of the manuscript tradition, proponents of the originality of the Words of Institution must explain when, how, and why (if ever) they were dropped from the anaphora. Macomber accounted for the "when" and "how" when he suggested that Patriarch Isho'yahb III (649–59) excised them in the course of his widespread reforms of the East Syrian baptismal and Eucharistic liturgies.[142] The claim that Isho'yahb *abbreviated* the liturgy, however, comes

---

141. Spinks, *Mar Nestorius and Mar Theodore the Interpreter*, 15–16. From an analysis of the *Catechetical Homilies*, Spinks has demonstrated that the anaphora(s) upon which Theodore commented is of the Syro-Byzantine type, i.e., "where the epiklesis comes after the anamnesis and before the intercessions." In *Addai and Mari*, as we have seen, the intercessions come before the *epiclesis*.

142. William F. Macomber, "The Maronite and Chaldean Versions of the Anaphora of the Apostles," *Orientalia Christiana Periodica* 37 (1971): 56, 74; id., "A History of the Chaldean Mass," *Worship* 51 (1977): 112ff.; see also Gelston, *Eucharistic Prayer of Addai and Mari*, 73–74.

much later in a biographical note furnished by the eleventh-century author Ibn aṭ-Tayyib († 1043).[143]

To explain why Isho'yahb removed the dominical words, Lang points to Macomber, who, following Botte, proposed that the development of a formal Spirit *epiclesis* rendered the Institution Narrative comparatively unimportant and expendable.[144] Lang furthered the suggestion by highlighting the emphasis Theodore of Mopsuestia placed on the consecratory effect of the *epiclesis*. Given Theodore's stature as "the most authoritative theologian in the Church of the East," Lang believed "Isho'yahb III may therefore have considered the Institution Narrative in *Addai and Mari* dispensable."[145] The problem with this line of reasoning is that it assumes the *epiclesis* in *Addai and Mari*[146] does not belong to the primitive core, that it was added later to displace a preexisting Institution Narrative. Given the archaic form of the *epiclesis* in that anaphora, however, and its clear affinities with the early baptismal *epicleses* of the Syriac *Acts of the Apostles*, it seems likely that the *epiclesis* indeed belongs to the earliest stratum.[147] Moreover, if the introduction of an *epiclesis* were the motivation for removing the Institution Narrative from *Addai and Mari*, then we may ask why

143. Wilhelm Hoenerbach and Otto Spies, eds., *Fiqh an-nasraniya: "Das Recht der Christenheit,"* Corpus Scriptorum Christianorum Orientalium 167–68 (Louvain: L. Durbecq, 1956–57), 90, 93.

144. Botte, "L'Anaphore chaldéenne des Apôtres," 274.

145. Lang, "Eucharist without Institution Narrative?" 48–49.

146. Gelston, *Eucharistic Prayer of Addai and Mari*, 54–55: Section H—56 And let thy Holy Spirit come, O my Lord, and rest upon this offering of thy servants, 57 and bless it and sanctify it that it may be to us, O my Lord, for the pardon of sins 58 and for the forgiveness of shortcomings, and for the great hope of the resurrection from the dead, 59 and for new life in the kingdom of heaven with all who have been pleasing before thee.

147. Gelston includes it in his hypothetical reconstruction in ibid., 122–23; section H. See also Gabriele Winkler, "Further Observations in Connection with the Early Form of the Epiklesis," in *Studies in Early Christian Liturgy and its Context* (Aldershot: Ashgate, 1997), essay IV; Sebastian P. Brock, "Invocations to/for the Holy Spirit in Syriac liturgical texts: some comparative approaches," in *Comparative Liturgy Fifty Years after Anton Baumstark (1872–1948)*, R. F. Taft and G. Winkler, Orientalia Christiana Analecta 265 (Rome: Pontifical Oriental Institute, 2001); reprinted in id., *Fire from Heaven*, IX:385ff.; id., *The Holy Spirit in the Syrian Baptismal Tradition*, Gorgias Liturgical Studies 4 (Piscataway: Gorgias Press, 2008), passim.

Isho'yahb did not do likewise to the anaphoras of *Theodore* and *Nestorius*, which contain both elements. Finally, from the standpoint of comparative liturgy, there is to my knowledge no example of an anaphora jettisoning the Words of Institution when a pneumatic *epiclesis* was added, even when bolstered by patristic commentaries stressing the significance of the invocation of the Spirit over the gifts.

Ironically, Lang claimed further support for the originality of the Institution Narrative from *Theodore* and *Nestorius*. Earlier scholarship considered these anaphoras lightly modified translations of preexisting Greek exemplars. However, Lang points to recent research that has argued that both were originally composed in Syriac.[148] From this Lang averred that, since the anaphoras of *Theodore* and *Nestorius* were modeled in part on *Addai and Mari*, "it would seem odd to assume that *Addai and Mari* did not have an Institution Narrative at a time when it was used as a source for two new anaphoras of the East Syrian rite that contained the dominical words as an integral part of the Eucharistic prayer."[149] While this research argues soundly for Syriac composition, it points to the many features borrowed from Greek anaphoras. Gelston, for instance, cites several studies that see the anaphora of

148. Jacob Vadakkel, *The East Syrian Anaphora of Mar Theodore of Mopsuestia: A Critical Edition*, Oriental Institute of Religious Studies Publications 129 (Vadavathoor: Kottayam, India, 1989); Pierre Yousif, "The Anaphora of Mar *Theodore*: East Syrian, Further Evidences," in *ΕΥΛΟΓΗΜΑ: Studies in Honor of Robert Taft*, ed. E. Carr, S. Parenti, A. A. Thiermeyer, and E. Velkovska, Studia Anselmiana 110, Analecta Liturgica 17 (Rome: Centro Studi S. Anselmo, 1993), 571–91; Anthony Gelston, "The Relationship of the Anaphoras of *Theodore* and *Nestorius* to that of *Addai and Mari*," in *Tuvaik: Studies in honour of Revd Dr Jacob Vellian*, ed. G. Karukaparampil, Syrian Churches Series 16 (Kottayam: 1995), 20–26; id., "The Origin of the Anaphora of *Nestorius*: Greek or Syriac?" *Bulletin of the John Rylands University Library of Manchester* 78 (1996): 73–86; id., "The Biblical Citations in the Syriac Anaphoras of James and the Twelve Apostles," *Studia Patristica* 35 (2001): 271–74; Spinks, *Mar Nestorius and Mar Theodore the Interpreter*, 9–12. It is interesting that Lang willingly accepts this recent shift in scholarly opinion while remaining suspicious of the scholarly shift suggesting *Addai and Mari* never contained an Institution Narrative: "Many liturgists today contend that it did not have one; however, until recently there seems to have been a consensus among scholars that *Addai and Mari* in its early form contained the words of Institution" (Lang, "Eucharist without Institution Narrative?" 36).

149. Lang, "Eucharist without Institution Narrative?" 50.

Nestorius as a fusion of the anaphoras of *Basil* and *Chrysostom* with that of *Addai and Mari*.[150] It is a specious argument, therefore, to insist that what is found in *Theodore* and *Nestorius* must have been found in *Addai and Mari*. Gelston also notes that the anaphoral repertoire was more varied before the reforms of Isho'yahb. Anaphoras of *Chrysostom*, *Ephrem*, *Narsai*, and *Barsauma* are mentioned by several later medieval sources.[151] Though Gelston does not suggest as much, perhaps Isho'yahb's reputation for liturgical pruning may have had something to do with the desuetude of these anaphoras following his catholicosate.

Finally, it is worth noting that Isho'yahb's reforms brought the East Syrian tradition up to date with liturgical trends elsewhere. It was his initiative, for instance, that introduced a postbaptismal anointing to the rites of initiation; previously East Syria knew only anointing *before* the water bath.[152] Thus, it would seem quite inconceivable for him to have removed the Words of Institution from *Addai and Mari* since doing so would have isolated his Church further from the liturgical practices of other communions. Why would he have chosen to imitate on baptismal practice while dissociating on patterns of Eucharistic praying? Admittedly, one might then ask, if *Addai and Mari* never contained the dominical words, why did Isho'yahb not feel compelled to add them? Perhaps, through the belief in its apostolic origin and its centuries of use, *Addai and Mari* had acquired both a relatively fixed form and a canonical status. Or perhaps the desire to pray the dominical words was sated by *Theodore* and *Nestorius*. One can only speculate.

CONCLUSION

Over the past decade, a stream of critics has questioned the pontifical decrees sanctioning intercommunion between the Church of the East and its Sister Church, the Chaldean Catholic Church. The decision to allow Chaldean Catholics to receive the Eucharist at a liturgy celebrated using an anaphora without the Words of Institution appeared to these critics to undermine centuries of traditional Roman Catholic

---

150. Gelston, *Eucharistic Prayer of Addai and Mari*, 24.

151. Ibid., 24.

152. See Maxwell E. Johnson, *The Rites of Christian Initiation: Their Evolution and Interpretation*, 2nd ed. (Collegeville: Liturgical Press, 2007), 144; Joseph Chalassery, *The Holy Spirit and Christian Initiation in the East Syrian Tradition* (Rome: Mar Thoma Yogam, 1995), 88.

sacramental theology and long-held assumptions of liturgical history. To combat this perceived threat, Gherardini, Santogrossi, Lang, and others argued that (1) the unqualified conviction of the universal Church is that consecration is accomplished in and by the recitation of the dominical words, and that (2) *Addai and Mari* always contained them until recently when they had disappeared out of ignorance or neglect.

Recent liturgical scholarship has shown that neither claim can be sustained. Attempts to paint late medieval scholastic theology as the unbroken tradition of both East and West strain the patristic evidence to the breaking point. We find patristic writers variously attributing the change of the bread and wine to the Words of Institution, to the *epiclesis*, and to the anaphora as a whole. Their aim was not to dogmatize one or another of these elements as *the* moment of consecration. Their intent, rather, was to probe the depths of the sacrament from several vantage points, each contributing to the vista and none exhausting completely the fullness of the mystery.

Equally erroneous is the belief that Roman Catholic scholastic theology and the *Canon Missae* are the benchmark against which all forms of Eucharistic praying must be vetted. If *Addai and Mari* is "defective" for its lack of an Institution Narrative, then the Roman Canon must be deficient for its lack of a proper *epiclesis*. Rather than passing such subjective and historically unfounded aspersions on these anaphoras, today's liturgical scholar places them in their appropriate context on the continuum of anaphoral evolution. *Addai and Mari* has no Institution Narrative because it was composed at a very early date—no extant contemporaneous pre-Nicene Eucharistic prayers contained it—and because it was influenced by Semitic forms of prayer. Likewise, the Roman Canon lacks an *epiclesis* because it was redacted, in large part, prior to the pneumatological controversies of the late fourth century.

Neither can it be proved that *Addai and Mari* originally and always contained a Narrative of Institution. While the debate will and should continue, the emerging consensus among liturgical historians is that the anaphora never contained the dominical words. The conspicuous silence of the manuscripts and the East Syrian liturgical commentators, coupled with general insights into the way Eucharistic prayers evolved, tip the scales heavily against an Institution Narrative. As such, *Addai and Mari* as prayed for nearly two millennia by the Church of the East represents a traditional and authentic celebration of the Lord's Supper by an apostolic Church with "true sacraments, and above all, by apostolic succession, the priesthood and the Eucharist."[153] The Roman Catholic Magisterium had no choice but to accept the functional intercommunion of these two Churches and it ought to stand by that decision.

To reverse these decrees would fly in the face of scholarship, have disastrous implications for ecumenical dialogue, and threaten further the spiritual lives of an already beleaguered community. Whether in diaspora throughout the world or under duress in their homeland, the only consolation many Iraqi Christians have is the nourishment they share in the one bread and one cup that gushes from the wellspring of their common ancestral apostolic tradition. While the historians and canonists continue the debate, let them be reminded: *suprema lex salus animarum est*—the salvation of souls is the greatest law.

153. *Unitatis redintegratio,* § 15.

* To these tragedies can be added the recent attack on the Syrian Catholic cathedral in Baghdad in October, 2010. The initial raid and ensuing botched hostage crisis, which occurred just as this collection of essays was going to press, claimed the lives of 53 worshippers and clergy. See the following (accessed November 8, 2010) for an account: http://www.bbc.co.uk/news/world-middle-east-11463544#story_continues_1 and http://www.nytimes.com/2010/11/08/world/middleeast/08baghdad.html. Though the Syrian Catholic Church is a separate ecclesial entity from the Chaldean and Assyrian Churches, the incident serves nonetheless to underscore again the disturbing trend of unchecked anti-Catholic violence in the region. The funeral liturgy was presided over by the Chaldean Catholic Patriarch Emmanuel III Delly.

III. The Mystery of the Holy Leaven (*Malka*) in the East Syrian Tradition

The *Malka* (*melka*) or mystery of the Holy Leaven is unique to the Church of the East. The word *malka* literally means "king," but in liturgical usage it refers to a special dough powder, a small part of which is added to the Eucharistic bread. Like most Eastern Churches, the Church of the East uses leavened bread in communion. According to R. M. Woolley, the bread is "round in shape, 2-2¼ inches across by ½ inch thick, and are stamped with a crosslet and four small crosses."[1] But it is to this bread that the *Malka* is added prior to baking. Although known as the Holy Leaven, *Malka* has several ingredients but ironically none of them are leaven. The *Malka* is renewed in a special rite on Maundy Thursday, and the rubric specifies its ingredients thus: "First, on the Thursday of Pascha they shall bring fine wheaten flour that is '*smidha*,' two thirds and one third of fine pure pounded salt, and they shall pour upon it a little fine preserved olive-oil and three drops of water, and they shall mix them together on the carved Eucharistic slab, the Sacristan and another priest or more and the deacons with them."[2] The *Malka* is a raza, a mystery, and is singled out by Mar Abdisho of Nisibis and Armenia (thirteenth century) as a mystery (= sacrament) alongside ordination, baptism, oil of unction, the Eucharist itself, absolution, and the sign of the cross.[3]

It would seem that the first reference to this practice is found in the patriarchal canons of Yohanan bar Abgareh († 905), two of which specified the use of the *Malka*. Thus Canon 15 stated: "A priest is obligated to prepare the Eucharistic bread for the Holy Qurbana and to mix the Holy Leaven with it, in addition to the simple leaven."[4] Here

---

1. R. M. Woolley, *The Bread of the Eucharist* (Milwaukee: Young Churchman Co., 1913), 58–59.
2. Ibid., 66–67.
3. Mar Abdisho, *The Book of Marginitha (The Pearl)*, ET Mar Eshai Shimun XXIII (Ernakulum [India]: Mar Themotheus Memorial Printing House, 1965), 45.
4. Soro, art. cit., Joseph Kelaita, ed., *The Liturgy of the East* (Mosel, 1928), 211.

a distinction is made between the Holy Leaven and simple leaven. An explanation for the origin of the *Malka* is found in the thirteenth-century work *Book of the Bee* by Shlemon of Basra:

> Some men have a tradition that when our Lord broke his body for his disciples in the upper room, John the son of Zebedee hid a part of his portion until our Lord rose from the dead. And when our Lord appeared to his disciples and to Thomas with them, he said to Thomas, "Hither with your finger and lay it on my side and be not unbelieving, but believing." Thomas put his finger near to the Lord's side and it rested upon the mark of the spear, and the disciples saw the blood from the marks of the spear and nails. And John took that piece of consecrated bread, and wiped up that blood with it; and the Easterns, Mar Addai and Mar Mari, took that piece, and with it they sanctified this unleavened bread which has been handed down among us.[5]

A much more complex account of its origin is given by Johannan Bar Zobi in the fourteenth century:

> I confess two sacraments in the holy Church—one the sacrament of Baptism, and the other the sacrament of the Body and Blood. The foundation of these two is laid in the flesh of our Lord, and it is fit that I should explain this for the edification of the sons of the Church. Peter the Apostle wrote this account, and I am therefore bound to record it without any alteration. When our Saviour was baptized of John in the river Jordan, John beheld his greatness, i.e., His Divinity and humanity, and understood that he did not submit to be baptized on his own account, but in order to set us an example that we should be baptized even as he was. And the blessed John was graciously inspired to take from Christ's baptism a little leaven for our baptism. So when the Lord went up out of the water whilst the water was yet dripping from his body, John approached our Lord, and collected these drops in a phial; and when the day of his martyrdom arrived he committed it to his disciple, and commanded him to preserve it with great care until the time should come when it would be required. This disciple was John the son of Zebedee, who he knew would become our Lord's steward. Accordingly, after his baptism, our Lord called John, and made him his beloved disciple; and when he was about to close his dispensation, and his passion and death drew nigh, on the evening preceding the Friday

---

5. Shlemon of Basra, *Book of the Bee*, ed. and trans. E. A. Wallis Budge (Oxford, 1886), 102, accessed at http://www.sacred-texts.com/chr/bb/bb47.htm.

he committed his Passover to his disciples in the bread and wine, as it is written, and gave to each a loaf; but to John he gave two loaves, and put it into his heart to eat one and to preserve the other, that it might serve as leaven to be retained in the Church for perpetual commemoration. After this, when our Lord was seized by the Jews, and the disciples through fear hid themselves, John was the only one who remained. And when they crucified the Lord in much ignominy with the thieves, John alone was present, determined to see what would become of him. Then the chief priests ordered that the crucified ones should be taken down from the cross, and that their legs should be broken, in order that if yet alive they might die outright. The soldiers did this to the thieves, but when they came to our Lord and found that he was dead already, they brake not his legs, but one of them with a spear pierced his side, and straightway there came out blood and water, of which John was witness. Now this blood is a token of the sacrament of the body and blood in the Church, and the water is a token of the new birth in believers. John was the only one who perceived this separateness of the water and the blood, and he bears witness thereof, as he says, that we might believe. He declares that he saw them unmixed, in that he did not take of them together, but of each separately. He took of the blood upon the loaf, which he had reserved from the paschal feast, and he took of the water in that same vessel which had been committed to him by John the Baptist. The very blood of his body, therefore, mixed with the bread, which he had called his body, and the water from his side mingled with the water from his baptism. After he rose from the grave and ascended up in glory to His Father, and sent the grace of his Spirit upon his disciples to endow them with wisdom, he commanded his apostles to ordain in his Church that same leaven which they had taken from his body to be for the sacrament of his body, and also for the sacrament of baptism. And when the disciples went forth to convert the nations, they divided this leaven amongst themselves, and they took oil of unction and mixed it with the water, which was kept in the vessel, and they divided this also amongst themselves to be a leaven for baptism. The loaf which John had, and which was mixed with the blood which flowed from his side, they bruised into powder, then mixed it with flour and salt, and divided it among them, each portion being put into a separate vessel to serve as leaven for the body and blood of Christ in the Church. This is the account which I have read, which bore the sign of Peter, and I have written it as I found it for the benefit of such as may read this our epistle.[6]

6. Cited in G. P. Badger, *The Nestorians and their Rituals*, vol. 11 (London: Masters and Co., 1853), 151–53.

Of course, this interesting midrash is different from Shlemon of Basra's account, and suggests, as Paul Bradshaw has observed, that when we find more than one account for the origin of a custom or tradition, it usually means that the origin has been entirely forgotten.[7] What might have been the origin of the *Malka* custom? Given the missionary activity of this Church, which reached not only India but also Mongolia and China, it may have been some symbolic means of expressing unity of the Church of the East, which at least, christologically, was rejected by Chalcedonians and "monophysite" Churches alike. It could be that the patriarchate of Seleucia-Ctisiphon instituted this sort of dehydrated, long-life, dried dough powder (a sort of liturgical "Twinkie") to symbolize unity of all Eucharistic celebrations of the Church of the East. In other words, its origin may be similar to the rite called fermentum at Rome. Scholarly opinion on the latter is certainly not of one mind, but however that Roman rite functioned, it served to symbolize the one Eucharist presided over by the bishop of Rome.[8] The tradition preserved in the Church of the East in India, which is for the bishop to consecrate the *Malka* on Maundy Thursday, may reflect the original custom, thus linking every Eucharist to the institution of the Supper. In this respect, the *Malka* takes on a further symbolic significance. It will be recalled that the Church of the East has three anaphoras—Nestorius, Theodore the Interpreter (Mopsuestia), and the most ancient of all, and almost certainly the oldest Eucharistic prayer still in use, Addai and Mari. The former two were probably composed by Mar Aba the Great circa 535, and that named after Nestorius seems to have been inspired by the Greek anaphoras of St. John Chrysostom and St. Basil. Both contain a narrative of institution. Addai and Mari, which is used throughout most of the year, is notorious for the fact that this ancient anaphora has no institution narrative. The only reference to the Last Supper is indirect: "And we also, O Lord (three times) your lowly, weak and miserable servants who are gathered together and stand before you at this time have received by tradition of the example which is from you rejoicing, and glorifying, and magnifying, and commemorating and praising, and performing this great and

7. Paul Bradshaw, *The Search for the Origins of Christian Worship* (New York: Oxford University Press, 2002), 19–20.

8. For the views of Nautin and Taft, Saxer, and the "Common opinion," see John F. Baldovin, "The Fermentum at Rome in the Fifth Century: A Reconsideration," *Worship* 79 (2005): 38–53.

dread mystery of the passion and death and resurrection of our Lord Jesus Christ."

The functions of an institution narrative within a Eucharistic prayer may be several, but one of them is that the narrative relates what is being done *now* in the present Church celebration to what was done *then* in the upper room. In many ways the *Malka*, with its midrashic origin given by Bar Zobi, fulfills in material element and symbol what the narrative of institution does in words. In Addai and Mari at least, the *Malka* serves to relate and link what the Church is doing now with what was done then in the upper room. It is the Holy Leaven rather than a spoken narrative that provides continuity with what was done at the Last Supper. Symbol takes the place of words. Canon law in requiring the use of the *Malka* for a valid Eucharist expresses the sacramentality of the *Malka*. Just as the omission of the Words of Institution in the Roman rite would render the Mass invalid, so without the *Malka*, the Church of the East celebration would not be a legitimate and valid Eucharist, because the continuity with the Last Supper would be lost.

The rite for renewal of the *Malka* was witnessed by Lady E. S. Drower in 1944, and her detailed account is worth rehearsing:

> The prayers always said at the making of the holy bread and consecration of wine and water preceded the ceremony, in itself simple. A small table stood in the sanctuary to the south facing south. Upon this, spread with a white cloth, was a wide metal dish, silvered over. Into the centre of this the bishop sprinkled a heap of flour—I was told two handfuls. It had been freshly ground by a virgin girl. Over this the bishop sprinkled a layer of salt, the proportion being about two-thirds flour to one-third salt. To this he added three drops of olive oil and three drops of water just drawn from the river. After he had mixed all thoroughly together he rubbed his hands with a towel. All this was performed in silence. A silver cross lay on the table to the east of the dish. The bishop, priest and two deacons then turned eastwards and began the chant of "Holy, holy, holy," sung in antiphon, followed by three *hulalas* (groups of psalms). A deacon brought a box containing incense to the bishop, who took incense from it thrice and placed it in the censer held by the deacon standing at the north side of the sanctuary. Chanting, censing and prayers continued at some length and, when the benediction was given, it took an unusual form, that is, the bishop held his hands together palm to palm and made a gesture of benediction, turning himself and bowing to the east, north and south, but not west.

He ended by facing the congregation and blessing it in the usual manner and saying, "Peace be with you."

Next, he traced a cross thrice with his forefinger on the *melka*, bent in silent prayer at the altar, and then, erect again, chanted. All in the sanctuary faced the altar whilst the censer swung gently and the bishop prayed inaudibly. After chanting he turned again to the *melka*, signed it with the sign of the cross again thrice and, going to the *giuts*, took therefrom the chalice containing the *melka* of the previous year. This, or some of it, he added to the new mixture on the plate, working them together thoroughly.

After more prayer and chanting, the new mingled with the old were placed in the cup, held aloft before the altar as if in offering, and placed in the *giuta*, which had remained open whilst the mixing was performed. The door was then shut.[9]

The rite given by Woolley, which normally is performed by a priest, begins with a variant sanctus and the Lord's Prayer, and is followed by psalms and anthems, and contains the creed and a litany.[10] A *gehanta* prays:

O Lord God Almighty (repeat) assist my weakness by thy mercies, and by the help of thy grace make me worthy by thy help to draw nigh and sign this matter with the sign of the cross to sanctify it; that it may be for the signing and the perfecting of the dough of the body of our Lord Jesus Christ.[11]

The actual prayer of blessing opens in a similar manner to the East Syrian anaphoras. It asks for the alighting of the Holy Spirit and the priest says:

Signed and sanctified and mixed is this new leaven with this holy and old leaven of our Lord Jesus Christ, which has been handed down to us from our spiritual fathers, Mar Mari and Mar Addai and Mar Thoma, the blessed Apostles, teachers of this Eastern Country, and has been carried from place to place and from country to country for the perfecting and the mixing of the living Bread of the life-giving myster-

9. E. S. Drower, *Water into Wine. A Study of Ritual Idiom in the Middle East* (London: John Murray, 1956), 58–59. Lady Drower, a noted anthropologist, did not specify where this was during her visit to Iran and Iraq.

10. Woolley, *Bread of the Eucharist*, 66–78.

11. Ibid., 73.

ies, as often as reason of necessity requires, in the name of the Father, and of the Son, and of the Holy Ghost.[12]

A slightly different rite is represented in the *Taksha* translated by M. J. Birnie and described by Bawai Soro. A prayer is offered as an introduction to Psalm 84:

> Glory to you, O Most High, who descended and put on the body of our humanity and fulfilled your dispensation for the sake of our salvation. On holy Passover you broke bread and gave to us, then delivered yourself up to redemptive suffering, undergoing the Cross of shame; and through the blood and water which flowed from your side you purged, washed away, and purified our defilements through your grace and mercies, O Lord of all.[13]

An alternative *gehanta* prays:

> You who appointed in your holy Church spiritual stewards . . . and the Apostles gave this symbol, delivering it to the priests and leaders of the flock of Christ, and on the strength of authority we too . . . through the grace of the Holy Spirit, are perfecting and renewing this holy Leaven, that it may impart holiness to the mingling of the holy and life-giving Mysteries.[14]

And a final *gehanta*:

> In your name, O Lord God, compassionate Father, and in the name of your Only-begotten Son, our Lord Jesus Christ, the Merciful One, and in the name of your living and holy Spirit, we call upon you and beseech you to send the power of your grace, with the gift of the Holy Spirit, the Paraclete, to bless the Leaven and sanctify it, that your Godhead may dwell in it and your Lordship be honored in it, so that the life-giving Mysteries, which on the Throne of your Lordship are offered, may be filled with it and perfected by it for the pardon and forgiveness of sins, amen.[15]

---

12. Ibid., 74–75.
13. Bawai Soro, "The Sacrament of the Holy Leaven 'Malka' in the Church of the East," *Fifth Pro-Oriente Non Official Dialogue within the Churches of the Syriac Tradition, Holy Apostolic Assyrian Church of the East*, 1–16, 11.
14. Ibid., 12.
15. Ibid., 13.

In the rite of making the bread for the communion, the priest takes some of the *Malka* and says:

> This dough is signed and hallowed with the old and holy leaven of our Lord Jesus Christ, which was given and handed down to us by our holy fathers Mar Addai and Mar Mari and Mar Thoma the Apostles, who made disciples of this eastern region: in the name of the Father and of the Son and of the Holy Ghost.[16]

He then signs the dough, and then adds *Malka* also to the priest's loaf and says, "This broken portion is signed and hallowed with this Holy Leaven in the name of the Father and of the Son and of the Holy Ghost."[17]

This raza/mystery, unique to the Church of the East, thus gives some continuity and unity to every Eucharistic celebration, enabling the whole Church to feast on bread mixed with fragments believed, at least from the time of Shlemon and Bar Zobi, to be ultimately in tactile succession to the loaves of the upper room itself.

16. Woolley, *Bread of the Eucharist*, 63.
17. Ibid.

Matthieu Smyth

IV. The Anaphora of the So-called "Apostolic Tradition" and the Roman Eucharistic Prayer[1]

The anaphora found in the midst of a small church order (chapter 4) and translated from Greek into Latin and recopied in Venetia in the fifth century in a palimpsest Verona, Bibl. Cap. 55 (*olim* 53),[2] as well as in an Ethiopian version of an Alexandrian *Synodos*,[3] has been of special interest for the historians of the liturgy. This canonical-liturgical collection of miscellaneous heterogeneous elements, combined without any real concern for unity, is erroneously known under the name of the *Apostolic Tradition* of Hippolytus of Rome,[4] although the preferred title

---

1. This essay appeared originally as "L'anaphore de la prétendue 'Tradition Apostolique' et la prière eucharistique Romaine," *Revue des sciences religieuses* 81, 1 (2007): 95–118. It was translated expressly for this volume by Michael S. Driscoll.

2. This fragment, first edited by Hauler in 1900, has been updated in a new edition: E. Tidner, ed., *Didascaliae apostolorum*, Texte und Untersuchungen zur Geschichte der altchristlichen Literatur (TU) 75 (Berlin, 1963); concerning the paleographic dimension, see E. A. Lowe, *Codices Latini Antiquiores. A Palaeographical Guide to Latin Manuscripts Prior to the Ninth Century* (Oxford, 1934–60), n. 508.

3. G. Horner, ed., *The Statutes of the Apostles or Canones Ecclesiastici* (London, 1904); H. Duensing, ed., *Der aethiopische Text der Kirchendornung des Hippolyt nach 8 Handschriften herausgegeben und übersetz* (Göttingen, 1946); we find in Latin a convenient synoptic presentation of different versions of the anaphora in P. Cagin, *L'Eucharistia* (Paris, 1912), with that of the Syriac *Testamentum Domini* and of some later Ethiopian anaphoras (see below, note 51).

4. B. Botte, ed., *La Tradition Apostolique de Saint Hippolyte. Essai de reconstruction*, Liturgiegeschichtliche Quellen und Forschungen 39 (Münster, 1989); P. F. Bradshaw, M.E. Johnson, and L.E. Phillips, *The Apostolic Tradition. A Commentary*, Hermeneia (Minneapolis, 2002). The second work is more preferable since it presents the texts in synoptic form and not in a haphazard reconstruction.

is *Diataxeis tôn hagiôn apostolôn.*[5] No attempt should be made to find any attribution, as is the case in the other documents of this genre.[6] Its renown is so important that it came to influence the current Roman liturgy deeply. Reputed to come from the pen of the Roman presbyter Hippolytus († 235),[7] a prayer distantly inspired by his anaphora took its place among the Eucharistic prayers authorized by the Latin Church (*Prex Eucharistica II*) as the most ancient witness of the Roman liturgical tradition.

I will not linger on the flimsiness of the attribution to Hippolytus.[8] How can we maintain this supposition regarding such a heterogeneous document coming from the pen of a precise author? How could we forget that liturgical collections and prayers that they contain reflect a tradition of one or several communities, and not the handiwork of one author? The hypothesis rests moreover on the confusion

5. Under this title the florilegia *Ochrid 86* and *BNF gr. 900* offers a fragment of this text. See M. Richard, "Quelques fragments des Pères anténicéens et nicéens," *Symbolae Osloenses* 38 (1963): 76–83; J. Magne, "La prétendue tradition apostolique d'Hippolyte de Rome s'appelait-elle *Ai diataxeis tôn hagiôn apostolôn—Les statuts des saints apôtres?*" *Ostkirchliche Studien* 14 (1965): 35–67; *Tradition apostolique sur les charismes et Diataxeis des saints apôtres. Identification des documents et analyse du rituel des ordinations,* Origines Chrétiennes 1 (Paris, 1975); "En finir avec la 'Tradition d'Hippolyte,'" *Bulletin de Littérature Ecclésiastique* 89 (1988): 5–22.

6. Regarding canonical-liturgical collections, see A. Faivre, "La documentation canonico-liturgique. Bilan et prospective," in *La Documentation patristique. Bilan et prospective,* ed. J.-C. Fredouille and R.-M. Roberge (Québec/Paris, 1995), 41.

7. According to the argument first put forward by E. Schwartz, *Uber die pseudoapostolistischen Kirchenordnungen,* Strasbourg 1910, later by R. H. Connolly, *The So-Called Egyptian Church Order and Derived Documents,* Texts and Studies VIII/4, Cambridge 1916, of which Bernard Botte subsequently became the great defender to the point of creating a historiographical orthodoxy.

8. Others before me have made the same argument. Beyond the works cited in note 4, we read M. Metzger, "Nouvelles perspectives pour la prétendue 'Tradition apostolique,'" *Ecclesia Orans* 5 (1988): 241–59; "Enquêtes autour de la prétendue 'Tradition apostolique,'" *Ecclesia Orans* 9 (1992): 7–36; "A propos des règlements ecclésiastiques et de la prétendue Tradition apostolique," *Revue des sciences religieuses* 66 (1992): 249–61; "La prière eucharistique de la prétendue Tradition apostolique," in *Prex Eucharistica III/1. Studia. Ecclesia antiqua et occidentalis,* ed. A. Gerhards et al., Spicilegium Friburgense 42 (Fribourg, Switzerland, 2005), 263–80; Chr. Markschies, "Wer schrieb die sogennante *Traditio Apostolica,*" in *Tauffragen und Bekenntnis,* W. Kinzig et al. (Berlin, 1999), 1–74.

between our canonical-liturgical collection, a work by its nature composite and anonymous like others of this genre, and the lost work, *The Apostolic Tradition of Hippolytus on the Charisms*. This latter must precede the *Diataxeis* within a larger collection, in the same fashion as The Way of Life does in another canonical collection, the *Apostolic Ordinance*.[9] In the midst of this enlarged collection, the treatise *On the Charisms* ensures the transition with the end of this same *Ordinance*, to which (*Ap. Ord.* 16) the ritual of episcopal ordination of the *Diataxeis* (§ 4) refers, according to the plan that remains underlying in the midst of *Apostolic Constitutions* VIII. Left over, an extract of this treatise *On the Charisms* still seems to open the *Diataxeis* (or rather what remains of it) in *Apostolic Constitutions* VIII, 1–2, in a fragmentary and revised form.[10] A scribe would have provided a colophon at the end of this exposé on the charisms indicating its first author, which would explain the presence of the name of Hippolytus in three of the documents passing on to us part of the *Diataxeis* (the *Canons of Hippolytus*, the *Epitome* of the *Apostolic Constitutions* and the Arabic *Octateuch of Clement*).[11]

Whatever it may be, the question here is not to examine the entirety of the *Diataxeis* but to specify the relationship, or rather its absence, between its anaphora and that of the Roman tradition. It is a matter of demonstrating why this prayer could not date to the beginning of the third century and even less be Roman, and to indicate what is in fact more likely.

THE ROMAN EUCHARISTIC PRAYER

As far as we can go back in the assuredly Roman sources, and as far as we can go in the sources influenced by the Roman liturgy, always

9. Th. Schermann, *Die allgemeine Kirchenordnung, früchristliche Liturgien und kirchliche Ueberlieferung*. II. *Die allgemeine Kirchenordnung des zweiten Jahrhundert* (Paderborn, 1914).

10. M. Metzger, ed., *Les Constitutions apostoliques*, Sources Chrétiennes (SC) 320, 329, and 336 (Paris, 1985–87); see the argument of Magne, *Tradition apostolique*, first part, which is not necessary to follow in its entirety to appreciate his remarks regarding the "orthodoxy" of Botte.

11. The pertinent texts are found in Bradshaw, Johnson, Phillips, *Apostolic Tradition*; see, however, Horner, *Statutes*, as well as J. Périer and A. Périer, *Les 127 Canons des apôtres*, Patrologia Orientalis (PO) 8/4 (Paris, 1912), for the *Octateuch*; F. X. Funk, ed., *Didascalia et Constitutiones Apostolorum* II (Paderborn, 1905), 72–96, for the *Epitome*; R.-G. Coquin, ed., *Les Canons d'Hippolyte*, PO 31 (Paris, 1966).

and without exception we encounter as a Roman prayer the only and unique tradition of the Roman Canon, with its structure and its distinctive speech, whether it be in one version or another. Here it is such as it was recited in Rome in the seventh century, after the reforms of Gregory the Great (✝ 604), an ordinary day, with the *praefatio communis* and the commemoration of the dead:[12]

> It is truly fitting and right, our duty and our salvation, that we should always and everywhere give you thanks, O Lord, holy Father, almighty eternal God, through Christ our Lord; through whom angels praise your majesty, dominions adore, powers fear, the heavens and the heavenly hosts and the blessed seraphim, joining together in exultant celebration. We pray you, bid our voices also to be admitted with theirs, beseeching you, confessing, and saying: "Holy, holy, holy . . ."
>
> We therefore pray and beseech you, most merciful Father, through your Son Jesus Christ our Lord, to accept and bless these gifts, these offerings, these holy and unblemished sacrifices; above all, those which we offer to you for your holy catholic church; vouchsafe to grant it peace, protection, unity, and guidance throughout the world, together with your servant *N.* our pope.
>
> Remember, Lord, your servants, men and women, and all who stand around, whose faith and devotion are known to you, who offer to you this sacrifice of praise for themselves and for all their own, for the redemption of their souls, for the hope of their salvation and safety, and pay their vows to you, the living, true, and eternal God.
>
> In fellowship with and venerating above all the memory of the glorious ever-Virgin Mary, mother of God and our Lord Jesus Christ, and also of your blessed apostles and martyrs Peter, Paul, Andrew, . . . Cosmas and Damian, and all your saints; by their merits and prayers grant us to be defended in all things by the help of your protection; through Christ our Lord.

12. L. Eizenhofer, ed., *Canon missae romanae* l, Rerum Ecclesiasticarum Documenta, Subsidia Studiorum 1 (Rome, 1954). Here I give the reading notably attested in the sacramentaries called "Gregorian," elaborated at Rome between the pontificates of Honorius I (625–39) and Gregory II (715–31); see J. Deshusses, ed., *Sacramentaire Grégorien d'après ses principaux manuscrits*. I. *Le Sacramentaire, supplément d'Aniane*, Spicilegium Friburgense 16 (Fribourg, Switzerland, 1979); for the *memento* of the dead, which will remain for some time consigned to a separate *libellus*, we rely on the insular sacramentaries or other later sources.

Therefore, Lord, we pray you graciously to accept this offering made by us your servants, and also by your whole family; and to order our days in peace; and to command that we are snatched from eternal damnation and numbered among the flock of your elect; through Christ our Lord.

Vouchsafe, we beseech you, O God, to make this offering wholly blessed, approved, ratified, reasonable, and acceptable; that it may become to us the body and blood of your dearly beloved Son Jesus Christ our Lord; who, on the day before he suffered, took bread in his holy and reverend hands, lifted up his eyes to heaven to you, O God, his almighty Father, gave thanks to you, blessed, broke, and gave it to his disciples, saying, "Take and eat from this, all of you; for this is my body." Likewise after supper, taking also this glorious cup in his holy and reverend hands, again he gave thanks to you, blessed and gave it to his disciples, saying, "Take and drink from it, all of you; for this is the cup of my blood, of the new and eternal covenant, the mystery of faith, which will be shed for you and for many for forgiveness of sins. As often as you do this, you will do it for my remembrance."

Therefore also, Lord, we your servants, and also your holy people, having in remembrance the blessed passion of your Son Christ our Lord, likewise his resurrection from the dead, and also his glorious ascension into heaven, do offer to your excellent majesty from your gifts and bounty a pure victim, an unspotted victim, the holy bread of eternal life and the cup of everlasting salvation.

Vouchsafe to look upon them with a favorable and kindly countenance, and accept them as you vouchsafed to accept the gifts of your righteous servant Abel, and the sacrifice of our patriarch Abraham, and that which your high priest Melchizedek offered to you, a holy sacrifice, an unblemished victim.

We humbly beseech you, almighty God, bid these things be borne by the hands of your angel to your altar on high, in the sight of your divine majesty, that all of us who have received the most holy body and blood of your Son by partaking at this altar may be filled with all heavenly blessing and grace; through Christ our Lord.

Remember also, Lord, the names of those who have gone before us with the sign of faith, and sleep in the sleep of peace. We beseech you to grant to them and to all who rest in Christ a place of restoration, light, and peace; through Christ our Lord.

To us sinners your servants also, who trust in the multitude of your mercies, vouchsafe to grant some part and fellowship with your holy Apostles and martyrs, with John, Stephen, Matthias, . . . Anastasia, and all your saints: into whose company we ask that you will admit us, not weighing our merit, but bounteously forgiving; through Christ our Lord.

Through him, Lord, you ever create, sanctify, quicken, bless, and bestow all these good things upon us. Through him and with him and in him all honor and glory is yours, O God the Father almighty, in the unity of the Holy Spirit, through all the ages of ages. Amen.

The Roman euchological sources without exception (and numerous Italian sources) offer no Eucharistic prayer other than the *canonica prex*. Other readings are to be found, but we do not come across traces of another competing form of Roman anaphora. In the hybrid documents (Milanese, Gallican, Hispanic, and Irish) the Roman Canon finds itself alongside some anaphoras of a very characteristic Gallican type easily distinguishable one from another, and no other. Nor do we find any translation from the Eastern anaphoras, other than some formulae having been borrowed here and there (even if the base of the Roman Canon results from such a translation[13]). The Roman tradition, with its emblematic canonical prayer, appears thus in a splendid euchological isolation, an isolation that is only broken by its obvious family ties to the Alexandrian Eucharistic prayers, represented by the anaphora of St. Mark[14] and that of the Sacramentary of Sarapion.[15]

Therefore we will not be surprised greatly that all those who try to reconstruct the history of the Roman Eucharist, taking as a point of departure the anaphora of the so-called "Apostolic Tradition of Hippolytus of Rome," supposedly in use in the city at the beginning of the third century, collide with insurmountable difficulties. In fact, as much by their structure as by their respective texts, the anaphora of the *Diataxeis tôn hagiôn apostolôn* and the Roman Canon represent different traditions. The two Eucharistic prayers resemble each other only on a minor point (which we will look at below).

Furthermore, reliance has been placed on the baptismal order of the *Diataxeis*, 21, of which some traces, notably its Creed, its triple immersion without formula other than the interrogatory, and its two postbaptismal anointings, do evoke the Roman ritual; but this double

13. M. J. Moreton, "Rethinking the Origin of the Roman Canon," *Studia Patristica* 26 (1993): 63–66.

14. G. J. Cuming, *The Liturgy of Saint Mark*, Orientalia Christiana Analecta (OCA) 234 (Rome, 1990). On the relationship between Mark and the Roman Canon, see the essay in this collection by Walter Ray, 99–127 below.

15. M. E. Johnson, *The Prayers of Sarapion of Thmuis. A Literary, Liturgical, and Theological Analysis*, OCA 249 (Rome, 1995).

anointing, with its identical duplicated formula, differs from that of Rome, which gives two quite distinct formulae. The formula with chrism "I anoint you with the holy oil in the name of Jesus Christ" from the *Diataxeis* has absolutely no Roman vestiges. And the other coincidences can be better explained by the fact that the structure of the Roman baptismal order belongs (contrary to its Eucharistic prayer) to a widely disseminated liturgical family (from which East Syria is disassociated).[16]

COMPARATIVE LITURGY

The first striking elements in the Roman Canon, even in its later versions, are its archaisms. When it is not purely theological, as in the case of certain prayers of praise at the beginning of the Alexandrian anaphora of St. Mark, the theology of the *canonica prex* is binitarian: it is based on a relation of Father-Son (as unique mediator), where the Holy Spirit is the figure of the odd one out. A number of its concerns reveal an older Judeo-Christian theology.

Two archaic versions, one cited in *De sacramentis* IV.21–27 of Ambrose[17] and the other in some Spanish liturgical books,[18] describe the Eucharistic elements respectively as "the figure of the body and the blood of our Lord" and as "the image and likeness of the body and

---

16. P. F. Bradshaw, "Redating the Apostolic Tradition: Some Preliminary Steps," in *Rule of Prayer, Rule of Faith*, ed. N. Mitchell and J. F. Baldovin (Collegeville: Liturgical Press, 1996), 3–7, 10–15; and especially M. E. Johnson, "The Postchrismal Structure of Apostolic Tradition 21, The Witness of Ambrose of Milan, and a Tentative Hypothesis Regarding the Current Reform of Confirmation in the Roman Rite," *Worship* 70 (1996): 16–34.

17. B. Botte, ed., *Ambroise de Milan. Des sacrements. Des mystères. Explication du Symbole*, SC 25 bis (Paris, 1994); see, for example, Chr. Mohrmann, "Quelques observations sur l'évolution stylistique du canon de la messe romaine," reprinted in *Études sur le latin des chrétiens. III. Latin chrétien et latin liturgique* (Rome, 1965), 23–41; Ch. Coebergh, "Il canone della messa ambrosiana. Una riforma romana a Milano," *Ambrosius* 29 (1953): 138–50; G. G. Willis, *A History of Early Roman Liturgy to the Death of Pope Gregory the Great*, Henry Bradshaw Society Subsidia 1 (London, 1994), 23–32.

18. M. Férotin, ed., *Le "Liber ordinum" en usage dans l'Eglise visigothique et mozarabe d'Espagne du cinquième au onzième siècle* 2, Bibliotheca Ephemerides Liturgicae (BEL) 83 (Rome, 1996), col. 321; and *Le "Liber mozarabicus sacramentorum" et les manuscrits mozarabes* 2, BEL 78 (Rome, 1995), 1440.

blood of Jesus Christ"[19] (a later mention removed from the *canonica prex*). The Canon insists on the theme of pure and spiritual sacrifice, that is, noncarnal, as well as on the sacrificial biblical typology of this same pure sacrifice in the *Quam oblationem*, "Vouchsafe, we beseech you, O God, to make this offering wholly blessed, approved, ratified, reasonable, and acceptable"; and in the *Supra quae*, "a holy sacrifice, a spotless victim" (the offering of the "pure victim, holy victim, spotless victim" that we find following the anamnesis is a later borrowing like all this section of the Canon). This typology is incarnated through the Old Testament figures in the same *Supra quae*: "and accept them as you vouchsafed to accept the gifts of your righteous servant Abel, and the sacrifice of our patriarch Abraham, and that which your high priest Melchizedek offered to you."

The rest of this prayer (*Supplices te rogamus*) is happy to evoke, in terms that come strictly from Jewish apocalyptic literature, the exchanges of the Archangel of God established between the earthly and heavenly altars: "We humbly beseech you, almighty God, bid these things be borne by the hands of your angel to your altar on high, in the sight of your divine majesty, so that each time from this altar of sanctification . . ." (here according to the insular and Milanese versions older than the received recensions, called "Gregorian," that do not distinguish very well between the earthly and heavenly altars). This Archangel is none other, without a doubt, than the figure of Christ the heavenly mediator, the *deuteros theos* who stands between God and his creation, drawn from Jewish Hellenistic theology.[20]

Furthermore, the composite (meaning chaotic) construction of the Roman Canon that makes it sometimes unintelligible (especially around the *Communicantes*) seems to be a good witness to a very old prayer that has been given a face-lift quite often without ever attempting to modify it deeply. The most recent textual additions, like the Sanctus, the institution narrative (the Last Supper account) or the anamnesis, appear there more like the intrusions that they truly are. It is flagrant in the case of the Sanctus, which was left without any embo-

19. Pope Gelasius († 496) confirms this same formula: "the image and the similitude of the body and blood of Christ is celebrated in the mysterious action" (*Contre Eutyches*, 14).

20. See notably Philo, *Questions and Answers on Genesis* II.62; a recent study in D. Boyarin, "The Gospel of the *Memra*: Jewish Binitarianism and the Prologue to John," *Harvard Theological Review* 94 (2001): 243–84.

lism, *Vere sanctus*, to connect it to what follows. The frequent recourse to the redactional contrivance of the *Wiederaufnahme*, around the theme of oblation, serves only to underline this. The rewriting of the *canonica prex*, following the criteria of the Ciceronian *cursus*, during the fifth century[21] did not affect it too deeply.

Certainly the anaphora of the *Diataxeis* also presents some no less evident archaisms:

- a direct address to the Father ("We thank you, O God, through your beloved servant, Jesus Christ") comparable to that of *Didache* 9, and anterior to the diffusion of the rhetorical catchphrase ("it is right and just to give you thanks," *Axion kai dikaion . . .*) of narrative style

- mention of the especially archaic Christological title of "servant" (*pais*) taken from *Didache* 9, a title already outdated by the time of the redaction of the New Testament, where it is only witnessed in the early records of Acts 3:13-26 and 4:27-30

- the vestige from *Didache* 9–10 ("gathering them in unity") at the heart of the intercessions

- the presence in the oration of *carmen Christo quasi deo* woven from characteristic concepts notably to be found in pre-Nicene paschal homilies (illustrated from *On the Pascha* of Pseudo-Hippolytus and of Melito of Sardis), and marked by the New Testament Christological rhetoric of the antithetical parallels humbling/exaltation ("while suffering to deliver from suffering")[22]

21. G. G. Willis, *Essays in Early Roman Liturgy*, Alcuin Club Collections 46 (London, 1964), 111–17.

22. E. Mazza, *L'anafora eucaristica. Studi sulle origine*, BEL Subsidia 62 (Rome, 1992): 120–41 (= *The Origins of the Eucharistic Prayer* [Collegeville: Liturgical Press, 1995], 102–29), concerning the "angel of your will" (Ps.-Hippolytus, 46–47); "you sent him from heaven into the womb of a virgin" (Melito, 66); "he whom you sent to us from heaven in these last times" (Melito, *Additamentum*); "your inseparable Word" (Ps.-Hippolytus, 45); "through whom you made all things" (Melito, 47); "gaining for you a holy people, he spread out his hands while he suffered" (Ps.-Hippolytus, 63, 50 and 38; Melito, 47); "while he suffered to deliver from suffering" (Ps.-Hippolytus, 1 and 49; Melito, 66 and 100); "while he gave himself over to suffer willingly" (Ps.-Hippolytus, 57); "in

- the absence of the Sanctus and the epiclesis for the transformation of the gifts

- the soberness of the anamnesis in relation to other later anaphoras

Nevertheless, next to these venerable vestiges, our anaphora presents numerous characteristics of "theological advances," if one can call it that. The relatively late character of the collection of *Diataxeis*, in the stage that it has come down to us, is well established. According to Georg Kretschmar, "the principal prayers of ordination of bishop and of priest, as well as the Eucharistic prayer, cannot be called archaic."[23]

Certainly the narration of the *magnalia dei* of the anaphora, this long Christological praise in a paschal tonality, goes back as we have just seen to the second century, to the time when the prayer of thanksgiving becomes "Christological" and "paschal," at the same time that a Eucharistic approach to the Christian Pascha is spreading. But from a certain point of view, it is a matter of a sign of relative "modernity."

Moreover, the *carmen Christo* seems to be the result of the fusion of two texts and has undergone several successive redactions engendering one or two expansions. A *Wiederaufnahme* rhetoric ("you sent us from heaven"/"you sent from heaven") is connected to a soteriological section on the discourse about the heavenly Christ: "He whom in these last times you sent to us as saviour and redeemer and angel of your will; who is your inseparable Word, through whom you made all things, and in whom you were well pleased. You sent him from heaven into a virgin's womb; and conceived in the womb, he was made flesh and manifested as your Son, being born of the Holy Spirit and the Virgin." The double awkward mention of the virginal conception suggests that "born of the Holy Spirit and of the Virgin" is a secondary interpolation, marked by later trinitarian concerns.

The Roman Canon as well as its cousin the anaphora of St. Mark betray in themselves an earlier stage of evolution of the Christian

---

order to destroy death" (Ps.-Hippolytus 3, 49, 57 and 62; Melito, 66, 102 and 68); "breaking the chains of the devil" (Ps.-Hippolytus, 45 and 48; Melito, 68); "stamp out hell" (Ps.-Hippolytus, 62; Melito, 102); "lead the righteous to the light" (Ps.-Hippolytus, 48; Melito, 112); "to show the resurrection" (Irenaeus, *Démonstration*, 38).

23. G. Kretschmar, "Early Christian Liturgy in the Light of Contemporary Historical Research," *Studia Liturgica* 16 (1986–87): 33.

prayer, anterior to the paschal reading of the Eucharist already at work in the narrative of the Last Supper of the Synoptics.[24] The anaphora of St. Mark, in particular, has kept intact a Judeo-Christian theocentric thanksgiving prayer, praising God the creator and only mentioning Christ with regard to his role as cosmic mediator: "[It is right and just Lord God] to bless you day and night, you who made heaven and all that is in it, the earth and what is on earth, seas and rivers and all that is in them; you who made man according to your own image and likeness. You made everything through your wisdom, the true light, your only Son, our Lord and Saviour Jesus Christ" (*oratio* of the anaphora of St. Mark from the Strasbourg Papyrus gr. 254, from the fourth century).

In keeping with the Eucharist of *Didache* 9–10, the themes of the Christian Pascha and of the saving work accomplished through Christ are absent. Mention is limited to his mediation. The other known Alexandrian anaphoras, that of the Sacramentary of Sarapion and that of the Barcelona Papyrus,[25] entail little more marked Christological developments. As for the Roman Canon, it seems to have long since lost its original thanksgiving in favor of the adoption at Rome of the principle of euchological variability (the prayers vary with the liturgical calendar), without doubt no later than 400.[26] This principle entails the introduction of the prayers of praise (the "prefaces") that thank God for all sorts of reasons, sometimes distant from the paschal mystery. We also find, notably at Easter, a Eucharist that commemorates the

24. K. Gerlach, *The Antenicene Pascha. A Rhetorical History*, Liturgia Condenda 7 (Louvain, 1998).

25. R. Roca-Puig, ed., *L'Anafora de Barcelona i altres pregaries (Missa dei Segle IV)* (Barcelona, 1994).

26. According to J. Janini, *S. Siricio y las Cuatro Temporas. Una investigacion sobre las fuentes de la espiritualidad seglar y dei Sacramentario Leoniano* (Valencia, 1958), Siricius († 399) would be the instigator of this "liturgical revolution" (E. Bourque, *Etude sur les sacramentaires romains. 1. Les textes primitifs* [Rome, 1949], 32). Whatever may be the case, Ch. Coebergh demonstrated that the Leonine Sacramentary contains pieces that go back to the time of Pope Gelasius († 496): "Le pape saint Gélase Ier auteur de plusieurs messes et préfaces du soi-disant sacramentaire léonien," *Sacris Eruditi* 4 (1952): 214–37. See also G. Pomarès, ed., *Gélase 1er. Lettre contre les Lupercales et XVIII messes du Sacramentaire Léonien*, SC 65 (Paris, 1959).

economy of salvation dispensed through Christ.[27] However, the *prae-fatio communis* (see above) is purely theological. Likewise a Gallican Sacramentary from the beginning of the eighth century, the *Missale Gothicum (Vat. Lat. Reg.* 317),[28] maintains, under the Gallican term *contestatio*, several archaic Roman prefaces remaining also purely theological and thanking God the Creator, without mentioning the Pascha of Christ:

> It is right and just to give you thanks, holy Father, eternal and all powerful God; to address to your majesty praises with devotion; to proclaim with the veneration of a devout spirit the indescribable praise to your high doings. You therefore are incomprehensible, ineffable and always fearful, Lord and Creator of all things, we acknowledge you, we believe in you, we obey you, and we pray to you, through Jesus Christ your son, our God, master and saviour. Through him we offer to your glory this pure sacrifice. (*Miss. Goth.* 492; see also 481, 503)

The narration of the *Diataxeis* blends without clash in a nonscriptural Christological institution narrative followed by a narrative of the Last Supper. These diverse sections of the Eucharist make in effect the object of an astute editorial fusion: we thank the Father for sending his Son, "he who" became incarnate and suffered his salutary passion while instituting the Eucharistic rite: "While he gave himself to death . . . to . . . fix the rule [of his sacrifice][29] . . . taking bread." The nar-

27. L. C. Mohlberg, ed., *Liber sacramentorum romanae ecclesiae ordinis anni circuli (Cod. Vat. Reg. lat. 316, Paris B.N. lat. 7193,41/56) (Sacramentarium gelasianum)*, Rerum Ecclesiast. Doc., Ser. Maior, Fontes 4 (Rome, 1981): 466.

28. E. Rose, ed., *Missale gothicum e codice Vaticano Reginensis latino 317 editum*, Corpus Christianorum, Series Latina 159D (Turnhout, 2005).

29. Elsewhere I have used the version by Dom Botte reconstructed ostensibly from the Latin text of the Verona fragment, but not here (see Metzger, *Constitutions apostoliques* III, p. 197, footnote). There is an evident analogy with the nonscriptural narrative in the anaphora of Addai and Mari ("We also [. . .] servants who are gathered together before you, Lord, we who have received through tradition the 'model' [of this offering] that comes before you," see below, footnote 61). Regarding the nonscriptural narratives as a primitive element of the anaphora, see E. Mazza, *L'Action eucharistique. Origine, développement, interprétation*, Liturgie 10 (Paris, 1999): 60, 106–8; C. Giraudo, "Le récit de l'institution dans la prière eucharistique a-t-il des précédents?" *Nouvelle Revue Théologique* 106 (1984): 513–35; E. J. Cutrone, "The Liturgical Setting of the Institution Narrative in the Early Syrian Tradition," in *Time and Community*, ed.

rative here is the logical sequel to the *carmen Christo* of the Eucharist. Likewise, the anamnesis as well as an offering prayer, which elsewhere would conclude the thanksgiving, overlap in a unique formula, creating a harmonious sequel to the narrative.

Moreover, the Last Supper narrative, as well as its concluding anamnesis, are latecomers to the core of euchology;[30] and the anamnesis of the *Diataxeis* recalling "the death and the resurrection" of Christ is already more developed than the Gallican anamnesis that limits itself to commemorate only the Passion.[31] While the first, in keeping with other Eastern anamneses, adopts a narrative and descriptive tone, the second, the Gallican, holds to a factual and synthetic statement.

On the other hand, the institution narrative of the Roman Canon, like that of the anaphora of St. Mark, breaks abruptly the rhetorical flow of the prayer. Nothing connects it to the preceding prayer of praise nor to any *carmen Christo*; it clings without much rhetorical coherence to a series of intercessions and offertory prayers. If we remove the Last Supper narrative from the anaphora of St. Mark and the Roman Canon, they would seem more harmonious.[32] The text of the Roman narrative, the *Qui pridie*, furthermore does not belong to the same liturgical tradition as that of the *Diataxeis*. The former is fundamentally Matthean with some adaptation and some Pauline additions, in keeping with other Latin narratives, with the exception of the Spanish that are Pauline, a little like the East. Here we come across the African text of the *Vetus Latina*. It follows a typically Latin chronology, inspired from Luke 22:15, placing the Last Supper on "the eve before his suffering" and not "the night when he was given over."[33] On the other hand, the *Diataxeis* proposes an ecclesiastical composition more difficult to connect to a precise New Testament text relating to the Last

J. N. Alexander (Washington, 1990), 105–14; M. Smyth, *La Liturgie oubliée. Les prières eucharistiques en Gaule et dans l'Occident non-romain pendant l'Antiquité* (Paris, 2003), 402–6, 537–47.

30. See the bibliography in the preceding note.

31. As B. Botte himself recognized ("Problèmes de l'anamnèse," *Journal of Ecclesiastical History* 5 [1954]: 15)! Regarding the anamnesis of a Gallican type ("This is what we do, Lord, in obedience to this precept and in commemoration of your passion"), see Smyth, *La Liturgie oubliée*, second part.

32. Mazza, *L'Action eucharistique*, 79.

33. E. C. Ratcliff, "The Institution Narrative of the Roman *Canon Missae*. Its Beginnings and Early Background," *Studia Patristica* 2 (1957): 64, 82; Willis, *A History*, 45–50.

Supper: it follows freely a Pauline framework supplied with a Matthean addition regarding the cup.

As for the pneumatological epiclesis of the *Diataxeis*, it witnesses to a much more advanced stage of theological development than that of the Roman Canon and some other Eucharists that in keeping with that of the Sacramentary of Sarapion would continue to ignore the pneumatological epicleses. The pneumatological epiclesis, imitated from some invocations over the baptismal water, is most probably not much older than the beginning of the fourth century. It is the result of the evolution of ancient Christological invocations over the oblations (of a *maranatha* type) and of some prayers over the participants of this same oblation.[34] The received text of the Roman Canon does not possess a pneumatological epiclesis. The prayer *Supplices te rogamus* concluding the *Supra quae*, which corresponds to what became in other liturgies the epiclesis, remained a binitarian prayer (*a deo per Christum*) over the sacrifice and over the assembly: "We humbly beseech you, almighty God, bid these things be borne by the hands of your angel to your altar on high, in the sight of your divine majesty, so that each time we receive from this altar of sanctification the most holy body and blood of your Son, we may be filled with all heavenly blessing and grace" (Insular and Milanese use). This formula demonstrates that the substratum of the Roman Canon is undoubtedly more ancient than the final redaction of the anaphora of the *Diataxeis*, which, according to Ratcliff,[35] should be pushed well into the fourth century judging from its epiclesis.

It is interesting to note that the manuscript tradition reports two ancient examples, those of the Spanish books and of the *Missale Gothicum*, of some additions of a pneumatological epiclesis to the Canon: if the latter (*Miss. Goth.* 527) is a Gallican interpolation, the former is Italian, maybe even Roman, but it hardly has any relation to the epiclesis of the *Diataxeis*:

---

34. See R. Taft, "From Logos to Spirit: The Early History of the Epiclesis," in *Gratias agamus. Studien zum eucharistischen Hochgebet. Festschrift Balthasar Fischer*, ed. A. Heinz and H. Rennings, Questiones Disputatae 120 (Fribourg-in-Breslau, 1992), 489–502; G. Winkler, "Further Observations in Connection with Early Forms of the Epiklesis," reprinted in *Studies in Early Christian Liturgy and Its Context* (Aldershot, 1997), chap. IV.

35. E. C. Ratcliff, "The Sanctus and the Pattern of the Early Anaphora," 29–36, 125–34.

We pray and beseech you also to accept and bless this offering as you accepted the gifts of your righteous servant Abel, the sacrifice of our patriarch Abraham, and that which your high priest Melchizedek offered to you. May the blessing descend invisibly . . . that comes from you as it descended at other times visibly on the offerings of the Fathers. May this suave perfume rise in the sight of your divine majesty to your altar on high by the hands of your angel, and may your Holy Spirit be brought to us in this liturgy; the one who sanctifies the people here present who offer to you [this oblation], along with these gifts and vows; in order that each of us who receive this body may receive the substance of the soul. (Liber Moz. Sacr. 627)[36]

Whatever it may be, this epiclesis does not succeed in implanting itself definitively into the liturgy of the city. Possibly it was only adopted in some churches (maybe suburban), leaving elsewhere in force an older usage, on this point (but not on others), of the *Supplices te rogamus*. The Roman tradition of the binitarian epiclesis was too ancient, too vigorous, to be thus supplanted by a newcomer.

In sum, one of the essential differences between these two Eucharistic prayers consists in that the Roman Canon, in its final form, appears to be a clumsy collection of disparate pieces disfiguring a still visible archaic substructure, while the anaphora of the *Diataxeis* presents itself as a (relatively) homogeneous and ordered discourse (some strands still remaining visible), but happily preserving some ancient parts welded to other later elements (*carmen Christo* as such, Last Supper narrative, anamnesis, pneumatological epiclesis). Certainly it

36. It may be that Gelasius knew this epiclesis: "How would it happen that the celestial Spirit is invoked for the consecration of these divine mysteries, if the pontiff, the same one who implores the presence of this Spirit, is condemned because he is fully in a criminal act" (*Ep. Fragm.* 7); see Kl. Gamber, "Zur Textgeschichte des romischen Canon Missae," reprinted in *Sakramentarenstudien*, Studia Patristica et Liturgica 7 (Ratisbonne, 1978), 62–63, which indicates a Beneventan vestige of the epiclesis from the *Lib. Moz. Sacr.* 627 placed alongside a preanaphoral prayer *Veni sanctificator* in the midst of the full ordinary missal copied at Montecassino at the end of the twelfth century, *Vat. Lat. 6082*, ed. V. Hala, "Der Ordo missae im Vollmissale des Cod. Vat. lat. 6082," *Zeugnis des Geistes. Gabe zum Benediktus-Jubiläum*, no. 39 (Beuron, 1947): 180–84 (Kl. Gamber, *Codices Liturgici Latini Antiquiores* l, no. 455 [Fribourg, Switzerland, 1968]).

rests upon some ancient elements,[37] but these latter were reworked in depth and incorporated into a later rhetorical ensemble than what constitutes the framework of the Roman Canon.

Let me repeat: the *canonica prex*, whether it may be through patristic witnesses (Zeno of Verona,[38] the *De sacramentis* IV.21–27 of Ambrose,[39] Ambrosiaster,[40] the Venerable Bede,[41] and the *Liber pontificalis*[42]), those of the decretals of Innocent to Decentius of Gubbio[43] and Vigilius to Profuturus of Braga,[44] or those of the sacramentaries (Leonine, Gregorian, Gelasian . . .),[45] refers us back to Rome, or at least to

---

37. According to Bradshaw, "Redating the Apostolic Tradition," 8–10, and "The Evolution of Early Anaphoras," in *Essays on Early Eastern Eucharistic Prayers*, ed. P. F. Bradshaw (Collegeville: Liturgical Press, 1997), 10–14; the theological substratum goes back to the second century but it underwent some modifications until the fourth century (the commentary in Bradshaw, Johnson, and Phillips, *Apostolic Tradition*, is more circumspect).

38. *Tract.* 1.3 (notably); see G. Jeanes, "Early Latin Parallels to the Roman Canon? Possible References to a Eucharistic Prayer in Zeno of Verona," *Journal of Theological Studies* 37 (1986): 427–31.

39. See notably Willis, *A History*, 23–32.

40. *Quaestiones Veteris et Novi Testamenti* 109.21; this anonymous Italian of the fourth century draws attention to the fact that "the high priest Melchizedek" of the Canon is, according to him, a bad translation of *hiereus upsistou*: "the priest is designated as the one from the Most High God and not as the supreme pontiff, contrary to that which our people have had the presumption to do during the oblation." As a matter of fact, it may not have been a bad translation since the *Targum* calls Melchizedek a "high priest." See R. Le Déaut, "Le titre de 'sumus sacerdos' donné a melchisedech est-il d'origine juive?" *Recherches de sciences religieuses* 50 (1962): 222–29.

41. *Hist. eccl.* II.1, regarding the addition *diesque nostros* by Gregory the Great; a testimony confirmed by the *Liber pontificalis*: see L. Duchesne, ed., *Liber pontificalis* 1 (Paris, 1886), 312.

42. Regarding the amplification *sanctum sacrificium immaculatam hostiam* of the *Unde et memores* attributed to Pope Leo, see Duchesne, ibid., 239.

43. R. Cabié, ed., *La Lettre du Pape Innocent à Decentius de Gubbio (19 mars 416). Texte critique, traduction et commentaire* (Louvain, 1973).

44. PL 69, col. 18.

45. Moreover, the Stowe Missal (Ireland, ninth century; G. F. Warner, ed., *The Stowe Missal MS D.II, 3 in the Library of the Royal Irish Academy*, Henry Bradshaw Society 31 and 32, Dublin/London 1906 and 1915), gives the Roman Canon under the name of "Canon of Pope Gelasius"; see J. H. Crehan, "*Canon dominicus papae Gelasi*," *Vigiliae Christianae* 12 (1958): 45–48.

Italy.[46] The only significant parallels that we can find lay in the Alexandrian anaphoras and the converse is true. The Alexandrian euchological tradition moreover is not less idiosyncratic than the Roman. One can only identify, for one or the other tradition, some later borrowings from anaphoras of a West Syrian type, especially from that of St. James and that of St. John Chrysostom.

THE ANAPHORA OF THE *DIATAXEIS* AND THE WEST SYRIAN EUCHOLOGICAL TRADITION

As for the anaphora of the *Diataxeis*, it points us to the East, and more particularly toward West Syria.[47] How could it be that a so-called Roman prayer does not possess the least relationship to the West, neither at Rome nor elsewhere? It would be necessary to suppose that it was in use in some Roman communities at the beginning of the third century (abstraction made by its epiclesis that absolutely forbids in reality such dating), then that it disappeared without leaving the smallest trace in favor of a rival older tradition—at the least improbable, and all the more so as it does not lack some parallels in the East, notably in Ethiopia and especially in Syria.

West Syria appears moreover as the sure birthplace of the *Diataxeis*,[48] in keeping with two other later liturgical-canonical documents that revised it: profoundly in the case of Book VIII of the *Apostolic Constitutions* (end of the fourth century), expanding it in the case of the

46. Th. Klauser, "Der Übergang der römischen Kirche von der griechischen zur lateinischen Liturgiesprache," in *Misc . . . Mercati* 1, Studi e Testi 121 (Vatican City, 1946), 467–82, basing himself on the testimony of Ambrose, maintains the hypothesis of a Milanese origin for the Roman Canon that would have thus supplanted the anaphora of the alleged *Apostolic Tradition*. He was harshly criticized by Chr. Mohrmann, "*Rationabilis—Logikos*," reprinted in *Études sur le Latin des chrétiens* 1. *Le Latin des chrétiens* 2 (Rome, 1961), 182ff.

47. J.-M. Hanssens, *La Liturgie d'Hippolyte* I et II (Rome, 1965–70), attributes to it an Alexandrian origin, but the document has no significant parallels in the ancient Alexandrian euchological texts, which distinguish themselves radically, like the Roman, from the anaphora of the *Diataxeis*.

48. This has already been suggested by M. H. Shepherd, "The Formation and Influence of the Antiochene Liturgy," *Dumbarton Oak Papers* 15 (1961): 25–44, followed by M. A. Smith, "The Anaphora of Apostolic Tradition Reconsidered," *Studia Patristica* 10 (1970): 426–30; see also in this vein, Mazza, *L'Action eucharistique*, 64ff.

Testamentum Domini (fifth century).[49] *Apostolic Constitutions* VIII.12.6–51 puts forward a glossed version of the anaphora of the *Diataxeis* amalgamated with several other Eucharists, within a large formulary of the West Syrian type. The Eucharistic prayer of the *Testamentum Domini* still remains close to its model of the *Diataxeis*.[50] Its epiclesis seems even to be based upon an older reading of the text of the anaphora: it lacks the request for the "sending" of the Spirit.[51]

The presence of the anaphora of the *Diataxeis* in Ethiopia, under the name anaphora of the Twelve Apostles and the anaphora of the Saviour,[52] can be explained if one imagines the considerable influence that the Syrian liturgical and canonical texts played in Egypt from the fourth century on, and through its mediation in Ethiopia. The anaphora of the *Testamentum Domini* was moreover adapted in Coptic under the name the anaphora of St. Matthew.[53] Various elements of this canonical-liturgical family, from the *Diataxeis* and the *Testamentum Domini*, gathered respectively in the midst of the collection of the Alexandrian

49. I. E. Rahmani, ed., *Testamentum Domini nostri Jesu Christi* (Mainz, 1899), Syriac version; see also R. Beylot, ed., *Testamentum Domini éthiopien. Edition et traduction* (Louvain, 1984).

50. See L. Ligier, "L'anaphore de la 'Tradition apostolique' dans le *Testamentum Domini*," in *The Sacrifice of Praise. Studies on the Themes of Thanksgiving and Redemption in the Central Prayers of the Eucharist and Baptismal Liturgies*, ed. B. D. Spinks, BELS 19 (Rome, 1981), 91–106.

51. Already noted by G. Dix, *Apostolike Paradosis. The Treatise on the Apostolic Tradition of Saint Hippolytus of Rome* (London, 1937), 75–77, followed by L. Bouyer, *Eucharistie* (Paris, 1968), 170–76, 185. The attempt of B. Botte to disqualify this witness, very embarrassing for his thesis, is more ingenuous than convincing: "L'épiclèse de l'anaphore d'Hippolyte," *Recherches de Theolologie Ancienne et Médiévale* 22 (1947): 241–51. Its refutation of Bouyer, as caustic as it may be, is no more convincing either: "À propos de la Tradition apostolique," ibid. 33 (1966): 183–85.

52. Texts in Cagin, *L'Eucharistia*; see H.-I. Dalmais, "La Tradition apostolique et ses dérivés dans les prières eucharistiques éthiopiennes," *Augustinianum* 20 (1980): 109–17. For recent studies on the Ethiopian anaphora, see Gabriele Winkler, *Das Sanctus. Über den Ursprung und die Anfänge des Sanctus und sein Fortwirken*, Orientalia Christiana Analecta 267 (Rome, 2002). See also the essay by M. E. Johnson, "Recent Research on the Anaphoral *Sanctus*: An Update and Hypothesis," in this collection, 161–88 below.

53. E. Lanne, ed., *Le Grand Euchologe du Monastère Blanc*, PO 28 (Paris, 1958): 348–50.

Synodos and the Clementine *Octateuch*, were also translated into Ethiopian. Still more significant, the anaphora of the *Diataxeis* offers numerous parallels in the euchology of the West Syrian type, which is difficult to explain without supposing a local common tradition at the base. One is struck first of all by the paschal and Christological narrative character of the *narratio* of our anaphora, characteristic of this euchological family. We also find here some great themes common to the ante-Nicene Easter homilies, as is still the case in the *Post Sanctus* of the anaphoras of the Twelve Apostles/St. John Chrysostom, St. Basil, and St. James:[54] "Holy are you and all-holy, and magnificent is your glory, for you so loved the world that you gave[55] your only-begotten Son for it, that all who believe in him may not perish but have eternal life" (*XII Ap. Syriac*).

The *narratio* of the *Diataxeis* even finds some direct parallels in the theological prayer and the *Post Sanctus* of the anaphora of *Apostolic Constitutions*	
VIII:[56]*Diataxeis* 4	*Apostolic Constitutions* VIII
the angel of your will	the angel of your great plan
through whom you created all things	through whom everything exists (12.7)
It is he who fulfilling your will	he fulfilled your will (12.32)
to deliver from suffering	to dissolve passions . . . and
to destroy death and break the	break the fetters of the devil (12.33)
fetters of the devil.	

All the anaphoras of the West Syrian type share a characteristic literary structure, of which the *Diataxeis* appears quite simply to represent a stage barely more ancient:

54. The texts of the principal West-Syrian anaphoras are collected in A. Hänggi and I. Pahl, eds., *Prex Eucharistica* 1. *Textus e variis liturgiis antiquioribus*, Spicilegium Friburgense 12 (Fribourg, Switzerland, 1998).

55. The *Post Sanctus* of Chrysostom adapts the theme of the "sending" of the Son, common to a majority of ancient anaphoras (of which the *Diataxeis* is one); see Smyth, *Liturgie oubliée*, second part, and M. Arranz, "L'économie du salut dans la prière *Post-Sanctus* des anaphores de type antiochéen," *La Maison-Dieu* 106 (1972): 46–75. The mission of the Son was undoubtedly present in the primitive form of the anaphora of St. Basil; see J. K. R. Fenwick, *The Anaphoras of St Basil and St James. An Investigation into their Common Origin*, OCA 290 (Rome, 1992): 107–8.

56. R. Graves, "The Anaphora of the Eighth Book of the Apostolic Constitutions," in Bradshaw, *Essays on Early Eastern Eucharistic Prayers*, 178–79.

Eucharistic Address to the Father: "We thank you, O God, through your beloved servant, Jesus Christ."

Economic praise in a Christological tonality: "whom you have sent from heaven in these last times, as saviour, redeemer, and angel of your will; who is your inseparable Word through whom you have created all things; whom in your good pleasure you have sent into the womb of a virgin and who, having been conceived, became flesh and showed himself to be your son, born of the Holy Spirit and of the Virgin. It is he who, fulfilling your will and winning for you holy people, extended his hands while suffering to deliver from suffering those who have faith in you."

Primitive nonscriptural Historical Narrative (here: "in order . . . to fix the rule [of this sacrifice]"): "While he willingly gave himself to suffering, in order to destroy death and break the fetters of the devil, to crush hell underfoot, to lead the righteous to the light, to fix the rule [of this sacrifice] and to make the resurrection known."

Secondary Institution Narrative (Last Supper Narrative): "Taking bread, he gave you thanks and said: 'Take, eat, this is my body which is broken for you': in the same way the chalice, saying: 'This is my blood which is poured out for you. When you do this, you do it in memory of me.'"

Anamnesis: "Therefore remembering his death and resurrection."

Act of offering: "We offer you this bread and this cup, thanking you for counting us worthy to stand before you and to serve you as priests."

Pneumatological Epiclesis: "And we beseech you to send your Holy Spirit on the oblation of the holy church."

Intercessions: "Thus in gathering them in unity, give to those who participate in that which is sanctified, to be filled with the Holy Spirit, to confirm their faith in the truth, in order that we may praise and glorify you through your servant Jesus Christ."

Doxology: "Through him be glory and honour to you with the Holy Spirit in the holy church now and forever. Amen."

The later West Syrian anaphoras, without exception, developed the elements of this scheme. It later would be supplemented with a thanksgiving of "theological" content developing the address to the Father, the Sanctus hymn with its long angelic protocol and its embolism of the type *Vere sanctus*, and finally the recitation of the diptychs to the intercessions. This distinctive scheme clearly differs from the East Syrian scheme, from the Alexandrian, from the Western non-Roman (even if the East Syrian and Egypt quickly came to imitate it).

The anamnesis and epiclesis of the *Diataxeis* in particular are typical of the West Syrian anaphora. The first displays a narrative and descriptive concern that cannot be mistaken. This type of anamnesis again finds some supplementary glosses in all the anaphoras of the family down to its most distant derivations. In fact, the addition of the anamnesis ("Therefore remembering . . .") in the anaphora concluding the historical narrative, as well as that of the Last Supper account, are originally Syrian. In the anaphoras of the West Syrian kind, the anamnesis plays a special role, because it became (with the institution narrative) interpolated between the thanksgiving and the *commendatio oblationis*, a very ancient element for the Eucharistic prayer, which thereafter supplied a rhetorical link with the epiclesis. This specific construction is first encountered in the *Diataxeis*: "Therefore remembering his death and resurrection, we offer you the bread and the cup, thanking you for counting us worthy to stand before you and to serve you as priests."

We again discover this structure in the first place in the anaphoras of *Apostolic Constitutions* VIII and of St. John Chrysostom, and in its Syrian version called "of the Twelve Apostles," which depends upon a common but missing Greek anaphora by the same name:

> Remembering then his passion and death and resurrection from the dead, his return to heaven and his future second coming, in which he comes with glory and power to judge the living and the dead, and to reward each according to his works, we offer you, King and God, according to his commandment, this bread and this cup, giving you thanks through him that you have deemed us worthy to stand before you and to serve you as priests. And we beseech you to look graciously upon these gifts set before you, O God who need nothing, and accept them in honour of your Christ. (*Apostolic Constitutions* VIII.38–39)

> While therefore we remember, Lord, your saving command and all your dispensation which is for us: your cross, your resurrection from

the dead on the third day, your ascension into heaven and your session at the right hand of the Father, and your glorious second coming, in which you will come in glory to judge the living and the dead, and to repay each one according to their works with compassion—for your church and your flock beseech you, saying through you and with you to your Father, saying, Lord, we who have received your graces, we give thanks and confess you on behalf of all for all things. (Twelve Apostles)

We therefore, remembering this saving commandment and all the things that were done for us: the cross, the tomb, the resurrection on the third day, the ascension into heaven, the session at the right hand, the second and glorious coming again; offering you your own from your own, in all and for all. We offer you also this spiritual worship. (Anaphora of St. John Chrysostom)

We therefore, remembering his holy sufferings, and his resurrection from the dead, and his ascension into heaven, and his session at the right hand of the Father, and his glorious and fearful coming to us, have set forth before you your own from your own. (Anaphora of St. Basil, Egyptian version)

We therefore, remembering his death and his resurrection from the dead on the third day and his return to heaven and his session at your right hand, his God and Father, and his glorious and awesome second coming when the universe will be judged with equity, when each person will be rewarded according to his works, we offer you this awesome and pure sacrifice. (Anaphora of St. James, Syriac version)

Paradoxically, it is a narrative anamnesis of this kind that was inserted in a rather unsightly way and much later (but before the end of the fourth century) in the middle of the Roman Canon (as well as in the anaphora of St. Mark). It is already found in these two primitive versions of the Roman Canon incorporated, on the one hand, in the *Missale Gothicum* and, on the other hand, in the *De sacramentis* of St. Ambrose, which follows a text already somewhat glossed:

Therefore, remembering the most glorious passion of the Lord and of his resurrection from the dead, we offer to you this spotless victim, spiritual (*rationalem*) victim, bloodless victim, this holy bread and this cup of eternal life. (*Miss. Goth.* 527)

Therefore, remembering his most glorious passion and resurrection from the dead, and ascension into heaven, we offer to you this spotless victim, reasonable victim, bloodless victim, this holy bread and this cup of eternal life. (*De sacr.* IV.27)

Later these borrowings from the West Syrian model, one that is close to the anaphora of St. John Chrysostom in this particular case, continued with difficulty in the middle of the anamnesis of the Roman Canon, of which here the received text (note the very developed narrative anamnesis):

For this reason, we your servants, but also your holy people, remember, Lord, our Christ your son, the Lord our God: as much his blessed passion as his resurrection from the dead, but also his glorious ascension into heaven; his own and present gifts, we offer to your majesty the pure victim, the holy victim, the immaculate victim, the consecrated bread of eternal life and the cup of salvation without end.

We do not need to look further for the one apparent connection regarding the relationship of the Roman Canon and the *Diataxeis*, 4.

In the same way, the epicleses of the anaphora of *Apostolic Constitutions* VIII and of St. John Chrysostom/Twelve Apostles seem to depend directly on that of the *Diataxeis* (even though it does not even involve the request of the transformation of the gifts that will characterize the second part of the Eastern epiclesis at the end of the fourth century), the usage of the verb "to send" is characteristic of this family of anaphoras:

And we beseech you to send your Holy Spirit on the oblation of your holy church. (*Diataxeis* 4)

And we beseech you to look graciously upon these gifts set before you, O God who need nothing; and send (*katapempsès*) down your Holy Spirit upon this sacrifice, the witness of the sufferings of the Lord Jesus, that he may make this bread body of your Christ, and this cup blood of your Christ. (*Apostolic Constitutions* VIII.12.39)

We ask you therefore . . . that you send (*katapempson*) your Holy Spirit upon these offerings set before you, and show this bread to be the venerated body of our Lord Jesus Christ, and this cup the blood of our Lord Jesus Christ, that they may be to all who partake of them for life and resurrection. (Twelve Apostles/Chrysostom)

This form influences to differing degrees the Alexandrian anaphora of St. Mark and the Palestinian anaphora of St. James, which nonetheless involve an older and distinctive epiclesis claiming the "coming" of the Holy Spirit. By contrast, the request "to send" is entirely absent in the West Syrian anaphoras (and in the anaphora of St. Basil), which instead prefers the characteristic "that he may come."[57] The West knew the rare *emitte*, but used especially for the Eucharist epicleses of a type "pour out" or "that he may descend," in line with the epiclesis, cited above, in a primitive version of the Roman Canon collected in the Spanish books.[58]

That the anaphora of the *Diataxeis* follows a relatively primitive euchological scheme does not at all prevent proposing a dating as late as other more "evolved" formularies, with which it could have coexisted very well in Syria. Other later Syrian anaphoras, their adaptation of the *Testamentum Domini*, the so-called anaphora of Epiphanius[59] and what is cited by Narsai (*Hom.* 17),[60] attributing it to Theodore of Mopsuestia, still omit the Sanctus hymn.[61] In East Syria, the anaphora of Addai and Mari omits even today the Last Supper narrative.[62] Liturgical uniformity around a "received" West Syrian model was progressive.

CONCLUSION

In spite of this incertitude, we can situate without much risk the final editing of our anaphora to the first half of the fourth century, somewhere west of Antioch and Palestine, or perhaps more to the north in the direction of Asia Minor, at the time when all the first pneumatic epicleses began to spread in West Syria. If absolutely necessary, we could imagine that its composition was completed a little later in a conservative milieu, at a gap in relation to the general euchological evolution of the East, like that of the Arians from which the *Apostolic Constitutions* came. In this regard, the anaphora of the *Diataxeis*,

---

57. See above, note 33.

58. Smyth, *La Liturgie oubliée*, second part.

59. As Smith has noted in "The Anaphora."

60. G. Garritte, "Un opuscule grec traduit de l'arménien sur l'addition d'eau au vin eucharistique," *Le Muséon* 73, 298–99, and B. Botte, "Fragments d'une anaphore inconnue attribuée à Saint Epiphane," ibid., 311–15.

61. R. H. Connolly, ed., *The Liturgical Homilies of Narsai*, Texts and Studies VIII/1 (Cambridge, 1909), XLIX.

62. M. Smyth, "Une avancée œcuménique et liturgique: la note romaine concernant l'Anaphore d'Addaï et Mari," *La Maison-Dieu* 233 (2003): 137–54.

4, owing to its archaisms, remains a document of inestimable value for the historian of the liturgy. It constitutes the first known example of a West Syrian anaphoral model, more precisely that of the anaphora of the Twelve Apostles/St. John Chrysostom, as the characteristic epiclesis built on the request to the Father to send the Spirit suggests. It is thus safe to see it as a representative document. The "classical" West Syrian model is already clearly identifiable, in spite of the absence of the address of the *Axion (ôs alèthôs) kai dikaion* type, of the Sanctus and the diptychs; in spite of the still embryonic character of the theological prayer of the epiclesis and intercessions; and in spite of the euchological vestiges present from the time of the *Didache*. The *Diataxeis hagiôn apostolôn* therefore conveys a hinge document, of which the pseudo-apostolic literature is the guardian.

As for the Western liturgy, it was not influenced by this anaphora, even though the Latin world had a translation of the *Diataxeis* in the fifth century at its disposal. The West had been making use for centuries of its own euchological traditions, already well structured. The liturgies of the Gallican and Roman kind received diverse Syro-Palestinian contributions. But with regard to anaphoras, let us mention the address *(Vere) Dignum et iustum est*, the Sanctus with its own protocol and its embolism or the pneumatic epiclesis (but not in the Canon in the two last cases).

It was only in the twentieth century that the organism placed in charge by Rome to put into effect the liturgical reforms, the *Consilium ad exsequendam Constitutionem de sacra liturgia*, which had been voted upon by Vatican II, decided to compile an anaphora inspired by the *Diataxeis* anaphora, at the instigation of one of its eminent members, Dom Bernard Botte. The purpose was to enrich the patrimony of Eucharistic prayers of the Church of Rome,[63] what was done being based on the belief of the Romanitas and of the supposed antiquity of this document, which Botte had defended with so much ardor. What a paradox for a document that in reality never had a relationship with the city and that in many respects was less ancient than the Roman Canon, the authentic Eucharistic prayer proper to the Church of Rome! Less primitive in certain respects than the ancient core of the anaphoras of the Gallican kind, as well as their characteristic anamnesis indicates ("Recalling his passion"), or the East Syrian anaphora of Addai and

---

63. B. Botte, "L'Anaphore brève," in *Anaphores nouvelles*, Assemblées du Seigneur 2 (Paris, 1968): 21–33.

Mari and its institution narrative lacking the Last Supper account ("we also . . . who have received through tradition the model [of this offering] which comes from you"). Less, much less, ancient than the theocentric Eucharist of the anaphora of St. Mark. And much less ancient also than the Eucharist of the *Didache* and its adaptation, the "mystical Eucharist" (incorporated in *Apostolic Constitutions* VII.25–26).

In any case, what would become Eucharistic Prayer II of the Roman Missal was destined to be adapted to the taste of the day. The address was equipped with a rhetorical protocol *Vere dignum et iustum est* in the place of the very direct "We thank you." The "servant" became the "son," playing upon the ambiguous character of *pais*, which formerly led the Latin translators of the *Veronensis* to write "child." The great Christological praise was relieved of all concepts that the experts of the *Consilium* judged unsuitable for the contemporary mentality: *exeunt* "the last times," the "inseparable Word," the manifestation of the Son, the victory over hell, the deliverance from suffering, the institution of the "rule" of the sacrifice—misunderstood at the time of Botte—the enlightenment of the just, etc. They considered it good to leave the choice to the presider of replacing what remained of this praise by a "preface": in other words, in this case nothing remains of the original body of the anaphora, the thanksgiving being the central element of the Eucharistic prayer from which this last maintained its quality as "Eucharistic."[64] The liturgical reform, still dominated by the medieval vision putting the entire accent on the institution narrative, the "consecration," constituted this Eucharistic prayer as if its praise were only a secondary protocol. A Sanctus with the added protocol and the (variable) embolism was placed at the end of the "preface." The epiclesis no longer called for the sending of the Holy Spirit over the gifts and was doubled before the institution narrrative (in the *Vere sanctus*) by a preparatory epiclesis to the so-called consecration, imitating the Roman *Quam oblationem*, out of fear that someone could have imagined that the original epiclesis was "consecratory." The Last Supper account was enriched in such a way that no one could doubt its "validity." The intercessions were developed and equipped with the prayers over the *nomina*.

64. A. Verheul, "La valeur consécratoire de la prière eucharistique," *Studia Liturgica* 17 (1987): 221–31; G. J. Cuming, "The Shape of the Anaphora," *Studia Patristica* 20 (1989): 333–45; B. Neunheuser "Das eucharistische Hochgebet als Konsekrationsgebet," in *Gratias agamus*, ed. Heinz and Rennings, 315–26.

Some will regret that we have thus changed such a venerable text. On the other hand, those who would be more tempted to deplore the abrupt introduction in a hierarchical manner of a Eucharistic prayer foreign to the Latin tradition in the midst of Western euchology would be able to console themselves by considering that the *Prex Eucharistica II* is in reality an original composition, painted in bright colors, the creative fruit of experts of the *Consilium* who took the anaphora of the *Diataxeis* as their point of departure. Its features, stamped by their West Syrian structure and by their archaisms, are henceforth almost unrecognizable, but faithfully reflect the concerns of a small group of liturgists in the middle of the twentieth century.

Walter D. Ray

V. Rome and Alexandria:
Two Cities, One Anaphoral Tradition

Scholars have long noted a close relationship between the Roman Canon and the Alexandrian anaphora of St. Mark (MARK).[1] Louis Bouyer says that "with the exception of the special position of the body of intercessions in the Roman canon, it seems indeed that the other apparent differences between Rome and Alexandria are merely differences between two variants of the same tradition, and the 'Roman' tradition must have existed at Alexandria at an early time just as it did at Rome."[2] Similarly, Enrico Mazza says that "the Alexandrian and Roman anaphoras are two different developments beginning from a single point."[3] Bouyer, however, while listing all the close verbal parallels between the Canon and MARK, relies heavily for his structural comparison on the regional Egyptian anaphoras of the Deir Balyzeh papyrus (DB) and, especially, the prayer book of Sarapion of Thmuis, thinking they preserve an older Alexandrian usage than the received text of MARK. Mazza is the first to attempt a structural comparison using the Strasbourg Papyrus (STR) as a complete Eucharistic prayer and the earliest witness to MARK. Through such a comparison Mazza believes that he can "situate the Roman Canon at a precise point in the development of the anaphoric texts and show from which anaphoric structure it derives," which turns out to be "an anaphoric text

---

1. For verbal parallels see Anton Baumstark, "Das 'Problem' des römischen Messkanons," *Ephemerides Liturgicae* 53 (1939): 204–43; Louis Bouyer, *Eucharist: Theology and Spirituality of the Eucharistic Prayer*, trans. Charles Underhill Quinn (Notre Dame: University of Notre Dame Press, 1968), 214–43; and more recently, M. J. Moreton, "Rethinking the Origin of the Roman Canon," *Studia Patristica* 26 (1993): 63–66.

2. Bouyer, *Eucharist*, 216.

3. Enrico Mazza, *The Origins of the Eucharistic Prayer* (Collegeville: Liturgical Press, 1995), 282.

analogous to that represented by the Strasbourg Papyrus."[4] "We can conclude, then," Mazza writes, "that the Canon is still a witness to the ancient paleoanaphoric structure of two eucharists and one petition."[5] Mazza has demonstrated significant structural parallels between STR and the Canon. He errs, however, by trying to compare STR to the Canon as a whole. This causes him to overlook other important structural and verbal parallels between them. In this essay, I will build on Mazza's many valuable insights while avoiding the weaknesses in his method to come up with a new understanding of the development of the Canon and its relationship to the Alexandrian prayer.

Mazza's principal insight is the importance of structure in identifying relationships among prayers. Through structure, the way prayers are put together, we can get at a community's prayer habits. Prayer habits ensure that even when content varies, prayers will use familiar sequences of topics, ways of connecting prayer units, pet phrases, etc., all of which can help identify prayer traditions. Here I will attempt a more systematic and rigorous structural analysis than Mazza achieves. I will start with a structural analysis of STR. Then I will present the structural parallels identified by Mazza between STR and the first half of the Canon. Next I will look at the parallels between STR and the second part of the Canon, many of which Mazza fails to notice. Only then will I consider the relationship between MARK and the Canon as a whole. Besides the received text of the Canon,[6] I will use the oldest fragments identified by scholars: the fourth-century Mai fragments;[7] quotations from Ambrose's *De sacramentis* from the late fourth century;[8] the prefaces from the sixth-century Verona sacramentary used by Mazza;[9] and two *"Post-pridie"* from the seventh-

4. Ibid., 243.

5. Ibid., 285.

6. Text in Anton Hänggi and Irmgard Pahl, *Prex Eucharistica: Textus e Variis Liturgiis Antiquioribus Selecti* (Fribourg: Éditions Universitaires, 1968), 424–38, hereafter cited as PE; English translation adapted from R. C. D. Jasper and G. J. Cuming, *Prayers of the Eucharist: Early and Reformed* (Collegeville: Liturgical Press, 1990), 163–66, hereafter cited as PEER.

7. PE 422; PEER 156–57.

8. PE 421–22; PEER 157–58.

9. Texts cited from Mazza, *Origins*, 257–58, my translations; citations from the Verona sacramentary use item numbers from the edition of L. C. Mohlberg, *Sacramentarium veronense* (Cod. Bibl. Capit. Veron. 85 [80]), Rerum ecclesiasticarum documenta—Fontes 1 (Rome, 1956).

century Mozarabic *Liber ordinum*, one, misidentified, corresponding to the *Te igitur* through *Quam oblationem* of the first part of the Canon,[10] the other an actual *Post-pridie*, corresponding to the Canon's *Unde et memores, Supra quae* and *Supplices*.[11] For MARK,[12] besides STR[13] we have a sixth-century papyrus fragment at the John Rylands Library in Manchester, England,[14] and an eighth-century wooden tablet from the British Museum,[15] both of which contain the second part of MARK, beginning with the introduction to the Sanctus. There is a Coptic translation of MARK, the anaphora of St. Cyril (by convention, Coptic MARK).[16] I will also make use of the regional prayers of Sarapion[17] and DB,[18] as well as the recently published Barcelona papyrus,[19] which contains a complete prayer, part of which is also preserved in a now lost Coptic fragment from Louvain published by L. Th. Lefort.[20]

10. PE 428 n. 1; PEER 157.

11. PE 433 n. 1; PEER 158.

12. Received text in PEER 101–15; PE 59–65.

13. First edition in M. Andrieu and P. Collomp, "Fragments sur papyrus de l'Anaphore de saint Marc," *Revue des sciences religieuses* 8 (1928): 489–515. The text can also be found in a new edition by Jürgen Hammerstaedt, *Griechische Anaphorenfragmente aud Ägypten und Nubien*, Papyrologica coloniensia 28 (Wiesbaden: Westdeutscher Verlag, 1999): 22–24; and in PE 116–18. My English translation is adapted from PEER 52–54.

14. PE 120–23.

15. Coptic edition in Hans Quecke, "Eine saïdische Zeuge der Markusliturgie (Brit. Mus. Nr. 54 036)," *Orientalia Christiana Periodica* 37 (1971): 40–54; English translation, with elements from the Rylands papyrus, in PEER 54–56.

16. Latin translation in PE 135–39.

17. Recent edition and English translation in Maxwell E. Johnson, *The Prayers of Sarapion of Thmuis*, OCA 249 (Rome: Pontifical Oriental Institute, 1995), 46–49; text and Latin translation in PE 128–33; English translation in PEER 75–78.

18. PE 124–27; PEER 80–81.

19. R. Roca-Puig, *Anàphora de Barcelona i alters pregàries (Missa del segle IV)* (Barcelona, 1994). See also the corrected, and more accessible, edition and English translation by Mikhael Zheltov, "The Anaphora and the Thanksgiving Prayer from the Barcelona Papyrus: An Underestimated Testimony to the Anaphoral History in the Fourth Century," *Vigiliae Christianae* 62 (2008): 47–64.

20. Coptic text in L. Th. Lefort, "Coptica Lovansiensia," *Le Muséon* 53 (1940): 22–24; Latin text in PE 140; English translation in PEER 81.

The idea that STR, though missing elements common to later Eucharistic prayers, such as Sanctus, institution narrative, anamnesis, and epiclesis, is nevertheless a complete Eucharistic prayer, and not just an early version of the first part of MARK as its early editors argued, was first proposed by Edward Kilmartin in 1974 and developed independently by G. J. Cuming and H. A. J. Wegman.[21] Briefly, presuming that STR is a complete prayer would explain the unusual placement of the intercessions in MARK. Cuming, with the aid of STR, showed that MARK's intercessions, which come before the Sanctus/epiclesis, institution narrative, anamnesis, and consecratory epiclesis, were integral to MARK's structure and not just an infelicitous intrusion as was previously thought. If STR is a complete prayer, then the intercessions originally did come at the end of the prayer, as they do in virtually all other Eucharistic prayers, except the Roman Canon. As Cuming and others have noted, STR's tripartite structure is analogous to the complete prayers of *Didache* 9–10 and Addai and Mari, as well as to the *Birkat ha-Mazon*, the Jewish after-meal blessing that many scholars think is the ancestor of the later Christian Eucharistic prayers.[22] The impression that STR is a complete prayer is strengthened by the fact that it occupies one complete sheet and concludes with a doxology. Critics of the growing consensus have pointed to prayers with intermediate doxologies like *Didache* 9 and 10 and Addai and Mari and suggested that there may have been additional sheets after the single sheet of STR that contained the rest of the MARK.[23] But even

21. For references and a summary of arguments, see Walter D. Ray, "The Strasbourg Papyrus," in *Essays on Early Eucharistic Prayers*, ed. Paul F. Bradshaw, 39–44 (Collegeville: Liturgical Press, 1997).

22. See Geoffrey J. Cuming, *The Liturgy of St. Mark*, OCA 234 (Rome: Pontifical Oriental Institute), XXV–XXVI; Mazza, *Origins*, 187–94.

23. See Bryan D. Spinks, "A Complete Anaphora? A Note on Strasbourg Gr. 254," *Heythrop Journal* 25 (1984): 51–55; and more recently Mikhael Zheltov, "The Anaphora and the Thanksgiving Prayer from the Barcelona Papyrus: An Underestimated Testimony to the Anaphoral History in the Fourth Century," *Vigiliae Christianae* 62 (2008): 47–64; and Zheltov and A. Yu. Vinogradov, review of Roca-Puig, *R. Anàfora de Barcelona i altres pregàries: Missa del segle IV* (Barcelona, 1994; 19962; 19932. 151 pp.), Khristianskij Vostok n.s. 3 (2002), in Russian. Zheltov points in particular to the fourth-century Barcelona papyrus, which contains a complete Eucharistic prayer of clearly Egyptian origin that contains all the parts of such a prayer missing in STR: Sanctus and first

supposing we had the pages following STR, if there were any, and these indeed contained the rest of MARK, given the odd placement of the intercessions and the doxology that follows them, we might still reasonably conclude that the portion ending in the doxology at one time constituted a complete prayer. More significantly, as I will show here, both MARK and the Roman Canon presuppose and depend upon the STR structure not only for the first part of the prayer but also for the second, of which it is a development. In other words, MARK itself presupposes the prior existence of a complete STR-like anaphora.

As Mazza and others have noted, STR has a tripartite structure consisting of praise, offering, and petitions.[24] (For the text, see tables 1–3, column 1.) Each part or strophe is governed by a present-tense verb or set of verbs: "It is" meet to praise, etc.; "we offer"; and "we pray and beseech." The strophes are connected to each other through the use of relative clauses: "though whom . . . ," "over which . . ." The prayer concludes with a doxology, also tied to what precedes it with a relative clause, "through whom." The result is a continuous whole.[25] Some have argued, and I have suggested elsewhere, that the

---

epiclesis, institution narrative, anamnesis and second epiclesis, arguing that "the very fact of the existence of an anaphora with a full structure already in a fourth-century source, that is, older than the Strasbourg Papyrus . . . deprives the witness of the latter of probative force" (Review of Roca-Puig, 567–68). We should not presume, however, that development in the Eucharistic prayer took place everywhere at the same pace. Older prayers could coexist with more recent prayers, even within a single region.

24. Mazza, *Origins*, 186; cf. H. A. J. Wegman, "Une anaphore incomplète? Les fragments sur Papyrus Strasbourg Gr. 254," in *Studies in Gnosticism and Hellenistic Religion*, ed. R. Van Den Broek and M. J. Vermaseren, studies presented to Gilles Quispel on the occasion of his 65th birthday (Leiden: Brill, 1981), 435; Maxwell E. Johnson, *The Prayers of Sarapion of Thmuis: A Literary, Liturgical and Theological Analysis*, OCA 249 (Rome: Pontifical Oriental Institute, 1995), 255; Ray, "Strasbourg Papyrus," 55.

25. This strictly grammatical analysis of the literary structure is a step that cannot be skipped, as Thomas Talley does when he tries to find in both STR and the prayer in Apostolic Tradition 4 a bipartite prayer based on a thematic division into thanksgiving/anamnesis and supplication/epiclesis following the taxonomy of Cesare Giraudo. To fail to observe the literary structure is to do what Talley has shown Giraudo to have done with respect to the prayer in Jubilee 22, *Didache* 10, and the anaphora of Addai and Mari. Thomas J. Talley, "The Literary Structure of the Eucharistic Prayer," *Worship* 58 (1984): 404–20,

transitional relative clauses may be remnants of doxologies such as we find in *Didache* 10 (which are not, however, introduced by relative clauses).[26] Whatever their remote origin, in the present structure they serve a very different purpose, which is integral to the prayer. In the continuous form in which it has come down to us, they serve to highlight Christ's role as mediator between God and creation, which is the pivot of the entire prayer. In the first strophe creation comes from God through Christ. The first transitional phrase redirects the movement as the offering of thanksgiving ascends through Christ to God. The second transitional phrase continues this upward movement, tying the petitions to the offering. The doxology concludes the movement. The relative clauses carry the thread of the prayer's movement from beginning to end: "You created all things through . . . Christ, through whom . . . , giving thanks, we offer you this sacrifice . . . , over which offering and sacrifice we pray and beseech you . . . , accept our prayer through Christ, through whom glory to you."

Whether one compares STR with the *Birkat ha-Mazon* or the early Christian after-meal prayer in *Didache* 10, as Mazza does,[27] it is likely that the three strophes of STR were once discrete units. The second strophe likely began, "We give thanks," as does the second strophe in both the *Birkat ha-Mazon* and *Didache* 10. We can also compare it with the second strophe of the tripartite prayer of David in 1 Chronicles 29:10-19, the content of which is the offering the people are making for the temple that begins, "And now we give thanks." In STR the finite verb of thanksgiving has been reduced to a participle and the focus transferred to the act of offering. The third strophe of STR likely began simply with the request, "Remember," as in *Didache* 10. As in *Didache* 10, the first object of petition is the Church. This strophe has been greatly augmented in STR with petitions along the lines suggested in 1 Timothy 2:1-2. Though the papyrus is badly damaged at this point, it is clear that the petitions conclude with a petition for the acceptance of the offerers and their offering.

---

esp. 419; cf. Cesare Giraudo, *La struttura lettaria della preghiera eucaristica: Saggio sulla genesi letteraria di una forma—tôdâ vetrotestamentaria, beraka guidaica, anaphora Cristiana*, Analecta Biblica 92 (Rome: Biblical Institute, 1981).

26. See Ray, "Strasbourg Papyrus," 47, 50–51. If intermediate doxologies have been suppressed in STR, then the final doxology carries even weight in the argument for the completeness of the prayer.

27. Mazza, *Origins*, 152–54.

THE STR STRUCTURE AND THE FIRST PART OF
THE ROMAN CANON

Mazza identified several early Roman prefaces with significant structural parallels to STR, including the fragments published by Cardinal Mai and several prefaces from the Verona sacramentary. Several of these are presented along with STR in table 1. These prefaces have a bipartite structure of praise and offering. We see that the parallels with STR involve those structural elements where STR appears to be innovating, in particular, a participial phrase that introduces the offering, verbs of asking that introduce the petitions, and relative clauses tying the petitions to the offering in an upward movement through the mediator Christ. We should also notice the use of the relative pronoun (*qui*)

TABLE 1: STR AND THE EARLY ROMAN PREFACES ADDUCED BY MAZZA

STR	Mai Fragment	Ver. n. 718 4th Mass of Sixtus	Ver. n. 202 In pentecosten ascendentibus a fonte	Ver. n. 29
[It is truly meet and right . . .] . . . you who made heaven and all that is in it, the earth and all that is in it, seas and rivers and all that is in them; you who made humanity in your own image and likeness. You made everything through your wisdom, your true light, your Son, our Lord and Savior	It is meet and right, equitable and just, that we give you thanks for all things, Lord, Holy Father . . . , who (*qui*) deigned . . . that light should shine by sending us Jesus Christ . . . , who (*qui*), humbling himself for our salvation, gave himself up to death . . .	It is meet (*Uere dignum*): Who (*qui*) this day has crowned as a faithful martyr the holy Xystus, priest of the apostolic see,	It is meet (*Uere dignum*): Who (*qui*) ascended above the highest heavens and, sitting at your right hand, pours out the promised Holy Spirit of adoption.	It is meet (*Uere dignum*): Who (*qui*) thus destroyed the enemy's ancient siege engines . . .

STR	Mai Fragment	Ver. n. 718 4th Mass of Sixtus	Ver. n. 202 In pentecosten ascendentibus a fonte	Ver. n. 29
Jesus Christ, *through him to you* with him and with the Holy Spirit	For whose mercy to your great generosity we are not sufficient to give thanks with any praise,	For which work and your many gifts		whose glory on this feast day
Giving thanks, *we offer the reasonable sacrifice and this bloodless service,* which all the nations offer you [Mal 1:11] . . .	**asking (*pe-tentes*)** of your great and merciful goodness to hold acceptable *this sacrifice which we offer to you,* standing before the face of your divine goodness,	**rejoicing in thanksgiving (*gratiarum actione laeta-ntes*)** *we offer you sacrifices of praise* (hostias tibi laudis offerimus): *through (per).*	Therefore (*Unde*) **rejoicing (*laetantes*)** before your altar, Lord of powers, *we offer you sacrifices of praise* (hostias tibi laudis offerimus), etc.	**recalling (*re-colentes*)** *we offer you sacrifices of praise* (hostias tibi laudis offeri-mus), With the angels.
over which sacrifice and offering *we pray and beseech* . . .	*through (*per) Jesus Christ, our Lord and God,* *through whom* (per quem) *we pray and beseech* (peti-mus et roga-mus) . . .			

to expand the praise in the first strophe. This pattern provided a structure that could be adapted to different circumstances. While some wording became more or less standardized—for example, *hostias tibi laudis offerimus, per quem, petimus et rogamus*—the structure remained flexible enough to accommodate the various occasions remembered in the first part of the variable preface. We see this especially in the different participles used to tie this first part of the preface to the offering: *laetentes, recolentes, celebrantes,*[28] *uenerantes.*[29] That in the background to these participles is the idea of thanksgiving is suggested even by the participle seemingly most removed from this idea, the *petentes* of the Mai fragment, which is also the earliest example. The plea for the acceptance of the offering is made necessary precisely because we cannot give thanks as we should, as would be required at this point in the prayer.

Mazza shows how this pattern of preface construction disappeared over time, though it is still present in a limited way in the Gelasian sacramentary.[30] The offering itself disappeared from the preface, to be replaced by the Sanctus.[31] That the pattern Mazza discovered was more significant in Rome than the few remaining instances of it might indicate is suggested by the fact that elements of it—the prepositional phrase and asking verbs introducing the petitions—have become permanently fixed in the *Te igitur* of the received Canon, along with the request for acceptance of the offering, long after the offering itself disappeared from the preface. Though Mazza suggests that the offering "shifted" to the *Te igitur,*[32] what we find there is not an offering but a *commendatio oblationis*, a prayer for acceptance of the offering such as we find in one form or another among the petitions following the offering in virtually all Eucharistic prayers.[33] We find one also, as we will see, in the second half of the Canon.

The full *Te igitur*, in the earliest form in which we have it, in a mislabeled Mozarabic *"Post pridie"* in the *Liber Ordinum,*[34] contains petitions both for the Church and for acceptance of the offering. These two petitions should probably be seen as the core supplications in this

---

28. Ver. n. 314: "Uere dignum: . . . Inter que praeceptis nos apostiolicis pariterque cognoscimus praesidiis erudiri. Et idcirco horum sollemnia *celebrantes* hostias tibi laudis offerimus: per."

29. Ver. 728: "Uere dignum: adest enim nobis sancti sacerdotis et martyris tui Xysti desiderata festiuitas; quam annua recursione *uenerantes* hostias tibi laudibus offerimus. Cum angelis."

30. Mazza, *Origins*, 260.

31. This is preferable to Mazza's idea that the offering moves to the *Te igitur*; see below.

32. Mazza, *Origins*, 260–62.

33. In the Mai fragment we see the opposite of the movement presupposed by Mazza, the drift into the offering of the petition for its acceptance.

34. PE 428 n. 1; PEER 157.

type of prayer. Like STR, the received Canon follows its petition for the Church with prayers for the living, in the *Memento Domine*, before asking (again) for the acceptance of the offering in the *Hanc igitur* and *Quam oblationem*. This last petition concludes the first part of the Canon. It stands in the same place in the Canon as the concluding petition for acceptance of the offering in STR (see table 2). This petition appears almost as a doublet or continuation of the petition for acceptance in the *Te igitur*. The first petition for acceptance of the offering is the only structural difference between STR and the Canon. If the first petition is the duplication and the *Quam oblationem* the original, then whenever it used one of the early prefaces, the structure of the first part of the Canon mirrored almost exactly that of STR.

TABLE 2: STR AND ROMAN CANON PART I (PETITIONS FROM *TE IGITUR*)

STR	Mozarabic *"Post-pridie"* (with equivalent prayers from the Canon)
. . . over which sacrifice and offering we pray and beseech you, remember *your holy* and only *Catholic Church*, all your peoples and your flocks. *The peace which is from heaven* bestow on all our hearts, and *grant us* also the *peace* of this life. The [king of] the land, peaceful things towards us, and towards your holy name, the prefect of [the province], the army, the princes, councils . . . [15–20 lines missing] . . . [for seedtime and] harvest . . . preserve, for the poor of [your] people, for all of us who call upon [your] name, for all who hope in you. Give rest to the souls of those who have fallen asleep; remember those of whom we make mention today both those	(*Te igitur*) Through whom we pray and beseech you, almighty Father, vouchsafe to accept and bless these offerings and these unblemished sacrifices, above all, those which we offer to you for *your holy Catholic Church*: vouchsafe to *grant it peace*, spread through the whole world in *your peace*.

whose names we say [and] whose we do not say . . .	
[Remember] our orthodox fathers and bishops everywhere; and grant us to have a part and lot with the fair . . . of your holy prophets, apostles, and martyrs;	(Memento Domine/Communicantes) Remember, Lord, also your servants who in honor of the Saints NN pay their vows to the living and true God, for the forgiveness of all their sins.
[through] their petitions . . . [receive] . . . [make worthy] . . . that which is received . . . grant to them through our Lord,	(Quam oblationem) Vouchsafe to make their offering blessed, ratified, and reasonable; it is the image and likeness of the
through whom glory to you to the ages of ages.	body and blood of Jesus Christ, your son and our redeemer.

STR AND THE SECOND PART OF THE ROMAN CANON

His desire to compare the whole of the Roman Canon with the whole of STR prevents Mazza from observing that the entire structure of STR can be accounted for in the first part of the Canon alone. Even more interesting, the structure is found again in the second half of the Canon, beginning with *Qui pridie*, the Canon's institution narrative. Mazza misses this, however, because he has eliminated the institution narrative and the anamnesis that follows it from the comparison since they are not found in STR. Mazza justifies the elimination of the institution narrative in part on the basis of his prior analysis of the Apostolic Tradition, from which "we know . . . that the account of institution entered into the anaphora as the last part of the preface." To know what an anaphora was like "before this practice imposed itself on all the texts," Mazza suggests, it is simply necessary to eliminate the account of institution.[35] But in doing this, he misses some of the most interesting verbal parallels between MARK and the Canon, especially in what Mazza takes as its earliest witness, the prayer quoted by Ambrose in *De sacramentis* 4. More important, he misses the structural parallels not only between the second part of the Canon and STR but also between the second and first parts of the Canon itself.

35. Ibid., 255.

These structural parallels become apparent when we view the texts in synoptic form (table 3). All that's missing from Ambrose's text is a *Vere dignum* before the *Qui pridie* to make the parallel complete. We observed that expanding the praise section by use of the relative pronoun *qui* was a standard practice in Rome. We also find the practice in Egypt, especially in the Barcelona papyrus. Had he not eliminated the institution narrative *a priori*, Mazza's own conclusion that the institution narrative entered the anaphora as the last part of the preface might have led him to see that the pattern was beginning again. It is quite possible that the *Qui pridie* is what remained of the praise section of an STR-like structure when it was appended to the first part of the Canon.

TABLE 3: STR, THE EARLY ROMAN PREFACE PATTERN, AND
ROMAN CANON PART II

Strasbourg Gr. 254/St. Mark	Veronense: In pentecosten ascendentibus a fonte.	Ambrose, *De sacramentis* IV
[It is truly meet and right . . . to praise] you [to hymn you,] to bless you, [to confess you] night and day, you who made heaven and all that is in it, the earth and all that is in it, seas and rivers and all that is in them; you who made humanity in your own image and likeness. You made everything through your wisdom, your true light, your Son, our Lord and Savior Jesus Christ,	It is meet (*Uere dignum*):	
through whom to you with him and with the Holy Spirit	Who (*qui*) ascended above the highest heavens and, sitting at your right hand, pours out the promised Holy Spirit of adoption.	Who the day before (*qui pridie*) he suffered took bread in his holy hands . . . Likewise, after supper, the day before he suffered, he took the cup . . .

Strasbourg Gr. 254/St. Mark	Veronense: In pentecosten ascendentibus a fonte.	Ambrose, *De sacramentis* IV
		As often as you do this, you do it in my remembrance.
Giving thanks,	Therefore, **rejoicing** (*unde laetantes*) before your altar, Lord of powers,	Therefore, **remembering** (*ergo memores*) his most glorious Passion and resurrection from the dead, and ascension into heaven,
we offer the reasonable *sacrifice and this bloodless service*, which all the nations offer you, "from the rising to the setting of the sun," from south to north, [for] your "name is great among the nations, and in every place incense is offered to your holy name and a pure sacrifice,"	*we offer* you the sacrifice of praise, etc.	*we offer to you* this spotless sacrifice (*hostiam*), *reasonable sacrifice, bloodless sacrifice*, this holy bread and this cup of eternal life;
over which sacrifice and offering *we pray and beseech you,*	[Mozarabic "*post-pridie*": Through whom *we pray and beseech you*, almighty Father, vouchsafe to accept and bless these offerings and these unblemished sacrifices, above all, those which we offer to you for *your holy Catholic Church*:	And *we pray and beseech you*
remember *your holy* and only *Catholic Church*, all your peoples and your flocks. *The peace which is from heaven* bestow on all our hearts, and *grant us* also the *peace* of this life. . . .	vouchsafe to *grant it peace*, spread through the whole world in *your peace*. Remember, Lord, also your servants who in honor of the Saints *NN* pay their vows to the	

Strasbourg Gr. 254/St. Mark	Veronense: In pentecosten ascendentibus a fonte.	Ambrose, *De sacramentis* IV
	living and true God, for the forgiveness of all their sins.	
[only in MARK: . . . *Receive*, O God, *the thank offerings* of those who offer the sacrifices, *at your spiritual altar in heaven by the ministry of your archangels . . . , as you accepted the gifts of your righteous Abel, the sacrifice of our father Abraham*, and the widow's two mites . . .]	Vouchsafe to *make their offering blessed, ratified, and reasonable*; it is the image and likeness of the body and blood of Jesus Christ, your son and our redeemer.]	to *receive this offering* on *your altar on high by the hands of your angels, as you vouchsafed to receive the gifts of your righteous servant Abel, and the sacrifice of our patriarch Abraham*, and that which the high priest Melchizedek offered to you. . . .

If the institution narrative concludes the first strophe of an STR-like structure, the "anamnesis" constitutes the second strophe. *Memores* in Ambrose is an adjective with the force of a participle. It no doubt translates the Greek participle μεμνημένοι found in the anamneses of most of the Greek anaphoras. As in the prefaces examined above, the redactors of this structure have done nothing more than choose a participle to suit the occasion and the Christological narrative that precedes it, with its concluding affirmation: "As often as you do this, you do it for my memory until I come again." With the new participle, the thanksgiving-offering of STR and the early Roman prefaces becomes the anamnesis-offering familiar from so many later Eucharistic prayers. The main verb, however, is still "we offer." And the content of the offering in Ambrose—pure, reasonable, and bloodless sacrifice—is remarkably like STR's reasonable sacrifice and bloodless worship. Only in Ambrose and in one *Post secreta* in the *Missale gothicum*, which is clearly dependent on Ambrose, do we find the term "bloodless sacrifice" in an early Western anaphora. The *immaculatam hostiam* of Ambrose may reflect the "pure sacrifice" (θυσίαν καθαράν) that concludes the quotation of Malachi 1:11 in the Strasbourg Papyrus.

The affinity of Ambrose's text with the Alexandrian anaphoral tradition is secured by the significant parallel between the petition that follows in Ambrose, introduced as expected by twin verbs of asking, and the *commendatio oblationis* that replaces the simple formula of STR in the developed anaphora of MARK. Both ask God to receive the offering on the heavenly altar through the hands of angels, just as he received "the gifts of the righteous Abel" and "the sacrifice of our father Abraham." Though this petition is not found in STR itself, it is found in what is clearly a development of STR in Alexandria.[36] It is, moreover, of a piece with STR's and Ambrose's offering of "reasonable and bloodless sacrifice." The narrative background for both can be found in the second-century Jewish-Christian Testament of Levi. In this story Levi has a vision in which he is taken up through the seven heavens.

> In the uppermost heaven of all dwells the Great Glory in the Holy of Holies superior to all holiness. There with him are the angels of the presence, who serve and propitiate before the Lord for all the sins of ignorance of the righteous. And they offer the Lord a pleasing odor, a reasonable and bloodless offering (λογικὴν καὶ ἀναίμακτον προσφοράν). (TL 3.3–6)[37]

This background suggests that the original context for both the offering and petition for acceptance of the offering was the kind of sacrifice of thanksgiving that we find in STR, MARK, and the early Roman prefaces. The "reasonable and bloodless sacrifice" is the worship of the angels, the sacrifice of praise. It does not have in view the sacrifice of Christ on the cross or the commemoration of that sacrifice. This is

---

36. Klaus Gamber, "Das Papyrusfragment zur Markusliturgie und das Eucharistiegebet im Clemensbrief," *Ostkirchliche Studien* 8 (1959): 35, thought a reference to "your heavenly altar" would fit in the lacunae of STR's petition for acceptance of the offering. Geoffrey J. Cuming accepts Gamber's reconstruction in his own work on St. Mark: *Liturgy of St. Mark*, 70.

37. Text in M. de Jonge, *The Testaments of the Twelve Patriarchs: A Critical Edition of the Greek Texts* (Leiden: Brill, 1978); translation by H. C. Kee in James H. Charlesworth, *The Old Testament Pseudepigrapha I: Apocalyptic Literature and Testaments* (Garden City, NY: Doubleday, 1983), 788–95. I will not enter into the question of a possible Jewish *Vorlage* for this passage. I accept Marinus de Jonge's judgment that the work as we have it is a Christian document. I will also not foreclose on the possibility that the Testament is here alluding to an already existing prayer. That is, I am not claiming that the Testament is the source of the euchological wording. What interests me is that the Testament and the Eucharistic prayers share a narrative world. It is perhaps interesting that one late ms. of TL from Mt. Athos has "holy angels," like Ambrose, while another group of mss. has "archangels," like Mark.

perhaps why the phrase did not have a long career in the West.[38] Ambrose's offering of reasonable and bloodless sacrifice was replaced in the received Canon with an offering "from your own gifts and bounty, a pure victim, a holy victim, an unspotted victim." The petition for acceptance was also rearranged in the received Canon to bring the human sacrifices of Abel, Abraham, and Melchizedek (*Supra quae*) to the fore. The angelic worship (*Supplices*) comes second. It therefore seems more likely that the institution narrative in Ambrose was added to an existing prayer comparable to STR, which already had the elements in question, than that these elements were chosen to round out a section of prayer whose primary content was the commemoration of Christ's passion. This suggests that the second part of the Canon was not composed by simply following the habitual pattern, perhaps because of the felt need to incorporate an institution narrative, but was adapted from an existing Strasbourg-type prayer, one that had already acquired such a narrative.

We don't know what followed the petition for the acceptance of the offering in Ambrose's prayer. In the received Roman Canon there follow two petitions, for the departed (*Memento etiam*) and again for the offerers (*Nobis quoque*). The originality of both these petitions has been questioned. But as Bouyer points out, though the *Memento etiam* is missing from many early manuscripts, the *Nobis quoque*, which presupposes the *Memento etiam*, is always present. The prayer for the departed may often be missing because it was not said on Sundays.[39] Bouyer also points out that these prayers closely parallel the concluding petitions of Sarapion and MARK's petitions before the *commendatio oblationis*.[40] Mazza makes the same observation with respect to STR.[41]

---

38. The use of *sacrificium laudis* and *hostia laudis* also diminished over time, being confined in the received Canon mainly to the commemoration of the living (*Memento Domine*); see the lists of instances of these terms compiled by Geoffrey Grimshaw Willis, "Sacrificium laudis," in *The Sacrifice of Praise: Studies on the Themes of Thanksgiving and Redemption in the Central Prayers of the Eucharistic and Baptismal Liturgies in Honor of Arthur Hubert Couratin*, ed. Bryan Spinks, 82–86 (Rome: Edizioni Liturgiche, 1981). The general use of the plural (sacrifices of praise) in the Verona sacramentary, while the source text (Heb 13:15) has the singular, may suggest that the phrase was already being redirected and no longer refers primarily to the Eucharist being celebrated.

39. Bouyer, *Eucharist*, 241.

40. Ibid., 240.

41. Mazza, *Origins*, 272–73.

Though Mazza accepts the theory that the *Memento etiam* is a late addition, he nevertheless includes both it and the *Nobis quoque* in his comparative tables, transposing them with Ambrose's prayer for the acceptance of the sacrifice to make the parallels more apparent.[42] Such a transposition may be justified, though it misses parallels this second part of the Canon has with the first (see table 4).[43]

TABLE 4: PETITIONS IN STR AND ROMAN CANON PARTS I AND II

STR	Canon, Part I (Mozarabic "*Post-pridie*")	Canon, Part II
over which sacrifice and offering *we pray and beseech you,* remember **your holy** and only **Catholic Church**, all your peoples and your flocks. **The peace which is from heaven** bestow on all our hearts, and **grant us** also the **peace** of this life. . . .	(=*Te igitur*) Through whom *we pray and beseech you,* almighty Father, vouchsafe to *accept and bless these offerings* and these unblemished sacrifices, above all, those which we offer to you for **your holy Catholic Church**: vouchsafe **to grant it peace**, spread through the whole world in your peace.	[Ambrose: *And we pray and beseech you* *to receive this offering* on your altar on high by the hands of your angels, as you vouchsafed to receive the gifts of your righteous servant Abel, and the sacrifice of our patriarch Abraham, and that which the high priest Melchizedek offered to you. . . .]
Give rest to the souls of *those who have fallen asleep;* remember those of whom we make mention today both those whose names we say [and] whose we do not say . . .	(=*Memento Domine*) Re-**member, Lord, also** your servants who in honor of the Saints *NN* pay their vows to the living and true God, for the forgiveness of all their sins.	[Received text: (*Memento etiam*) **Remember also, Lord**, the names of *those who* have gone before us with the sign of faith, and *sleep in the sleep of peace*. We beseech you to grant to them and to all who rest

42. Ibid., 278–79.

43. The parallel between the first and second parts of the Canon would be even more significant if we included the *Communicantes* and *Hanc igitur* after *Memento Domine*. Even if these are later additions to the prayer, they show, I think, a conscious desire to balance the petitions in each part of the prayer.

STR	Canon, Part I (Mozarabic "*Post-pridie*")	Canon, Part II
[Remember] our orthodox fathers and bishops everywhere; and *grant us to have a part and lot with the fair* . . . of your holy prophets, *apostles, and martyrs;*		in Christ a place of restoration, light, and peace; through Christ our Lord. (*Nobis quoque*) To us sinners your servants also, who trust in the multitude of your mercies, vouchsafe to *grant some part and fellowship with your holy Apostles and martyrs*, NN, and all your saints: into whose company we ask that you will admit us, not weighing our merit, but bounteously forgiving; through Christ our Lord.]
[through] their petitions . . . [*receive*] . . . [**make worthy**] . . . **that which is received** . . . grant to them through our Lord,	(=*Quam oblationem*) Vouchsafe to **make their offering blessed, ratified, and reasonable;** it is the image and likeness of the body and blood of Jesus Christ, your son and our redeemer.	

It will be remembered that even in its first part, the Canon is anxious to ask that the offering be received, making this its first request in the *Te igitur*. The Canon appears to be following the same pattern in its second part. In other words, it may well be that the Canon itself has transposed the petitions found in its STR-like model in order to conform to its own pattern, established in its first part. Unlike the first part, however, the second part does not repeat the petition for acceptance of the offering.[44]

Even if we do not include these petitions in the comparison, but especially if we do, we see that the second part of the Canon, like the first, comprises a complete STR-like structure. In this second part, in fact, un-

44. It may be that the final petition for acceptance in the first part of the Canon, the *Quam oblationem*, was retained primarily because it became the hook for adding the institution narrative and the second part of the prayer. See more below.

like the first part, the parallels are not simply structural but also verbal, suggesting that the prayer from which it derives is closely related to STR itself. Had STR acquired the prayer for acceptance it has in MARK and an institution narrative with the requisite participial phrase before the offering, at the same time losing the long quotation of Malachi 1:11 (as no longer necessary, since the offering is explained by the institution narrative), then it would be very close to the second part of the Canon as cited by Ambrose. In our study of the early Roman prefaces, we observed the flexibility of the STR structure in adapting to differing circumstances. It is not unlikely that on occasion or in certain places such adaptation included the use of an institution narrative.[45] The resulting prayer would have provided a model known to the redactors of both MARK and Ambrose, which they could use when, for whatever reason, it became necessary to include an institution narrative on every occasion.

Such a possibility seems all the more likely when we notice the close relationship between Ambrose's institution narrative and MARK's (table 5).

TABLE 5: INSTITUTION NARRATIVES:
MARK AND THE ROMAN CANON (AMBROSE)

MARK (British Museum Tablet)	Ambrose
For our Lord and Savior and King of all, Jesus Christ, in the night when he was betrayed and willingly underwent death, took bread in his *holy* and undefiled [and] blessed *hands, looked up to heaven to you, the Father of all*, blessed, gave thanks over it, sanctified, broke [and] gave it to *his disciples [and] apostles*,	Who the day before he suffered took bread in his *holy hands, looked up to heaven to you, holy Father, almighty*, eternal God, gave thanks, blessed, and broke it, and handed it when broken to *his apostles and disciples*, saying, "Take and eat from this, all of

45. There was certainly more than one such prayer. In a recent article, I argue that Apostolic Tradition 4 presents another STR-like prayer that acquired an institution narrative. See Walter D. Ray, "The Strasbourg Papyrus and the Roman Canon: Thoughts on Chapter 7 of Enrico Mazza's *The Origins of the Eucharistic Prayer*," *Studia Liturgica* 39 (2009): 54–58. Its institution narrative is different than MARK's and the Canon's. DB, which is structurally like MARK with a duplication of the STR structure, and the Barcelona papyrus, which maintains a tripartite structure and is closely related to STR, have similar institution narratives from yet a third source.

MARK (British Museum Tablet)	Ambrose
saying, "Take and eat of this, all of you; this is my body, which is given for you for the forgiveness of your sins. Do this for my remembrance." Likewise, after supper, he took a cup,	you; for this is my body, which will be broken for many."
	Likewise, after supper, the day before he suffered, he took the cup, looked up to heaven to you, holy
blessed, sanctified, [and] gave it to them, saying, "Take this and drink from it all of you; this is my blood, which is shed for many for the forgiveness of their sins. Do this for my remembrance. For as often as you eat this bread and drink this cup, you proclaim my death [and] confess my resurrection."	Father, almighty, eternal God, gave thanks, blessed, and handed it to his apostles and disciples, saying, "Take and drink from this, all of you; for this is my blood."
	As often as you do this, you do it in my remembrance.

Most of the differences between them can be ascribed to the tendency, which was carried out differently in each of them, toward greater parallelism in the words spoken over the elements and closercitation of Scripture. Of the early extant Eucharistic prayers, Jesus looks up to his Father in heaven only in these two and Apostolic Constitutions VIII, the sources of which are obscure. The looking up is not generally a feature of Antiochene prayers. It is in Greek James, but not the Syriac, which seems to preserve the older usage. Of later prayers, it is found in the Egyptian anaphoras of Basil (the Greek version, but not, presumably, the earlier Sahidic) and Gregory, in two anaphoras from the White Monastery in Upper Egypt,[46] in several Ethiopian prayers, and in several Syrian Orthodox prayers for which Egyptian influence is possible.[47] "Disciples **and** apostles" together as the direct object of Christ's giving is rare, but appears in Byzantine Basil, Chrysostom, and

46. Emmanuel Lanne, *Le grand euchologe du Monastère Blanc*, Patrologia Orientalis 28/2 (Paris: Fimrin-Didot, 1958).

47. See the comparative tables compiled by Paul Cagin, *L'Euchologue latine étudiée dans la tradition de ses formules et de ses formulaires. L'Eucharistie, canon rimitif de la messe ou formulaire essential et premier de toutes les liturgies.* Scriptorium Solesmense II (Paris: Brotherhood of St. John the Evangelist, 1912), 225–44.

James and their Syriac counterparts, as well as in most of the Egyptian, Ethiopian, and Syrian Orthodox prayers that also have Christ looking up. In the West, however, we find disciples and apostles together only in Ambrose, and not even in the received Roman Canon. Whatever the origin of this institution narrative, it made its way into a prayer very much like STR, and from there into both Ambrose and MARK.

MARK AND THE ROMAN CANON

In Bouyer's estimation, the significant structural difference between MARK and the Canon is the position of the intercessions. In the Canon the intercessions follow the Sanctus; in MARK they precede it.[48] He tries to trace the differing placement of the Sanctus and intercessions to differences in the use of the *Qedushah* (the Sanctus) in synagogue ritual. Conservative Roman Jews said the *Qedushah* before the *Tefillah*, the Jewish Eighteen Blessings that Bouyer thinks lies behind the Christian anaphoral intercessions, while Alexandrian Jews inserted the *Qedushah* into the *Tefillah*. Mazza also thinks that the difference between these prayers can be accounted for by where they placed the Sanctus and the institution narrative, both of which he thinks are late insertions. From his comparison of STR and the Canon, Mazza concludes that MARK "added at the end, by simple coupling, any new part that the anaphora received in its development,"[49] whereas "the Canon did not juxtapose texts through mere addition, one simply following the other, but sought the most appropriate location within the anaphora."[50] Both sets of conclusions depend heavily on the presuppositions of their respective authors.

A more rigorous structural analysis shows that, on the contrary, MARK and the Canon developed in very similar ways. Both, in fact, appear to have developed "by simple coupling," or rather, by doubling their original tripartite structures. The Canon appears to have done this by taking a whole prayer, very similar to STR but with an institution narrative, suppressing its introductory praise, and appending it to the end of its original tripartite structure. The first two strophes of the first structure, the "Preface," remained flexible while the second structure, which may originally have been one of the occasional variants of STR, became fixed. MARK's development was somewhat more

48. Bouyer, *Eucharist*, 218.
49. Ibid., 283.
50. Ibid., 284.

complicated, but not essentially different. It apparently used the same source as the Canon. But because MARK began with STR, which had probably already become a fixed prayer, it already had STR's offering of reasonable sacrifice and bloodless worship. It probably also had the petition for the acceptance of the offering. If it didn't, and instead took this petition from the same source as its institution narrative, it logically put the petition in that part of the prayer in which the bloodless sacrifice was offered. In any case, MARK obtained a new offering, with a new introduction of the offering to complement the institution narrative in order to round out the structure in its second part. MARK's redactor could have done this either by borrowing from elsewhere or by new composition, or some of both. He apparently had plenty of material to work with, even in his own tradition. The offering "from your own gifts" is fairly widespread; in Egypt it is found in Sahidic Basil and the Barcelona papyrus. The additional qualification of "this bread and this cup," a commonplace for Western Christians, in the East is found only in Egypt and in prayers derived from Apostolic Tradition 4, where bread and cup are the only things offered.[51] The use of the participle "proclaiming" to introduce the anamnesis/offering is unique to Egypt and certainly originated there. The consecratory Spirit epiclesis that forms the petitions, introduced as usual by the verbs "we ask and beseech," is shared by MARK, DB, and Barcelona and has features unique to Egypt, especially the request that the wine become the "blood of the new covenant." MARK's epiclesis may have been also influenced by the Jerusalem anaphora of James, with which it shares the unique verb ἐξαποστέλειν. But wherever MARK got its materials, it is likely that, since the redactor evidently found the tripartite structure to be important, the structure was added all at once rather than piecemeal.

One difference between the Roman Canon and MARK is the way the new structure is connected to what precedes it. In the Canon, the connection is clear. The redactors simply kept the relative pronoun the institution narrative would have had in a preface, referring it now to

---

51. This fact would seem to confirm that the place of origin for ApTrad 4 is either Rome or Egypt. It is not likely that ApTrad is the source for this expression of offering for Rome. If it were, one might expect that Rome would also have taken over ApTrad's epiclesis. ApTrad might have taken its expression from Rome and given it to Egypt. Given the close relationship of these two regions, however, it is more likely that "bread and cup" belonged to their common stock of offering terminology, whence ApTrad also took it.

the immediately preceding reference to Christ in the *Quam oblationem.* This petition for the acceptance of the offering, which concludes the original structure, perhaps ended with "through Christ our Lord," like the preceding *Hanc igitur* in the received text.[52] The *Quam oblationem* would have been altered so that its offering referred to the institution narrative. MARK introduces its narrative with an explanatory "for" or "because" (ὅτι). What MARK's narrative explains, however, is not clear. In the received text it follows the post-Sanctus epiclesis, which in the British Museum tablet reads: "Fill, O God, this sacrifice also with the blessing from you through the descent of your Holy Spirit." Coquin thinks that the institution narrative was originally connected to the offering, as it appears to be in Sarapion. The petitions, Sanctus, and post-Sanctus epiclesis would all have been later insertions.[53] But as Cuming showed, the petitions are an integral part of the primitive structure. Coptic MARK adds a sentence to the Greek text: "And with blessing bless and with sanctifying sanctify these your precious gifts which we have placed before you, this bread and this cup." This sentence provides an adequate hook for the institution narrative, which would then explain the offering of bread and wine. At the same time it produces a clear division between the two parts of the prayer. The post-Sanctus petition to fill the sacrifice looks back to the earlier offering, which in Coptic MARK is still reasonable sacrifice and bloodless worship.[54] The added petition in Coptic MARK for the blessing of the gifts looks forward to the institution narrative and the offering of "these your gifts."

Most scholars have seen the unique Egyptian Sanctus/epiclesis, which follows the intercessions and precedes the institution narrative, as the main structural difference between the Roman Canon and

52. The *Hanc igitur*, which appears to be a later addition, duplicates the theme of acceptance of the offerers found in the early Mozarabic equivalent of the *Quam oblationem* and in the *Nobis quoque* at the end of the petitions in the second half of the Canon. It is possible that it draws on material that once appeared in the *Quam oblationem* after the latter was altered to accommodate the institution narrative.

53. R.-G. Coquin, "L'anaphore alexandrine de Saint Marc," *Le Muséon* 82 (1969): 334.

54. In Greek MARK the word "sacrifice" has disappeared from the first offering. Its post-Sanctus epiclesis must look forward to the institution narrative to provide an understanding of the sacrifice to be filled.

MARK. The Egyptian Sanctus is unique in not having the *Benedictus* "Blessed is he that comes in the name of the Lord" but rather an epiclesis that picks up on the word "full" in the Sanctus. In MARK the sequence is "Heaven and earth are *full* of your glory. *Full* in truth are heaven and earth . . . *Fill* also this sacrifice . . ." Not all the witnesses have the transitional middle sentence. MARK and Sarapion do, but DB does not. I will not go into the unique theology of the Egyptian Sanctus, which has suggested to some that the Sanctus was introduced quite early into the Alexandrian prayer.[55] Instead I will focus on the structural question of the unit's placement in the prayer and what this might tell us about how the unit entered the anaphora. While the text of this unit is quite stable among the various Egyptian prayers, there is no agreement among them about its placement. In terms of the STR pattern, MARK and Deir Balyzeh attach the unit after the petitions, while Sarapion and Barcelona have it before the offering.

What was the original location of the Egyptian Sanctus? Our observations of MARK's relationship with the Roman Canon may provide a clue. Bouyer compares MARK's post-Sanctus epiclesis to the Canon's *Quam oblationem*, the petition for acceptance of the offering that concludes the first part of the Canon. He also suggests that this post-Sanctus epiclesis is a continuation of MARK's earlier *commendatio oblationis* at the hands of archangels. He calls these two prayers a two-part epiclesis, comparable to the *Hanc igitur* and *Quam oblationem* of the Canon, between which the Sanctus has been interposed.[56] While the comparison cannot hold because of the apparently late development of the *Hanc igitur*, the idea that the two petitions in MARK belong together is worth pursuing. Bouyer might also have pursued his observation of the idea of an exchange of heavenly blessings for earthly things that he finds in both the Alexandrian and Roman versions of the petition for the acceptance of the offering.[57] This is explicit in MARK, where after being asked to receive the offerers' sacrifice at the

55. For discussion, see Gregory Dix, "Primitive Consecration Prayers," *Theology* 37 (1938): 270–77; Bryan D. Spinks, *The Sanctus in the Eucharistic Prayer* (Cambridge: Cambridge University Press, 1991), 86–88; Johnson, *Prayers of Sarapion*, 208–15; Robert F. Taft, "The Interpolation of the Sanctus into the Anaphora: When and Where? A Review of the Dossier, Part II," *OCP* 58 (1992): 88–95.

56. Bouyer, *Eucharist*, 215.

57. Ibid., 209.

hands of archangels, God is asked to "give them imperishable things for perishable, heavenly things for earthly, eternal for temporal." Following the comparable petition for acceptance in the Roman Canon (i.e., the *Supra quae* and *Supplices*), God is asked "that all of us who have received the most holy body and blood of your Son by partaking at this altar *may be filled* (repleamur) *with all heavenly blessing and grace*" (emphasis added). Another version, from an early Mozarabic *Post-pridie*, asks that God's "blessing descend here invisibly" and that God's "holy Spirit be borne down upon those solemn things." These western petitions recall MARK's post-Sanctus epiclesis, which asks that God "fill this sacrifice also with the blessing from you through the descent of your Holy Spirit." The closeness of MARK's epiclesis to the western prayers would seem to lend support to Bouyer's hunch that the Egyptian post-Sanctus epiclesis indeed once immediately followed the earlier petition for acceptance of the sacrifice. If so, then it was part of the prayer before the Sanctus was. Perhaps it already used the word "fill," as the Roman petition does.

Though it does not appear explicitly in the Testament of Levi, the idea of an exchange of God's blessing for angelic worship seems to have been part and parcel of the Eucharistic "bloodless sacrifice" narrative. Further evidence can be found in the preanaphoral prayer for the offering in the Byzantine liturgy of St. Basil, showing that this exchange tradition circulated more widely than just Egypt and Rome (emphasis added):

> Accept us who draw near to thy holy Altar, according to the plenitude of thy mercy, that we may be worthy to offer unto thee this reasonable and unbloody sacrifice, for our own sins, and for the errors of the people: which do thou accept upon thy holy, and heavenly and supersensual Altar for the savour of a sweet odour. *Send down upon us the grace of thy Holy Spirit.* Look upon us, O God, and behold this our service, and accept it as thou didst accept the gifts of Abel, the sacrifices of Noah, the burnt-offerings of Abraham.[58]

58. Translation from Isabel Florence Hapgood, *Service Book of the Holy Orthodox Catholic Apostolic Church* (Englewood, NJ: Antiochian Orthodox Christian Archdiocese of North America, 1983). See also the current Byzantine post-anaphoral litany: "That our God . . . receiving them on his holy, heavenly and ideal altar as an odor of spiritual fragrance, will send down in return divine grace and the gift of the Holy Spirit." This exchange idea is also found in the prayers for incense in several traditions, including the Alexandrian liturgy

Whenever the Alexandrian church decided to add the hymn of the seraphim to its Eucharistic prayer, right after the reference to the angelic liturgy at the heavenly altar would have been a reasonable place to put it. In the form it takes in Egypt, the Sanctus is understood to be the content of the sacrifice. In the pre-Sanctus God is asked to receive the Sanctus in the same terms as he is asked to receive the people's offerings at the heavenly altar. The Sanctus is the people's participation in the heavenly, bloodless sacrifice. Sarapion takes this understanding one step further, moving the Sanctus into the offering itself. But the post-Sanctus epiclesis suggests that its original location was after, or rather part of, the prayer for acceptance of the offering.[59]

The whole prayer for acceptance with Sanctus would have looked something like this, using the simplest form it has come down to us, from Sarapion:

> Receive, O God, the thank offerings of those who offer the sacrifices, at your spiritual altar in heaven by the ministry of your archangels as you accepted the gifts of your righteous Abel and the sacrifice of our father Abraham.
>
> For you are far above every principality and power and virtue and dominion and every name that is named, not only in this age but in the age to come.
>
> Beside you stand thousands of thousands and myriads of myriads of angels and archangels.[60] Beside you stand the two most honorable seraphim with six wings, which cover the face with two wings, and the feet with two, and fly with two; and they cry, "Holy."

---

of St. Mark. But the Eucharistic bloodless sacrifice tradition antedates the use of incense in Christian worship. "A pleasing odor" already characterizes the bloodless offering in the Testament of Levi.

59. In the *textus receptus* of MARK, the "fill" epiclesis unit is separated from the petition for acceptance not only by the Sanctus but also by a number of further petitions. But these all appear to have been added later, some coming from the three prayers after the gospel in the Alexandrian liturgy, some borrowed from the anaphora of James, and some taken from 1 Clement (cf. Cuming, *Liturgy of St. Mark*, 116–18). They were probably added after the post-Sanctus epiclesis came to be more closely associated with the institution narrative than with what preceded it. MARK's present "exchange" petition in the *commendatio oblationis* was perhaps also added after the epiclesis was separated from it.

60. I have omitted Sarapion's expansion of the list of angelic powers, which are absent from MARK.

With them receive also our cry of "Holy," as we say:

Holy, holy, holy, Lord of Sabaoth; heaven and earth are full of your glory. Full in truth are heaven and earth of your holy blessing through our Lord and God and Savior Jesus Christ.

Fill, O God, this sacrifice also with the blessing from you through the descent of your Holy Spirit.

If this suggestion is correct, then the structural difference posed by the Sanctus/epiclesis is more apparent than real. Originally, the Sanctus would have been nothing more than an expansion of the petition for acceptance of the offering concluding the first part of the prayer.

It is fairly well established that the Sanctus was a late insertion into the Roman Canon and it need not detain us here.[61] As for the differing positions of the intercessions that Bouyer was concerned about, it should be clear that the double structure of both MARK and the Canon offers two places for petitions, at the end of each part of the prayer. Neither MARK nor the Canon wanted to duplicate the intercessions. MARK kept them where they were in STR. The Canon elected to divide its intercessions. Those for the living went into the first half; those for the dead, into the second half. The result is a more balanced prayer.

CONCLUSIONS

Structural analysis of their Eucharistic prayers would seem to confirm what others have asserted, that Rome and Alexandria indeed belonged to the same anaphoral tradition. We can be much more specific in our description of the shape of that tradition than Mazza's "two thanksgivings and one petition" structure. The first thanksgiving, if that's what it was and not a blessing, depending on the ancestry one gives the prayer, presented the occasion or cause for the thanksgiving. In the shared tradition, the second thanksgiving had become an offering introduced by a participle of thanksgiving. The participle could vary to match the content of the opening strophe. This was an important development, for it was the precursor to the common anamnesis/ offering of later Eucharistic prayers. Though the anamnesis is an all but universal feature of later prayers, it had to originate someplace, and I would argue that it originated in this tradition when it would include an institution narrative in its opening praise. The common

61. Spinks, *The Sanctus*, 93–96.

practice of following the anamnesis/offering with an epiclesis of the Holy Spirit may also have arisen in this tradition. This could have come about in two ways. It could have developed from the petition for the Church, like what opens the petitions in STR. In this case the role of the Spirit would be to bring life to God's people. Or the epiclesis could have originated in a petition for the acceptance of the offering. Such a petition would conclude the petitions in an STR-like prayer. But we saw that the Roman penchant was to move or duplicate this petition right after the offering. In this kind of epiclesis the Spirit is invoked primarily on the Eucharistic elements. Though Rome itself did not develop such an epiclesis, others may have imitated the Roman placement of the *commendation oblationis*. In any case, the common practice is to introduce the epiclesis with (usually two) verbs of offering such as the pair that opens the petitions in STR. That what results from the insertion of an institution narrative into the first strophe of an STR-like prayer is a structure commonly known as "Antiochene" is a question worth pondering but beyond the scope of this paper.

Finally, we can ask how these two cities came to share a single anaphoral tradition. Bouyer thinks their common tradition derives from a common form of synagogue worship. The basic tripartite prayer structure does perhaps have a Jewish antecedent, as Mazza has also argued. But the elements that characterize this tradition, and distinguish it from other Christian traditions with tripartite prayers, such as the traditions behind *Didache* 9–10 and the East Syrian anaphora of Addai and Mari, are distinctively Christian: the particular Christological narrative and the structural adaptations it entails, including the relative clauses connecting the strophes. It may be Jewish-Christian in its formation, but it is a fully formed Christian tradition that these churches share. Perhaps one church derived it from the other. Or perhaps they both derived from it from a common source. It is possible that this prayer tradition encompasses more than these two cities. If we think the latter more likely, then Jerusalem seems a possible candidate for the common source. Cuming was of the opinion that behind the Eucharistic prayer of Cyril of Jerusalem lay a prayer very much like STR.[62] Jerusalem also offered bloodless sacrifice, over which it offered petitions. We observed similarities between the institution narrative and epiclesis of MARK and those of the Jerusalem anaphora

62. G. J. Cuming, "The Anaphora of St. Mark: A Study in Development," *Le Muséon* 95 (1982): 129.

of James. To think of these as Egyptian elements in the Jerusalem liturgy, however, as Cuming also did,[63] may get the direction of influence wrong. If Jerusalem is the common source for the anaphoral tradition of Alexandria and Rome, then we must be approaching a very early form of Christianity. I am not proposing that Jerusalem is the source of this tradition, but I offer it as a possibility worthy of further consideration.

63. G. J. Cuming, "Egyptian Elements in the Jerusalem Liturgy," *JTS* n.s. 25 (1974): 117–24.

Paul F. Bradshaw[1]

VI. The Barcelona Papyrus and the Development of Early Eucharistic Prayers

Scholars have been aware of what has come to be known as the Barcelona Papyrus for more than forty years, although a full text was first published only in 1994.[2] Dated by papyrologists to either the first or second half of the fourth century, it contains among other liturgical material a complete Eucharistic prayer. Because such texts from this early period are so rare, it is perhaps surprising that the world of liturgical scholarship has so far paid this discovery little attention. Spurred on by a recent article on this material by the Russian scholar Michael Zheltov, which includes both a critical edition and a translation,[3] I propose to try to fill that lacuna now and attempt to situate it in its place within the evolving patterns of Eucharistic praying of the time.

The few who have studied it have regarded Egypt as its place of origin, partly because it has been recognized as being an original Greek version of the Coptic Louvain Papyrus, which consists of part of a Eucharistic prayer, from the end of the Sanctus to the end of the institution narrative, dating from circa AD 600,[4] but also because it contains several features that are characteristics of Egyptian anaphoras.

---

1. I would like to express my gratitude to my colleague Maxwell Johnson and to members of the Problems in Early Liturgy Seminar of the North American Academy of Liturgy for their helpful comments on an earlier draft of this paper.

2. Ramón Roca-Puig, *Anàfora de Barcelona i alters pregàries* (Barcelona, 1994). It was first announced in idem, "Sui Papiri di Barcellona," *Aegyptus* 46 (1966): 91–92.

3. Michael Zheltov, "The Anaphora and the Thanksgiving Prayer from the Barcelona Papyrus: An Underestimated Testimony to the Anaphoral History in the Fourth Century," *Vigiliae Christianae* 62 (2008): 467–504.

4. See Sebastià Janeras, "L'Original grec del fragment copte Lovaina Núm. 27 en l'Anàfora de Barcelona," *Miscellània Litúrgica Catalana* 3 (Barcelona: Institut d'Estudis Catalans, 1984), 13–25.

These are (a) praise for creation incorporating a quotation from part of Psalm 146:6, "heaven and the earth, the sea and all that is in them"; (b) a pre-Sanctus unit that refers to "thousands of thousands and myriads of myriads of angels, archangels," and connects the heavenly praise to its earthly counterpart; (c) the absence of an accompanying *Benedictus qui venit* to the Sanctus; and (d) an epiclesis on the Eucharistic elements after the Sanctus and before the narrative of institution.

While these elements certainly point to an Egyptian connection of some sort, they are not necessarily decisive with regard to its ultimate origin, especially as other features of the text differ significantly from what eventually became the dominant pattern in Egyptian anaphoras. First, the prayer includes not just praise for creation but also for redemption, something more characteristic of prayers of the West Syrian tradition than of Egypt, where—with the exception of two extant examples that do make brief reference to aspects of redemption, the mid-fourth-century *Sacramentary of Sarapion* and a fragmentary prayer preserved on two ostraca in the British Museum[5]—the prevailing tradition was to restrict the focus to creation alone.[6]

Second, the pre-Sanctus unit is much less developed than in the other examples of Egyptian prayers that are extant, and in particular mentions the cherubim and seraphim before speaking of the thousands of thousands and myriads of myriads of angelic beings, whereas the rest have the reverse order and preface it with a quotation from Ephesians 1:21, "above every principality and power and virtue and dominion and every name that is named, not only in this age but in the age to come," as well as extending the reference to the cherubim and seraphim to include the details of how they dispose their six wings from Isaiah 6:2.[7] One other significant difference in this pre-Sanctus unit is also worth noting. The Barcelona text includes a short citation of Colossians 1:16, "thrones and dominions." Although

5. See R. C. D. Jasper and G. J. Cuming, *Prayers of the Eucharist: Early and Reformed*, 3rd ed. (Collegeville: Liturgical Press, 1987), 76; Hans Quecke, "Das anaphorische Dankgebet auf den koptischen Ostraka B.M. Nr. 32 799 und 33 050," *Orientalia Christiana Periodica* 37 (1971): 391–405. I am indebted to Alistair Stewart-Sykes for the reference to this latter example.

6. Compare the English translations of the relevant Egyptian texts in Jasper and Cuming, *Prayers of the Eucharist*, 53 and 59 with examples of those of the West Syrian type, ibid., 70–71, 91, 104–8, 116–18, 125–26, 131–32.

7. Ibid., 64, 77, 80.

this does also occur in a longer form on the Coptic ostraca and in the *Sacramentary of Sarapion*[8] and the Coptic version of the anaphora of St. Basil,[9] it is not otherwise found in Egyptian prayers, but a similar quotation does appear in some anaphoras of West Syrian and Jerusalem origin.[10]

Third, it lacks the characteristic post-Sanctus verbal link found in other Egyptian texts, namely, "full are heaven and earth . . . fill this sacrifice . . . ," and its post-Sanctus offering language and epiclesis are much more developed than the earliest examples of other Egyptian prayers that we possess. Here it is explicitly the bread and the cup that are offered and then God is asked to send the Holy Spirit on them to make them the body and blood of Christ. On the other hand, what is usually believed to be the oldest Egyptian prayer, the Strasbourg Papyrus, simply offers "the reasonable sacrifice and this bloodless service" and has no epiclesis at all.[11] The anaphora in the *Sacramentary of Sarapion* similarly uses the expression "this living sacrifice, the bloodless offering" and at this point in its prayer merely asks God to fill the sacrifice with power. When later in that text, after the institution narrative, it does refer explicitly to the bread and cup, it is to ask God to "let" the Logos "come" that they may become "body of the Word" and "blood of the truth."[12] The earliest known examples of prayers from anywhere that ask God to actually *send* the Holy Spirit and specify what the Spirit is expected to do in relation to the Eucharistic elements all date from the last quarter of the fourth century onwards, and that includes some Egyptian anaphoras.[13]

Fourth, like the pre-Sanctus material, its narrative of institution differs from other Egyptian texts. It lacks the characteristic Egyptian linkword "for," and at first sight may appear to be simply an adaptation of

8. See further Maxwell E. Johnson, *The Prayers of Sarapion of Thmuis: A Literary, Liturgical, and Theological Analysis*, Orientalia Christiana Analecta 249 (Rome: Pontifico Istituto Orientale, 1995), 208, 215.

9. See Jasper and Cuming, *Prayers of the Eucharist*, 70.

10. Ibid., 85, 90, 108, 117.

11. Ibid., 53–54.

12. Ibid., 77–78.

13. The earliest quotation seems to be in Cyril of Jerusalem, *Mystagogical Catechesis* 5.7 (Jasper and Cuming, *Prayers of the Eucharist*, 85–86), though the author may here be giving a gloss on the text rather that citing the actual words of the prayer known to him. Other examples in Jasper and Cuming, *Prayers of the Eucharist*, 56, 65–66, 93, 111, 119–20, 127, 133.

the Matthean version of the Last Supper. But while it shares with the other early Egyptian prayers the record of Jesus' words over the cup as having begun "Take, drink . . . ," against Matthew's "Drink of it, all (of you) . . . ," it differs from them in not including any interpretative words over the bread, "which is given (or 'broken') for you for forgiveness of sins." However, the same is also true of a number of other citations of the Eucharistic words of Jesus in several early Christian sources from various parts of the East and ranging from the second to the fourth centuries.[14] These quote the words over the bread in the simple form, "Take, eat; this is my body," which suggests that the Barcelona text may represent an earlier stage in the line of development of the wording of the narrative in a liturgical context than other Egyptian examples. It is also worth noting that the linking passage at the end of the narrative, which seems to be influenced by 1 Corinthians 11:25-26, appears to be addressed not to God the Father like the rest of the prayer but to Christ: "we also do the same in *your* remembrance." Could this whole section have been drawn from another Eucharistic prayer that was addressed to Christ throughout?

Fifth, and finally, the prayer does not end with wide-ranging intercession for all sorts of people and needs but instead restricts itself to petitions for the communicants. This contrasts with all other extant Egyptian prayers, except for one that is found scratched on a wooden tablet of the eighth century in the British Museum and in even more fragmentary form on a sixth-century parchment in the John Rylands Library, Manchester, but which has been thought to date from around 400, and therefore apparently later than the Barcelona Papyrus, and so more likely to have been influenced by it than to have been an influence on it.[15]

Taken as a whole, these differences suggest that the original nucleus of the prayer either was not composed in Egypt or alternatively represents a variant tradition there that was probably subject to some significant influence from elsewhere. Is it possible, therefore, to attempt to reconstruct the process by which the anaphora came to assume its final form? There is a growing consensus among liturgical scholars

---

14. Pierre Nautin, ed., *Homélies pascales* 1, Sources chrétiennes 27 (Paris: Éditions du Cerf, 1950), no. 49; Origen, *Comm. in Joh.* 32.24; *Hom. in Jer.* 12; Eusebius, *Demonstratio evangelica* 8.1.78; Cyril of Jerusalem, *Mystagogical Catechesis* 4.1.

15. See Jasper and Cuming, *Prayers of the Eucharist*, 54–56.

that in other extant early Eucharistic prayers both the Sanctus with its surrounding material and also the institution narrative were usually fourth-century additions to an older core, [16] and that seems to be the case here too, especially because the pre-Sanctus and Sanctus units effectively bisect the praise for redemption. Moreover, as noted earlier, a developed epiclesis of this type is also generally acknowledged to be a fourth-century development. I have therefore placed all three of these elements in italics in the accompanying table on pages 134–35[17] so as to help reveal more clearly what appears to have been the older nucleus of the prayer, a tripartite pattern of praise, offering, and petition. This structure is comparable to what appears to underlie several other ancient prayers, including the Strasbourg Papyrus and the *Sacramentary of Sarapion*. But both of these differ markedly in content from the Barcelona text. Are there any others that might offer a closer parallel?

One possibility might be with the Egyptian version of the anaphora of St. Basil, which has often been believed to have been brought from Cappadocia to Egypt by Basil himself in AD 357, but is generally considered to have antedated him.[18] While parts of this anaphora do resemble the Barcelona Papyrus to some extent—the inclusion of praise for redemption, a simpler introduction to the Sanctus that also quotes Colossians 1:16, an explicit offering of bread and cup with prayer for descent of the Spirit on them—there are also enough marked differences from it to cast serious doubts on whether the two have a close relationship. The rest of the pre-Sanctus material is not the same; the institution narrative occurs at a different point in the prayer and has much more developed language; the offering of bread and cup is in the past tense; the petition for the Holy Spirit is nowhere near as explicit as to its object; and as well as prayer for the communicants, the prayer ends with more general intercessions.

---

16. See, for example, Johnson, *Prayers of Sarapion of Thmuis*, 205, 254–76.

17. The translation of the Barcelona anaphora is adapted from that in Michael Zheltov's article; the translation of the anaphora from the *Apostolic Tradition* is that of the Latin version in Paul F. Bradshaw, Maxwell E. Johnson, and L. Edward Phillips, *The Apostolic Tradition: A Commentary* (Minneapolis: Fortress Press, 2002), 38–40; and the translations of the other texts are from Jasper and Cuming, *Prayers of the Eucharist*, 53, 56, 77.

18. Ibid., 67–73. On the origin of the prayer, see Hieronymus Engberding, *Das Eucharistische Hochgebet der Basileiosliturgie* (Münster: Aschendorff, 1931), lxxxiv–lxxxv.

Comparison of the Anaphora of the Barcelona Papyrus with Extracts from Other Contemporary Examples

Apostolic Tradition	Barcelona Papyrus	Strasbourg Papyrus
We render thanks to you, God, through your beloved child Jesus Christ, whom in the last times you sent to us as savior and redeemer and angel of your will, who is your inseparable word, through whom you made all things and it was well pleasing to you,	It is fitting and right to praise you, to bless you, to hymn you, to give you thanks, O Master, God Pantocrator of our Lord Jesus Christ, who created all things from nonexistence into being, all heaven and the earth, the sea and all that is in them,	to bless [you] . . . [night] and day . . . [you who made] heaven [and] all that is in [it, the earth and what is on earth,] seas and rivers and [all that is] in [them]; [you] who made man [according to your] own image and likeness. You made everything through your wisdom, the light [of?] your true Son, our Lord and Saviour Jesus Christ. Giving thanks through him to you with him and the Holy Spirit, we offer the reasonable sacrifice and this bloodless service. . . .
[whom] you sent from heaven into the virgin's womb, and who conceived in the womb was incarnate and manifested as your Son, born from the Holy Spirit and the virgin; who fulfilling your will and gaining for you a holy people stretched out [his] hands when he was suffering, that he might release from suffering those who believed in you; who when he was being handed over to voluntary suffering, that he might destroy death and break the bonds of the devil, and tread down hell and then illuminate the righteous, and fix a limit and manifest the resurrection,	through your beloved child Jesus Christ, our Lord, through whom you have called us from darkness into light, from ignorance to knowledge of the glory of his name, from decay of death into incorruption, into life eternal; *who sits on the chariot, cherubim and seraphim before it; beside whom stand thousands of thousands and myriads of myriads of angels, archangels, thrones and dominions, hymning and glorifying, with whom we are also hymning, saying: Holy, holy, holy, Lord of Sabaoth, heaven and earth are full of your glory, in which you have glorified us through your Only-Begotten, the firstborn of every creature, Jesus Christ our Lord,* who sits on the right hand of your greatness in heaven, who is coming to judge the living and the dead,	**Sacramentary of Sarapion** . . . Beside you stand thousands of thousands and myriads of myriads of angels, archangels, thrones, dominions, principalities, and powers. Beside you stand the two most honourable seraphim with six wings, which cover the face with two wings, and the feet with two, and fly with two; and they cry "Holy." With them receive also our cry of "Holy," as we say: "Holy, holy, holy, Lord of Sabaoth; heaven and earth are full of your glory." Full is heaven, full also is earth of your excellent glory, Lord of the powers. Fill also this sacrifice with your power and your partaking; for to you we offered this living sacrifice, this bloodless offering. . . .
taking bread [and] giving thanks to you, he said: "Take, eat, this is my body that will be broken for you." Likewise also the cup, saying, "This is my blood that is shed for you. When you do this, you do my remembrance." Remembering therefore his death and resurrection,		

		British Museum/John Rylands
we offer to you the bread and cup, giving thanks to you because you have held us worthy to stand before you and minister to you. And we ask that you would send your Holy Spirit in the oblation of [your] holy church,	through whom we offer you these your creatures, the bread and the cup: *we ask and beseech you to send on them your Holy and comforter Spirit from heaven to represent them materially and to make the bread the Body of Christ and the cup the Blood of Christ of the New Covenant,*	. . . we set before you these gifts from your own, this bread and this cup.
	as he himself, when he was about to hand [himself over], having taken bread and given thanks, broke it and gave it to his disciples, saying: "Take, eat, this is my body"; likewise after supper, having taken a cup, having given thanks, he gave it to them, saying: "Take, drink the blood which is shed for many for remission of sins." And we also do the same in your remembrance, like those—whenever we meet together, we make the remembrance of you, of the holy mystery of our Teacher and King and Saviour Jesus Christ.	We pray and beseech you to send your Holy Spirit and your power on these [your?] [gifts] set before you, this bread and this cup, and to make the bread the body of Christ and [the cup the blood of the] new [covenant] of our Lord and Saviour Jesus Christ
[that] gathering [them] into one you will give to all who partake of the holy things [to partake] in the fullness of the Holy Spirit, for the strengthening of faith in truth, that we may praise and glorify you through your child Jesus Christ, through whom [be] glory and honor to you, Father and Son with the Holy Spirit, in your holy church, both now and to the ages of ages. Amen.	Even so we pray to you, Master, that in blessing you will bless and in sanctifying, sanctify . . . for all communicating from them for undivided faith, for communion of incorruption, for communion of the Holy Spirit, for perfection of belief and truth, for fulfilment of all your will, so that in this and again we will glorify Your all-revered and all-holy name, through Your sanctified child, our Lord Jesus Christ through whom glory [be] to You, power unto the un-blended ages of ages. Amen.	that [they may be to all of us who] receive for faith, for sobriety, [for healing, for joy, for sanctification,] for renewal of soul, body, [and spirit, for sharing in eternal life,] for self-control and of [sic] immortality, for . . . [that] in this also as in all [may be glorified and hymned and sanctified your] holy and honored and all . . . [name . . .].

Another possible parallel is the Eucharistic prayer in the so-called *Apostolic Tradition* of Hippolytus. This work was definitely known in some part of Egypt in the first half of the fourth century, if not earlier, because it formed the basis of another church order composed there at that period, the *Canons of Hippolytus*, but as that does not include a Eucharistic prayer at all, we have no way of knowing whether one already had a place in the *Apostolic Tradition* or not, and even if it did, how it might have been worded at this point in time.[19] In terms of close verbal parallels, there is little connection between the two prayers. While the *Apostolic Tradition* does also have an explicit offering of bread and cup followed by a petition for God to "send the Holy Spirit on the offering," it does not go on to specify the purpose as being to make them the body and blood of Christ, and in any case this epiclesis is commonly thought to be a late addition to the text of the *Apostolic Tradition*.[20]

If, however, we go on to compare the structure of what appears to have been the oldest core of the Barcelona text with what seems to have been the earliest form of the anaphora in the *Apostolic Tradition*, the similarities are more striking. Both begin with brief praise for creation and more extended praise for redemption. Both then offer the bread and the cup, and both end with prayer for the communicants alone and not more general intercession. Both of them also construct the first part of the prayer in the same way, by using successive relative clauses, and both use the word "child/servant" rather than "Son" in relation to Jesus at the beginning and end of the prayer, an expression that is otherwise found in works usually dated no later than the middle of the second century, that is, the *Didache*, *1 Clement*, the *Epistle of Barnabas*, and the *Martyrdom of Polycarp* (although some would place the final recension of this last work in the third century). The coupling of this word with "beloved," as here in the Barcelona text, occurs uniquely in *1 Clement* as well as in a prayer in the *Martyrdom of Polycarp* and also in the ordination and Eucharistic prayers of the *Apostolic Tradition*. However, it appears that *1 Clement* rather than the *Apostolic Tradition* is the direct source for the inclusion of this particular phrase, as Zheltov has identified the first part of the praise for redemption in the Barcelona text, "through your beloved child Jesus Christ, our Lord, through whom you have called us from darkness

19. See Bradshaw, Johnson, and Phillips, *Apostolic Tradition*, 37.
20. Ibid., 42.

into light, from ignorance to knowledge of the glory of his name," as being virtually identical to a passage in *1 Clement*.[21]

This is not to suggest that the Barcelona prayer is actually derived from that in the *Apostolic Tradition*, or vice versa, but rather that both originate out of a shared tradition of anaphoral construction, and one that seems more likely to have been in West Syria than in Egypt,[22] although the existence of such a variant tradition in Egypt cannot be entirely ruled out. The only real parallel with early Egyptian texts in the nucleus of the Barcelona prayer is the use of Psalm 146:6, "heaven and the earth, the sea and all that is in them," and that could be a later addition, and in any case that phrase is commonly found in biblical texts[23] even if it does not feature in any extant anaphora as such outside Egypt. There is nothing in this core material that would require us to posit a fourth-century date for its composition, and every reason to suppose that, like the earliest form of the *Apostolic Tradition* anaphora, it might go as far back as the second century.

Into this nucleus would subsequently have been inserted the three further elements, although it is impossible to be completely sure in what sequence this might have taken place. Two of them—the institution narrative and the epiclesis—have parallels in the anaphora in the *Apostolic Tradition*, but differences in form seem to preclude any direct dependency. The institution narrative is unlikely to have been added to either prayer before the first half of the fourth century, as the oldest other example of a similar narrative occurs in the *Sacramentary of Sarapion* and even later in the century the custom had apparently not yet spread to all prayers.[24] The Barcelona text and the *Apostolic Tradition* each use a somewhat differently worded version and locate it at a different point in the prayer, the *Apostolic Tradition* before the statement

21. *1 Clement* 59.2. The only variation is that Clement has "his" beloved . . . , instead of "your." See Zheltov, "The Anaphora and the Thanksgiving Prayer from the Barcelona Papyrus," 488, n. 66.

22. On the West Syrian character of the anaphora of the *Apostolic Tradition*, see Matthieu Smyth, "L'anaphore de la prétendue 'Tradition apostolique' et la prière Eucharistique romaine," *Revue des sciences religieuses* 81 (2007): 213–28, translated into English in this collection of essays, pp. 71–98 above.

23. Also found in Exodus 20:11; Nehemiah 9:6; Acts 4:24; 14:15; Revelation 10:6; 14:7.

24. In particular, the anaphora of Addai and Mari and the prayers known to the author of the *Mystagogical Catecheses* and to Theodore of Mopsuestia: see Jasper and Cuming, *Prayers of the Eucharist*, 42–44, 85–86, 135–37.

of offering, with an anamnetic clause to form the link back to that, and the Barcelona Papyrus after the mention of the offering of the bread and cup. Similarly, the petition for the Holy Spirit is more precisely worded as to its effects in the Barcelona Papyrus than is the version in the *Apostolic Tradition*, although it is quite possible that it was originally similar in form and then expanded rather later.

Wherever the rest may have originated, the pre-Sanctus and Sanctus unit, which the *Apostolic Tradition* never added, seems definitely to belong on Egyptian soil, but from an earlier phase of development than those in the *Sacramentary of Sarapion* and other prayers from this region. In order to smooth the transition back to Christ's session in heaven, the redactor has apparently created a linking clause at the end, "in which you have glorified us through your Only-Begotten, the firstborn of every creature, Jesus Christ our Lord," the phrase "firstborn of every creature" being drawn from Colossians 1:15, the verse preceding the reference to "thrones and dominions" used in the pre-Sanctus.[25]

The emergence of all these features is thus entirely consistent with the verdict of papyrologists on the dating of the material on which the prayer is written. While its original core appears to be among the oldest Eucharistic prayers known to us, it seems to have reached its final form around the same period as the anaphoras in the *Sacramentary of Sarapion* and the *Apostolic Tradition* in their fully developed manifestations. It therefore deserves serious attention in connection with any theory concerning the evolution of early Eucharistic prayers.

25. See also Sebastià Janeras, "Sanctus et Post-Sanctus dans l'anaphore du P.Monts. Roca inv. n° 154b-155a," *Studi sull'Oriente Christiano* 11 (2007): 9–13, who proposes that a copyist has accidently omitted the repetition of the phrase "for full is heaven of your holy glory" immediately after the Sanctus.

John Paul Abdelsayed

VII. Liturgical Exodus in Reverse:
A Reevaluation of the Egyptian Elements in
the Jerusalem Liturgy

In 1974, Geoffrey Cuming persuasively demonstrated that Egypt was a dominant liturgical source in the development of the Eucharistic liturgy and other liturgical rites in Jerusalem. Elements such as institution narrative, intercessions, and sanctus, all of which—with the possible exception of the sanctus—are absent from early Syrian liturgies, were inserted into the Jerusalem liturgy from older Egyptian anaphoras.[1] He concluded that it is more probable that the trajectory of influence extended from Egypt to Syria via Jerusalem rather than vice versa.[2] Bryan Spinks responded to many of Cuming's arguments, even though he ended up agreeing that Egyptian influence on Jerusalem could not be ruled out.[3] Indeed, the last thirty years of liturgical scholarship have revealed an increasing acknowledgment of Egyptian roots within Jerusalem's anaphoral constructions—establishing a liturgical "Exodus in Reverse."[4]

This study will demonstrate that, although individual liturgical elements taken singly are generally not probative, the totality of the structural analysis, linguistic comparisons, and thematic evaluations within the Jerusalem rite are highly indicative of Egyptian origins,

---

1. Geoffrey J. Cuming, "Egyptian Elements in the Jerusalem Liturgy," *Journal of Theological Studies* (1974): 117–224 (hereafter, "Egyptian Elements").

2. Ibid., 121.

3. Bryan Spinks, "The Jerusalem Liturgy of the Catechesis Mystagogicae: Syrian or Egyptian?" *Studia Patristica* 18:2 (1989): 391–96.

4. This term was used by Maxwell E. Johnson in his *Liturgy in Early Christian Egypt*, Alcuin/GROW Liturgical Study 33 (Cambridge: Grove Books Limited, 1995), 5, 50.

with later additions from Antioch and Syria.[5] While the vagaries of these liturgical elements and their respective developments cannot be examined in detail, this study will argue for a reassessment of Cuming's "Egyptian connection" thesis in light of current liturgical scholarship. After examining that there was some strong connection between Egypt and Jerusalem, I will then explore how and why such a unique connection might have evolved.

EGYPTIAN INFLUENCE ON THE EARLY JERUSALEM ANAPHORA

The anaphoral structure, language, and theme of Mystagogical Catecheses (MC) 4 and 5 forcefully advance the hypothesis that the Jerusalem rite adopted several distinctively Egyptian elements. John Fenwick observes a parallel between Egyptian and Jerusalem anaphoras, up to 70 percent in some sections, which he attributed to an Egyptian influence on the Jerusalem rite.[6] The following looks at the relevant sections of the Jerusalem anaphora in light of those elements.

Lavabo *and* Pax

> Ye saw then the Deacon give to the Priest water to wash, and to the Presbyters who stood around God's altar. He gave it, not at all because of bodily defilement; no; for we did not set of the Church with defiled bodies. But this washing of hands is a symbol that ye ought to be pure from all sinful and unlawful deeds; for since the hands are a symbol of action, by washing them we represent the purity and blamelessness of our conduct. . . . Then the Deacon cries aloud, RECEIVE YE ONE ANOTHER; AND LET US KISS ONE ANOTHER. . . . The kiss therefore is reconciliation, and for this reason holy: as the blessed Paul has in his Epistles urged; *Greet ye one another with a holy kiss;* and Peter, *with a kiss of charity.*[7]

5. This argument is an extension of Baldovin's arguments for and against an institution narrative in MC. John F. Baldovin, *Liturgy in Ancient Jerusalem*, Alcuin/GROW Liturgical Study 57 (Bramcote, Nottingham: Grove Books Limited 1989), 27.

6. Fenwick enumerates that the post-sanctus and institution narrative shares 70 percent of its material with Egyptian Basil, and 50 percent for the intercessions, 35 percent for pre-sanctus, and 30 percent of the anamnesis. John Fenwick, *Fourth Century Anaphoral Construction Techniques*, Grove Liturgical Study 45 (Bramcote, Nottingham: Grove Books Limited, 1986), 33.

7. MC 5.2–3. ET from F. L. Cross, *St. Cyril of Jerusalem: Lectures on the Christian Sacraments* (Crestwood: St. Vladimir's Seminary Press, 1977), 71–72.

Cuming asserts that the *lavabo* before the *pax* in MC coincides with that of Coptic Mark and Syriac James.[8] Robert Taft, Hans Lietzmann, and Anton Baumstark agree that this is most probably the original rubric. This *lavabo* is strangely absent from Greek Mark and Greek James, and distinct from *Apostolic Constitutions* (*ApConst*) 8.11 (after the *pax*) and Theodore of Mopsuestia (during the *pax*).[9] Spinks disputes such a comparison, since Cyril is the first known reference to the *lavabo* practice, and argues that the simultaneity of the actions may account for a diversity of usage.[10] Despite such claims, it is precisely the simultaneity of actions that makes this comparison so essential! That the *lavabo* was conducted "quickly and without fuss"[11] should not signify that variant practices should be disregarded but rather suggests a unique and valuable liturgical link. On this basis, Taft acknowledged a similar link between Theodore of Mopsuestia and Pseudo-Denys, who "present basically the same tradition."[12] Therefore, the similarity among MC, Coptic Mark, and Syriac James—compared with the variations in Syria and Antioch—may in fact demonstrate a tight, liturgical bond between Egypt and Jerusalem in the fourth and fifth centuries.

Sanctus

> We make mention of heaven, and earth, and sea; of the sun and moon; of the stars and all the creation, rational and irrational, visible and invisible; of Angels, Archangels, Virtues, Dominions, Principalities, Powers, Thrones; of the Cherubim with many faces . . . We make mention also of the Seraphim, whom Esias by the Holy Ghost beheld encircling the throne of God, and with two of their wings veiling their countenance,[13] and with two their feet, and with two flying, who cried, HOLY, HOLY, HOLY, LORD GOD OF SABAOTH.[14]

---

8. Cuming, "Egyptian Elements," 121.

9. Ibid.

10. Spinks, "Jerusalem Liturgy," 392–93; Robert F. Taft, *The Great Entrance*, OCA 200 (Rome: PIO, 1975), 47–51, 163–64.

11. Taft, *Great Entrance*, 50.

12. Ibid., 47.

13. The Greek word here is πρόσοπον (*prosopon*), singular for "face" or "countenance." Church's translation incorrectly renders this as a plural, "countenances." I have corrected the translation accordingly.

14. MC 5.5–6; ET from Cross, *St. Cyril of Jerusalem*, 73–74.

Gregory Dix and Georg Kretschmar were among the first to argue for an Egyptian origin of the sanctus.[15] Robert Taft restored the plausibility of the initial Egyptian provenance, dating the sanctus in the Egyptian anaphoral structure to sometime around 350.[16] MC's sanctus is particularly in line with Egyptian anaphoras, since it lacks *Benedictus qui venit*, a common trait of Syrian and Byzantine anaphoras.[17] As with Sarapion, Deir Balyzeh, the British Museum Tablet, the John Rylands parchment, the Louvain Coptic Papyrus, and the Barcelona Papyrus, MC 5.7 connects the epiclesis with the conclusion of the sanctus.[18] While Ratcliff,[19] Botte,[20] and Macomber in 1966[21] argued that the sanctus interrupts the thought of the first anaphoral prayer in

15. Dom Gregory Dix, *The Shape of Liturgy* (New York: Continuum International Publishing, 2005), 165; Georg Kretschmar, *Studien zum frühchristlichen Trinitätstheologie* (Tübingen, 1956), 164.

16. Robert F. Taft, "The Interpolation of the Sanctus into the Anaphora: When and Where? A Review of the Dossier, Part I," *Orientalia Christiana Periodica* 57 (1991): 281–308; idem, "The Interpolation of the Sanctus into the Anaphora: When and Where? A Review of the Dossier, Part II," *Orientalia Christiana Periodica* 58 (1992): 83–121.

17. While it is true that Theodore also lacks a Benedictus as well as the Syrian Apocryphal Acts of the Apostles, this is due to the variation of early anaphoral prayers, as Bradshaw asserts.

18. Johnson, *Liturgy in Early Christian Egypt*, 23, notes 2–4. On the Barcelona Papyrus, see the recent work of Michael Zheltov, "The Anaphora and the Thanksgiving Prayer from the Barcelona Papyrus: An Underestimated Testimony to the Anaphoral History in the Fourth Century," *Vigiliae Christianae* 62 (2008): 467–504, and the preceding essay by Paul Bradshaw, "The Barcelona Papyrus and the Development of Early Eucharistic Prayers," pp. 129–38 above.

19. E. C. Ratcliff, "The Original Form of the Anaphora of Addai and Mari: A Suggestion," *Journal of Theological Studies* 30 (1929): 23–32.

20. Bernard Botte, "L'anaphore chaldéenne des Apôtres," *Orientalia Christiana Periodica* 15 (1949): 259–76; idem, "Problèmes de l'anaphore syrienne des Apôtres Addaï et Mari," *L'Orient Syrien* 10 (1965): 89–106.

21. William F. Macomber, "The Oldest Known Text of the Anaphora of the Apostles Addai and Mari," *Orientalia Christiana Periodica* 32 (1966): 347–48; cited in Nicholas V. Russo, "Reconstructing Addai and Mari: A Review of the Dossier & Implications for the Sanctus Debate," unpublished paper (December 6, 2003), 7.

Addai and Mari, Engberding,[22] Sauget,[23] and Macomber's later work[24] more convincingly demonstrated that MC's sanctus was a natural element.

Even if the sanctus in MC 5.6 is a foreign element or insertion,[25] its characteristics are far more Egyptian than Syrian or Byzantine. Like the Egyptian sanctus structure, MC emphasizes the union of heaven and earth in praise of God as two choirs united in one, while the Byzantine-Syrian sanctus prayers dichotomize the heavenly and earthly praise, distinguishing between God's work for the angels on the one hand and mankind on the other.[26]

Moreover, MC 5.6 not only uses "the face" of Seraphim, as the early Egyptian pattern in Origen's *De Principiis* 4.14, Sarapion, and Deir Balyzeh, but also speaks of several cherubim, another parallel with Coptic Cyril, James, Qumran, *Apostolic Constitutions* (*ApConst*) 8, and Byzantine Basil.[27] While the possibility of a common use of the LXX may explain the reference to the Seraphim with two wings covering "the face" as Spinks argues,[28] Isaiah 6:2 is not the only biblical quotation used to construct this pre-sanctus. The text more closely follows the uniquely Egyptian Colossians 1:16–Isaiah 6 pattern. However, instead of speaking of the "eyes" of the cherubim (as present in Deir Balyzeh and Coptic Cyril), MC 5.6 refers to their "faces." Spinks doubts that MC is influenced from the Egyptian anaphoras since it lacks any reference to Ephesians 1:21. However, Origen (*De Principiis* IV.14), the Barcelona Papyrus, and *ApConst* 12.27 lack this as well, which could

22. Hieronymus Engberding, "Urgestalt, Eigenart und Entwickelung eines altantiochenischen eucharistischen Hochgebets," OrChr, Series 3, vol. 7 (1932): 32–48; idem,"Zum anaphorischen Fürbittgebet der ostsyrichen Liturgie der Apostel Addaj und Mar(j)," *Oriens Christianus* 41 (1957): 102–24.

23. J. M. Sauget, *Anaphora syriaca Sancti Petri Apostoli tertia, Anaphoras syriacae quotquot in codicibus adhuc repertae sunt, II* (Rome, 1973), 273–329.

24. William F. Macomber, "The Ancient Form of the Anaphora of the Apostles," *East of Byzantium: Syria and Armenia in the Formative Period* (Washington, DC: Dumbarton Oaks, 1982), 73.

25. "For the reason of our reciting this confession of God, delivered down to us from the Seraphim, is this, that so we may be partakers with the hosts of the world above in their Hymn of praise."

26. Macomber, "Ancient Form," 76–77, 82; Russo, "Reconstructing Addai and Mari," 6.

27. See Kretschmar, *Studien*; Johnson, *Liturgy in Early Christian Egypt*, 210ff.

28. Spinks, "Jerusalem Liturgy," 393.

indicate an earlier Egyptian pattern. These elements make MC's preface much closer to the Egyptian than Theodore's preface, which focuses on a Philippians 2 theme.

Spinks attempts to demonstrate that Cyril's sanctus was influenced by that of Theodore of Mopsuestia (ca. 383–92 AD), and not by the Egyptian sanctus prayers, since Theodore also lacks a Benedictus. While his argument is at first convincing, Spinks does not attempt to explain why Theodore's anaphora lacks a sanctus in the 380s, while Asterios Sophistes includes one several years earlier (335–41). It is quite reasonable that Asterios's sanctus included the Benedictus because his Easter homilies were delivered after the celebration of Pascha between 335–41,[29] while Theodore's catechetical homilies were given during the Lenten season, before the feast of Palms. Since Egeria mentions that the Benedictus was added to the normal antiphons on the feast of Palms,[30] it is quite probable that a similar insertion was made to the sanctus. Spinks is certainly aware of Auf de Maur's conclusion that the Benedictus entered into the Eucharistic prayer via the Easter Vigil anaphora around the time of Asterios, but assumes that this was done in every liturgy thereafter in the tradition. But Taft posits a transition such that the Benedictus was inserted first into Morning Prayer, then into the Easter Vigil, and finally into every Eucharistic prayer.[31] Such a gradual inclusion of the Benedictus, then, demonstrates how MC's sanctus (and maybe even Theodore's) was originally Egyptian. Thus, the later Antiochian anaphoras added a Benedictus while the Egyptian anaphoras remained without it.

Day's recent work confirms that the Benedictus was inserted into the Jerusalem liturgy after MC 5 and Egeria, but before James.[32]

---

29. Taft dates it to ca. 337. Taft, "Interpolation of the Sanctus" (1992), 83–121, 97.

30. "As the eleventh hour draws near, that particular passage from Scripture is read in which the children bring palms and branches come forth to meet the Lord, saying, 'Blessed is He Who comes in the Name of the Lord.' The bishop and all the people rise immediately and then everyone walks down from the top of the Mount of Olives, with the people preceding the bishop and respond continually with 'Blessed is He Who comes in the Name of the Lord' to the hymns and antiphons" (Egeria, 31.2–4; John Wilkinson, *Egeria's Travels*, 3rd ed. [Oxford: Oxbow Books, 1999], 152).

31. Taft, "Interpolation of the Sanctus" (1992), 104.

32. Juliette Day, "The Origins of the Anaphoral Benedictus," *Journal of Theological Studies* 60:1 (2009): 193–211.

This, however, contradicts her own hypothesis that Jerusalem was the source of the insertion. If this was inserted before or with James, then either Cyril or Egeria predates Asterios (335–41). If not, then Cyril and Egeria continue following the Egyptian sanctus that lacks a Benedictus, while James accepts the Antiochian insertion. In fact, to confirm her theory that Egeria and MC date to the 390s or later, she must adopt a later date of James than Fenwick, and completely ignore the reference to Asterios. In light of Asterios's sanctus, Day is forced either to date Egeria, MC, and James earlier or to accept that the Benedictus is not a Jerusalem creation but an interpolation from elsewhere.

Based on the plural "faces" of the cherubim, the inclusion of the two seraphim, a sanctus without Benedictus, and the address only to the Father, Taft concluded that it is not unreasonable to demonstrate a hagiopolite anaphoral sanctus from Alexandria in the second half of the fourth century.[33] This Taftian restoration of the Dix-Kretschmar hypothesis makes highly plausible an Egyptian origin for the sanctus, not only in Jerusalem but for other anaphoras at the end of the third century. Perhaps the only element that could discount an Egyptian provenance of Jerusalem's sanctus would be if Wolfram Kinzig's conclusion is verified that the Asterios is actually a Nicene Orthodox from Palestine or Antiochia.[34] While, according to Spinks, the sanctus-epiclesis unit in Egypt remains an "enigma," we are not fully persuaded to abandon a theory of Egyptian roots.[35] And, indeed as the recent work of Michael Zheltov has argued, the sanctus and narrative of institution themselves are already part of some Egyptian Eucharistic prayers in the early fourth century.[36]

33. Taft, "Interpolation of the Sanctus" (1992), 108.

34. Taft, "Interpolation of the Sanctus" (1992), 105. This debate between Kinzig and Karl-Heinz Uthemann on this is so complex and inconclusive, Taft does not even enter into that debate. See W. Kinzig, "Asterius Sophista oder Asterius Ignotus? Ene Antwort," *Vigiliae Christianae* 45 (1991): 389–98. Uthemann's review thereof in *Vigiliae Christianae* 45 (1991): 194–203.

35. Bryan Spinks, "The Integrity of the Anaphora of Sarapion of Thmuis and Liturgical Methodology," *Journal of Theological Studies* 49 (1998): 136–44, 140.

36. Zheltov, "Anaphora and the Thanksgiving Prayer," 495–96.

> Then having sanctified ourselves by these spiritual Hymns, we call
> upon the merciful God to send forth His Holy Spirit upon the gifts
> lying before Him; that He may make the Bread the Body of Christ,
> and the Wine the Blood of Christ; for whatsoever the Holy Ghost has
> touched is sanctified and changed.[37]

In both structure and language, MC's epiclesis prayers (MC 4.2, 5.7)
point to Egypt. Johnson has cogently argued for an Egyptian origin of
the Jerusalem sanctus based upon a parallel structure of the epiclesis
prayers in Sarapion and MC 5.6 that employ Colossians 1:16 and Isaiah 6.[38] As in most Egyptian anaphoras, MC's epiclesis immediately
follows the sanctus. More specifically, MC's pattern mirrors the consistent epicletic pattern found in the Louvain Papyrus, Deir Balyzeh,
Coptic Mark, and Greek Mark.[39]

Perhaps the most convincing evidence is the linguistic similarities
between MC/James and Egyptian anaphoras. Spinks attempts to dif-
ferentiate MC's epiclesis from Egyptian ones because it lacks an introductory *plenum-pleres*, "full-fill" (that is, heaven and earth are *full . . .
now fill* these gifts), into the epiclesis. A closer examination of Cyril's
three verbs, however, reveals a unique parallel to the Egyptian epiclesis prayers. While Cyril's phrase "having sanctified ourselves" is
not an exact match to the Egyptian *pleres*, its appeal to God to "send"
the Holy Spirit in order to "make" the transformation possible is more
in line with the Egyptian theme.

When comparing the Basilian anaphoras, Fenwick discovered the
closest epiclesis prayer to Jerusalem was the Sahidic version, which
asks for the Holy Spirit to come (ἐλθεῖν), sanctify (ἁγιάσαι), and
change/appoint (ἀναδεῖξαι) the gifts.[40] Indeed, MC 5.7 is virtually
identical to the Egyptian tripartite request found in the Barcelona
Papyrus, Louvain Papyrus, and Deir Balyzeh:

---

37. MC 5.7; ET from Cross, *St. Cyril of Jerusalem*, 74.

38. Maxwell E. Johnson, "The Origins of the Anaphoral Use of the Sanctus and Epiclesis Revisited," in *Crossroads of Cultures*, ed. H. J. Feulner, E.
Velkovska, and R. F. Taft, 405–42 (Rome: Pontificio Instituto Orientale, 2000).

39. Johnson, *Liturgy in Early Christian Egypt*, 26.

40. Fenwick, *Fourth Century Anaphoral Construction Techniques*, 17–22.

Barcelona (350?)	Louvain Papyrus (4th c.)	Cyril, MC 5.7	Deir Balyzeh
We ask and beseech You to send onto them Your Holy and Paraclete Spirit from Heaven to represent them materially and to make the bread the Body of Christ and the cup the Blood of Christ of the New Covenant.	We pray and beseech You to send out over them Your Holy Spirit, the Paraclete, from heaven . . . to (make?) the bread the body of Christ and the cup the blood of Christ of the New Covenant.	Then having sanctified ourselves by these spiritual Hymns, we beseech the merciful God to send forth His Holy Spirit upon the gifts lying before Him; that He may make the Bread the Body of Christ, and the Wine the Blood of Christ . . .	Fill us too with Your glory! And deign to send Your Holy Spirit on these offerings that You have created, and make this bread the Body of our Lord and Savior Jesus Christ and this chalice the Blood of the New Testament of our Lord, God and Savior Jesus Christ.

This Egyptian-Jerusalem parallel is quite distinct from the East Syrian pattern, which requests the Holy Spirit to "come" or "dwell" on the gifts. Sebastian Brock has demonstrated that epiclesis petitions for the Holy Spirit to "come" is the more ancient form found in East Syrian texts and the Greek anaphoras of Basil and James.[41] Moreover, Gabriele Winkler rightly distinguished the Syrian invocations with what she believes to be later Greek interpolations to "send" the Holy Spirit in *Apostolic Tradition* (hereafter, *ApTrad*) 4 and MC 5:7.[42] But, whether the Egyptian or Syrian pattern is, in fact, earlier, the "Egyptian connection" is practically incontestable. Indeed, the strong correlation between MC and Egyptian anaphoras in style, structure, and theology demonstrates this connection over and against Syrian counterparts.

41. Sebastian Brock, *Fire from Heaven: Studies in Syriac Theology and Liturgy* (Burlington, VT and Aldershot, Hampshire: Ashgate Publishing, 2006), 213–15.

42. Gabriele Winkler, "Das Sanctus: Über den Ursprung und die Anfänge des Sanctus und sein Fortwirken," *Orientalia Christiana Analecta* 267 (Rome: Pontificio Instituto Orientale, 2002); idem, "Nochmals zu den Anfängen der Epiklese und des Sanctus im Eucharistischen Hochgebet," *Theologische Quartalschrift* 174 (1994): 214–31.

> Then, after the spiritual sacrifice is perfected, the Bloodless Service upon that Sacrifice of Propitiation, we entreat God for the common peace of the Church, for the tranquility of the world; for kings; for soldiers and allies; for the sick; for the afflicted; and, in a word, for all who stand in need of succour we all supplicate and offer this Sacrifice. Then we commemorate also those who have fallen asleep before us, first, Patriarchs, Prophets, Apostles, Martyrs, that at their prayers and intervention God would receive our petition. Afterwards also on behalf of the holy Fathers and Bishops who have fallen asleep before us, and in a word of all who in past years have fallen asleep among us.[43]

Egypt seems to have also played a significant role in the development of intercessions in the Jerusalem anaphoras of Cyril and James. The anaphora of Mark contains two sets of intercessions: a short cluster between its preface and sanctus, and a longer section following the epiclesis. Cuming argued that an early strand of Egyptian petitions is among the many second-century variations of 1 Clement.[44] He posited that the manuscript variation of intercessions in the anaphora of Mark suggest a clear development from the short petitions in Strasbourg, MS 1970 and MS 2281 that echo 1 Clement 59.4, to the "enormously enlarged" intercessions that are found in medieval manuscripts.[45] Moreover, Origen's references to intercessory petitions for fellow citizens and the emperor could also demonstrate the third-century status of this development in Caesarea and/or Egypt.[46] As Cuming and Fenwick have argued, the closer correspondence in order and proximity between Cyril's six intercessions with Coptic Mark, and Cyril's list of departed with Greek Mark, corroborates this "Egyptian link."[47] This link is closer between Cyril and Mark than with James.

With a similar approach, Fenwick concluded that the ten successive anaphoral intercessions in MC 5.8–9 were conflated with the intercessions of Egyptian (Sahidic) Basil to yield the result found in

---

43. MC 5.9; ET from Cross, *St. Cyril of Jerusalem*, 74.

44. This includes as well variations of the "Bread prayer" in the Didache. Geoffrey J. Cuming, *The Liturgy of St. Mark* (Rome: Pontificum Institutum Orientalium, 1990), 118.

45. Cuming, *Liturgy of St. Mark*, 118, 109–18, 131–36.

46. Origen, *Contra Celsum*, 8.13, 45, 73.

47. Cuming, "Egyptian Elements," 122.

James.[48] These ten groups of intercessions are the compilation of four intercessions from Sahidic Basil, three intercessions unique to James, and three others from various versions of Basil. Therefore, if Cuming and Fenwick are correct, Egyptian Mark and Egyptian Basil are the main source for the intercessions found both in Cyril and James.

Institution Narrative?

Scholarly debate on whether the anaphora of MC contained an institution narrative has effectively reached an impasse. Gregory Dix stated long ago that the earlier Jerusalem anaphora consisted of four main sections: a preface, sanctus, epiclesis, and intercessions.[49] Bryan Spinks argues that MC 5.5–8 follows this early pattern, and moves directly from an epiclesis to a set of intercessions.[50] According to Doval, this demonstrates MC's early date and makes it similar to Addai and Mari and the Strasbourg Papyrus.[51] However, Yarnold claims that rejecting a narrative in MC "rests on very insubstantial evidence."[52]

Alternative interpretations have also been proffered. Georg Kretschmar hypothesized that the narrative was recited inaudibly with other portions.[53] Cuming asserted that an institution narrative (located in between the epiclesis and intercessions) may be inferred from a number of factors. First, MC 4 is based on 1 Corinthians 11:23ff, which is the text used for introducing this lecture. Also, MC 5.8's use of ὅτι and "the completion (ἀπαρτισθῆναι) of the spiritual sacrifice" correlates well with other references to a narrative in Chrysostom,

48. Fenwick, *Fourth Century Anaphoral Construction Techniques*, 26–28; see also J. R. K. Fenwick, "The Significance of Similarities in the Anaphoral Intercession Sequence in the Coptic Anaphora of St. Basil and Other Ancient Liturgies," *Studia Patristica* 18:2 (1989): 355–62.

49. Dix, *Shape of Liturgy*, 188–96.

50. Spinks, "Integrity of the Anaphora of Sarapion," 136–44.

51. Alexis James Doval, *Cyril of Jerusalem, Mystagogue: The Authorship of the Mystagogic Catechesis* (Washington, DC: Catholic University of America Press, 2001), 152–53.

52. Edward J. Yarnold, "Anaphoras without Institution Narratives?" *Studia Patristica* 30 (1997): 395–410, 400.

53. Georg Kretschmar, "Die frühe Geschichte der Jerusalemer Liturgie," *Jarbuch fur Liturgie and Hymnologie* 2 (1956): 30–33; Fenwick, *Fourth Century Anaphoral Construction Techniques*, 13–14.

Sarapion, Deir Balyzeh, Louvain Papyrus, and Coptic Mark.[54] However, Spinks points to Theodore's fifteenth homily to demonstrate that Chrysostom's use of "perfecting" and "completing" the sacrifice does not exclusively refer to a narrative.[55] And, of course, Emmanuel J. Cutrone, in his magisterial work on this topic, has argued persuasively that the presence of an institution narrative in MC 5 simply does not fit with the overall "eikon-mimesis" ("image-imitation") approach taken to the theology of the rites of Christian initiation in general through the MCs.[56]

Nevertheless, the Egyptian connection with Jerusalem still holds true. If MC lacks a narrative, as seems to be the most likely conclusion, given the work of Cutrone, then Cyril has either added an epiclesis as an extension of Strasbourg's "offering," a prayer that Cuming believed lay at the structural root of the Jerusalem anaphora,[57] or is simply dependent upon other Egyptian anaphoras. Such an "early Strasbourg" document could be the "pre-Basilian" anaphora that Fenwick believes is the root of Basil and James. This development, in line with the work of Cuming and Fenwick, does not contradict the contributions of Winkler, Spinks, and Brock. For, it is still possible that such a Strasbourg Urtext could have Syrian roots. However, since this "Syrian Strasbourg" document remains a matter of conjecture, the actual Egyptian Strasbourg Papyrus must suffice. Indeed, it is becoming more probable that such an Urtext was some version of the Strasbourg Papyrus

54. Cuming, 118-119; Baldovin, 27. For additional examination of this debate, see F.E. Brightman and C.E. Hammond, *Liturgies Eastern and Western* (Oxford: Clarendon Press, 1896), 496; Dix, *Shape of Liturgy*, 197–98; E.J. Cutrone, "Cyril's Mystagogical Catechesis and the Evolution of the Jerusalem Anaphora," *Oriental Christiana Periodica* 44 (1978): 52-64; Hanz Lietzmann, *Mass and Lord's Supper: A Study in the History of the Liturgy*, trans. Dorothea H. G. Reeve (Lieden; Brill, 1953), 20-40; Doval, *Cyril of Jerusalem, Mystagogue*, 150–51; A. Gelston, ed. and trans., *The Eucharistic Prayer of Addai and Mari* (Oxford: Clarendon Press, 1992), 72-6.

55. Spinks, "Integrity of the Anaphora of Sarapion," 392.

56. "Cyril's Mystagogical Catecheses and the Evolution of the Jerusalem Anaphora," *Orientalia Christiana Periodica* 44 (1978). See also his "The Liturgical Setting of the Institution Narrative in the Early Syrian Tradition," in *Time and Community: In Honor of Thomas Julian Talley*, ed. J. N. Alexander, 105–14 (Washington, DC: The Pastoral Press, 1990).

57. See G. J. Cuming, "The Shape of the Anaphora," *Studia Patristica* 20 (1989): 333–45.

(or something similar to *ApTrad*), which was reworked into Basil for the Byzantine rite; into James for the Jerusalem rite, in consultation with MC and Egeria; and into Cyril in the Coptic rite.[58] For the latter, Sarapion, Barcelona Papyrus, and other Egyptian documents would be intermediate steps along the path of anaphoral development.

Liturgy as "Sacrifice"

As a second-century topos, a liturgical theology of "sacrifice" is located in Justin and Irenaeus, however quite undeveloped.[59] While sacrifice is a common theme of the early Church,[60] this strong tradition may have distinct features in Egyptian anaphoras, with especial regard to Malachi 1:11. In fact, this Egyptian theme found in the Strasbourg Papyrus, Sarapion, and Coptic Cyril[61] may well be the origin of Cyril's language of "spiritual sacrifice, the bloodless service" (MC 5.8).

In the second century, Athenagorus cites Malachi 1:11 in arguing that Christians do not offer sacrifices of blood, but bloodless and reasonable sacrifice:

> And first, as to our not sacrificing: the Framer and Father of this universe does not need blood, nor the odor of burnt-offerings, nor the fragrance of flowers and incense, forasmuch as He is Himself perfect fragrance, needing nothing either within or without; but the noblest sacrifice . . . And what have I to do with holocausts, which God does

58. Maxwell E. Johnson, "Christian Initiation in Fourth Century Jerusalem and Recent Developments in the Study of the Sources," in *Inquiries into Eastern Christian Worship: Acts of the Second International Congress of the Society of Oriental Liturgy*, ed. Basilius J. Groen and Steven Hawkes Teeples (Rome, September 17–21, 2008), Eastern Christian Studies, vol. 10, in press.

59. Justin Martyr, *Dialogue with Trypho*, 41, 117; Irenaeus, *Against the Heresies*, 4.17.5.

60. Cf. Kenneth Stevenson, *Eucharist and Offering* (New York: Pueblo Publishing Co., 1986); Robert J. Daly, *Christian Sacrifice* (Washington, DC: Catholic University of America Press, 1978); idem, *The Origins of the Christian Doctrine of Sacrifice* (Philadelphia: Fortress Press, 1978), 132.

61. "We offer the reasonable sacrifice and this bloodless service which all the nations offer You" (Mal 1:11). In the Strasbourg Papyrus, this immediately precedes the peace of the church, "over this sacrifice and offering we pray and beseech you, Remember Your holy and only Catholic Church." Also, Sarapion's post-sanctus prayer states, "we offered this living sacrifice, this bloodless offering." In Sarapion, this immediately precedes the institution narrative.

not stand in need of? . . . though indeed it does behoove us to offer a bloodless sacrifice and reasonable worship.[62]

Moreover, Didache 14.3's language of "pure sacrifice" refers both to giving of thanks, the Eucharist, and the breaking of bread in the community. In contrast, Syrian anaphoras lack this "sacrificial" language found in early Egyptian and Jerusalem anaphoras. Theodore refers to the sacrifice as "awe-inspiring," "offering," or "delivering"[63] but does not use the same adjectives of "spiritual," "unbloody," or "rational" (Hom. 15). This sacrificial language of Malachi 1:11 is more than simply linguistic parallel. It is a thematic hallmark of these early liturgies in approximately the same location. This too can demonstrate a precise Egyptian-Jerusalem connection not easily found elsewhere.

Pre-communion, Communion, and Post-Communion Rites

> Then, after these things, we say that Prayer which our Saviour delivered to His own disciples, with a pure conscience styling God our Father, and saying, OUR FATHER WHICH ART IN HEAVEN. . . .

> After this ye hear the chanter, with a sacred melody inviting you to the communion of the Holy Mysteries, and saying, "O taste and see that the Lord is good" [Ps 34:8]. Trust not the decision to thy bodily palate; no, but to faith unfaltering; for when we taste we are bidden to taste, not bread and wine, but the sign [*antitypon*] of the Body and Blood of Christ.

> Approaching, therefore, come not with thy wrists extended, or thy fingers open; but make thy left hand as if a throne for thy right, which is on the eve of receiving the King. And having hollowed thy palm, receive the Body of Christ, saying after it, Amen. . . . Then . . . approach also the cup of His Blood; not stretching forth thine hands, but bending and saying in the way of worship and reverence, Amen. . . .

---

62. Athenagorus, *A Plea for the Christians*, chap. 13, ANF, v. 2, 134–35. For more, see Walter D. Ray, "The Strasbourg Papyrus," in *Essays on Early Eucharistic Prayers*, ed. Paul F. Bradshaw, 39–56, 47–49 (Collegeville: Liturgical Press, 1997); see in the same volume G. J. Cuming, "The Liturgy of St. Mark: A Study of Development," 57–72, esp. 64–65.

63. Yarnold notes how this literally is translated from the Syriac "sending up," which could be a Syriac translation of the Greek "anaphora." Edward Yarnold, *The Awe-Inspiring Rites of Initiation: The Origins of the R.C.I.A.*, 2nd ed. (Collegeville: Liturgical Press, 1994), 225, n. 83.

Then wait for the prayer, and give thanks unto God, who hath accounted thee worthy of so great mysteries.[64]

Robert Taft's valuable work on the pre-communion rites demonstrates how difficult it is to piece together the status of liturgical affairs in the fourth century. On several points, however, the evidence suggests influence from Egypt to Antioch and Syria and not vice versa.

The first substantial witness of the pre-communion *ordo* (after the preliminary traces in Justin's *Apology*, 1.65–67 and *ApTrad* 22) is the Euchologion of Sarapion of Thmuis, 2–3.[65] Sarapion provides the first witness to the pre-communion inclination and the earliest extant prayer of blessing over the congregation before communion.[66] Because no such inclination is mentioned by Chrysostom, *ApConst* 8.13, nor Theodore of Mopsuestia, Hom. 16, 21–22, Taft surmises that it was inserted into Chrysostom's anaphora at the turn of the century.[67] This in turn influences Chrysostom's pre-communion prayer, and the later Armenian, West-Syrian, and Ethiopian rites.[68]

The vague description regarding the breaking of bread during communion in Justin's *Apology* 1.65, 67 and *ApConst* 8.13 indicates an apparent "soft point." Again, at least two of the three earliest, indisputable references come from Egypt: *ApTrad* 21–22, Sarapion 2, and Timothy of Alexandria (381).[69] Once again, the second group of sources is Syrian/Antiochian: St. John Chrysostom in Constantinople (398–404), *ApConst* 8, 13:14, Ephrem, and Theodore of Mopsuestia.[70]

The insertion of the pre-communion "Our Father" poses one significant exception. The first evidence of this prayer is found in MC

---

64. MC 5.11–22; ET from Cross, *St. Cyril of Jerusalem*, 75–80.

65. Robert F. Taft, *A History of the Liturgy of St. John Chrysostom, Volume V: The Precommunion Rites*, OCA 261 (Rome: Pontificio Instituto Orientale, 2000), 59–60; Maxwell E. Johnson, *The Prayers of Sarapion of Thmuis: A Literary, Liturgical and Theological Analysis*, OCA 249 (Rome: Pontificio Instituto Orientale, 1995), 50–51.

66. Ibid., 177.

67. Ibid., 194.

68. Ibid., 105–6, 111–13, 176.

69. Ibid., 320–25; Johnson, *Prayers of Sarapion of Thmuis*, 50–51; F. X. Funk, *Didascalia et Constitutiones apostolorum*, vol. 2 (Paderborn, 1905), 176; G. J. Cuming, "Thmuis Revisited. Another Look at the Prayers of Bishop Sarapion," *Theological Studies* (1980): 568–75.

70. Ibid., 321–27.

5.11–18, not Sarapion. Years later, Chrysostom mentions its recital in Antioch (398) and Constantinople (398–404).[71] While it is uncertain whether Egyptian anaphoras contained this pre-communion prayer, it is most probable that the direction of influence was from Jerusalem to Syria and Antioch, and not vice versa.

Summary
While the precise source of MC's liturgical structure remains a mystery, its unique liturgical connection with Egypt is inescapable. Thus, Cuming's original conclusion stands and is worth quoting still today:

> The balance of probability is heavily in favor of the reading having originated in Egypt and made its way to Syria via Jerusalem, rather than vice versa . . . [Thus,] the Jerusalem rite, though showing clear signs of Syrian influence, is basically akin rather to the Egyptian Liturgy of St. Mark.[72]

WHY EGYPT?

The first portion of this study analyzed the voluminous scholarship that recognizes that various anaphoral elements were exported from Egypt to Jerusalem, and much of the Christian world. In comparison, however, little study has been devoted to examine why or how Egypt would have established such an influence on the Jerusalem rite. I wish to examine some of these unique factors regarding the church and liturgy of Egypt that could account for such a unique, liturgical relationship with Jerusalem.

Travel and Trade
The major travel routes that connected Egypt with the rest of the ancient world passed through the natural land bridge of Palestine.[73] Such trade routes fostered the relationship between the theological and ecclesiastical leaders of Alexandria and Jerusalem in their exile or personal travel. Throughout his five exiles, Athanasius traversed Jerusalem on several occasions. Origen also traveled to Arabia (215,

---

71. Ibid., 62–64.
72. Cuming, "Egyptian Elements," 121, 117.
73. "Travel," in *Tyndale Bible Dictionary*, ed. Walter A. Elwell and Philip Wesley Comfort (Carol Stream, IL: Tyndale House Publishers, 2001), 1272.

244 AD),[74] Cappadocia (ca. 235), Antioch, Athens,[75] and Greece via Caesarea Palestine.[76] In Jerusalem (216 AD), he was welcomed by Bishop Alexander and his successor Theoctistus.[77]

These trade routes also facilitated the transport of voluminous correspondence between the two ancient sees. Jerusalem was probably the first large city to receive the bishop of Alexandria's festal letters and other ecumenical pronouncements regarding heresies. Talley notes how highly influential the festal letters of the bishop of Alexandria and his correspondence exchanged with the bishops of Palestine were in this regard, which can be traced back to at least the late second century.[78] For example, when Alexander of Alexandria sent his famous letter to the bishops to warn them about the Arian heresy, Macarius of Jerusalem is explicitly mentioned.[79] Moreover, the Library of Caesarea also housed volumes of Origen's letters that demonstrate his ubiquitous influence throughout the ancient world.[80]

74. Eusebius states that Origen, along with several bishops, was invited to Arabia "for a conference" with Beryllus, which subsequently convinced him and converted him back to the "true doctrine" (Eccl. Hist. 6.33.1–2). A visit to Arabia is also mentioned after the conversion of Ambrose from the Marcionite camp (Eccl. Hist. 6.18–19).

75. "Being at that time in Athens, he finished his work on Ezekiel and commenced his Commentaries on the Song of Songs, which he carried forward to the fifth book. After his return to Cæsarea, he completed these also, ten books in number" (Eusebius, Eccl. Hist. 6.32).

76. "At this time Origen was sent to Greece on account of a pressing necessity in connection with ecclesiastical affairs, and went through Palestine, and was ordained as presbyter in Cæsarea by the bishops of that country" (Eusebius, Eccl. Hist. 6.23.4).

77. For more complete history, see Henri Crouzel, *Origen*, trans. A. S. Worrall (Edinburgh: T&T Clark, 1989). This last visit angered Demetrius of Alexandria, who disapproved of a layman expounding the Scriptures before bishops and large assemblies. See Eusebius, Eccl. Hist. 6.32.9–19 and accompanying notes in NPNF, s. 1, v. 1, 267–68.

78. Thomas Talley, *The Origins of the Liturgical Year*, 2nd emended ed. (Collegeville, MN: Liturgical Press, Pueblo, 1991), 168.

79. Epiphanius mentions this letter in his Haer. 69.4, 730. Saint Athanasius also refers to Macarius of Jerusalem as an example of "the honest and simple style of apostolical men" (*Cont. Ar.* 1, 291).

80. Eusebius of Caesarea, Eccl. Hist., Book 6: "The little I have to say about him I will put together from letters and from information supplied by those of his friends who are still alive."

The "School" and Deans of Alexandria

Nicaea designated Alexandria's bishop to announce the dates of Epiphany and Pascha because of its accuracy in astronomical calculations. Egypt also became a liturgical point of reference, both for its dynamic and vast liturgical tradition and prominent theologians: Clement, Origen, Dionysius, and others. Without question, Origen is one of the most valuable witnesses to the structure of the early Eucharistic liturgies.[81] Origen's comments on the liturgy have always been the source of controversy and consternation. One major methodological difficulty is ascertaining whether his comments reflect actual liturgical rubrics, or are simply spiritual meditations. A second is distinguishing whether Origen is speaking of liturgical practices in Egypt, Caesarea, or both. One also must distinguish between his authentic writings, adjustments made by Latin translators, and other additions made by his adversaries and admirers.[82]

The liturgical link between Egypt and Jerusalem can be further traced through the fourth-century bishops. As the patriarchal deacon of Bishop Alexander, Athanasius probably met Macarius of Jerusalem at the Council of Nicaea.[83] Much later, when Eastern bishops met at Philippopolis (modern Plovdiv) to confirm the condemnation of Athanasius and depose Julius of Rome and Hosius of Córdoba, Macarius of Jerusalem met with Western bishops at Sardica in 339 to reinstate Athanasius as patriarch.[84] It has also been asserted that Macarius attended with his promising deacon, Cyril.[85] A similar circumstance

---

81. Origen's *Contra Celsum* 8 contains several intimations of a full Eucharistic prayer, including the calling of peace (*Corpus Scriptorum* [hereafter, CS], 8.14), incense offered at the altar (CS 8.17–20), sanctus (8.32, 34, 36), offering (προσάγειν) of the Eucharistic gifts (CS 8.33), an epicletic prayer over the Eucharistic loaves (ἄρτους) (CS 8.32–33), "intercessions to God" for fellow citizens (CS 8.45) and the emperor (CS 8.73), and a final doxology (CS 8.75).

82. These and other methodological problems are discussed more thoroughly by Harold Buchinger, "Early Eucharist in Transition? A Fresh Look at Origen," in *Jewish and Christian Liturgy and Worship: New Insights into its History and Interaction*, ed. Albert Gerhards and Clemens Leonhard, 212–13 (Leiden/Boston: Brill, 2007).

83. Sozomen, Hist. Eccl., 1.17; Theodoret, Hist. Eccl. 1.15.

84. Alden A. Mosshammer, *The Easter Computus and the Origins of the Christian Era* (New York: Oxford University Press, 2008), 183.

85. Jerome, Chron. Ann., 349 (350 AD); Abraham Terian, *Macarius of Jerusalem: Letter to the Armenians, Avant 4* (Crestwood, NY: St. Vladimir's Seminary Press, St. Nersess Armenian Seminary, 2001), 122.

took place several years later. When Athanasius returned from his exile of 346, Maximus III of Jerusalem (333–50 AD) restored him to communion with a synod of sixteen Palestinian bishops gathered at Jerusalem.[86] One would presume such restoration took place within a Eucharistic celebration, which naturally could have involved some sort of theological dialogue or discussion of ritual practice. The virtually identical circumstances demonstrate a consistent and unique relationship between the two sees throughout the fourth century.

This influence continued during the time of Cyril of Jerusalem. Egyptian bishops were present for the Council of Tyre and consecration of buildings on Golgotha in 335.[87] At the Council of Constantinople (381)—which Cyril attended—Pope Timothy of Alexandria was asked a series of liturgical questions, his responses to which were adopted in canonical form. However, since the minutes of the council are not extant and the contents of Timothy's *Canonical Responses* contain minimal liturgical information, we can only speculate on the extent of Timothy's liturgical influence on Cyril. Nonetheless, many have identified an Alexandrian influence in Cyril's writings. Kent Burreson asserts, "Cyril was certainly influenced by the Alexandrian theological tradition in his educational training, presumably in Caesarea (Palestine) and Jerusalem."[88] Leonel Mitchell also contends that anywhere from four through eighteen of Cyril's catechetical lectures were outlined and modeled after Origen's *Peri Archon*, possibly a result of his academy in Caesarea (Palestine).[89]

Liturgical Documents

Many of the earliest and most influential Eucharistic prayers and liturgical references come from Egypt. As Johnson notes, "No early

---

86. Socrates Scholasticus, Eccl. Hist., 2.24.

87. Edmund Bishop, "Liturgical Comments and Memoranda," *Journal of Theological Studies* 14 (1912): 23–50, 38; Spinks, "Integrity of the Anaphora of Sarapion," 394.

88. Kent J. Burreson, "The Anaphora of the Mystagogical Catechesis of Cyril of Jerusalem," in *Essays on Early Eucharistic Prayers*, 131–51, 133.

89. Leonel L. Mitchell, "The Development of Catechesis in the Third and Fourth Centuries: From Hippolytus to Augustine," in *A Faithful Church: Issues in the History of Catechesis*, ed. John H. Westerhoff III and O.C. Edwards Jr., 54 (Wilton, CT: Morehouse-Barlow, 1951); see also Anthony A. Stephenson, "St. Cyril of Jerusalem and the Christian Gnosis," *Studia Patristica* 1 (1957): 149; Burreson, "Anaphora of the Mystagogical Catechesis of Cyril," 134.

Christian liturgical tradition has left us with more anaphoral texts and fragments than has the Egyptian tradition."[90] The anaphoras of Strasbourg Papyrus, Sarapion (ca. 359), Greek and Coptic Mark, the Barcelona Papyrus, Deir Balyzeh, the John Rylands parchment, the Louvain Coptic Papyrus, and the British Museum Tablet (ca. 400) demonstrate a uniquely Egyptian anaphoral structure, quite distinct from the "West Syrian" or "Antiochene."

Most recently, Johnson and Day have reopened the possibility that *ApTrad* is an Egyptian document, or some version thereof that was influential in the Eucharistic rite. Although he thought it to be of Hippolytan authorship, Lanne recognized that *ApTrad* had much more influence in Egyptian baptismal rites than it did in Rome.[91] Bradshaw's and Baldovin's work on *ApTrad* may even verify that the Canons of Hippolytus are more Egyptian than Syrian.[92] Developing the work of J. M. Hanssens[93] and Day, Johnson suggests that *ApTrad* or some Egyptian derivative not only influences Macarius and Cyril but also Sarapion, CH, and *ApConst*.[94] But he can only speculate whether a document like *ApTrad* is driving Macarius of Jerusalem's insistence of keeping the tradition, which he believes comes directly "from the accounts of the apostles."[95]

CONCLUSION

In Leviticus 18, God specifically commanded the Israelites not to keep the practices of the Egyptians but to follow his commands and judgments. God brought them out of Egypt to establish his special

---

90. Johnson, *Liturgy in Early Christian Egypt*, 20.

91. E. Lanne, "La confession de foi baptismale à Alexandrie et à Rome," in *La liturgie expression de la foi: conference Saint-Serge XXV Semained'Études Liturgiques Paris 1978*, ed. A. Triacca and A. Pistoia, BEL Subsidia 16 (Rome 1979), 215.

92. Paul F. Bradshaw, *The Canons of Hippolytus*, Alcuin/GROW Liturgical Study 2 (Bramcote, Nottingham: Grove Books Limited, 1987); John Baldovin, "Hippolytus and the Apostolic Tradition," *Theological Studies* 64, no. 3 (2003): 520–42.

93. Jean Michel Hanssens, *La liturgie d'Hippolyte, Ses documents, son titulaire, ses origines et son charactère*, 2nd ed., *Orientalia Christiana Analecta* 155 (Rome, 1965); idem, *La liturgie d'Hippolyte, documents et études* (Rome: Libreria Editrice dell'Università Gregoriana, 1970).

94. Johnson, "Christian Initiation in Fourth Century Jerusalem."

95. Terian, *Macarius of Jerusalem, Letter to the Armenians*, 225.8, p. 89.

people with true worship of the true God ultimately centered in Jerusalem. Centuries later, however, the reverse seems to be the case. It is the worship of the Egyptian Christians that influenced the worship of Jerusalem through its theologians, dates, rubrics, and liturgical customs. When examining any point of the liturgy in Jerusalem, one cannot reach any definitive conclusion without consulting Egypt. The liturgical journey to the Jerusalem rite naturally passes through Egyptian lands. Even Spinks admitted that his study "in no way rules out the possibility that the rites described in MC were influenced by Egypt."

Certainly, many pieces of the liturgical puzzle are yet to be properly assembled. Does MC have an institution narrative that can be traced to Egypt? Does Origen reflect the sanctus or intercessory petitions in Egypt, Caesarea, or both? Until such questions are answered, we can only continue to speculate how the liturgical documents, ritual practices, and liturgical theology in Egypt influenced Jerusalem. Nevertheless, much like the original Exodus of the Israelites from Egypt, for the liturgical exodus in reverse to Egypt the specifics concerning the route have yet to be ascertained.

Maxwell E. Johnson

VIII. Recent Research on the Anaphoral *Sanctus*: An Update and Hypothesis

*Dedicated to Gabriele Winkler on the occasion of her 70th birthday and
in grateful recognition of her groundbreaking scholarship on
the* Sanctus *in the Eucharistic prayer*

> The Seraph could not touch the fire's coals with his fingers,
> But just brought it close to Isaiah's mouth;
> The Seraph did not hold it, Isaiah did not consume it,
> But us our Lord has allowed to do both.
>
> —*On Faith 73, by St. Ephrem the Syrian*

The question of the entrance of the *Sanctus* of Isaiah 6:3 into the Eucharistic prayer or anaphora—the when and the where—has long been an unresolved issue in Eucharistic praying, an "unresolved puzzle," in the words of Enrico Mazza.[1] Up to and until only more recent and highly detailed scholarly studies, there have been two primary theories on how this took place.[2] The first, the "Egyptian theory," advanced and popularized by Gregory Dix,[3] held that the origins of the anaphoral use of the *Sanctus* were to be found in Alexandria, where it existed by the middle of the third century, a location

---

1. Enrico Mazza, *The Origins of the Eucharistic Prayer* (Collegeville: Liturgical Press, 2005), 202.

2. Much of the first part of this essay is a summary of my chapter "The Origins of the Anaphoral use of the Sanctus and Epiclesis Revisited: The Contribution of Gabriele Winkler and its Implications," in *Crossroad of Cultures: Studies in Liturgy and Patristics in Honor of Gabriele Winkler*, ed. H-J. Feulner, E. Velkovska, and R. Taft, Orientalia Christiana Analecta 260, 405–42 (Rome: Pontifical Oriental Institute, 2000).

3. Gregory Dix, "Primitive Consecration Prayers," *Theology* 37 (1938): 261–83.

and date witnessed to, presumably, in Origen of Alexandria's *De principiis* I and IV. As nuanced further by Georg Kretschmar,[4] namely, that an anaphoral use of the *Sanctus* did not yet exist in Origen's day but that Origen's *theology* strongly influenced its shape when it *was* adopted for anaphoral use later in the third century, this "Egyptian theory" has had a strong and long-lasting effect on liturgical scholarship. The second theory, the so-called "climax theory," advocated by E. C. Ratcliff in an important 1950 essay,[5] argued that the anaphoral *Sanctus* went back to the very origins of Christian Eucharistic praying itself, and that it originally functioned as the *conclusion* of an anaphoral pattern that consisted only of a lengthy thanksgiving for creation and redemption followed by a thanksgiving for the admission of earthly worshipers into that of the angels of heaven. In part, Ratcliff's argument was based on the line *"adstare coram te et tibi ministrare"* in the anaphora of *Apostolic Tradition* 4,[6] which he interpreted as a remnant of an introduction to the *Sanctus* that had once followed at this point. While most scholars today[7] do not accept Ratcliff's "climax theory," some version of the "Egyptian theory," as we shall see below, is supported still by others.

---

4. Georg Kretschmar, *Studien zum früchristlichen Trinitätstheologie* (Tübingen, 1956), 164.

5. E. C. Ratcliff, "The Sanctus and the Pattern of the Early Anaphora," *Journal of Ecclesiastical History* 1 (1950): 29–36, 125–34.

6. For a Latin text of the anaphora of *Apostolic Tradition* 4, see Anton Hänggi and Irmgard Pahl, *Prex Eucharistica: Textus e Variis Liturgiis Antiquioribus Selecti* (Fribourg: Éditions Universitaires, 1968), 80–81; hereafter PE.

7. There is a nuanced sense in which Ratcliff's theory is still in vogue among those scholars whom Bryan Spinks identifies as comprising the "English School" of liturgical scholarship, who argue that one early anaphoral pattern (cf. the Strasbourg Papyrus) consisted of short ascriptions of praise and thanksgiving and was concluded with a doxology. To this were later added, in piecemeal fashion, the *Sanctus* in place of the concluding doxology and the Institution Narrative, the Anamnesis, the epiclesis(es), and expanded intercessions, thus ultimately producing some of the characteristic or "classic" Eucharistic prayers of Christian antiquity. See Spinks, *The Sanctus in the Eucharistic Prayer* (Cambridge: Cambridge University Press, 1991), 104–11. For examples, see especially G. J. Cuming, "Four Very Early Anaphoras," *Worship* 58 (1984): 168–72, and J. Fenwick, *Fourth Century Anaphoral Construction Techniques*, Grove Liturgical Study 45 (Bramcote, Notts., 1986).

THE CONTRIBUTIONS OF ROBERT TAFT AND BRYAN SPINKS, AND THE EARLIER WORK OF GABRIELE WINKLER

In a highly important two-part article in 1991 and 1992, Robert Taft offered a strong defense of the "Egyptian theory" for the interpolation of the *Sanctus* into the anaphora.[8] He argued that the Egyptian form of the *Sanctus*, without *Benedictus*, as witnessed to, for example, by Greek St. Mark—and attached to an immediate epiclesis connecting "heaven and earth are full of your holy glory" to the invocation "fill, O God, this sacrifice also with the blessing from you through the descent of your [all-] holy Spirit"[9]—to be the more primitive form since it appeared to be integral to the structure of the Egyptian anaphora overall. Similarly, along with Kretschmar, he dated its interpolation into the anaphora to be in the second half of the third century in a form highly influenced by Origen of Alexandria's theology of the biblical *Sanctus* of Isaiah 6. Origen writes in *De principiis*:

> My Hebrew teacher also used to teach as follows, that since the beginning or the end of all things could not be comprehended by any except our Lord Jesus Christ and the Holy Spirit, this was the reason why Isaiah spoke of there being in the vision that appeared to him two seraphim only, who with two wings cover the face of God, with two cover his feet, and with two fly, crying one to another and saying "Holy, holy, holy is the Lord of hosts; the whole earth is full of thy glory" [Isa 6:2-3]. For because the two seraphim alone have their wings over the face of God and over his feet, we may venture to declare that neither the armies of the holy angels nor the holy thrones, nor the dominions, nor principalities, nor powers can wholly know the beginnings of all things and the ends of the universe. (*De principiis* IV.3, 14)[10]

For Taft, as for Dix, the place to see this interpolation of the *Sanctus* into the anaphora most clearly in its Origenist interpretation was in the anaphora of that mid-fourth-century collection of prayers known

---

8. Robert Taft, "The Interpolation of the Sanctus into the Anaphora: When and Where? A Review of the Dossier," Part I, OCP 57 (1991): 281–308; Part II, OCP 58 (1992): 531–52.

9. See R. C. D. Jasper and G. J. Cuming, *Prayers of the Eucharist: Early and Reformed*, 3rd ed. (Collegeville: Liturgical Press, 1987), 64, hereafter, PEER.

10. Origène, *Traité des principes*, 394. Trans. from G. W. Butterworth, *Origen on First Principles* (London: Peter Smith Publisher, Inc., 1936), 311.

as the *Sacramentary*, *Euchologion*, or *Prayers of Sarapion of Thmuis*, where the introduction to the *Sanctus* through the post-*Sanctus* epiclesis reads:

> For you are above all rule and authority and power and dominion and every name which is named, not only in this age but also in the coming one. Beside you stand a thousand thousands and a myriad myriads of angels, archangels, thrones, dominions, principalities and powers.
>
> Beside you stand the two most-honored six-winged seraphim. With two wings they cover the face, and with two the feet, and with two they fly, sanctifying. With them receive also our sanctification as we say:
>
> Holy, holy, holy Lord of Sabaoth;
> heaven and earth are full of your glory.
>
> Full is heaven and full also is the earth of your majestic glory, Lord of powers. Fill also this sacrifice with your power and with your participation. For to you we offered this living sacrifice, the unbloody offering.[11]

Taft concluded, then, by claiming that the *idea* of interpolating the *Sanctus* into the anaphora came from Egypt, while the *form* the *Sanctus* took in other traditions, like that of Syria with the added *Benedictus*, came from Christianized versions of Jewish synagogue prayer.

At the same time that Taft was preparing his essay on the topic, Bryan Spinks' important study *The Sanctus in the Eucharistic Prayer* appeared.[12] Therein, Spinks rejected both of the standard theories of Ratcliff and Dix, claiming that the origins of the anaphoral use of the *Sanctus* were more likely Syrian than Egyptian and its use was probably derived—directly or even indirectly—from synagogue liturgy (Jewish or Christianized), Jewish (*merkavah*) mysticism, or simply from biblical language itself, taking different forms in different places. Diametrically opposed to the work of Taft, Spinks argued that the earliest anaphoral use of the *Sanctus* is in the Syrian anaphora of *Addai*

---

11. Maxwell E. Johnson, *The Prayers of Sarapion of Thmuis; A Literary, Liturgical, and Theological Analysis*, Orientalia Christiana Analecta 249 (Rome, 1995), 47.

12. Bryan Spinks, *The Sanctus in the Eucharistic Prayer* (Cambridge: Cambridge University Press, 1991).

and Mari, already in the third century. And against what would be one of Taft's primary arguments, Spinks claims, against both Dix and Kretschmar, that there is "little justification for seeing the theology of Origen" behind Sarapion's text at all.[13] According to Spinks, Sarapion's reference to "the two most-honored six-winged seraphim" merely reflects an Alexandrian identification of the two living creatures in the LXX version of Habakkuk 3:2 (ἐν μέσῳ δύο ζῴων) with the seraphim of Isaiah 6:3, an identification known by both Clement of Alexandria (*Stromateis* 7:12)[14] and Athanasius (*In illud omnia mihi tradita sunt* 6).[15] Consequently, Spinks claimed that:

> This link, together with the strange petition which introduces the pericope, might suggest to the speculative mind Origen's theology equating seraphim with the Son and Spirit. However, the text does not actually make this equation and is perfectly consistent with the understanding found in Clement and Athanasius that the two living creatures were the seraphim. The thought of the Thmuis eucharistic prayer seems to be: Christ and the Holy Spirit speak in us, so that we, like the living creatures [seraphim] who stand beside you, may praise you with the Holy, holy, holy.[16]

A few years later, however, Spinks nuanced this position a bit, saying that the Dix-Kretschmar approach, as embraced and furthered by Taft, was "suggestive and plausible," claiming that Sarapion's petition (i.e., "let the Lord Jesus speak in us and let the holy Spirit also hymn you through us") is to be "interpreted more naturally as simply reflecting the indwelling of the Son and Spirit. . . . We cannot join the heavenly worship unless Christ and the Holy Spirit make their dwelling in us."[17] I also entered into the fray on this question, arguing "that the text [of Sarapion] in question *does* say quite clearly that it is the Son and Spirit themselves, who sing *in* and *through* the assembly as they 'hymn *God* through us.' Hence . . . the 'heavenly worship' in which the liturgical

---

13. Spinks, *Sanctus*, 87.

14. *Ante-Nicene Fathers*, vol. 2 (Grand Rapids, MI: Eerdmans, 1967), 546.

15. *Nicene and Post-Nicene Fathers*, series 2, vol. 4, (Grand Rapids, MI: Eerdmans, 1971), 90.

16. Spinks, *Sanctus*, 89.

17. "The Integrity of the Anaphora of Sarapion of Thmuis and Liturgical Methodology," *Journal of Theological Studies* 49 (1998): 141.

assembly joins appears to be precisely that which is offered by the Son and Holy Spirit *to* the Father."[18]

Gabriele Winkler has taken a different methodological approach to our question and she has done this in two phases. First, of her many significant contributions to the study of early Christian liturgy, one major emphasis has been her thorough and detailed analysis of the Syrian *Acts of the Apostles* and the attention she has drawn to their often overlooked importance and role within liturgical development in general. This has especially been the case with her work on the evolution and theological interpretation of the early rites of Christian initiation.[19] In three key articles on the origins of the anaphoral use of both the *Sanctus* and epiclesis,[20] she turns precisely to these important sources within their overall Christian initiation context, where she argues that two of these elements emerged in early Syria as portions of the prayers for the consecration of the prebaptismal oil and water. With particular attention to the initiation materials appearing in the *Acts of John*, she notes that the *Sanctus*, addressed only to God, the Father, appears in a close relationship to the prebaptismal oil of anointing. This, according to Winkler, was the distinctive ritual

18. Maxwell E. Johnson, "The Baptismal Rite and Anaphora in the Prayers of Sarapion of Thmuis: An Assessment of a Recent 'Judicious Reassessment,'" *Worship* 73, 2 (March 1999): 140–68.

19. Cf. her monumental work *Das armenische Initiationsrituale. Entwicklungsgeschichtliche und liturgievergleichende Untersuchung der Quellen des 3. bis 10. Jahrhunderts*, Orientalia Christiana Analecta 217 (Rome, 1982); id., "The Original Meaning of the Prebaptismal Anointing and Its Implications," *Worship* 52 (1978): 24–45; and id., "Confirmation or Chrismation? A Study in Comparative Liturgy," *Worship* 58 (1984): 2–17. Both of the articles are reprinted in M. E. Johnson, ed., *Living Water, Sealing Spirit: Readings on Christian Initiation* (Collegeville: Liturgical Press, 1995), 58–81 and 202–18, respectively.

20. "Nochmals zu den Anfängen der Epiklese und des Sanctus im Eucharistischen Hochgebet," *Theologisches Quartalschrift* 74, 3 (1994): 214–31; id., "Further Observations in Connection with the Early Form of the Epiklesis," *Le Sacrement de l'Initiation: Origines et Prospectives, Patrimoine Syriaque Actes du colloque III* (Antelias, Lebanon, 1996), 66–80; and id., "Weitere Beobachtungen zur frühen Epiklese (den Doxologien und dem Sanctus), Über die Bedeutung der Apokryphen für die Erforschung der Entwicklung der Riten," *Oriens Christianus* 80 (1996): 177–200.

high point of Christian initiation in the early Syrian tradition.[21] In the *Acts of John* the *Sanctus* is connected further to the appearance of fire, an element that "goes back to a very ancient strand of the tradition," found in other early Syrian sources, in which fire appeared in the Jordan itself at the baptism of Jesus. Indeed, it is this connection between the appearance of fire, Jesus' own baptism, and Christian baptism as assimilation to Jesus' own baptism that may have suggested the inclusion of the *Sanctus* here in the first place. This combination of the *Sanctus* and the appearance of fire, both associated with the prebaptismal oil here, suggests to Winkler that here we have reflected a very old stratum of the tradition. Furthermore, two other elements are of particular significance here. First, it is important to note that the text of the *Sanctus* in the relevant passages from the *Acts of John* does not contain any form of the *Benedictus*, a fact that, according to Winkler, demonstrates that the *Benedictus* was also not a part of the *Sanctus* in the early Syrian tradition. Second, and most important, Winkler underscores the overall initiation context of the *Sanctus* in the early Syrian tradition and suggests that it is from here that it would pass eventually into anaphoral usage. But how?

While the connection between the *Sanctus* and the prebaptismal anointing for Syria is indicated only within the *Acts of John*, an overall initiation context for the *Sanctus* is suggested in other Eastern sources as well. As Winkler notes, the *Sanctus* continues to be present in the East Syrian baptismal rite for the consecration of oil, the West Syrian baptismal rite at the consecration of the baptismal water, the Maronite rite for the consecration of the waters at Epiphany, and the East Syrian Night Office (*Leyla*) for Epiphany, all of which tie the use of the *Sanctus* to the celebration of Jesus' own baptism—his pneumatic birth and assimilation of "Adam"—in the Jordan.[22] And early Eastern sources elsewhere make a similar connection between the

---

21. Winkler, "Nochmals zu den Anfängen," 223. Here she refers also to her essay "Die Licht-Erscheinung bei der Taufe Jesu und der Ursprung des Epiphaniefestes," which appears now in English translation by David Maxwell as "The Appearance of the Light at the Baptism of Jesus and the Origins of Epiphany: An Investigation of Greek, Syriac, Armenian, and Latin Sources," in *Between Memory and Hope: Readings on the Liturgical Year*, ed. M. E. Johnson (Collegeville: Liturgical Press, 2000), 291–348.

22. For texts and references, see Winkler, "Nochmals zu den Anfängen," 225–29.

Sanctus and Christian initiation. In the homilies of Asterios Sophistes of Cappadocia, for example, it is precisely within the context of the Easter Vigil that reference is made both to neophytes and to all the assembly singing the *Sanctus* in the anaphora (now, though, in its "later" form with the *Benedictus*). While a similar reference occurs in Gregory of Nyssa, Winkler draws special attention to *Mystagogical Catechesis* 5:6 of Cyril (John) of Jerusalem, where the *Sanctus*, without *Benedictus*, is directed to God the Father (as in the *Acts of John*), and where it has entered the anaphora itself at the conclusion of the initiation rites. According to her, the very fourth-century change in the meaning of the prebaptismal anointing from pneumatic assimilation to Christ to an exorcistic purification in preparation for the gift of the Holy Spirit by the water bath and subsequent *postbaptismal* anointing suggests to her that this may have caused the *Sanctus* to be shifted from its prebaptismal location to the Eucharistic liturgy, the culminating rite of initiation. Such an "original baptismal context" for the anaphoral use of the *Sanctus* in Syria, Cappadocia, and Syro-Palestine is paralleled in the West as well. Indeed, it is *because* the Eucharist itself is an integral part of the overall complex of Christian initiation rites that such a connection between the anaphora and initiation rites can be suggested in the first place.

Second, since the appearance of those essays, Winkler's long-awaited monograph, *Das Sanctus: Über den Ursprung und die Anfänge des Sanctus und sein Fortwirken*,[23] was published in 2002 but has yet to receive the detailed attention it deserves. Herein she moves the question beyond the context of Christian initiation in the early Syrian tradition and out of the Syrian *Acts* into Old Testament Pseudepigraphal and other Jewish and Jewish-Christian sources from which the anaphoral *Sanctus* may have been derived in the first place, a research direction taken earlier by Spinks in the first three chapters of his already mentioned study, although Winkler makes use of additional sources. While, according to her, Syria remains the place of origin for the anaphoral use of the *Sanctus*, comparative support is sought within other geographical and ecclesial locales, most notably that of Ethiopia, which, according to her, deserves much greater attention than past scholarship has normally given it.

---

23. G. Winkler, *Das Sanctus. Über den Ursprung und die Anfänge des Sanctus und sein Fortwirken*, Orientalia Christiana Analecta 267 (Rome, 2002).

In her recent detailed investigation of the wider Jewish context of
the *Qedushah/Sanctus*, Winkler directs our attention to the fact that
the *Qedushah/Sanctus* can and does appear both with and *without* the
added quotation of or reference to Ezekiel 3:12 ("and blessed be the
glory of the Lord"), the equivalent to the *Benedictus.* Hence, according
to her, neither the presence nor the absence of the *Benedictus* within
an anaphoral *Sanctus* can be taken as a sign of antiquity within a
particular anaphoral tradition, since there is clear Jewish precedent
for both in the sources. At the same time, allusion to the *Benedictus*
may well be present within certain anaphoras that appear to lack it.
In *Addai and Mari*, for example, the listing of the Cherubim before
the Seraphim in the short introduction to the *Sanctus* suggests to her
that there is here a missing or "hidden" *Benedictus* since it is the case
in Jewish Hekhalot literature beginning with the Hebrew version of
Enoch, and also in Pseudo-Dionysius and in Syriac hymns of the fifth
through the sixth centuries, that the Cherubim are associated always
with the *Benedictus* and not with the *Sanctus.*[24]

While Winkler clearly accepts the scholarly view of some, especially
as articulated by Bryan Spinks, that the anaphora of *Addai and Mari*
already contained the *Sanctus* in the third century, her work now directs us to Ethiopia and particularly to the Ethiopian anaphora of the
Apostles in its relationship to the book of Enoch in the Pseudepigrapha. In chapter 39 of Ethiopic Enoch (the *Book of the Parables*), which,
according to Winkler, reflects the oldest Enoch tradition (although the
date of the Ethiopian translation varies from the fourth to the seventh
centuries), there appears a bipartite *Qedushah* consisting of Isaiah 6:3
and Ezekiel 3:12 (= *Benedictus*), which functions as the culmination of
Enoch's vision of the heavenly angelic liturgy:

Ethiopic Enoch 39:[25]
Those who do not sleep bless thee,
they stand before your glory

---

24. On this, see *Das Sanctus*, 107–8, 129–36, and 154–55.

25. Text as quoted by Winkler, "A New Witness to the Missing Institution
Narrative," in *Studia Liturgica Diversa: Essays in Honor of Paul F. Bradshaw*, ed.
M. E. Johnson and L. E. Phillips, 123 (Oregon: The Pastoral Press, 2004).

and they bless, glorify, and exalt [Thee] saying
"Holy! Holy! Holy! . . ." [Isaiah 6:3]

And here my eyes saw all those who do not sleep,
they stood before him and blessed him and said:
"Blessed art Thou"
and "Blessed be the name of the Lord for ever and ever"
[= further *variant* to Ezekiel 3:12]

Having noted this bipartite *Qedushah* in a context where there is no discernible Christian influence, Winkler next compares this text with the *Sanctus* and previously "undetected *Benedictus*" in the Ethiopian anaphora of the Apostles with the following result:[26]

Ethiopic Enoch (*Qedusha*):	Ethiopic Anaphora of the Apostles (*Sanctus + Benedictus*)
Holy, holy, holy (**cf. Isaiah 6:3**)	Holy, holy, holy
Is the Lord of spirits,	perfect Lord of hosts,
He fills the earth with spirits	heaven and earth are full
	Of the holiness of thy glory . . .
Blessed art Thou . . .	
And:	
Blessed be the name of the Lord	*Blessed be the name of the Lord*
(**cf. Ezekiel 3:12**)	
	and blessed be
	the name of his glory
	for ever and ever.
	So be it. So be it.
	So be he blessed.

If, however, the *Sanctus/Benedictus* of the Ethiopian anaphora of the Apostles comes from chapter 39 of Ethiopic Enoch, the problem is that in the anaphora itself the *Sanctus* and *Benedictus* are not connected but are actually separated by several other elements. That is, *between* the *Sanctus* and *Benedictus* the Ethiopian anaphora of the Apostles contains what she calls a "short transition" to an Institution Narrative, an

---

26. Ibid., 125–26.

Anamnesis, a short petition, and a full consecratory epiclesis. Hence, Winkler argues that at a very early point in Ethiopian anaphoral development the *Sanctus/Benedictus* would have been an integral unit that later became divided by the interpolation of these other anaphoral units. That is, in the Ethiopian liturgical tradition, the Institution Narrative, Anamnesis, and Epiclesis are all later interpolations into an earlier anaphoral pattern that, like *Addai and Mari* in Syria, already contained the *Sanctus* but, unlike *Addai and Mari*, also contained an integral and connected *Benedictus*. She writes that:

> The possibility of comparison between the *Qedussah* of Ethiopic Enoch with the Sanctus of the Ethiopic "Anaphora of the Apostles," especially the verbatim agreements concerning the "Blessed/Benedictus" of Ethiopic Enoch and the Ethiopic "Anaphora of the Apostles," does not allow the assumption that the "Blessed" (= "Benedictus") of the anaphora can be considered a secondary interpolation. The Benedictus formed part of the Ethiopian "Anaphora of the Apostles" from the beginning. Only the fact that the Benedictus became separated from the Sanctus through the interpolation of the Institution Narrative (with its Antiochene position of the epiclesis) can be considered secondary. The dependence of the Ethiopic Anaphora on Ethiopic Enoch, especially with regard to the "Blessed," is quite obvious: the Sanctus-Benedictus of the Ethiopic "Anaphora of the Apostles" emerged from the Jewish *Qedussah* of Ethiopic Enoch.[27]

And she claims further that:

> both the Syriac and Ethiopic "Anaphora of the Apostles" reflect an ancient layer, the Syrian "Anaphora of the Apostles" going back to the third century, and the form of the Sanctus-Benedictus of the Ethiopic "Anaphora of the Apostles" being exceptionally old and preserving features of the Jewish *Qedussah*.[28]

According to Winkler, therefore, the *idea* of the anaphoral *Sanctus* came from Syria, first attested in *Addai and Mari*, but the particular *form* it took in Ethiopia was from Ethiopian Enoch, which included

---

27. Winkler, *Das Sanctus*, 96. English translation by G. Winkler, "A New Witness to the Missing Institution Narrative," in *Studia Liturgica Diversa*, 126–27.
28. Winkler, *Das Sanctus*, 143.

a form of the *Benedictus*, a form that ultimately also reflects Syrian origins since Ethiopian Enoch is but a translation of Aramaic Enoch. And, of equal importance, the anaphoral use of the *Sanctus-Benedictus* had to have been "exceptionally old" also in Ethiopia, old enough for it to be split in two by the addition of the Institution Narrative, Anamnesis, and Epiclesis.

In the second part of her book, which need not concern us in detail here, Winkler turns to a descriptive analysis not only of the presence but of the overall formative influence of the *Sanctus* throughout Eastern Christian liturgy. Here she argues that in many ways it is the *Sanctus* itself, which has been influential in determining the various contents not only of the anaphora but also of the entire Divine Liturgy. That is, Isaiah 6:3 appears to have provided for the emergence of the *Trishagion* as the Entrance *Troparion*, at the entrance of the gospel, the entrance with the gifts, the *Sanctus* itself, and even the *sancta sanctis* before communion. In other words, for Winkler, who provides a detailed analysis of the various troparia and chants in this section, the "Holy" functions as a "thread" running through all of Eastern liturgy that serves to mark its essential stages.[29] And closely related to this is the fact that several Eastern Christian anaphorae, in differing traditions, are known by some form of the word *Qedushah*, "sanctification," or "making holy," rather than "anaphora" or "prosphora" in their titles.

COMMENTS AND REFLECTIONS

There are several issues that Winkler's impressive work raises for liturgical scholarship on the question of the anaphoral use of the *Sanctus*. Here, however, because of my own work on the Egyptian liturgical tradition, especially that of Sarapion of Thmuis,[30] I will limit my comments to the *Sanctus* and "split *Benedictus*" of the presumably related Ethiopian anaphoral tradition. To do so, of course, it is necessary to have in front of us the full text, at least of the relevant portions, of the Ethiopian anaphora of the Apostles. In what follows, the portions of the text from the Ethiopic version of the *Apostolic Tradition* are in regular print with all additions to that text, including the *Sanctus* and *Benedictus*, in italics:

29. See *Das Sanctus*, 196.
30. See Johnson, *Prayers of Sarapion*.

The Ethiopian Anaphora of the Apostles[31]

We give thee thanks, O Lord, in thy beloved Son our Lord Jesus, whom in the last days thou didst send unto us, thy Son the Saviour and Redeemer, the messenger of thy counsel, this Word is he who is from thee, and through whom thou didst make all things by thy will.

Intercessions

Introduction to the Sanctus

There stand before thee thousand thousands and ten thousand times ten thousand and the holy angels and archangels and thy honourable beasts, each with six wings. [Deacon: Look to the east]. With two of their wings they cover their face, with two of their wings they cover their feet, and with two of their wings they fly from end to end of the world. [Deacon: Let us give heed]. And they all constantly hallow and praise thee with all them that hallow and praise thee; receive also our hallowing which we utter unto thee:

Sanctus

Holy holy holy, perfect Lord of hosts, heaven and earth are full of the holiness of thy glory.

Post-Sanctus

Truly heaven and earth are full of the holiness of thy glory through our Lord and our God and our Saviour Jesus Christ thy holy Son. He came and was born of a virgin that he might fulfill thy will and make a people for thee.

Remember us, Lord, in thy kingdom; remember us, Lord, Master, in thy kingdom; remember us, Lord, in thy kingdom, as thou didst remember the thief on the right hand when thou wast on the tree of the holy cross.

He stretched out his hands in the passion, suffering to save the sufferers that trust in Him.
Who was delivered to the passion that he might destroy death, break the bonds of Satan, tread down hell, lead forth the saints, establish a covenant and make known his resurrection.

---

31. Trans. from M. Daoud, *The Liturgy of The Ethiopian Church* (Cairo: The Egyptian Book Press, 1959), 69–76. A critical edition of the Ethiopian text is in process by Richard Meßner and Martin Lang. See their study, "Ethiopian Anaphoras. Status and Tasks in Current Research Via an Edition of the Ethiopian Anaphora of the Apostles," in *Jewish and Christian Liturgy and Worship: New Insights into its History and Interaction*, ed. Albert Gerhards and Clemens Leonhard, Jewish and Christian Perspectives 15, 185–206 (Leiden/Boston: Brill, 2007).

Institution Narrative

Anamnesis

Now, Lord, we remember thy death and thy resurrection. *We confess thee and* we offer unto thee this bread and this cup, giving thanks unto thee; and thereby thou hast made us worthy of the joy, standing before thee and ministering to thee.

Epiclesis

We pray thee and beseech thee, Lord, that thou wouldest send the Holy Spirit *and power* upon this bread and upon this cup. *May he make them the body and blood of our Lord and our God and our Saviour Jesus Christ, world without end.*

Amen; Lord have pity upon us, Lord spare us, Lord have mercy upon us.

With all the heart let us beseech the Lord our God that he grant unto us the good communion of the Holy Spirit.

As it was, is and shall be unto generations of generations, world without end.

Grant it together unto all them that take of it, that it may be unto them for sanctification and for filling with the Holy Spirit and for strengthening of the true faith, that they may hallow and praise thee and thy beloved Son, Jesus Christ with the Holy Spirit.

Grant us to be united through thy Holy Spirit, and heal us by this oblation that we may live in thee for ever.

Blessed be the name of the Lord, and blessed be he that cometh in the name of the Lord, and let the name of the Lord, and let the name of his glory be blessed. So be it, so be it, so be it blessed.

Send the grace of the Holy Spirit upon us.

Winkler's hypothesis that the current *textus receptus* of the Ethiopian anaphora of the Apostles reflects the later interpolation of the Institution Narrative, Anamnesis, and Epiclesis into an earlier anaphoral core, which very early on contained a connected *Sanctus* and *Benedictus* with a close ("verbatim") literary relationship to the *Qedusha* of Ethiopic Enoch, is intriguing. Hence, it may well be that it is the Ethiopian anaphoral pattern that ultimately explains the Alexandrian or Egyptian anaphoral pattern. That is, immediately following the *Sanctus* in the *textus receptus* of the Ethiopian anaphora of the Apostles, the post-*Sanctus* transition to the Institution Narrative, picking up on "heaven and earth are *full* of the holiness of thy glory" from the *Sanctus*, begins with the sentence *"Truly heaven and earth are full of the holiness of thy glory through our Lord and our God and our Saviour Jesus Christ thy holy Son."* If this transition sentence (*without* an Epiclesis!), Institution Narrative, Anamnesis, and Epiclesis are what originally divided the *Sanctus* and *Benedictus*, causing the *Benedictus* to function now as a concluding doxology, and if the connected *Sanctus/Benedictus* was part of the Ethiopian anaphora of the Apostles from the beginning, then the "unique" anaphoral pattern of Egypt with its post-*Sanctus* Epiclesis may have been simply a further development and expansion of this model. *"Truly heaven and earth are full of the holiness of thy glory through our Lord and our God and our Saviour Jesus Christ thy holy Son"* becomes expanded in Egypt into a petition for the Holy Spirit to "fill" the Eucharistic gifts as in the anaphora of St. Mark. What all of this means ultimately, of course, even if indirectly, is that Egypt originally received the *Sanctus* from Syria since the relevant Pseudepigraphal literature has an original Aramaic or Syrian provenance.

Winkler's major point here, of course, is that the *form* of the *Sanctus/ Benedictus* in the Ethiopian anaphora of the Apostles comes from the *Qedushah* in chapter 39 of Ethiopian Enoch, which in Ethiopian anaphoral prayer was split apart. Her point is *not* that this particular anaphora in its current form is ancient but, primarily, that the Ethiopian anaphora of the Apostles reflects in its structure the result of that earlier split.

The problem, however, is that we have no evidence of Ethiopian anaphoral prayer, construction, or structure prior to this particular anaphora of the Apostles and, as is well known, apart from the conversion and baptism of the Ethiopian Eunuch in Acts 8:26-40, the origins of Christianity in Ethiopia, first via Egyptian evangelization and then via Syrian monasticism, are usually dated as beginning in the fourth century, a time in which all kinds of liturgical influence from diverse locales is possible.[32] Hence, while "early" Ethiopian anaphoral prayer

---

32. See Aziz S. Atiya, *History of Eastern Christianity* (Notre Dame, IN: University of Notre Dame Press, 1968), 146–66; Adrian Hastings, *The Church in Africa: 1450–1950* (Oxford: Clarendon Press, 1994), chaps. 1, 4, 6. Elizabeth Isichei, *A History of Christianity in Africa from Antiquity to the Present* (London: SPCK, 1995).

may well have included an integral and connected *Sanctus/Benedictus*, which later was divided by further anaphoral construction, there are no early Ethiopian *liturgical* texts beyond the Enoch literature allowing us to know that with any degree of certainty. A recent essay by Richard Meßner and Martin Lang, "Ethiopian Anaphoras. Status and Tasks in Current Research Via an Edition of the Ethiopian Anaphora of the Apostles," in fact, argues against Winkler's approach, claiming that the *Benedictus* at the conclusion of the prayer was *not* due to a split in an earlier united *Sanctus-Benedictus* inherited from Ethiopic Enoch, but was taken directly from the concluding doxology of the *Ethiopic Testamentum Domini*, which has no *Sanctus* whatsoever but *only* a concluding *Benedictus*. They write:

> The . . . sentence ("blessed who comes in the name of the Lord"), a quotation from Ps 118:26, but directly taken over from the NT (Matt 21:9), where it is related to Christ entering Jerusalem, gives a Christological interpretation to the doxology. The reference point in this sentence is Christ's coming in the Eucharistic communion. The last member of this berakha/doxology ("be blessed the name of his glory") is called in the TestDom "the seal of the Eucharist" and therefore obviously of the highest importance. It is certainly to be linked— though, of course, not genetically—with the famous berakha used in the temple worship after the uttering of God's name: . . . "Blessed the name of the glory of the kingdom for ever and ever." This is one of many examples for the reception of temple motives in Christian worship. The source of the berakha/doxology in the Anaphora of the Apostles is . . . the Testamentum Domini, not, as claimed by Gabriele Winkler, the Ethiopic Book of Henoch. The barukh formula in the Anaphora of the Apostles resp. in the Testamentum Domini as well as the formulae in 1 Henoch, adduced by G. Winkler, are both part of the reception history of Jewish berakhot, more precisely: of temple berakhot.[33]

They conclude further that far from being an "early" Eucharistic prayer, the "Anaphora of the Apostles is . . . an artificial product of a rather late date, redacted . . . certainly not earlier than the 14th century."[34]

---

33. Meßner and Lang, "Ethiopian Anaphoras," 199.
34. Ibid., 203.

More recently, however, and quite independently from Meßner and Lang, Winkler herself has nuanced her position, noting that the *current* form of the *Benedictus* in the Ethiopic anaphora of the Apostles is taken clearly from the Ethiopic *Testamentum Domini* and not directly from Ethiopian Enoch.[35]

Ethiopic Anaphora of the Apostles	Ethiopic Testamentum Domini
(Benedictus)	*(Concluding Doxology)*
Blessed be the name of the Lord,	*Blessed be the name of the Lord*
and blessed be he that cometh	*for ever . . . Blessed is he who comes*
in the name of the Lord,	*in the name of the Lord,*
and let the name of the Lord,	
and let the name of his glory be blessed.	*Blessed be the name of his glory . . .*
So be it, so be it, so be it blessed.	*So be it, so be it, so be it.*
Send the grace of the Holy Spirit upon us.	*Send the grace of the Spirit upon us.*[36]

As such, what it indicates is simply the use of the text of the *Testamentum Domini* by what Meßner and Lang refer to as the not-earlier-than-the-fourteenth-century redactor; it does not mean anything for what an earlier stratum of the anaphora itself may have contained. Rather, whatever the date and provenance of the much disputed *Testamentum Domini*,[37] it would seem that the unified *Sanctus-Benedictus* of Ethiopic

35. See G. Winkler, "Über das christliche Erbe Henochs und einige Probleme des Testamentum Domini," *Oriens Christianus* (2009); and id., *Liturgy of Sahak*, Anaphorae Orientales (Rome: Pontificio Istituto Orientales, forthcoming).

36. The text is taken from Grant Sperry-White, *The Testamentum Domini: A Text for Students, with Introduction, Translation, and Notes*, Alcuin/GROW Liturgical Study 19 (Cambridge: Gover Books, Ltd., 1991), 18. It should be noted that, while it is the *Ethiopic* version of the *Testamentum Domini* under discussion here, which is probably a translation of a Coptic version, the Syriac version also includes the same text of the *Benedictus* in this location. For an English translation of the Syriac Text, see James Cooper and Arthur J. Maclean, *The Testament of Our Lord Translated into English from the Syriac* (Edinburgh: T & T Clark, 1902), 75.

37. Grant Sperry White suggests a date around 381 AD. For a more recent approach, see Michael Kohlbacher, "Wessen Kirche ordnete das Testamentum Domini Nostri Jesu Christi?" in *Zu Geschichte, Theologie, Liturgie und Gegenwartslage der Syrischen Kirchen*, ed. Martin Tamcke and Andreas Heinz, Ausgewählte Vorträge des deutschen Syrologen-Symposiums vom. 2.-4. Oktober 1998 in Hermannsburg, Studien zur Orientalischen Kirchengeschichte

Enoch would have had to been split apart early enough for only the *Benedictus* to have been incorporated into the Ethiopic *Testamentum Domini*. Not surprisingly, then, after the split (or, for that matter, before or even independently), *Sanctus* and *Benedictus* could easily have circulated as independent liturgical units, with the interpolation of one not necessarily always demanding the interpolation of the other at the same time.[38] Consequently, Winkler's statement that "the *Benedictus* formed part of the Ethiopian 'Anaphora of the Apostles' from the beginning," or, at least, Eucharistic praying in Ethiopia, may, it seems, be vindicated rather than refuted by the text of the *Testamentum Domini*, no matter what the date of the anaphora of the Apostles itself. And it must be asserted further that the fourteenth-century date given by Meßner and Lang to the *textus receptus* of the Ethiopian anaphora of the Apostles can only be to its *final* form; it says nothing about an earlier form for which we must await subsequent research by those well versed in Ethiopic.

Nevertheless, the overall composition and structure of the final form of the Ethiopian anaphora of the Apostles may be explainable in another way. The core text of the Ethiopian anaphora of the Apostles, as indicated in the text above, is the anaphora of the Ethiopic version of the so-called *Apostolic Tradition*, which here parallels the fifth-century Verona Latin version closely, and which, according to Alessandro Bausi's recent work, is also closely paralleled in the newly discovered fifth- or sixth-century Ethiopian version of the document.[39] But prior to the existence of this text, certainly the words of Ernst Hammerschmidt, *Studies in the Ethiopic Anaphoras*, bear repeating. That is, while this

---

9 (Münster: Lit Verlag, 2000): 55–138; and especially G. Winkler, "Über das christliche Erbe Henochs."

38. Juliette Day has recently argued for the independent circulation of the *Benedictus* without *Sanctus*, claiming, in a manner akin to Anton Baumstark, that its anaphoral origins are not based on Ezekiel 3:12 but in the Matthean form (Matt 21:9), as used first in the fourth-century Jerusalem Palm Sunday acclamation. From there the *Benedictus* passed into the Liturgy of St. James and from there to the Eucharistic prayers both of East and West. Hence, the *idea* of the *Benedictus* may well rest in Jewish sources but its anaphoral form is Matthean. See Juliette Day, "The Origins of the Anaphoral Benedictus," *The Journal of Theological Studies* 60, 1 (2009): 193–211.

39. See Alessandro Bausi, "New Egyptian Texts in Ethiopia," *Adamantius* 8 (2002): 146–51. On the different versions of the AT see Paul F. Bradshaw, Maxwell E. Johnson, and L. Edward Phillips, *The Apostolic Tradition: A Commentary*, Hermeneia (Minneapolis: Fortress Press, 2002), 7–11, and for the anaphora, 37–49.

anaphora may certainly go back to the origins of Christianity in Ethiopia, before the time of Frumentius it may be the case that Christians in Ethiopia had already taken parts of a (Egyptian) Church Order as a basis for their liturgy, "but we do not want to concern ourselves with this question any further because it is not possible to go much beyond mere surmise."[40] Hence, while it is possible that at an early stage of its development this prayer may have simply been a short *eucharistia* that in Ethiopia included a unified *Sanctus/Benedictus*,[41] the text of the prayer in the Ethiopian anaphora of the Apostles already reflects the *textus receptus* of the anaphora in the *Apostolic Tradition*, which, in its final form at least, is now being dated in the mid-fourth, rather than early third, century.[42] And, when the additions to this possible core, reflected in italics in the text above, are analyzed (including the *Sanctus* but not the *Benedictus*), those additions for the most part appear to be *Alexandrian* or *Egyptian* in character. That is:

1. The prayer in its current form contains its intercessions in the "Alexandrian" location in the "preface";

2. The post-*Sanctus* "transition" is directly connected to the *Sanctus* (without *Benedictus*!) by a sentence that closely parallels the anaphora of St. Mark: "*Truly heaven and earth are full of the holiness of thy glory through our Lord and our God and our Saviour Jesus Christ thy holy Son*"; and

3. The (now consecratory) epiclesis refers to both the "Holy Spirit" and "power" ("send the Holy Spirit *and power* upon this bread and upon this cup"), a phrase paralleled closely in the Egyptian anaphora contained in the British Museum Tablet ("We pray and beseech you to send your Holy Spirit and your power on these [your?] gifts . . .").[43] So also, the

40. E. Hammerschmidt, *Studies in the Ethiopic Anaphoras*, 2nd rev. ed., *Athiopische Forschungen* 25 (Stuttgart: Franz Steiner Verlag Wiesdbaden GMBH, 1987), 340–41.

41. This would necessitate an argument similar to that of E. C. Ratcliff, "The Sanctus and the Pattern of the Early Anaphora," *Journal of Ecclesiastical History* 1 (1950): 29–36, 125–34.

42. See P. Bradshaw, M. Johnson, and L. E. Phillips, *The Apostolic Tradition*, Hermeneia (Minneapolis: Fortress Press, 2002), especially 37–48.

43. PEER, 56.

pre-institution epiclesis in the anaphora of Sarapion of Thmuis, picking up on "Lord of Sabaoth/powers" in the *Sanctus*, asks that God's "power and participation" might fill the Eucharistic gifts.[44]

Although there are no other "Egyptianisms," like the use of Alphonse Raes's "famous aorist"[45] in the Anamnesis, or the connection of the Institution Narrative to the anaphora by means of *hoti* ("therefore") or its equivalent, absences that are fully explainable by the use of the *Apostolic Tradition* anaphora as a core, Egyptian influence seems to me rather obvious in this text. In fact, could one not argue that the current form of the Ethiopian anaphora of the Apostles, whatever its prehistory might have been, was constructed precisely by combining the anaphora of Ethiopian *Apostolic Tradition* with *a* version of an Alexandrian-type anaphora? Or, in other words, what causes the *Qedushah* of Ethiopian Enoch to be split apart into *Sanctus* and *Benedictus* within Ethiopian anaphoral usage is the developing *Egyptian* or *Alexandrian* pattern of anaphoral construction. And if this is so, that it is the Egyptian pattern—including the *Sanctus* (without *Benedictus*)—which is interpolated into the anaphora of the Ethiopian *Apostolic Tradition* in order to form the Ethiopian anaphora of the Apostles, then it would also be true that Egypt already had to have the *Sanctus* itself before this could take place! Indeed, with the exception of the *Benedictus* at the end of the prayer, the entire text of the Ethiopian anaphora of the Apostles looks like an Egyptian-interpolated anaphoral pattern into the Eucharistic prayer of the Ethiopic version of *Apostolic Tradition*. Hence, it is not only that the *Sanctus/Benedictus* are split by the addition of other anaphoral units; it looks like they are split precisely by the Egyptian anaphoral structure such that the *Benedictus*, out of place before "full indeed," is now placed at the next most logical place as an appropriate substitute for the final doxology! Hence, the following might be said:

1. That the *Sanctus* and at least the idea of the *Benedictus* in the Ethiopian anaphora of the Apostles comes from the *Qedusha* in chapter 39 of Ethiopian Enoch seems quite plausible;

44. Johnson, *Prayers of Sarapion*, 47.
45. See Alphonse Raes, "Un nouveau document de la Liturgie de S. Basile," *Orientalia Christiana Periodica* 26 (1960): 401–10.

2. That at an early time in Ethiopia *Sanctus* and *Benedictus* may have been together in a Eucharistic prayer only to have been separated later by the interpolation of other anaphoral units is, indeed, plausible; and

3. That the *textus receptus* of the Ethiopian anaphora of the Apostles still reflects the remnant of that once-upon-a-time interpolation also follows logically and remains plausible.

In spite of the fact that Winkler's position is both plausible and compelling, I remain rather reluctant to leave the Egyptian anaphoral tradition out of this development altogether. As I have attempted to argue, I think it remains quite plausible to assert that it is the Egyptian anaphoral pattern that influences this development. If so, then Ethiopia received the *idea* and even the structural *location* of the anaphoral *Sanctus* from Egypt but the form it took in *Ethiopia* came from Ethiopian Enoch. The question here with this anaphora of the Apostles, of course, is not about the origins of the anaphoral *Sanctus* in general but the specific origins of its use in Ethiopia. Therefore, even if Syria, as represented by *Addai and Mari*, may have been the location of the original anaphoral use of the *Sanctus*, there is still a strong case that can be made that Egypt had the anaphoral *Sanctus* prior to Ethiopia and that Ethiopia received the *idea* and location of the *Sanctus* from Egypt, but the *form* it took, including a now concluding *Benedictus*, came from Ethiopian Enoch and eventually with regard to the form of the *Benedictus* from the Ethiopic *Testamentum Domini*.

TOWARD THE BEGINNINGS OF A NEW HYPOTHESIS?

As noted at the beginning of this essay, scholarship has focused on the when and where of the interpolation, or addition, of the *Sanctus* into the Eucharistic prayers of the Church. But has any final scholarly consensus on this been reached? No. After all the detailed work that has been done on this question in recent years by several preeminent scholars, we are still left with essentially two options: Syria and/or Egypt. And perhaps the most that can be said about this is no more than what Taft concluded in the early 1990s. While favoring an Egyptian origin for its interpolation, he nevertheless added, in view of the possibility of Syrian origins, "the evidence does not permit us to exclude the possibility that the Egyptians reworked the Syrian Sanctus on the basis of their native Origenist exegesis of Is 6:2-3, and only later referred to the Trinity in the Sanctus."[46] This is probably the furthest we can go on the question of its origins, especially because as the cliché has it, the evidence tends to be "six of one and a half dozen of the other."

In light of this I wonder if a somewhat different methodological approach from the perspective of theological interpretation might not be in order at this time. The earliest *undisputed* anaphoral texts having the *Sanctus* all date from sometime in the fourth-century Christian East. Those texts include the anaphora of Sarapion of Thmuis; early versions of the Basilian anaphoras (whether Egyptian, Syrian, or Armenian);[47] the anaphoral outline provided by Cyril (John) of Jerusalem; and now, most recently, thanks to the work of Michael Zheltov, the Greek Barcelona Papyrus of the Louvain Coptic Papyrus.[48] But with regard to the *Sanctus*, scholarship has been trying to get back behind these written documents to reconstruct in the most intelligible and plausible manner what the prehistory of the textual evidence was and from where and when in that prehistory the *Sanctus* entered into Eucharistic praying. Now if we attend to the theological context of those written sources themselves, there may well be a clue not so much as to the when or where but to the "why" of the addition of the *Sanctus* to the anaphora in the first place. And perhaps the why will provide a clue to the when or where.

What suggests this approach to me, in fact, is Winkler's conclusion regarding the presence of the *Sanctus* in the context of the consecration of the prebaptismal oil in the *Acts of John*. While Paul Bradshaw and others may well be correct in noting that elements such as the *Sanctus* and epiclesis "were standard prayer units in the tradition, and in parallel developments then became part of the consecration of bap-

46. Taft, "Interpolation," II, 116.

47. See Gabriele Winkler, *Die Basilius-Anaphora: Edition der beiden armenischen Redaktionen und der relevanten Fragmente, Übersetzung und Zusammenschau aller Versionen im Licht der orientalischen Überlieferungen,* Anaphorae Orientales 2 (Rome: Pontificio Istituto Orientale, 2005).

48. Michael Zheltov, "The Anaphora and the Thanksgiving Prayer from the Barcelona Papyrus: An Underestimated Testimony to the Anaphoral History in the Fourth Century," *Vigiliae Christianae* 62 (2008): 467–504. For a study of this anaphora, see Paul Bradshaw, "The Barcelona Papyrus and the Development of Early Eucharistic Prayers," pp. 129–38 above.

tismal oil and water and of Eucharistic prayers,"[49] Winkler provides the beginning of a *theological* answer to the question of why this happened. That is, as we have seen, the *Sanctus* is sung at the consecration of the prebaptismal oil because the prebaptismal anointing, according to her, was the very high point of the ritual. Indeed, it is the very place where the glory and presence, the *Shekinah*, of God is revealed. Note the following from the *Acts of John*:

> *II:9-12:* And straightaway fire blazed forth over the oil and the oil did not take fire, for two angels had their wings spread over the oil and were crying: "*Holy, holy, holy, Lord Almighty*" (cf. Isa 6:3).

> *IVl:6-10:* And in that hour fire blazed forth over the oil, and the wings of the angels were spread over the oil, and the whole assemblage was crying out, men and women and children, "*Holy, holy, holy, Lord Almighty of whose praises heaven and earth are full*" (cf. Isa 6:3).[50]

Thus, what she has done is to provide *not* a context in what we might today call "non-sacramental worship" (such as synagogue prayer, Jewish mysticism, etc.) but in the very context of divine and sacramental revelation in a liturgical event! It is a small step from there to the Eucharist.

Similarly, in the conclusion to his own study, Bryan Spinks himself suggests the theological *appropriateness* of the *Sanctus* in the anaphora:

> Although it is quite possible, and in some cases perhaps desirable, to compile eucharistic prayers *without* the sanctus, there is every reason to expect that this ancient chant will continue to be utilised in some form in the eucharistic prayer—not because of tradition, but because it is *appropriate*. For, in Christian theology, the glory of God was revealed in Christ whose love and grace is revealed in the eucharistic feast. In Christ the space of heaven and the region of the earth are united. In the eucharist the worshipper enters heaven through Christ, and is represented by our true High Priest. Here time and eternity intersect and become one, and this world and the world to come elide.[51]

49. Paul Bradshaw, *The Search for the Origins of Christian Worship*, 2nd ed. (London: SPCK, 2002), 137. See also id., *Eucharistic Origins* (New York: Oxford, 2004), 127–28.

50. Text from W. Wright, *Apocryphal Acts of the Apostles*, vol. II (London, 1871), as cited by Winkler, "Nochmals zu den Anfängen," 221–22.

51. Spinks, *Sanctus*, 206 (emphasis added).

And, significantly, Meßner and Lang, as we saw above, also draw attention to the relationship of the concluding *Benedictus* in the *Ethiopic Testamentum Domini* to the Eucharistic presence of Christ, saying:

> The . . . sentence ("blessed who comes in the name of the Lord"), a quotation from Ps 118:26, but directly taken over from the NT (Matt 21:9), where it is related to Christ entering Jerusalem, gives a Christological interpretation to the doxology. The reference point in this sentence is Christ's coming in the Eucharistic communion. The last member of this berakha/doxology ("be blessed the name of his glory") is called in the TestDom "the seal of the Eucharist" and therefore obviously of the highest importance. [52]

Is, then, the answer to the question of the anaphoral use of the *Sanctus* really a theological one at base? Is it only when the Eucharist itself becomes conceived of as *the* primary location and manifestation of the presence of Christ, the very dwelling of the *Shekinah* here and now, that the *Sanctus* enters into Eucharistic praying as the most "appropriate" Christological hymn—with or without *Benedictus*—to acclaim and glorify that presence? And when it does, is the language used not so much that of synagogue *berakoth* or domestic worship—Christianized or not—but from the closest biblical parallel to God's self-revelation to Isaiah in the temple, the experience of which still can only be called *mysterium tremendum et fascinans*, indeed, the language of, at least, the heavenly Temple, where Christ continually pleads his once-for-all sacrifice (Hebrews) and the four living creatures of Revelation 4:8 continually sing the *Sanctus*? In fact, as the great hymn *On Faith I. 73, 1* of St. Ephrem the Syrian demonstrates, it is not just the *Sanctus* but the very contents of Isaiah's encounter with God in Isaiah 6:2-3 that become interpreted in a Eucharistic manner, a manner that still governs one understanding of holy communion in the Christian East today:

On Faith 73, 1:

In your Bread there is hidden the Spirit who is not consumed,
in your Wine there dwells the fire that is not drunk;
the Spirit is in your Bread, the Fire in your Wine,
a manifest wonder, which our lips have received.

---

52. Meßner and Lang, "Ethiopian Anaphoras," 199.

When the Lord came down to earth to mortal men
he created them again in a new creation, like angels,
mingling Fire and Spirit within them,
so that in a hidden manner they might be of Fire and Spirit.

The Seraph could not touch the fire's coals with his fingers,
But just brought it close to Isaiah's mouth;
The Seraph did not hold it, Isaiah did not consume it,
But us our Lord has allowed to do both.

To the angels who are spiritual Abraham brought
food for the body, and they ate. The new miracle
is that our mighty Lord has given to bodily man
Fire and Spirit to eat and drink.

Fire descended in wrath and consumed sinners,
The Fire of mercy descended and dwelt in the bread.
Instead of that fire which consumed mankind,
You have consumed Fire in the Bread and you come to life.

Fire descended and consumed Elijah's sacrifice,
the Fire of mercies has become a living sacrifice for us:
Fire consumed the oblation,
And we Lord, have consumed your Fire in your oblation.[53]

And, recall that Cyril (John) of Jerusalem offers his own rationale for the singing of the *Sanctus*: "The reason why we sing this hymn of praise which has been handed down to us from the seraphim is that we may share with the supernatural armies in their hymnody."[54]

But even if we grant the rather obvious claim that the *Sanctus* is theologically appropriate to the Eucharist, can a theological approach to the question of the entrance of the *Sanctus* into the Eucharistic prayer help us with the when and the where of that entrance? Perhaps it can, especially, at least, for the when. For if it is the increasing focus on the Eucharist itself as the location where, in the words of Spinks, "the worshipper enters heaven through Christ, and is represented by our true High Priest," that attracts the appropriateness of the *Sanctus*, then it just may well be that it is the fourth-century, especially post-Nicene, context itself that provides the overall theological environ-

53. ET, S. Brock, *The Holy Spirit in the Syrian Baptismal Tradition* (New York: John XXIII Center, 1979), 12–13.

54. Text from PEER, 85.

ment for this. In his recent book, *Eucharistic Origins*, Paul Bradshaw writes of the great transformation of the Eucharist and its liturgy in the fourth century[55] taking place as a result of the massive social and cultural changes the Church itself experienced, as it was becoming a *cultus publicus*. In this context, Bradshaw suggests that certain anaphoral elements, such as the Institution Narrative, became added to the anaphora for catechetical reasons as the liturgy itself became increasingly catechetical and didactic. With that, other dramatic elements of liturgy were either highlighted or added, complete with various parts of the liturgy becoming interpreted in an increasingly allegorical "life of Christ" (Antiochene) or mystical and heavenly (Alexandrian) manner, contributing to what Alexander Schmemann called a "mysteriological piety" divorced now from true liturgical symbolism.[56] Also, combined with an increasingly noncommunicating attendance at the Eucharistic liturgy, the Eucharist itself came to be commonly interpreted in ways that underscored its "awesome" and "fearful" nature. Bradshaw writes:

> [T]here are signs of . . . attempts to instill in the congregation the right attitude of mind. These notes were struck in preaching and teaching about the Eucharist as well as in the liturgical rites themselves. Thus Chrysostom in his homilies repeatedly speaks of the "dreadful sacrifice," of the "fearful moment" when the mysteries are accomplished, and of the "terrible and awesome table" that should only be approached with fear and trembling. But the language of liturgical prayer also took on a more exalted tone, apparently with a similar intent.[57]

In addition, it is also well known that it was precisely from the fourth century on that literary descriptions of Jewish sacrificial worship and temple priesthood imagery influenced both liturgical practice and thought.[58]

With the possible exception of the anaphora of *Addai and Mari*, which *may* or may *not* have included the *Sanctus* originally, prior to the written anaphorae and other documents of the fourth century (e.g., The *Te Deum* and the *Acts of John*) our evidence for some kind of Chris-

---

55. Bradshaw, *Eucharistic Origins*, 139ff.

56. Alexander Schmemann, *Introduction to Liturgical Theology*, second edition (New York: St. Vladimir's Seminary Press, 1975), pp. 82ff.

57. Bradshaw, *Eucharistic Origins*, 140–41.

58. See Bradshaw, *Search*, 35.

tian possible liturgical—but non-Eucharistic—usage of the *Sanctus* is limited indeed. Within extant Christian literature, along with Revelation 4:8, it appears only in 1 Clement 34:5-8; The *Passion of Sts. Perpetua and Fecility* 12.2, narrating their entrance into heaven; and Tertullian's *De oratione* 3.3, the liturgical context of which, if any, is difficult to determine. Hence, whatever the case may have been in the third century, it is only in the fourth century, within that overall theological context summarized above, that we know with certainty the presence of the *Sanctus* within the anaphora. Indeed, in that context the addition of the *Sanctus* to the Church's public Eucharistic liturgy could do nothing other than underscore strongly and most appropriately that "awesome" rite now taking place on the altar, whether one would be communing or not. And when the *Sanctus* entered the anaphora sometime in the fourth century, it took different forms depending on locale and tradition. In Egypt, it reflected, without *Benedictus*, the Origenist theological interpretation given by Origen himself and reflected in the anaphora of Sarapion of Thmuis. In Syro-Palestine, as reflected in Cyril (John) of Jerusalem, it appears to have been similar. In Syria, the form it took was probably related, directly or indirectly, to Jewish synagogue usage or even to Christianized synagogue usage, as is shown, presumably, by the prayers in *Apostolic Constitutions* 7. And in Ethiopia, it came from Ethiopic Enoch 39, though with, I have suggested, also Egyptian structural influence on the final form of the anaphora of the Apostles in that tradition.

If theology, however, helps us in determining the "when" of the entrance of the *Sanctus* into the anaphora, does it help us in determining "where" this first took place? As Robert Taft has written regarding the theory that the *Sanctus* could have originated in different ways and different places unrelated to each other: "the suggestion that the Sanctus could have landed independently, in both Egypt and elsewhere, in basically the same place in the same shape of the anaphora, between the praise and institution account, cannot be taken seriously."[59] And, since someone had to be first, I continue to find it highly suggestive, although, of course, not conclusive, that the earliest fourth-century anaphorae we possess having the *Sanctus* are Egyptian, namely, the anaphora of Sarapion of Thmuis from the mid-fourth century, and, if Zheltov's recent dating of the Barcelona Papyrus is accepted,[60] the

59. Taft, "Interpolation," Part 2, 116.
60. Zheltov, "The Anaphora and the Thanksgiving Prayer," 495–96.

early fourth century. But wherever it first entered Eucharistic praying, certainly it is the overall theological context of the fourth century that encouraged its wider dissemination and use throughout the Churches of the Christian East.

CONCLUSION

The history of scholarship on the *Sanctus* and its entrance into Eucharistic praying has tended, quite understandably, to focus on the what, when, and where of this biblical hymn passing from a Jewish liturgical or other context into a Christian one. But no one I am aware of has attempted to address the issue of why. Why does a hymn from a nonmeal context, whether in Jewish circles or Christianized Jewish circles, pass from that context to become a constitutive component of Christian sacramental meal praying? Thanks, initially, to Gabriele Winkler's analysis of the presence of the *Sanctus* within the consecration of the prebaptismal oil in the *Acts of John*, as well as other scholars, like Spinks, emphasizing the Christological and, hence, Eucharistic appropriateness of the *Sanctus*, I have suggested that it is the overall great transformation of the Eucharist and Eucharistic liturgy taking place in the fourth century that needs to be acknowledged in answering this question. Why does the *Sanctus* enter the anaphora? Simply because the meal of the Christian assembly, the Eucharist itself, *is* the primary location where the heavenly Christ is now encountered most fully among us, salvifically present, in his Body and Blood, where heaven and earth are joined, and where the earthly Church and heavenly Church unite together now in their common hymn of the Seraphim, and in some places with the Cherubim as well, in singing "Holy, holy, holy." Whether this transition was already taking place in the late third century, either in Syria (e.g., in *Addai and Mari*) or in Egypt (sometime between Origen of Alexandria and Sarapion of Thmuis), we simply cannot account for its apparent popularity from the fourth century on both in East and West without serious and renewed scholarly attention to theology, to the why.

Hans-Jürgen Feulner

IX. The Armenian Anaphora of St. Athanasius

Dedicated to Gabriele Winkler on her 70th birthday

The *Anaphora of Athanasius*, used today as the only Eucharistic Prayer of the Armenian Church, is of considerable interest for three reasons: first, for its obvious dependence on the oldest Armenian redaction of the *Anaphora of Basil* in some parts of the anaphora; second, for its reflection of the Syrian tradition throughout various parts of the anaphora; and third, for the secondary Byzantine influence that is mirrored in the epiclesis.

ON THE ARMENIAN DIVINE LITURGY[1]

Introductory Remarks

The invention of an alphabet corresponding to Armenian phonemes[2] by the monk *Mesrop Maštoc'* (d. 440) at the beginning of the

---

1. Cf. also H.-J. Feulner, "On the 'Preparatory Rites' of the Armenian Divine Liturgy: Some Remarks on the Ritual of Vesting," in *Worship Traditions in Armenia and the Neighboring Christian East*, ed. R. R. Ervine, AVANT Series 3, 93–117, esp. 94–96 (New York: St. Vladimir's Orthodox Seminary Press, 2006); idem, "The Prayers of St. Gregory of Narek in the Divine Liturgy (*Surb Patarag*)," in *Saint Grégoire de Narek. Théologien et Mystique* [. . .], J.-P. Mahé and B. L. Zekiyan, eds., Orientalia Christiana Analecta (hereafter, OCA) 275 (Rome: Pontificio Istituto Orientale, 2006): 187–203, esp. 188–94.

2. On the creation of the Armenian alphabet, cf. S. Weber, *Die katholische Kirche in Armenien. Ihre Begründung und Entwicklung vor der Trennung* (Freiburg: Herder, 1903), 394–404; J. Marquart, *Über den Ursprung des armenischen Alphabets in Verbindung mit der Biographie des Hl. Maštoc'* (Vienna: Mechitharisten-Buchdruckerei, 1917); P. Peeters, "Pour l'histoire des origines de l'alphabet arménien," *Revue des Études Arméniennes* 9 (1929): 203–37 (= Idem, *Recherches d'histoire et de philologie orientales* I [Brussels: Société des Bollandistes, 1951] 171–207); Ch. Renoux, "Langue et littérature arméniennes," in *Christianismes Orientaux*, ed. M. Albert et al., 107–66, here 125

fifth century not only contributed to the development of a proper literature and national consciousness for the Armenian people. It also made possible worship entirely in Armenian.[3] We know this period as the so-called "Golden Age" of Armenian literature. The creation of a national liturgy then became the center of interest. In the part of Armenia outside the Roman Empire (*Armenia maior*), liturgical services had previously been conducted in the Syriac language until the beginning of the fifth century. Even after classical Armenian, or *Grabar*, had become the liturgical language, the Syrian form of the liturgy continued to have a great influence on the Armenian rite, although increasingly Byzantine and later on—via contact with the Crusaders—even Roman influences are to be observed. Thus, as the Armenian rite developed, it underwent the following important "waves" of *external* liturgical influence:[4]

(Paris: Les Éditions du Cerf, 1993); and esp. G. Winkler, *Koriwns Biographie des Mesrop Maštocʿ. Übersetzung und Kommentar*, OCA 245 (Rome: Pontificio Istituto Orientale, 1994), 226–68.

3. Cf. Weber, *Die katholische Kirche in Armenien*, 408–11; A. Baumstark, *Die christlichen Literaturen des Orients* II (Leipzig: G.J. Göschen'sche Verlagsbuchhandlung, 1911), 75–76; E. Hammerschmidt and J. Assfalg, "Abriß der armenischen Kultsymbolik," in *Symbolik des orthodoxen und orientalischen Christentums*, ed. E. Hammerschmidt et al., Symbolik der Religionen 10 (Stuttgart: Hiersemann, 1962): 235–54, here 239 and 248; V. Inglisian, "Die armenische Meßliturgie," in *Eucharistiefeiern in der Christenheit*, Th. Bogler, ed., 30–39, here 30–31 (Maria Laach: Ars liturgica, 1960); G. Winkler, "Zur Geschichte des armenischen Gottesdienstes im Hinblick auf den in mehreren Wellen erfolgten griechischen Einfluß," *Oriens Christianus* 58 (1974): 154–72, here 156–57; R. F. Taft, "The Armenian 'Holy Sacrifice (*Surb Patarag*)' as a Mirror of Armenian Liturgical History," in *The Armenian Christian Tradition. Scholarly Symposium in Honor of the Visit to the Pontifical Oriental Institute, Rome, of His Holiness Karekin I, Supreme Patriarch and Catholicos of All Armenians, December 12, 1996*, ed. R. F. Taft, OCA 254 (Rome: Pontificio Istituto Orientale, 1997), 175–97, here 178, etc.

4. See also Winkler, "Zur Geschichte"; Taft, "Armenian 'Holy Sacrifice,'" 175–79; H.-J. Feulner, "Die Vernetzung der armenischen Athanasius-Anaphora mit den benachbarten Liturgiebereichen," in *The Formation of a Millennial Tradition. 1700 Years of Armenian Christian Witness (301–2001). Scholarly Symposium in Honor of the Visit to the Pontifical Oriental Institute, Rome, of His Holiness Karekin II, Supreme Patriarch and Catholicos of All Armenians, November 11, 2000*, ed. R. F. Taft, OCA 271 (Rome: Pontificio Istituto Orientale, 2004), 43–64, here 45.

- In the foundational period of the Armenian Church, there was an East-Syrian and Cappadocian-Greek influence.[5]

- From the fifth century on we observe considerable hagiopolite influence on the Armenian liturgy, especially in the lectionary and calendar of feasts and commemorations, as Charles Renoux has shown in his very important studies.[6]

- From around the beginning of the second millennium, there was a stronger wave of Byzantine influence.

- Armenian Christians came into contact with the Crusaders as they passed through Asia Minor on their way to the Holy Land, and from the eleventh to the fourteenth centuries we

---

5. See. G. Winkler, *Das armenische Initiationsrituale. Entwicklungsgeschichtliche und liturgievergleichende Untersuchung der Quellen des 3. bis 10. Jahrhunderts*, OCA 217 (Rome: Pontificio Istituto Orientale, 1982); eadem, "The History of the Syriac Prebaptismal Anointing in the Light of the Earliest Armenian Sources," in *Symposium Syriacum 1976*, OCA 205 (Rome: Pontificio Istituto Orientale, 1978), 317–24; eadem, "Zur frühchristlichen Tauftradition in Syrien und Armenien unter Einbezug der Taufe Jesu," *Ostkirchliche Studien* 27 (1978): 281–306; eadem, "The Original Meaning of the Prebaptismal Anointing and Its Implications," *Worship* 52 (1978): 24–45; eadem, "Die Tauf-Hymnen der Armenier. Ihre Affinität mit syrischem Gedankengut," in *Liturgie und Dichtung. Ein interdisziplinäres Kompendium* I, ed. H. Becker and R. Kaczynski, Pietas Liturgica 1 (St. Ottilien: EOS Verlag, 1983): 381–419; eadem, *Über die Entwicklungsgeschichte des armenischen Symbolums. Ein Vergleich mit dem syrischen und griechischen Formelgut unter Einbezug der relevanten georgischen und äthiopischen Quellen*, OCA 262 (Rome: Pontificio Istituto Orientale, 2000); Feulner, "Die Vernetzung der armenischen Athanasius-Anaphora," 52–59.

6. Cf. A. Renoux, *Le codex arménien de Jérusalem 121* I–II, Patrologia Orientalis 35/1+36/2 (Turnhout: Brepols, 1969–71); idem, "Liturgie arménienne et liturgie hiérosolymitaine," in *Liturgie de l'Église particulière et liturgie universelle* [. . .], BEL. Subsidia 7 (Rome: Edizioni Liturgiche, 1976): 275–88; idem, "Liturgie de Jérusalem et lectionnaires arméniens. Vigiles et année liturgique," in *La prière des heures*, Lex Orandi 35 (Paris: Les Éditions du Cerf, 1963), 167–99, etc. See also G. Winkler, "Der armenische Ritus: Bestandsaufnahme und neue Erkenntnisse sowie einige kürzere Notizen zur Liturgie der Georgier," in *The Christian East: Its Institutions and Its Thought. A Critical Reflection. Papers of the International Scholarly Congress for the 75th Anniversary of the Pontifical Oriental Institute, Rome, 30 May–5 June 1993*, ed. R. F. Taft, OCA 251 (Rome: Pontificio Istituto Orientale, 1995), 265–98, here 265–67 (with footnote 2).

have Latin or Roman influence. This includes Armenian translations from the Dominican rite of the Order of Preachers, whose members were active in this area.[7]

The Corpus of Armenian Anaphoras[8]
Already at the beginning of the fifth century we find in the Armenian *Anaphora of Gregory the Illuminator*[9] an example of early Cappadocian or early Syrian influence.[10] And as Hieronymus Engberding demonstrated almost eighty years ago, this anaphora attributed to

7. Cf. G. Winkler, "Armenia and the Gradual Decline of Its Traditional Liturgical Practices as a Result of the Expanding Influence of the Holy See from the 11th to the 14th Century," in *Liturgie de l'Église particulière et liturgie universelle* [. . .], BEL.Subsidia 7 (Rome: Edizioni Liturgiche, 1976): 329–68; D. Findikyan, "L'influence latine sur la liturgie arménienne," in *Roma-Armenia. Grande Salle Sixtine, Bibliothèque Apostolique du Vatican, 25 Mars–16 Juillet 1999*, ed. C. Mutafian (Rome: Edizioni De Luca, 1999): 340–44.
8. See Winkler, "Zur Geschichte," 157–61, 170–72; eadem, "Armenischer Ritus," 274–77; F. Köckert, *Sowrb Patarag—"Heiliges Opfer." Texte und Untersuchungen zur Liturgie der armenisch-apostolischen orthodoxen Kirche*, unpublished doctoral thesis (Halle: 1986), 114–17; Taft, "Armenian 'Holy Sacrifice,'" 180–83; H.-J. Feulner, *Die armenische Athanasius-Anaphora. Kritische Edition, Übersetzung und liturgievergleichender Kommentar*, Anaphorae Orientales 1–Anaphorae Armeniacae 1 (Rome: Pontificio Istituto Orientale, 2001): 77–84; idem, "Zu den Editionen orientalischer Anaphoren," in *Crossroad of Cultures. Studies in Liturgy and Patristics in Honor of Gabriele Winkler*, ed. H.-J. Feulner, E. Velkovska, and R. F. Taft, OCA 260 (Rome: Pontificio Istituto Orientale, 2000), 251–82, here 277–80.
9. J. Catergian, *Die Liturgien bei den Armeniern. Fünfzehn Texte und Untersuchungen*, ed. J. Dashian (Vienna: Mxit'arean Tparan, 1897), 120–58 [Armenian text]; A. (Ch.) Renoux, "L'Anaphore arménienne de Saint Grégoire l'Illum[in]ateur," in *L'Eucharistie d'Orient et d'Occident. Semaine liturgique de l'Institute Saint-Serge* II, ed. B. Botte et al., Lex Orandi 47 (Paris: Les Éditions du Cerf, 1970), 83–108 [with French translation]; E. Renhart, "Die älteste armenische Anaphora," in *Armenische Liturgien. Ein Blick auf eine ferne christliche Kultur*, ed. E. Renhart and J. Dum-Tragut, Heiliger Dienst, Ergänzungsband 2 (Graz/Salzburg: Schnider Verlag, 2001): 93–241, here 148–79 [Armenian text with German translation].
10. See now G. Winkler, *Die Anaphora des Basilius. Edition der beiden armenischen Redaktionen und der relevanten Fragmente, Übersetzung und Zusammenschau aller Versionen im Licht der orientalischen Überlieferungen*, Anaphorae

Gregory the Illuminator in medieval manuscripts is actually an early redaction of the *Anaphora of Basil* translated into Armenian (= *arm Bas I*).[11] Liturgical translations into Armenian were abundant during this remarkably productive "Golden Age."[12] By the end of the fifth century, the Armenians had translated or even created four other anaphoras: the *Anaphora of Sahak* (= *arm Sah*),[13] the *Anaphora of Gregory of Nazianzen* (= *arm Greg*),[14] the *Anaphora of Cyril* (= *arm Cyr*),[15] and finally the *Anaphora of Athanasius* (= *arm Ath*).[16] The Armenian *Anaphora of Athanasius*, used today whenever the Eucharist or Divine Liturgy (*Surb Patarag*) is celebrated, seems to have replaced the other Armenian anaphoras by the end of the ninth century at the latest.

In this context it may be interesting to invite attention to five other Armenian translations or adaptations of non-Armenian Eucharistic liturgies: between the eleventh and fourteenth centuries the *Anaphora*

Orientales 2–Anaphorae Armeniacae 2 (Rome: Pontificio Istituto Orientale, 2005).

11. Cf. H. Engberding, *Das Eucharistische Hochgebet der Basileiosliturgie. Textgeschichtliche Untersuchung und kritische Ausgabe*, Theologie des christlichen Ostens 1 (Münster: Aschendorff , 1931), lxxxiii; Winkler, "Zur Geschichte," 157–59.

12. On the Armenian translations in antiquity, see L. Ter-Petrossian, *Ancient Armenian Translations* (New York: St. Vartan Press, 1992), 11ff.

13. Catergian and Dashian, 222–42; P. Ferhat, "Denkmäler altarmenischer Meßliturgie 2: Die angebliche Liturgie des hl. Katholikos Sahak," *Oriens Christanus* 11 (1913): 18–25 [Latin translation]; A. Hänggi and I. Pahl, eds., *Prex Eucharistica* I: *Textus e variis liturgiis antiquioribus selecti*, Spicilegium Friburgense 12, 3rd ed. (Fribourg: Éditions Universitaires,1998), 332–36 [Latin translation].

14. Catergian and Dashian, 244–54; P. Ferhat, "Denkmäler altarmenischer Meßliturgie 1: Eine dem hl. Gregor von Nazianz zugeschriebene Liturgie," *Oriens Christanus* 9 (1911): 205–13 [Latin translation]; Hänggi and Pahl, *Prex Eucharistica* I, 327–31 [Latin translation].

15. Catergian and Dashian, 256–367; A. Rücker, "Denkmäler altarmenischer Meßliturgie 4: Die Anaphora des Patriarchen Kyrillos von Alexandrien," *Oriens Christanus* 23 (1927): 256–67 [Latin translation]; Hänggi and Pahl, *Prex Eucharistica* I, 337–41 [Latin translation].

16. Catergian and Dashian, 616–721; F. E. Brightman, *Liturgies Eastern and Western* (Oxford: Clarendon Press, 1896), 412–57 [English translation]; Hänggi and Pahl, *Prex Eucharistica* I, 320–26 [Latin translation]. See the critical edition and German translation: Feulner, *Athanasius-Anaphora*, 174–223.

of Ignatius[17] and the *Anaphora of James;*[18] furthermore the Armenian *Anaphora of John Chrysostom* (= *arm Chrys*)[19] presumably translated from the Greek in the twelfth/thirteenth centuries; another Armenian translation of the developed Byzantine form of the *Anaphora of Basil* (= *arm Bas II*);[20] and the Roman-Latin *Ordo Missae*,[21] translated most likely by *Nersēs Lambronacʻi* (d. 1198) in the newly erected Armenian kingdom in Cilicia. We also have an Armenian translation of the Byzantine Lenten rite of the presanctified gifts.[22]

The Armenian Liturgical Commentaries on the Divine Liturgy

In addition to the manuscript texts of the *Armenian Liturgy of St. Athanasius* that have been in use, there are several commentaries on the Armenian Eucharistic liturgy that are to be counted among the most important historical sources for the study of the Armenian Divine Liturgy.[23] Such Armenian liturgical commentaries are explanations of the liturgical services composed by church writers, usually

17. Catergian and Dashian, 389–411; A. Rücker, "Denkmäler altarmenischer Meßliturgie 5: Die Anaphora des hl. Ignatius von Antiochien," *Oriens Christanus* 27 (1930): 58–79 [Latin translation].

18. Catergian and Dashian, 435–50; A. Baumstark, "Denkmäler altarmenischer Meßliturgie 3: Die armenische Rezension der Jakobusliturgie," *Oriens Christanus* 15/16 (1918): 13–27 [Latin translation]; Hänggi and Pahl, *Prex Eucharistica* I, 342–46 [Latin translation].

19. Catergian and Dashian, 353–84; G. Aucher, "La versione armena della Liturgia di San Giovanni Crisostomo," in Χ*PYCOCTOMIKA* (Rome: Pustet, 1908), 387–94 [Italian translation].

20. Catergian and Dashian, 180–216.

21. Ibid., 455–66.

22. Ibid., 414–29.

23. Cf. also Köckert, *Sowrb Patarag*, 112–13; A. Gerhards, "Der Stellenwert der Anaphora in den Liturgiekommentaren des Orients," *Ephemerides Liturgicae* 107 (1993): 209–23, here 218; A. (Ch.) Renoux, "Les commentaries liturgiques arméniens," *Mystagogie. Pensée liturgique d'aujourd'hui et liturgie ancienne* [. . .], ed. in A.M. Triacca – A. Pistoia, BEL.Subsidia 70 (Rome: Edizioni Liturgiche, 1993): 277–308, here 299–306; Winkler, "Armenischer Ritus," 276–77; Taft, "Armenian, 'Holy Sacrifice,'" 183–84. On the Byzantine liturgies, see the studies of R. Bornert, *Les commentaries byzantins de la Divine Liturgie du VII*e *au XV*e *siècle*, Archives de l'Orient chrétien 9 (Paris: Institut français d'études byzantines, 1966); and H.-J. Schulz, *Die byzantinische Liturgie. Glaubenszeugnis und Symbolgestalt*, Sophia 5, 3rd ed. (Trier: Paulinus Verlag, 2000) = *The Byzantine Liturgy: Symbolic Structure and Faith Expression* (New York: Pueblo, 1986).

monks or bishops. Since many of the available manuscripts of Eucharistic texts contain only the anaphoral section of the *Surb Patarag*, we must turn to the Armenian liturgical commentaries for the complete *Ordo*. Of the extant classic commentaries on the Armenian liturgy, only three of the nine that deal with the Eucharist have been published.

- The earliest extant text of the *Armenian Liturgy of St. Athanasius* is contained in a formulary dating from approximately 950. However, this formulary must be extracted from the liturgical commentary of Bishop *Xosrov Anjewac'i*, the father of *Grigor Narekac'i (= Gregory of Narek)*, whose explanation of the liturgical text begins after the Creed. He wrote it as a sort of liturgical catechism for the faithful of his diocese.[24] As our first witness to the Armenian *Anaphora of Athanasius*—the formulary that would eventually become the only Armenian Eucharistic Prayer in use—*Xosrov's* significance for the history of the Armenian liturgy cannot be overestimated.

- Compared with the commentary of *Xosrov Anjewac'i*, the liturgical commentary of *Nersēs Lambronac'i* on the *Armenian Liturgy of St. Athanasius* from 1192 is more extensive. In addition to the Anaphora, it contains the entire Liturgy of the Word and the preceding preparatory rites, including two prayers of *Gregory of Narek*.[25] *Nersēs Lambronac'i* was archbishop of Tarsus in

24. Catergian and Dashian, 276–92; Ł. Ališan, ed., *Meknut'iwn ałōt'ic' pataragin* (Venice: 1869) [Armenian]; P. Vetter, *Chosroae Magni episcope monophysitici explicatio precum missae* (Freiburg: Herder, 1880) [Latin translation]; S. Salaville, "L'explication de la messe de l'arménien Chosrov (959). Théologie et liturgie," *Échos d'Orient* 14 (1940/42): 349–82 [with a French translation]; S.P. Cowe, *Commentary on the Divine Liturgy by Xosrov Anjewac'i* (New York: St. Vartan Press, 1991), 95–231 [Armenian text with English translation and commentary]. On the person and works of Xosrov Anjewac'i, cf. N. Połarean, *Hay grołner* (Jerusalem: Tparan Srboc' Yakobeanc,' 1971), 141–43; Cowe, *Commentary*, 3–18.

25. Catergian and Dashian, 543–50; *Xorhrdacut'iwn srbazan pataragi bac'atrut'eamb Nersēsi Lambronac'woy* (Jerusalem: 1842) [Armenian]; *Xorhrdacut'iwnk' i kargs ekełec'woy ew meknut'iwn xorhrdoy pataragin* (Venice: 1847), 193–226 [Armenian]; E. Dulaurier, *Recueil des historiens des Croisades. Documents arméniens* I (Paris: Imprimerie Impériale, 1859), 569–78 [French translation of some parts]; B. Talatinian, "Florilegio dall'opera «Spiegazione della Santa Messe» di Nerses Lambronatzi, Arcivescovo armeno di Tarso (1152–1198)," in *Studia Hierosolymitana* III, ed. G.C. Bottini, Studium Biblicum Franciscanum. Collectio

Cilicia and nephew of the Armenian Catholicos *Nersēs Šnorhali* (d. 1173). He was influenced, apart from his own tradition, by the Byzantine and later also by the Latin-Roman liturgy.[26]

- Finally we have the liturgical commentaries of *Movsēs Erznkac'i* (d. ca. 1323)[27] and of *Yovhannēs Arčišec'i* (d. ca. 1330),[28] both amplifications of the commentaries of *Xosrov Anjewac'i* and of *Nersēs Lambronac'i*.[29] Other anonymous commentaries on the full liturgy surviving in later codices of the seventeenth century await identification and research.

THE STUDY OF ARMENIAN ANAPHORAS

The investigation of the Armenian anaphoras began on a large scale with the monumental study of the Armenian monks of the Viennese Mekhitarist Congregation, namely, Joseph Catergian (= Y. Gat'rcean) and Jacob Dashian (= Y. Tašean),[30] published in 1897 in Armenian.[31]

---

maior 30 (Jerusalem: Tip. PP. Francescani, 1982), 193–245 [Italian translation]; I. Kéchichian, *Nersès de Lambron (1153–1192). Explication de la Divine Liturgie*, Recherches 9, Nouvelle Série. B. Orient Chrétien (Beyrouth: Dar El-Machreq, 2000), 181–270 [French translation]. On the person and works of Nersēs Lambronac'i, cf. Połarean, *Hay grołner*, 253–59; B. L. Zekiyan, "Nersēs de Lambron," in *Dictionnaire de Spiritualité* XI (Paris: Beauchesne, 1982), col. 122–34.

26. Cf. Winkler, "Armenia and the Gradual Decline," 340–43; B. L. Zekiyan, "Les relations arméno-byzantines après la mort de St. Nersès Šnorhali," *Jahrbuch der österreichischen Byzantinistik* 32/4 (1982): 331–37, here 333–35; Köckert, *Sowrb Patarag*, 113; Renoux, "Commentaires," 303–4.

27. On his commentary of the Divine Liturgy dated 1293, cf. E. Petrosyan, "Movsēs Erznkac'u Hawak'umn hamaṙōt meknut'ean srboy pataragin, zor yaraǰagoyn arareal ē srboc' lusawor harc'n ašxatut'yunə," *Ejmiacin* (1973): 14–20 (I); (1973) 43–48 (II). On the person and works of Movsēs Erznkac'i, cf. Połarean, *Hay grołner*, 347–50.

28. Cf. Catergian and Dashian, 513–18; *Hamaṙōt Meknut'win Pataragi* (Constantinopel: 1717, 1799; Calcutta: 1839), Armenian. On the person and works of Yovhannēs Arčišec'i, cf. Połarean, *Hay grołner*, 354–55.

29. Cf. Renoux, "Commentaires," 305–6; Cowe, *Commentary*, 87–92.

30. Cf. J. Catergian, *Die Liturgien bei den Armeniern. Fünfzehn Texte und Untersuchungen*, ed. J. Dashian (Vienna: Mxit'arean Tparan, 1897). Cf. also G. Winkler, "On the Formation of the Armenian Anaphoras: A Preliminary Overview," in Ervine, *Worship Traditions in Armenia and the Neighboring Christian East*, 59–86, here 60–61.

31. This work came to the attention of F. C. Conybeare, who presented a short overview of it in 1898 in *The American Journal of Theology* 2 (1898): 705–7.

Armenian Anaphoras	Armenian Main Anaphora	Anaphoras from other Churches
• *Anaphora of Gregory the Illuminator*[32] (= first Armenian redaction of the *Anaphora of Basil* !) (Fragment of this anaphora in *Buzandaran Patmut'iwnk'* V, 28)[33]	**ANAPHORA OF ATHANASIUS**	*Byzantine Formularies:* • *Anaphora of Basil* (= second Armenian redaction of the *Anaphora of Basil*) • *Anaphora of Chrysostom* (• Rite of the Presanctified Gifts)
• *Anaphora of Sahak*		*Syrian Formularies:* • *Anaphora of James* • *Anaphora of Ignatius of Antioch*
• *Anaphora of Gregory of Nazianzen*		
• *Anaphora of Cyril of Alexandria*		*Roman-Latin Formulary:* • Canon Missae of the Roman Church

The significance of Catergian's and Dashian's edition and study of the Armenian anaphoras lies in their attempt to prove that the earliest Armenian anaphoras reflect close ties to patristic Greek texts of Cappadocia, above all those of *Gregory of Nazianzen*.[34] Catergian thought that several of these Armenian anaphoras derived from Cappadocia, where they allegedly constituted a "Codex Liturgicus" of the Church of Caesarea, which was subsequently translated into Armenian during the fifth century through the efforts of Catholicos *Yovhannēs Mandakuni* (478–90).[35] According to Catergian, the nucleus of the five anaphoras (of *Basil*, *Sahak*, *Gregory*, *Cyril*, and *Athanasius*) essentially goes back

32. In the Armenian manuscript tradition this anaphora is attributed to *Gregory the Illuminator*; cf. Catergian and Dashian, 130–35.

33. Cf. Catergian and Dashian, 96–98, 130–35; N. G. Garsoïan, *The Epic Histories Attributed to P'awstos Buzand (Buzandaran Patmut'iwnk'). Translation and Commentary* (Cambridge, MA: Harvard University Press, 1989), 208–9 (321, notes 7–13) and 24 with note 100.

34. Cf. Catergian and Dashian, 219, 252, 336–40.

35. Ibid., 217–19, 328–29, 336–40.

to *Gregory Nazianzen*,[36] a theory that did not find unconditional support even from Dashian, the coeditor.[37] The theory of the alleged Cappadocian underpinning of the earliest strata of the Armenian anaphoras was later extended to include the claim of major Byzantine influences on the Armenian rite.[38]

An enormous step in advancing our knowledge of one of the most significant anaphoras of the entire Christian tradition was taken in Hieronymus Engberding's famous doctoral dissertation of 1931 on the various redactions of the *Anaphora of Basil*. His stemma on the evolution of Basil proved the overriding importance of its two Armenian recensions for the study of this ancient anaphora.[39] In the late nineties, Gabriele Winkler broke new ground with her pioneering work on *Basil* and its various redactions, having subjected Engberding's findings[40] to closer scrutiny. She was able to prove that the Armenian text of the *Anaphora of Gregory the Illuminator* (Lusaworič')[41] (= *arm Bas* I) reflects the more original shape of Basil and that the Egyptian versions mirror its secondary evolution. She could also

36. Ibid.

37. Ibid., 340.

38. See also Winkler, "Zur Geschichte"; M. Findikyan, "Bishop Step'anos Siwnec'i: A Source for the Study of Medieval Armenian Liturgy," *Ostkirchliche Studien* 44 (1995): 171–96, here 172.

39. Cf. Engberding, *Das Eucharistische Hochgebet der Basileiosliturgie*, lxxxvi–lxxxvii.

40. Cf. G. Winkler, "Zur Erforschung orientalischer Anaphoren in liturgievergleichender Sicht I: Anmerkungen zur Oratio post Sanctus und Anamnese bis Epiklese," *Orientalia Christiana Periodica* 63 (1997): 363–420; eadem, "Zur Erforschung orientalischer Anaphoren in liturgievergleichender Sicht II: Das Formelgut der Oratio post Sanctus und Anamnese sowie Interzessionen und die Taufbekenntnisse," in *Acts of the International Congress "Comparative Liturgy Fifty Years after Anton Baumstark (1872–1948)."* Rome, 25–29 September 1998, ed. R. F. Taft and G. Winkler, OCA 265 (Rome: Pontificio Istituto Orientale, 2001), 671–88; eadem, "Zur Erforschung orientalischer Anaphoren in liturgievergleichender Sicht III: Der Hinweis auf die ,die Gaben' bzw. ,das Opfer' bei der Epiklese," in *Das Opfer. Biblischer Anspruch und liturgische Gestalt*, ed. A. Gerhards and K. Richter, Quaestiones Disputatae 186 (Freiburg: Herder, 2000): 216–33, etc.

41. So in both codices of the Armenian redaction, *Cod. 17* from Lyon and *Cod. 6* from Munich.

show the (East) Syriac features of that anaphora clearly reflected in the Armenian text. [42]

These findings had considerable repercussions for the hitherto held assumption of an exclusively Greek foundation for the Antiochene type of anaphoras.[43] Contrary to Catergian's claim that the *Anaphora of Athanasius* (= *arm Ath*) essentially went back to *Gregory Nazianzen*, and was then translated into Armenian during the fifth century by *Yovhannēs Mandakuni*,[44] two things were now clear: neither could this anaphora be associated with the fourth or fifth centuries, nor did it reflect pre-Byzantine Cappadocian connections.

ANALYTICAL REMARKS ON
THE *ANAPHORA OF ATHANASIUS*

Although *arm Ath* shows several connections with the first Armenian translation of the *Anaphora of Basil* (*arm Bas I*) that emerge at closer scrutiny, *arm Ath* is rather different from *arm Bas I*. This difference is quite obvious throughout the anaphora: its conspicuously short prayers before and after the *Sanctus*, the distinct transition to the *Sanctus*, the presence of the *Benedictus* (still missing in the first Armenian recension of Basil), as well as distinctions in the first part of the anamnesis, the epiclesis, and the intercessions. Borrowings from the first Armenian redaction of Basil are visible, for example, in the *Opening Dialogue* (see appendix I.),[45] the phrasing of the *Words of Institution* (see

---

42. Cf. G. Winkler, *Die Anaphora des Basilius. Edition der beiden armenischen Redaktionen und der relevanten Fragmente, Übersetzung und Zusammenschau aller Versionen im Licht der orientalischen Überlieferungen*, Anaphorae Orientales 2– Anaphorae Armeniacae 2 (Rome: Pontificio Istituto Orientale, 2005), [literature]. It should be noted that Gabriele Winkler is going to prepare critical editions of Armenian anaphoras (in the series "Anaphorae Armeniacae" of the Pontifical Oriental Institute in Rome), such as the *Anaphora of Sahak* and others. For the Egyptian redaction(s) of the *Anaphora of Basil*, see also A. Budde, *Die ägyptische Basilius-Anaphora. Text – Kommentar – Geschichte*, Jerusalemer Theologisches Forum 7 (Münster: Aschendorff, 2004).

43. See also the summary of G. Winkler, "On the Formation of the Armenian Anaphoras: A Preliminary Overview," in Ervine, *Worship Traditions in Armenia and the Neighboring Christian East*, 59–86, here 61–69.

44. Cf. Catergian and Dashian, 219, 338–39.

45. Cf. Feulner, *Athanasius-Anaphora*, 227–54.

app. V.),[46] the second part of the *Anamnesis* (see app. VI.),[47] and some elements of the *Anaphoral Intercessions* (see app. VIII.).[48] The inclusion in *arm Ath* of several features common in the Syrian tradition, some of them being present also in Ethiopian anaphoras, is of special interest, for these features seem to point to the sixth century as a possible date for the origin of *arm Ath*.

The Introduction to the Anaphora[49]

The *Exhortation of the Deacon* that immediately precedes the beginning of the anaphora (app. I.1.) stems in its sections "Let us stand in awe" and "Mercy and peace" either directly from the Byzantine tradition, in which these two appear together from of old, or is to be traced—through the mediation of the Armenian *Anaphora of Basil I* (= *arm Bas I*)—to a common pre-Byzantine source. The sections "to you, O God" and "offers himself as a sacrifice" were interpolated as Armenian particularities only later, before the tenth century. The initial salutation of the priest at the beginning of the *Opening Dialogue* (app. I.2.) in *arm Ath* ("The grace, the love") points to a trinitarian formula that strongly deviates from the Pauline salutation formula in 2 Corinthians 13:13, while being strongly similar to *arm Bas I* and *arm Greg*.

The second part of the *Opening Dialogue*, again, matches that of *arm Bas I* and *arm Greg*. The diaconal formula "lift up your minds" follows the Antiochian tradition with its *mitk'* (= "mind"). The addition "in the fear of God" is also found in *arm Bas I* and is probably of Armenian origin. The final part of the *Opening Dialogue* corresponds to most of the Armenian anaphoras. Here the Armenians appended the secondary "with the whole heart," which is likewise an Armenian particularity.

The diaconal exhortation "lift up your minds" is preceded in today's Armenian liturgy by the awkwardly interpolated "The doors, the doors! With all wisdom and good heed." This interpolation, evidenced in only a few of the oldest manuscripts, stems from the Byzantine rite.

46. Ibid., 306–36.

47. Ibid., 338–65.

48. Ibid., 412–53, esp. 446–50; idem, "Das anaphorische Fürbittgebet und die Diptychen nach der kritischen Edition der armenischen Athanasius-Anaphora," in Taft and Winkler, *Acts of the International Congress "Comparative Liturgy Fifty Years after Anton Baumstark (1872–1948),"* 623–70, esp. 660–65.

49. See appendix I. For details, see Feulner, *Athanasius-Anaphora*, 230–54.

There, however, it is placed just before the Creed—just as in the liturgical commentary of *Nersēs Lambronac'i.*

The Oratio ante Sanctus (Prayer Before the Sanctus) [50]

The *Oratio ante Sanctus* (app. II.) is prayed silently by the priest, with folded hands. Its theme is the praise of God (app. II.1.), which becomes one with the praise of the angels (app. II.2.) in the following hymn, the "Thrice-Holy" of the *Sanctus*. In *arm Ath* the *Oratio ante Sanctus* has essentially been determined by the redaction of *Nersēs Lambronac'i*, especially with regard to the various addresses utilized for God. As in many other anaphoras, the *Oratio ante Sanctus* latches on to the preceding *Opening Dialogue* with the words "It is truly proper and right." Compared to other Armenian anaphoras, here the theme of the praise of God is pursued rather briefly, with but two verbs ("to adore" and "to glorify").

The *Transition to the Sanctus-Benedictus* (app. II.2.) is also relatively brief. It is missing a detailed description of the angelic powers. Moreover, the term *vigilant ones* ("vigilant angels" [= "wakeful ones"]), which entered this anaphora through Syrian channels, is the only example of this term being used with reference to the angels within the Armenian anaphoral tradition.

The Sanctus-Benedictus [51]

As distinct from biblical witness (Isa 6:3), *arm Ath* created its own address: "Heaven and earth are full of *your* glory" (app. III.1.). One can assume that the *Benedictus* (app. III.2.), having originated in Syria, became commonplace in the Armenian liturgy in the ninth and tenth centuries at the latest. The biblical "Hosanna" is translated as *awrhnut'iwn* ("praise"). The underlying Greek participle ἐρχόμενος of the New Testament text (Matt 21:9) is divided into an imperfect and a future form: "who did come and are to come," which is typical of the Syrian liturgical realm. So here we can assume a further trace of Syrian influence on *arm Ath*.

The Oratio post Sanctus (The Prayer after the Sanctus I) [52]

In the *Oratio post Sanctus* (app. IV.), the theme of thanksgiving is in the foreground. This thanksgiving is devoted to God's economy for

---

50. See appendix II. For details, see Feulner, *Athanasius-Anaphora*, 256–71.
51. See appendix III. For details, see Feulner, *Athanasius-Anaphora*, 274–83.
52. See appendix IV. For details, see Feulner, *Athanasius-Anaphora*, 284–304.

the salvation of mankind, and the underlying structure is similar to the *post Sanctus* in *arm Bas I* and *arm Sah*. The *Oratio post Sanctus*, which is said by the priest quietly during the singing of the *Sanctus*, begins with the triple repetition of "Holy [*surb*]" (app. IV.1.), and thus dovetails with the immediately preceding *Sanctus-Benedictus*. This manner of repeating the *Sanctus* (app. IV.1.) is commonly found in West-Syrian anaphoras, so that we must presume a Syrian origin of this first part of the *Oratio post Sanctus*.

The following *Pars Oeconomiae Veteris Testamenti* (part containing the Old Testament saving economy) (app. IV.2.) is relatively brief, compared to many other anaphoras of the East. Here the salvific moments of the Old Testament are commemorated only summarily, by mentioning a few events; the human being who has fallen to sin is to be consoled by the prophets, the reception of the Law, etc.

The *Pars Christologica* (christological part) is divided into two sections: (a) the *Pars Christologica I* (app. IV.3.), which, on the one hand, with its strong Eucharistic theme (cf. also Heb 9 and 10) is to be traced to the period around or after the sixth century, and, on the other hand, with its conspicuous juxtapositions (debtor–debt, sacrificial victim–anointed one, etc.) betrays a closeness to Syrian sources; and (b) the soteriologically very significant *Pars Christologica II* (app. IV.4.), which, with its mention of the incarnation from the Virgin Mary, of the human life of Jesus with all its hardships, and of the voluntary death on the cross, seems to be based on the formulae of a baptismal creed. There are undeniable correlations between the christological part of the *Oratio post Sanctus* and the formulae of baptismal creeds of the East.

The mention of the "true" incarnation of the Lord "without illusion [*aṙanc' c'noric'*]" (app. IV.4.) and "through union *without confusion* [*anšp'ot' miut'iwn*]" of the divine and human natures must evidently be understood in an antidocetic vein. The human nature of Christ is described with all the suffering of human existence, but "without sin [*aṙanc' mełac'*]," which sums up the Armenian position from the sixth century on in the so-called "Aphthartodocetic" controversy.

The Words of Institution[53]

In the manuscript sources there are many deviations and variant readings of the *Words of Institution* (V.) in *arm Ath*. The form found in *Xosrov Anjewac'i* is relatively simple, while the *Words of Institu-*

---

53. See appendix V. For details, see Feulner, *Athanasius-Anaphora*, 306–36.

tion of *arm Ath*—as witnessed in the manuscript evidence—matches that of the liturgical commentary of *Nersēs Lambronac'i* (there are also similarities with *arm Bas I* and *arm Greg*). Many anaphoras have a "time-specification" (e.g., "on the night" or something similar) with reference to Jesus' Last Supper with his disciples. But in *arm Ath* there is no "time-specification" in the *Introduction to Words over the Bread* (app. V.1.), which rather subtly distinguishes this introduction from the preceding *Oratio post Sanctus*. It is in the *Introduction to Words over the Bread* (app. V.1.), and only here, that the mention of Jesus' hands is accentuated through five attributes ("holy, divine, immortal, spotless and creative"). This reflects a probable influence both of *arm Bas I* ("holy, spotless, immaculate, almighty") as well as and especially the liturgical commentary of *Nersēs Lambronac'i* ("holy, divine, immortal, creative"). Hence, the Lord's actions are in both the *Introductions to Words over the Bread and the Cup* (app. V.1. and V.3.) arranged with precise symmetry. Here *arm Ath* and *arm Cyr* correspond completely with each another.

The reference to those "who were seated [at the table]" (= the disciples) with Jesus (app. V.1. and V.3.) is made in the Armenian liturgy and is evidently influenced by *arm Bas I* (here only in the *Introduction to Words over the Bread*) and *arm Greg* (but this "seated [at the table]" is not found in the liturgical commentary of *Xosrov Anjewac'i*). The Armenian anaphoras also refer time and again to the disciples as "chosen [əntreal]." In addition to this, in *arm Ath* the mention of the disciples in both the *Introductions to Words over the Bread and over the Cup* is completely symmetrical. Through their conspicuous asymmetry, the *Dominical Words over the Bread and Cup* (app. V.2. and V.4.) differ noticeably from the intentionally strict symmetry of their preceding introductions. The only completely symmetrical segments are the statements of soteriological objective, namely, "for the expiation and remission of sins" at the *Dominical Words over the Bread and Cup*, which by reason of its duplication is probably of Syrian origin. The same duplication is also found in the epiclesis (app. VII.3.).

In most manuscripts of *arm Ath*, the *Dominical Words over the Bread* are comprised of a combination of Matthew 26:26 and Luke 22:19 (with 1 Cor 11:23). The *Dominical Words over the Cup*, on the other hand, clearly echo Matthew 26:27-28 (with Mark 14:24). Many manuscripts of *arm Ath* are curiously missing the word "take [aṙēk']" in the *Dominical Words over the Cup* (app. V.4.), which is to be explained by a secondary cessation of the preceding symmetry.

In summary, it can be said that the *Words of Institution* in *arm Ath* are not of particularly ancient origin, because of their parallels and strict coordination with Scripture. Furthermore, the respective structures of the *Introductions* and the *Dominical Words* seem somewhat developed, albeit to a rather humble extent. Overall, the *Words of Institution* (as well as the epicletic petitions) of *arm Ath* demonstrate the tendency of the Armenian liturgy toward *symmetry-construction*.

The Anamnesis and Oblation[54]

The *Anamnesis* of *arm Ath* comprises two anamnetic parts (app. VI.2. and VI.3.), which had already been brought together into one whole before the tenth century. In both parts it is *God the Father* who is addressed (in the liturgical commentary of *Xosrov Anjewac'i*, the one addressed is yet indefinite). The *Anamnetic Part I* (app. VI.2.) is dominated by the theme of Christ's descent into Hades with his human body. This *Descensus* motif, which stems from the Syrian tradition, was possibly originally located in the *Oratio post Sanctus*. It probably landed in the *Anamnesis* of *arm Ath* from *arm Bas I*, where this motif is found in the *Oratio post Sanctus* (which is primary).

The *Oblation* "And we offer to you yours of your own from all and for all" (app. VI.4.) of the *Anamnetic Part II* is still missing in the liturgical commentary of *Xosrov Anjewac'i*. According to manuscript evidence, however, this independent *Oblation* apparently entered *arm Ath* as a standard segment of its formulary by the twelfth century, regardless of the fact that several older manuscripts are still missing it. The *Anamnetic Part II* (app. VI.3.) has—already at its beginning—its first oblation formula, "bringing forth the saving mystery," which can be traced to the eighth century because of the slavish reproduction of its key phrase (*yaṙaǰ bereal*, "*while offering . . .*"). Thus it is older than the second *Oblation*, "And we offer to you yours."

The chronological commemoration of Christ's salvific deeds in the *Anamnetic Part II* (app. VI.3.) is arranged according to the Creed and is thematically reminiscent of *arm Bas I*. But the precise formulation of the separate commemorations corresponds largely to *arm Sah*. The *ekphonesis* (spoken aloud) "from all and for all," which is likewise still absent from the liturgical commentary of *Xosrov Anjewac'i*, is to be understood—as it is in all other anaphoras of the East—as an introduction to the ensuing praise and thanksgiving. The hymn of *Praise and*

---

54. See appendix VI. For details, see Feulner, *Athanasius-Anaphora*, 338–77.

Thanksgiving of *arm Ath* is influenced by *arm Bas I*. The earliest witness to its present-day form is *Nersēs Lambronacʿi*.

The clearly secondary construct of the *Transition to Epiclesis* (app. VI.6.), whose concluding doxology does not appear in full in all manuscripts, deals with both the unworthiness of the celebrant and God's forbearance. By thus severing the pristine unity of praise and epiclesis, this *Transition* betrays its later origins. And here, also, one finds thematic similarities to *arm Bas I*.

Another later interpolation in *arm Ath* is the *Hymn to the Father* (app. VI.1.), which is only evidenced in a small number of manuscripts beginning with the fourteenth century.

The Epiclesis[55]

The *Epiclesis* in *arm Ath* can be categorized as a *consecratory Spirit*-epiclesis (app. VII.), of the kind we already find in the so-called *Catechetical Lectures* of Cyril of Jerusalem (*Catech. Myst.* V, 7). As in other Eucharistic anaphoras of the Antiochian liturgical family, it is located in *arm Ath* between the *Anamnesis* and the *Intercessions*. In the liturgical commentary of *Xosrov Anjewacʿi*, the epiclesis (still without rubrics) is a comprehensive whole, without the repetition of certain petitions. The addressee of this epiclesis is *God the Father*, who is petitioned to send down the Holy Spirit, specifically upon *the congregation* and upon *the offered Eucharistic gifts*. Concerning the verb utilized for the *Epiclesis* (*aṙakʿea*, "send") in *arm Ath* (app. VII.3.a.), it conforms with all other Armenian anaphoras—with the sole exception of *arm Bas II*. The verb that describes the transformation of the Eucharistic gifts is *arascʿes*, which corresponds to the Greek verb ποιέω ("to make"). In the concluding formula of the entire consecratory prayer over the bread *and* wine (app. VII.3.c.), the consecratory moment is once again stressed through the verb *pʿoxarkem* ("to change"), which corresponds to the Greek verb μεταβάλλω. Here one must presume the influence of the Byzantine *Anaphora of Chrysostom* (= *byz Chrys*). The secondary *concluding consecratory formula*, "changing them by your Holy Spirit" (app. VII.3.c.), is taken directly from *byz Chrys* and is present in the Armenian epiclesis from the thirteenth century. The entire consecratory petition over the bread and wine is a later interpolation, probably only since *Nersēs Lambronacʿi*.

---

55. See appendix VII. For details, see Feulner, *Athanasius-Anaphora*, 378–411.

An additional interpolation, found only in a few manuscripts from the beginning of the fourteenth century, is the *Hymn to the Son* (app. VII.2.), which, together with the two other hymns to the Father and the Holy Spirit, forms one comprehensive piece that could possibly be traced to *Nersēs Šnorhali*.

The *Remission of Sins* in connection with the epiclesis is only found in a few Armenian anaphoras, and there it is only in the simplest form ("for remission of sins"). But in *arm Ath* this petition is duplicated as "for expiation and for remission of sins" (app. VII.3.d.), probably so as to match the corresponding *double-petition* for *Remission of Sins* found in the *Words of Institution* (app. V.2./4.). This prayer of absolution stems from Syro-Palestinian liturgical areas, where it was widespread. Here, once again, we can observe the characteristic tendency of Armenian liturgy toward *symmetry-construction*, expressed not only in the constructs of the *Words of Institution* but in the forms chosen for the epicletic petitions as well.

The Intercessions and Diptychs[56]

The *Anaphoral Intercessions* and the *Diptychs* (app. VIII.) present us with the most complicated questions of *arm Ath*, which can only be partly resolved here. According to the manuscript evidence of *arm Ath* and the *Textus receptus*, there is a duplication of the *Anaphoral Intercessions* (app. VIII.1. and VIII.3./5.), probably the result of the cross-pollination of two different traditions. Hieronymus Engberding supposed that the *Anaphoral Intercessions I* belonged to the more pristine text. One can agree with Engberding's conclusion, but not with the argumentation he uses to arrive at it. It must also be noted that *arm Bas I* influenced the development of *arm Ath*. Because of this duplication, the *Anaphoral Intercessions* (*I* and *II*) in *arm Ath* present us with a construct of great complexity, the likes of which we do not come across in any other Armenian anaphora.

The petition for "seasonableness" of weather and fertility of the fields is also found in *arm Bas I*. It actually belongs, however, in a *general petitionary prayer*, such as the Peace-Prayer of the Armenian Liturgy of the Word, or the petitionary prayer of the Divine Office.

It seems that the *Diptychs I* and *II* (app. VIII.2./4.) were proclaimed aloud by the deacon from the very beginning. In the oldest manuscript witnesses to *arm Ath*, they still have no accompanying function to the

---

56. See appendix VIII. For details, see Feulner, *Athanasius-Anaphora*, 412–53.

inaudibly recited *Anaphoral Intercessions* of the priest. The *Diptychs II* (app. VIII.4.), read aloud by the deacon, are evidenced in the manuscripts to be an interpolation. Thematically they echo the *Anaphoral Intercessions I (a)*. Some manuscripts show that the *Diptychs II* were originally read together with the *Diptychs I*.

CONCLUSION

The following six summary statements indicate the present state of the questions on the development and current shape of *arm Ath*.

1. In the *Transition to the Sanctus-Benedictus* of *arm Ath* (app. II.2.), we find a reference to a special category of angels, namely, those angels who never sleep, the "wakeful ones"/"vigilant angels" (*zuartʿunkʿ*),[57] which figure prominently in the early Syriac sources as *ʿir*. In the Armenian anaphoras, these angels, which belong to the highest ranks of angels before God's throne of glory, are mentioned only in the *Oratio ante Sanctus* of *arm Ath*, whereas they occur quite frequently in the Ethiopian anaphoras.[58] The presence of these angels in the context of the *Sanctus* in *arm Ath* undoubtedly derives from Syria. The reference to the cherubim and seraphim—in that order—in the anaphora is already attested very clearly (e.g., in the East-Syrian *Anaphora of Addai and Mari*). The sequence seraphim–cherubim (as witnessed, for example, in *arm Ath*) must have appeared only in connection with the introduction of the *Benedictus*. The inclusion in the *Oratio ante Sanctus* of the category of the "wakeful ones" very likely belongs to a time no earlier than the sixth century.[59]

2. Another intriguing trait in *arm Ath* is the wording of the *Benedictus* (app. III.2.). The "Praise in the highest" (*awrhnutʿiwn i barjuns*), which does not follow the Greek but the rather slightly different Armenian text of Matthew 21:9, implicitly reminds us also of the appearance of the angels to the shepherds in the field (Luke 2:14) to announce the incarnation with the "Gloria in excelsis" (*pʿaṙkʿ i barjuns*). In addition, the continuation of the *Benedictus* in *arm Ath* ("Blessed [are] you who

---

57. See Feulner, *Athanasius-Anaphora*, 256/257, 267–71; G. Winkler, *Das Sanctus. Über den Ursprung und die Anfänge des Sanctus und sein Fortwirken*, OCA 267 (Rome: Pontificio Istituto Orientale, 2002), 154, 189.

58. See Winkler, *Sanctus*, 80, 81, 84, 134, 184–85, esp. 153 (n. 97 + 99).

59. For this category of angels in the context of the cherubim and seraphim, see G. Winkler, "Beobachtungen zu den im ,ante Sanctus' angeführten Engeln und ihre Bedeutung," *Theologische Quartalschrift* 183 (2003): 213–38.

did come and are to come"), and also the transition from the *Sanctus* to the *Oratio post Sanctus*, clearly echo the Syrian tradition.[60]

3. The *Oratio post Sanctus* (app. IV.) consists of two distinct christological parts, the first including language of "sacrifice," which did not appear in Eucharistic Prayers of the East before the sixth century. Something similar has to be said about the second part, with its emphasis on the concept of Christ's "unity" (*miut'iwn*),[61] pointing to the sixth century as its time of origin.[62]

4. The increasing symmetry in connection with the introductory elements of the *Words of Institution* (app. V.) probably took place during the sixth century, a trait that we encounter as well in the Armenian Creeds at the beginning of the *Horologion* (*Žamagirk'*).[63]

5. The *Anamnesis* (app. VI.) unfolds in two parts.[64] The first part takes up the typical Syrian reference to the rupturing of the bars (*nigk'*) of hell,[65] which is absent from Latin or Greek sources. Moreover, as in the Armenian redaction of Basil, it is said that the Son descended into the regions of hell "with his body," an assertion also typical of the Syrian tradition.[66]

6. The wording of the *Epiclesis* (app. VII.) with its designation of the Holy Spirit as "co-essential" (*ēakic'*) is also attested in the Creed at the beginning of the *Horologion*. The concept of "essence," "co-essential" (*ēut'iwn, ēakic'*) as *termini technici* for the οὐσία and ὁμοούσιος of the Son, and subsequently the equality in being of the Holy Spirit, did not appear before the sixth century.[67] In addition, the petition to send the Spirit to both the gathering and the gifts ("send to us and to these

---

60. See Feulner, *Athanasius-Anaphora*, 281–82, 291, 294–96.

61. Ibid., 298–300.

62. Winkler, *Entwicklungsgeschichte*, 418, 422–25, 427.

63. Ibid., 204, 593, 597.

64. See Feulner, *Athanasius-Anaphora*, 338–41, 350–65.

65. Ibid., 338/339, 357–58; see in addition S. P. Brock, "Some Aspects of Greek Words in Syriac," in *Synkretismus im syrisch-persischen Kulturgebiet*, ed. A. Dietrich, Abhandlungen der Akademie der Wissenschaften in Göttingen 96 (Göttingen: Vandenhoeck & Ruprecht, 1975), 80–108, here 95–98.

66. See Feulner, *Athanasius-Anaphora*, 338/339, 352, 361 (n. 88); Winkler, *Entwicklungsgeschichte*, 528–30.

67. See Winkler, *Entwicklungsgeschichte*, 563–69; see in addition the testimony of several West Syrian anaphoras: S. P. Brock, "Towards a Typology of the Epicleses in the West Syrian Tradition," in Feulner et al., *Crossroad of Cultures*, 173–92, here 184.

gifts set forth, your co-eternal and co-essential [consubstantial] Holy Spirit"[68]) corresponds to the phrasing ("send to us and to these gifts") in several West-Syrian anaphoras.[69]

Looking through the evidence presented, one observes that a good many features of *arm Ath* echo a heritage typical for the Syrians, several elements of which stem from the sixth century. Thus we can hypothetically conclude that the roots of *arm Ath* may go back to the sixth century and that the Syrian heritage detectable throughout this Eucharistic Prayer is possibly moored in the close contacts of the Armenian Church with the Syrians during the middle of that century.[70]

An extensive Byzantine influence on *arm Ath* is also obvious. Byzantine influences are clearly demonstrable in the liturgical commentary of *Nersēs Lambronac'i* of the twelfth century. But insertions from the Byzantine liturgy are only additions to the Armenian prayers, not replacements of them: we can show such "Byzantinisms" in *arm Ath*, for example, in the ending of its *Epiclesis*.

So it may well be that the *Anaphora of Athanasius* was celebrated in some southern regions of Armenia, possibly side by side with the *Anaphora of Basil* (= *Anaphora of Gregory the Illuminator*), for quite some time and that in a slow process of several centuries the *Anaphora of Athanasius* slowly supplanted the *Anaphora of Basil*.

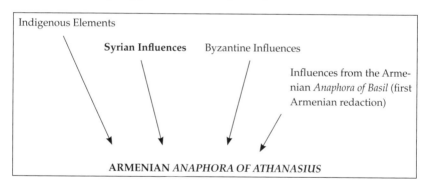

Indigenous Elements

Syrian Influences   Byzantine Influences

Influences from the Armenian *Anaphora of Basil* (first Armenian redaction)

ARMENIAN *ANAPHORA OF ATHANASIUS*

---

68. See Feulner, *Athanasius-Anaphora*, 380. The Armenian personal pronoun in the form of *i mez* (= accusative or locative) can either be translated "send *upon* us" (acc.) or "send *to* us" (loc.).

69. See Brock, "Towards a Typology of the Epicleses," 173–92.

70. See Winkler, *Entwicklungsgeschichte*, 213–19.

APPENDIX

THE ANAPHORA OF ST. ATHANASIUS[71]

[I. Introduction to the Anaphora]

[1. EXHORTATION OF THE DEACON BEFORE THE OPENING DIALOGUE]

The Deacon:
Let us stand in awe,
let us stand in the fear of the Lord,
let us stand straight,
let us attend with good heed

The Choir:
to you, O God,

The Deacon:
Christ, the spotless Lamb of God, offers himself as a sacrifice.

The Choir:
Mercy and peace and a sacrifice of praise.

[2. OPENING DIALOGUE]

The Priest:
✛ The grace, the love and the divine sanctifying power of the Father
and of the Son and of the Holy Spirit be with you all.

The Choir:
Amen. And with your spirit.

The Deacon:
The doors, the doors!
With all wisdom and good heed lift up your minds in the fear of God.

The Choir:
We have them lifted up to you, O Lord almighty.

The Deacon:
And give thanks to the Lord with the whole heart.

The Choir:
It is proper and right.

---

71. Adapted text from D. Findikyan, ed., *The Divine Liturgy of the Armenian Church* (New York: St. Vartan Press, 1999), 28–39.

[II. Oratio ante Sanctus]

[1. PRAISE OF GOD'S ECONOMY]

The Priest:
It is truly proper and right with most earnest diligence always to adore
and glorify you, Father almighty, who did remove the hindrance of the
curse by your imponderable Word, your co-creator, who, having taken
the Church to be a people to himself, made his own those who believe
in you, and was pleased to dwell among us in a ponderable nature, according to the dispensation through the Virgin, and as the divine master-
builder building a new work, he thereby made this earth into heaven.

[2. TRANSITION TO THE SANCTUS-BENEDICTUS]
For he, before whom the companies of vigilant angels [= "wakeful ones"]
could not bear to stand, being amazed at the resplendent and unap-
proachable light of his divinity, even he, becoming man for our salvation,
granted to us that we should join the heavenly ones in spiritual choirs,
And in one voice with the seraphim and the cherubim, we should
sing holy songs and make melodies and, boldly crying out, shout with
them and say:

[III. Sanctus-Benedictus]

[1. SANCTUS]

The Choir:
Holy, holy, holy Lord of hosts;
Heaven and earth are full of your glory.
Praise in the highest.

[2. BENEDICTUS]
Blessed are you who did come and are to come in the name of the Lord.
Hosanna in the highest.
Blessed [are] you who did come and are to come in the name of the Lord.
Hosanna in the highest.

[IV. Oratio post Sanctus]

[1. RESUMPTION OF THE SANCTUS-BENEDICTUS]

The Priest:
Holy, holy, holy are you truly and all-holy; and who is he that will presume to contain in words the outpouring of your infinite loving kind-
ness to us?

From the very beginning you did care for him who had fallen into sin and did comfort him in diverse manners by the prophets, by the giving of the law, by the priesthood and by the prefigurative offering of animals.

[3. PARS CHRISTOLOGICA I]
And at the end of these days, tearing up the sentence of condemnation for all our debts, you gave us your only-begotten Son, both debtor and debt, immolation and anointed, lamb and heavenly bread, high priest and sacrifice; for he is distributor and he himself is distributed always in our midst without ever being consumed.

[4. PARS CHRISTOLOGICA II]
For having become man truly and without illusion, and having become incarnate, through union without confusion, through the Mother of God, the holy Virgin Mary, he journeyed through all the passions of our human life without sin and came willingly to the world-saving cross, which was the occasion of our redemption.

[V. Words of Institution]

[1. INTRODUCTION TO WORDS OVER THE BREAD]

The Priest:
Taking the bread in his holy, divine, immortal, spotless and creative hands, he blessed it, gave thanks, broke it and gave it to his chosen, holy disciples, who were seated, saying:

[2. DOMINICAL WORDS OVER THE BREAD]
Take, eat; this is my body, which is distributed for you and for many, for the expiation and remission of sins.

The Choir:
Amen.

[3. INTRODUCTION TO WORDS OVER THE CUP]

The Priest:
Likewise taking the cup, he blessed it, gave thanks, drank and gave it to his chosen, holy disciples, who were seated, saying:

[4. DOMINICAL WORDS OVER THE CUP]
Drink this all of you. This is my blood of the new covenant, which is shed for you and for many for the expiation and remission of sins.

The Choir:
Amen.

[VI. Anamnesis with Oblation]

[1. HYMN TO THE FATHER]

The Choir:
Heavenly Father, who did give your Son to death for us, debtor for our debts, by the shedding of his blood, we beseech you, have mercy upon your rational flock.

[2. ANAMNETIC PART I]

The Priest:
And your only-begotten beneficent Son gave us the commandment that we should always do this in remembrance of him.
And descending into the lower regions of death in the body which he took of our kinship, and mightily breaking asunder the bolts of hell, he made you known to us the only true God, the God of the living and of the dead.

[3. ANAMNETIC PART II]
And now, O Lord, in accordance with this commandment, bringing forth the saving mystery of the body and blood of your Only-begotten, we remember his redemptive sufferings for us, his life-giving crucifixion, his burial for three days, his blessed resurrection, his divine ascension and his enthronement at your right hand, O Father; his awesome and glorious second coming, we confess and praise.

[4. OBLATION]
And we offer to you yours of your own from all and for all.

[5. PRAISE AND THANKSGIVING]

The Choir:
In all things blessed are you, O Lord. We bless you, we praise you; We give thanks to you; We pray to you, O Lord our God.

[6. TRANSITION TO EPICLESIS]

The Priest:
We do indeed praise you and give thanks to you at all times, O Lord our God, who, having overlooked our unworthiness, have made us ministers of this awesome and ineffable mystery. Not by reason of any good works of our own, of which we are always altogether bereft and at all times find ourselves void, but ever taking refuge in your overflowing forbearance, we make bold to approach the ministry of the body and blood of your Only-begotten, our Lord and Savior Jesus

Christ, to whom is befitting glory, dominion and honor, now and always and unto the ages of ages. Amen.

[*VII. Epiclesis*]

[1. INTRODUCTORY DIALOGUE]

The Priest:
✛ Peace to all.

The Choir:
And with your spirit.

The Deacon:
Let us bow down to God.

The Choir:
Before you, O Lord.

[2. HYMN TO THE SON]

The Choir:
Son of God, who are sacrificed to the Father for reconciliation, bread of life distributed among us, through the shedding of your holy blood, we beseech you, have mercy on your flock saved by your blood.

[3. PETITION TO SEND DOWN THE HOLY SPIRIT]
[a]

The Priest:
We bow down and beseech and ask you, beneficent God, send to [upon] us and to [upon] these gifts set forth, your co-eternal and co-essential [= "consubstantial"] Holy Spirit.

The Deacon:
Amen. Bless, Lord.
[b]

The Priest:
Whereby blessing this bread, make it truly the body of our Lord and Savior Jesus Christ. *[He repeats this three times]*
[c]
And blessing this cup, make it truly the blood of our Lord and Savior Jesus Christ. *[He repeats this three times]*
[d]
Whereby blessing this bread and this wine, make them truly the body and blood of our Lord and Savior Jesus Christ, changing them by your Holy Spirit. *[He repeats this three times]*

So that for all of us who approach it, this may be for acquittal, for expiation and for remission of sins.

The Choir:
Spirit of God, who, descending from heaven, accomplishes through us the mystery of him who is glorified with you, by the shedding of his blood, we beseech you, grant rest to the souls of those of ours who have fallen asleep.

[VIII. Intercessions and Diptychs]

[1. ANAPHORAL INTERCESSIONS I]

   [a. For the Living]

The Priest:
Through this grant love, stability and desirable peace to the whole world, to the holy Church and to all orthodox bishops, to priests, to deacons, to kings, to the princes of the world, to peoples, to travelers, to seafarers, to prisoners, to those who are in danger, to the weary and to those who are at war with barbarians.
Through this grant also seasonableness to the weather and fertility to the fields and a speedy recovery to those who are afflicted with diverse diseases.

   [b. For the Dead]

Through this give rest to all who long ago have fallen asleep in Christ: to the forefathers, the patriarchs, the prophets, the apostles, martyrs, bishops, presbyters, deacons and the whole company of your holy Church and to all the laity, men and women, who have ended their life in faith. With whom, O beneficent God, visit us also, we beseech you.

The Choir:
Be mindful, Lord, and have mercy.

[2. DIPTYCHS I]

The Priest:
That the Mother of God, the holy Virgin Mary, and John the Baptist, the first martyr Stephen and all the saints be remembered in this holy sacrifice, we beseech the Lord.

The Choir:
Be mindful, Lord, and have mercy.

The Deacon:

That the holy apostles, prophets, doctors, martyrs and all holy patriarchs, apostolic bishops, presbyters, orthodox deacons and all the
saints be remembered in this holy sacrifice, we beseech the Lord.

The Choir:

Be mindful, Lord, and have mercy.

The Deacon:

On Sundays of resurrection, say this:

We worship the blessed, praised, glorified, wondrous and divine
(resurrection) of Christ.

The Choir:

Glory to your (resurrection), O Lord.

On saints' days, say this:

That the holy and God-pleasing prophet (**or** patriarch, **or** apostle,
or martyr) _____, whose remembrance we have made this day, be
remembered in this holy sacrifice, let us beseech the Lord.

The Choir:

Be mindful, Lord, and have mercy.

The Deacon:

That our leaders and first enlighteners, the holy apostles Thaddeus
and Bartholomew, and Gregory the Enlightener, Areesdages, Vrtanes,
Hooseeg, Kreekorees, Nerses, Sahag, Daniel and Khat; Mesrob the Var-
tabed and Gregory of Nareg, Nerses of Kla, John of Vorodn, Gregory
and Moses of Datev, and Kreekor and Nerses and their companions
and all the pastors and chief-pastors of the Armenians be remembered
in this holy sacrifice, we beseech the Lord.

The Choir:

Be mindful, Lord, and have mercy.

The Deacon:

That the holy hermits, the virtuous and God-instructed monks Paulus,
Anthony, Paul, Macarius, Onophrius, Mark the Abbot, Serapion,
Nilus, Arsenius, Evagrius, Barsumas; John and Simeon and their companions; Vosgee and Sookyas and their fellow martyrs; and all the
holy fathers and their disciples throughout the world be remembered
in this holy sacrifice, we beseech the Lord.

The Choir:

Be mindful, Lord, and have mercy.

The Deacon:
That the devout kings, Saints Abgar, Constantine, Drtad and Theodosius and all saintly and pious kings and God-loving princes be remembered in this holy sacrifice, we beseech the Lord.

The Choir:
Be mindful, Lord, and have mercy.

The Deacon:
That all the faithful everywhere, men and women, old and young of every age, who in faith and holiness have fallen asleep in Christ, be remembered in this holy sacrifice, we beseech the Lord.

The Choir:
Be mindful, Lord, and have mercy.

[3. ANAPHORAL INTERCESSIONS IIA]

The Priest:
Be mindful, Lord, and have mercy and bless your holy, catholic and apostolic Church, which you have saved by the precious blood of your Only-begotten, and have freed by the holy cross. Grant her unshaken peace. Be mindful, Lord, and have mercy and bless all the orthodox bishops who impart to us the word of truth in orthodox doctrine.

[4. DIPTYCHS II]
And more specially grant us to have our chief bishop and venerable Patriarch of All Armenians lord _____ and the mindful Primate of this Diocese, His Eminence (Arch)bishop _____ for length of days in orthodox doctrine.

The Deacon:
Thanksgiving and glory we offer to you, O Lord our God, for this holy and immortal sacrifice which is on this holy altar, that you will grant it to be to us for holiness of life.
Through this grant love, stability and desirable peace to the whole world, to the holy Church and to all orthodox bishops and to our chief bishop and venerable Patriarch of All Armenians lord _____; and to the mindful Primate of this Diocese, His Eminence (Arch)bishop _____; and to the priest who is offering this sacrifice.
Let us pray for the forces and victories of Christian kings and pious princes.
Let us also beseech the Lord for the souls of those who are at rest, and especially for our prelates who are at rest, and for the founders of this holy church, and for those who are laid to rest under her shadow.

Let us ask deliverance for those of our brethren who have been made captive, and grace to the congregation here present, and rest for those who have ended their life in Christ with faith and holiness.

That these be remembered in this holy sacrifice, we beseech the Lord.

The Choir:
From all and for all.

[5. ANAPHORAL INTERCESSIONS IIB]

The Priest:
Be mindful, Lord, and have mercy and bless your people standing here before you and those who have offered these gifts, and grant them whatever is necessary and profitable.

Be mindful, Lord, and have mercy and bless those who have made vows and those who have brought gifts to your holy Church and those who are mercifully mindful of the poor. Render what is due to them, according to your natural bounty, a hundredfold here and in the world to come.

Be mindful, Lord, and have mercy and compassion on the souls of those who are at rest. Give them rest and enlighten them; reckon them among your saints in the kingdom of heaven and make them worthy of your mercy.

[For the dead:]
Be mindful, Lord, also of the soul of your servant _____ and have mercy on him/her according to your great mercy and by your visitation give him/her rest in the light of your countenance.

[For the dead:]
Deliver him/her from all the snares of soul and of body.

Be mindful, Lord, also of those who have commended themselves to us for remembrance in our prayers, of those who are living and of those who are at rest, and direct their will in their petitions as well as our will to what is right and abounding in salvation, and reward them all with your blessed bounties that pass not away.

And having cleansed our thoughts, make us temples fit for the reception of the Body and Blood of your Only-begotten and our Lord and Savior Jesus Christ, with whom to you, O Father almighty, together with the life-giving and liberating Holy Spirit, is befitting glory, dominion and honor, now and always and unto the ages of ages. Amen.

The Priest:
✛ And the mercy of our great God and Savior Jesus Christ be with you all.

The Choir:
Amen. And with your spirit.

Anne Vorhes McGowan

X. The Basilian Anaphoras: Rethinking the Question*

One of the earliest references to a liturgy associated with St. Basil comes from the mid-sixth century. Writing about 543 CE, Leontius of Byzantium states that the church at Constantinople used "the Liturgy of St. Basil and that of the Apostles" at the time of Theodore of Mopsuestia (c. 425–430).[1] Basil the Great died in 379, and, given the scope of his influence, it would not be surprising if a prayer attributed to him was used widely some fifty years after his death.[2] The bishop of Caesarea in Cappadocia (370–379) may well have had a role in redacting the core text of the *Byzantine* recension of the anaphora that bears his name; however, the questions surrounding this eucharistic prayer quickly increase in complexity when the various representatives of this anaphoral family are compared. For the designation "Anaphora of St. Basil" (hereafter BAS) applies not to a single textual tradition but to at least two related but distinct groups of witnesses: a shorter Egyptian form and a longer form extant in Greek, Syriac, and Armenian. Although Basil did visit Egypt c. 356–357 while still a layperson, there is no historical evidence that would suggest that Basil himself is the

---

* The author wishes to thank the members of the North American Academy of Liturgy's "Problems in the Early History of Liturgy" seminar group for their helpful feedback on an earlier draft of this essay.

1. The reference is in *Adv. Incorrupticolas et Nestor* 19, *PG* 86.1368C. Cited in John R. K. Fenwick, *The Anaphoras of St. Basil and St. James: An Investigation into their Common Origin*, Orientalia Christiana Analecta 240 (Rome: Pontificium Institutum Orientale, 1992), 23. Other early references to a Liturgy of St. Basil include a "quotation" of the Liturgy of Basil in a letter (c. 520) attributed to Peter the Deacon (although not all versions of the Anaphora of Basil contain the quoted text) and a mention of the Basilian liturgy in the canons of the Council "in Trullo" (692). See ibid., 23–24.

2. Ibid., 305.

219

ultimate source of the *Egyptian* prayers to which the name of Basil has become attached.

Given this probable context, D. Richard Stuckwisch has summarized the four basic questions that guided most twentieth-century scholarship on the Basilian anaphoras:[3]

(1) Where and how did the Egyptian form of Basil (E-BAS) originate, and where did it circulate once it did arise?

(2) Is E-BAS in any way "Egyptian"? (And, if so, what Egyptian features does it have?) This leads to a closely related question, namely, how—if at all—is E-BAS "Basilian"? If the prayer originated in Egypt, the attribution of an Egyptian prayer to Basil requires further explanation. If, on the other hand, the prayer originated with Basil (or at least closer to the milieu whence he came), one must propose a hypothesis to explain its eventual appearance in Egypt.

(3) What is the relationship between E-BAS and the other forms of Basil? The other forms seem to be, for the most part, variations on a hypothetical common source (designated Ω by P. Hieronymus Engberding), which is itself an expansion of E-BAS. As Stuckwisch indicates, "the question really has never been whether or not the anaphoras are related to each other, but only what is the nature and direction of their relationship."[4] Ω-BAS differs from E-BAS primarily in its considerable expansion of the text (achieved largely through the addition of Scriptural language and allusions) as well as its enhanced degree of theological precision, particularly in terms of its more explicit Trinitarian character.

(4) What is the connection between the Basilian anaphoras and the historical figure of Basil? Scholarly consensus generally grants that Basil could have played a role in the development of the anaphora, but exactly where and when this might have happened remains open for debate.

3. See D. Richard Stuckwisch, "The Basilian Anaphoras," in *Essays on Early Eastern Eucharistic Prayers*, ed. Paul F. Bradshaw (Collegeville, MN: Liturgical Press, 1997), 119–20.

4. Ibid., 113.

Achieving a greater degree of certainty regarding the answers to any or all of the aforementioned questions would provide crucial insights that could illumine the process of early anaphoral development. This essay will focus primarily on the third question, particularly through an examination of the trajectory of scholarly investigation into the relationship between E-BAS and the forms thought to derive from the hypothetical "Ω-BAS." The latter portion of the essay will be devoted to a critical overview of some substantial studies of BAS undertaken in the last decade by Gabriele Winkler and Achim Budde that invite a more radical paradigm shift in terms of rethinking questions of origins and influence surrounding the various representatives of the Basilian anaphoral tradition. Before launching into a survey of the scholarship on the anaphora, however, it will be helpful to pause briefly to glance at the structure of BAS and review its textual witnesses.

THE ANAPHORA OF BASIL AND WEST SYRIAN ANAPHORAL STRUCTURE

Despite variations in the date and provenance of the manuscripts that first attest to the several forms of BAS, the structure of BAS is highly consistent across the textual tradition, reflecting what eventually emerged (by the late fourth century) as the "standard shape" of the West Syrian or Antiochene anaphora.[5] Its purported "correspondence" with the Antiochene structure has been used as an argument against the ultimate Egyptian origin of the anaphora (since the intercessions of BAS are located toward the end of the anaphora, rather than after the preface as in the "Alexandrian" form typified by the Anaphora of St. Mark).[6] Stuckwisch proposes, however, that this full Antiochene "shape" only arises with BAS and is perpetuated mainly

---

5. R. C. D. Jasper and G. J. Cuming present an outline of this form in the introduction to their *Prayers of the Eucharist: Early and Reformed*, 3rd ed., revised and enlarged (Collegeville, MN: Liturgical Press, 1990), 6. Other anaphoras that fit this pattern, which is thought to have emerged by the late fourth century, include the Anaphoras of St. John Chrysostom and St. James as well as the *Apostolic Constitutions*. For further reflection on the correspondence of BAS with the "West Syrian" anaphoral pattern, see Fenwick, *The Anaphoras of St. Basil and St. James*, 13–17.

6. See, e.g., Leonel L. Mitchell, "The Alexandrian Anaphora of St. Basil of Caesarea: Ancient Source of 'A Common Eucharistic Prayer,'" *Anglican Theological Review* 58, no. 2 (1976): 204.

in liturgies that have been influenced by BAS; consequently, it seems that the shape of BAS is "paradigmatic" only for its own liturgical family—not for a universal form of the anaphora.[7]

John Fenwick presents the following outline of the structure of the Anaphora of Basil:[8]

Preface
Pre-Sanctus
Sanctus
Post-Sanctus
Institution Narrative
Anamnesis
Epiclesis
Intercessions
Doxology

After the opening dialogue, the preface (characterized by adoration of the immanent Trinity) moves into a relatively brief—especially in E-BAS—pre-Sanctus thanksgiving section, which refers to the worship of the angels and culminates in the Sanctus.[9] The post-Sanctus section

7. Stuckwisch, "The Basilian Anaphoras," 113.

8. Fenwick, *The Anaphoras of St. Basil and St. James*, 16. He cautions, however, that the designation of a "pre-Sanctus" and "post-Sanctus" section is based on later terminology that became standardized once the Sanctus had become a typical feature of most anaphoras. The material now located before and after the Sanctus may represent two originally independent units of thanksgiving rather than a single unit that was at some point "interrupted" by the insertion of the Sanctus. For a fuller discussion of the issue, see 15–16. Jasper and Cuming suggest that, based on the extremely brief introductory transition to the Sanctus (consisting of a mere nine words), it is possible that the Sanctus was a fairly recent addition, at least to E-BAS (see *Prayers of the Eucharist*, 68). Paul Bradshaw has observed that the general *structure* of the prayer (but not its content or probable compositional history) partially resembles a "hybrid" of the eucharistic prayers in the *Apostolic Tradition*, the Strasbourg papyrus, and the Sacramentary of Sarapion. See Paul F. Bradshaw, *Eucharistic Origins* (Oxford/New York: Oxford University Press, 2004), 151.

9. Jasper and Cuming note that the brief mention of creation found in the pre-Sanctus section of E-BAS is replaced, at least in the Byzantine version of BAS, by the phrase, "The whole rational and spiritual Creation does you service" (see *Prayers of the Eucharist*, 114). Paul Bradshaw has detected some

continues the theme of thanksgiving, recounting the saving deeds of Christ (extending to the Last Judgment) and incorporating a confession of the economic Trinity.[10] This section is greatly expanded in the longer recensions of BAS. The institution narrative follows, perhaps somewhat abruptly,[11] and the prayer continues with an anamnesis/offering formula that, while linking the Eucharistic sacrifice to the sacrifice of Christ, reiterates some of the material found in the post-Sanctus and also contains several parallels to the second article of the Creed.[12] The epiclesis prays to God that the Holy Spirit might descend upon the people gathered and upon the gifts to "make" them (literally "show [them] to be," ἀναδεῖξαι in the Greek) holy gifts for the sanctification of soul and body.[13] The intercessions follow, blending prayer specifically for the communicants with more general intercessions for the church and the world.[14] Once again, the intercessions

---

limited parallels in the pre-Sanctus section with the corresponding sections of the prayer of Sarapion of Thmuis; see *Eucharistic Origins*, 151. A detailed treatment of the pre-Sanctus section of the Byzantine version of the anaphora (with observations about how it differs from the pre-Sanctus of E-BAS) can be found in Cyprian Robert Hutcheon, "'A Sacrifice of Praise': A Theological Analysis of the Pre-Sanctus of the Byzantine Anaphora of St. Basil," *St. Vladimir's Theological Quarterly* 45, no. 1 (2001): 3–23.

10. Stuckwisch characterizes this confession as "one of the most distinctive features of BAS." See "The Basilian Anaphoras," 113.

11. For more on the connection between the post-Sanctus and the institution narrative, see below, pp. 242–44.

12. See Fenwick, *The Anaphoras of St. Basil and St. James*, 16 and Stuckwisch, "The Basilian Anaphoras," 112. The anamnesis/offering formula runs as follows: "We therefore, remembering his holy sufferings . . .[etc.] . . . and his glorious and fearful coming to us (again) have set forth before you your own from your own gifts, this bread and this cup" (quoted from the ET of E-BAS in Jasper and Cuming, *Prayers of the Eucharist*, 71).

13. According to Bradshaw, this reflects "a theological shift towards what has been called an 'epiphany' understanding of consecration, in which the Spirit is invoked on the gifts in order that the presence of Christ may be revealed in them" (*Eucharistic Origins*, 156).

14. In the Grottaferrata manuscript of Byzantine Basil (Grottaferrata Γβ VII, from the ninth or tenth century), the transition to the intercessions is prefaced with εὐχή, as if what follows originally comprised a separate prayer unit (which may have also been the case with E-BAS as well). See W. E. Pitt, "The Origin of the Anaphora of the Liturgy of St. Basil," *Journal of Ecclesiastical History* 12, no. 1 (1961): 1; and Jasper and Cuming, *Prayers of the Eucharist*, 115.

are considerably expanded in the later recensions of the prayer.[15] The anaphora concludes with a Trinitarian doxology.

ARM-BAS, BYZ-BAS, E-BAS, AND SYR-BAS: AN OVERVIEW OF THE TEXTS

The general shape of BAS outlined above is represented by textual witnesses that emerge from four distinct geographic areas (namely, "Byzantium," Armenia, Syria, Egypt) and represent several linguistic families.[16]

Byzantine Basil (Byz-BAS)

Byz-BAS is the most extensively documented of the four groups of Basilian texts. Over 250 Greek manuscripts of Byz-BAS exist; furthermore, there are about 150 additional manuscripts written in Slavonic, Syriac (Melkite), Arabic (Melkite), Georgian, and Armenian—all of which (except for the Armenian versions) correspond quite closely to the Greek texts.[17] Despite the lack of a Greek critical edition, the remarkably high degree of correspondence between descendants

---

Since the reference to "prayer" in this text is not a consistent feature of the textual tradition of BAS as a whole, however, it is perhaps wise not to make too much of this heading. The same sort of prudence that Robert F. Taft advises with respect to authorial attribution is likely warranted here as well: "In ancient texts, attribution and authenticity are far from synonymous and, with regard to religious texts, skepticism in the face of attributions of authorship is the prudent attitude." See Robert F. Taft, "St. John Chrysostom and the Byzantine Anaphora that Bears His Name," in *Essays on Early Eastern Eucharistic Prayers*, 197.

15. The shorter E-BAS introduces the prayer for the dead with the curious statement, "since, Master, it is a command of your only-begotten Son that we should share in the commemoration of your saints" (see Jasper and Cuming, *Prayers of the Eucharist*, 69). The addition of this non-Scriptural warrant to intercede for the dead may suggest that what follows is a relatively recent addition to the prayer, which, consequently, is in need of justification.

16. For a concise overview of the textual tradition, see Stuckwisch, "The Basilian Anaphoras," 110–12. Fenwick (see *The Anaphoras of St. Basil and St. James*, 49–57) provides a more thorough treatment of the significance and distribution of the various forms of BAS.

17. The most striking difference is due to the fact that the Armenian versions contain additional material not found in the other forms of Byz-BAS. They are discussed further below as "Arm-BAS II" in the Armenian section.

from the Byzantine family of manuscripts permits considerable confidence in the Greek text of BAS.[18] The oldest surviving representative is Codex Barberini Gr. 336, which dates to the eighth century; however, the text is unfortunately incomplete.[19] Subsequent editors of the text have therefore supplemented it with manuscripts from the ninth or tenth century (or later).[20] Compared to the versions of E-BAS, Byz-BAS exhibits both theological elaborations (likely formulated to counter views about the Holy Spirit that were condemned at the Council of Constantinople in 381) as well as an apparent preservation of a less developed text at certain points where the Syrian and Armenian versions have been expanded.[21]

Armenian Basil (Arm-BAS)

Given the connections between Armenia and Cappadocia in the third and fourth centuries, it is not surprising that a version of a liturgy attributed to Basil would surface in Armenia. Gabriele Winkler,

---

18. Fenwick, *The Anaphoras of St. Basil and St. James*, 55–56.

19. Basil's name occurs in this manuscript before the prayer of the Proskomide of the rite now attributed in its entirety to the fourth-century bishop. Regardless of what the name may or may not suggest about the prayer's relationship to the person of Basil, the presence of the name implies "a degree of antiquity" and the placement of the Liturgy of St. Basil at the very beginning of the codex "suggests that it enjoyed a priority of use in Constantinople at that period." See Fenwick, *The Anaphoras of St. Basil and St. James*, 24. For a recent critical edition of the Barberini Codex, see Stefano Parenti and Elena Velkovska, eds., *L'Eucologio Barberini gr. 336*, 2nd ed. (with Italian translation), Bibliotheca Ephemerides Liturgicae Subsidia 80 (Rome: C.L.V.-Edizioni Liturgiche, 2000).

20. F. E. Brightman uses Barberini 336, supplementing the lacuna with the Grottaferrata MS from the ninth or tenth century. See idem, ed., *Liturgies Eastern and Western*, vol. 1: *Eastern Liturgies* (Oxford: Oxford University Press, 1896), 309–44. Brightman's text is reproduced in Anton Hänggi and Irmgard Pahl, eds., *Prex eucharistica: textus e variis liturgiis antiquioribus selecti*, vol. 1, Spicilegium Friburgense 12 (Fribourg: Éditions Universitaires, 1968), 230–43, however, *without* indicating the precise point at which the newer manuscript intervenes in the central section of the prayer (see Fenwick, *The Anaphoras of St. Basil and St. James*, 57). An English translation of Brightman's text of Byz-BAS (which does specify the beginning and ending points of the interpolated manuscript) is available in Jasper and Cuming, *Prayers of the Eucharist*, 114–23.

21. See Fenwick, *The Anaphoras of St. Basil and St. James*, 57.

however, draws particular attention to the fact that there are really two distinct sets of Armenian witnesses to BAS. The first group, Arm-BAS I, is ascribed to Gregory the Illuminator (c. 257–c. 337), the missionary evangelizer and "founder" of the Armenian Church; these texts are generally less expanded than either Syr-BAS or Byz-BAS.[22] This form seems closer to an *Urtext* than do the more recent texts of Arm-Bas II (under Basil's name), which, as mentioned above, clearly demonstrate their dependence on the Byzantine tradition despite their incorporation of additional material.[23]

Winkler proposes that the texts of Arm-BAS II reflect, for the most part, a "fusion" of the Armenian and Byzantine traditions. Much of the "additional material" in Arm-BAS II relative to Byz-BAS can be accounted for by the reliance of Arm-BAS II on Arm-BAS I; however, Arm-BAS II may in some places preserve some very ancient traditional layers. Furthermore, according to Winkler, both versions of Arm-BAS also contain some characteristics that have parallels in the Egyptian textual forms of BAS.[24] Arm-BAS I survives in three medieval manuscripts, and an additional witness is provided by a partial quotation in Faustus of Byzantium's *History of the Armenians* (c. 425) in the context of a description of fourth-century events.[25] Arm-BAS II is represented by at least four manuscripts.[26]

22. Ibid., 55; for example, a number of words and phrases contained in Syr-BAS and Byz-BAS are not present in Arm-BAS I.

23. See Gabriele Winkler, *Die Basilius-Anaphora: Edition der beiden armenischen Redaktionen und der relevanten Fragmente, Übersetzung und Zusammenschau aller Versionen im Licht der orientalischen Überlieferungen*, Anaphorae Orientales 2 (Rome: Pontificio Istituto Orientale, 2005), 127–28. Winkler's *Die Basilius-Anaphora* includes a critical edition of the Armenian manuscripts (including fragments) of Arm-BAS I and Arm-BAS II. Winkler also provides an assessment of Erich Renhart's critical edition of Arm-BAS I (with German translation). See ibid., 25–27; and Erich Renhart, ed., "Die älteste armenische Anaphora: Einleitung, kritische Edition des Textes und Übersetzung," in *Armenische Liturgien: Ein Blick auf eine ferne christliche Kultur*, ed. E. Renhart and J. Dum Tragut, Heiliger Dienst, Ergänzungsband 2 (Graz/Salzburg: Schnider Verlag, 2001), 93–241.

24. Winkler, *Die Basilius-Anaphora*, 128.

25. Fenwick, *The Anaphoras of St. Basil and St. James*, 55. The citation seems to include part of the post-Sanctus and epiclesis.

26. For an overview of the manuscript tradition of Arm-BAS, see Winkler, *Die Basilius-Anaphora*, 130, and idem, "Ein Rätsel gelöst: Die Angaben zur

Syriac Basil (Syr-BAS)

The Syriac version of Basil (Syr-BAS) is preserved in a handful of manuscripts, only two of which have been published.[27] Most of the manuscripts are fairly late (from the thirteenth to the eighteenth centuries); however, the text preserved in one manuscript may be as old as the seventh or eighth century. The versions of Syr-BAS contain numerous interpolations, some rather extensive, particularly in the anamnesis and intercessions.[28]

Egyptian Basil (E-BAS)

Among the Basilian anaphoras, the various versions of Egyptian Basil (E-BAS) represent a decisively shorter form of BAS than do the other textual families. The oldest known form of Basil (sometimes called ES-BAS) is in Sahidic Coptic and exists only in a few fragments and one incomplete manuscript, which is missing the first third of the prayer, resuming at the end of the post-Sanctus.[29] The manuscript itself likely dates to the first half of the seventh century—Archbishop Benjamin, who is remembered in the intercessions, was patriarch of Alexandria from 622–662. The rest of the text contained in the manuscript, however, may largely date to the fourth century or perhaps even earlier.[30] Consequently, Fenwick can claim that it is "the earliest substantial witness to the anaphora of St. Basil which we possess."[31]

Venediger-Handschrift (V) der älteren armenischen Version der Basilius-Anaphora in den bisherigen Veröffentlichungen," *Zeitschrift für antikes Christentum* 10, no. 2 (2006): 313–19.

27. See I. Rahmani, ed., *Missale Syriacum iuxta ritum ecclesiae apostolicae Antiochenae Syrorum* (Sharfé: Typis patriarchalibus in Seminario Sciarfensi de Monte Libano, 1922), 172–96; and E. Renaudot, *Liturgiarum Orientalium Collectio*, 2nd [corrected] ed., vol. 2 (Frankfurt/London: Joseph Baer/John Leslie, 1847), 543–56.

28. See Fenwick, *The Anaphoras of St. Basil and St. James*, 54.

29. The critical edition of the most complete version of ES-BAS, sometimes dubbed the "Louvain fragment," was published by J. Doresse and E. Lanne, *Un témoin archaïque de la liturgie copte de S. Basile* (Louvain: Publications Universitaires, 1960), with a preface and accompanying essay ("Les liturgies 'basiliennes' et saint Basile") by B. Capelle. For an English translation of the Sahidic (supplemented by the Bohairic for the first portion), see Jasper and Cuming, *Prayers of the Eucharist*, 67–73.

30. See Doresse and Lanne, *Un témoin archaïque*, 2 and 4–5.

31. Fenwick, *The Anaphoras of St. Basil and St. James*, 49.

Other Egyptian versions of the text exist in Bohairic Coptic (EB-BAS, whose witnesses are *"extrêmement nombreux"*), as well as Greek (EG-BAS) and Ethiopic (each represented by only a handful of manuscripts and/or fragments).[32] All these manuscripts, however, are comparatively late (dating from the fourteenth to the nineteenth centuries), and, consequently, are relatively less important than ES-BAS for reconstructing the early history of BAS's development. ES-BAS, on the other hand, not only lacks all the additional material found in the Ω versions, but it further lacks several elaborations contained in EB-BAS and EG-BAS that were previously viewed as important features of the E-BAS tradition. For example, "ES-Basil contains no specific request in the Epiclesis for the elements to be transformed into the Body and Blood of Christ, nor does it commemorate any saint other than Mary. It also lacks clearly Egyptian features such as petitions concerning the rising of the Nile in the Intercessions."[33] Some potentially "Egyptian" features that remain include the use of Psalm 146:6, the phrasing of the offering in the aorist ("we . . . have set forth before you," implying perhaps an "offering" at a previous point in the liturgy), the unusual form of the doxology, and perhaps also the addition of the "Pauline comment" (cf. 1 Cor 11:26).[34] Recent scholarly consensus has generally granted that ES-BAS is probably the most faithful witness to an Egyptian *Urtext* of BAS.

The clear relationship between the multiple forms of BAS has inspired numerous hypotheses regarding the possible relationship and developmental history of the various texts.

OVERVIEW OF TWENTIETH-CENTURY SCHOLARSHIP

The Tradition of "Proclus" (A Sixteenth-Century Forgery Debunked)
Speculations about the relationship between the longer and shorter versions of Basil are nothing new, dating at least to the sixteenth century. The pseudo-tradition of Proclus, bishop of Constantinople (✝ 446), designates Basil (and others) as liturgical compilers and further claims that liturgies had once been much longer but that the

---

32. For an overview of these texts, see Doresse and Lanne, *Un témoin archaïque*, 7–10. A Latin translation of the Bohairic text can be found in Renaudot, vol. 1, 13-18. A version of the Greek text can be found in ibid., 63–71 (reproduced in Hänggi and Pahl, *Prex eucharistica*, 347–57).

33. Fenwick, *The Anaphoras of St. Basil and St. James*, 53.

34. Jasper and Cuming, *Prayers of the Eucharist*, 68.

diminished piety of those in later ages had led to the production of condensed versions as a pastoral accommodation.[35] Since this testimony (supposedly) came from a reliable source and was written not long after the death of Basil, it was presumed to be accurate; this implied that the shorter version of BAS (E-BAS) was a later redaction of the longer, more original Byz-BAS. In 1962, however, F. J. Leroy exposed the work attributed to Proclus as a sixteenth-century forgery by Constantin Palaeocappa.[36]

P. Hieronymus Engberding (1931)

After conducting a detailed study of the manuscript evidence available in the early twentieth century, P. Hieronymus Engberding published the first serious scholarly study on the anaphora of BAS (*Das Eucharistische Hochgebet der Basileiosliturgie*) in 1931.[37] A student of Anton Baumstark, Engberding recognized the short and long forms of BAS and applied his mentor's laws of liturgical development to cast suspicion on the tradition of Proclus. Engberding proposed that the direction of anaphoral development would likely have proceeded from short and simple to long and complex; consequently, the shorter version of BAS was probably more original, with the longer form developing from the shorter chiefly through theological enhancements and Scriptural citations.[38]

Engberding was also responsible for identifying the four geographical families discussed above, and he posited a schematic of their relationship.[39] The shorter form (which has been referred to here as E-BAS) Engberding designated Ä (for Ägypt[isch]), and he also proposed a common source (Ω) lying behind the surviving witnesses of the longer recension. Subunits of Ω included A (the "Old

---

35. Proclus, *Tractatus de traditione divinae missae*, PG 65, 849B-852B.

36. See F. J. Leroy, "Proclus, 'De Traditione Divinae Missae': un faux de C. Palaeocappa," *Orientalia Christiana Periodica* 28 (1962): 288–99.

37. P. Hieronymus Engberding, *Das Eucharistische Hochgebet der Basileiosliturgie: Textgeschichtliche Untersuchungen und kritische Ausgabe*, Theologie der Christlichen Ostens 1 (Münster: Verlag Aschendorff, 1931). Engberding's study identified (see XXVII ff.) and compared (see XXXVII) over four hundred manuscripts of BAS.

38. For an overview of Engberding's conclusions, see LXXIV ff; here LXXV–LXXVII.

39. See especially the chart on LXXXVII. (A key to the abbreviations used there can be found on XIII–XIV.)

Armenian," here called Arm-BAS I) and the hypothetical ψ (from which S [Syr-BAS] and B [Byz-BAS] were ultimately derived). Furthermore, Engberding suggested that all extant forms of BAS might be derivatives of an archetypical *Urgestalt*.[40] In Engberding's judgment, Basil was not the author of Ur-BAS but rather the editor-redactor (*Bearbeiter*) of Ω-BAS, which represented an expansion of the original prayer (Ur-BAS) by the addition of explicit Scriptural references and the incorporation of a more developed Trinitarian theology.[41] E-BAS, on the other hand, represented a separate Egyptian redaction of Ur-BAS, which resulted through the combination of the *Urgestalt* with local Egyptian prayers (which Engberding dubbed "*ägyptisches Heimatgut*").[42]

Engberding's conclusions were widely accepted and gained further support with the publication of a critical edition of the Louvain fragment (of ES-BAS) in 1960 and the exposure of the tradition of Proclus as a forgery in 1962. One weakness of Engberding's study, however, is that is dealt with only the preface, pre-Sanctus, Sanctus, and post-Sanctus of BAS, leaving over half of the anaphora critically unexamined.[43] A number of subsequent studies have sought to extend and refine the work on BAS that Engberding began.

Doresse and Lanne—and Capelle (1960)
The publication in 1960 of the critical edition of a recently discovered Sahidic Coptic fragment by J. Doresse and E. Lanne (accompanied by an essay written by Bernard Capelle), represents one of the

---

40. Engberding's conviction that the *Urtext* of the anaphora was in Greek prompted him to offer a retro-translation of the extant oriental versions (Coptic, Armenian, Syriac, and Ethiopic) into Greek, intending through linguistic analysis to trace the historical evolution of the respective redactions. See Gabriele Winkler, "On the Formation of the Armenian Anaphoras: A Preliminary Overview," in *Worship Traditions in Armenia and the Neighboring Christian East*, ed. Roberta R. Ervine (Crestwood, NY: St. Vladimir's Seminary Press and St. Nersess Armenian Seminary, 2006), 62.

41. Engberding, LXXXIV–LXXXV.

42. Ibid., LXXXVII.

43. In a series of later articles, Engberding took up an analysis of the intercessions in the various recensions of BAS. See H. Engberding, "Das anaphorische Fürbittgebet der Basiliusliturgie," *Oriens Christianus* 47 (1963): 16–52; and 49 (1965): 18–37; "Das anaphorische Fürbittgebet der syrischen Basiliusliturgie," *Oriens Christianus* 50 (1966): 13–18; and "Das anaphorische Fürbittgebet der älteren armenischen Basiliusliturgie," *Oriens Christianus* 51 (1967): 29–50.

most important developments in studies of the Basilian anaphoras.[44] Doresse and Lanne present the text of ES-BAS in four parallel columns: the Sahidic Coptic text, a Latin transliteration, a Greek retroversion (based on the assumption that the original prayer was composed in Greek), and a critical apparatus that explains what choices were made in the construction of the Greek retroversion.[45] This fourth column reveals that Doresse and Lanne reconstructed the Greek text using not only other versions of E-BAS but also early church orders such as the *Apostolic Tradition* and *Apostolic Constitutions*. This publication corroborated the work of Engberding (who obviously did not have access to ES-BAS), and led to the acceptance of ES-BAS as one of the earliest known eucharistic prayers.

Alphonse Raes (1958 and 1960)

Alphonse Raes reviewed Doresse and Lanne's critical edition of ES-BAS shortly after its publication. Whereas a few years earlier he had ascribed both E-BAS and Byz-BAS to Basil himself,[46] Doresse and Lanne's critical edition of an early *Sahidic* text convinced him that the Egyptian features of E-BAS were of decisive importance.[47] If E-BAS was originally written in Greek, either a Greek text was written in Egypt or a Greek text imported from elsewhere was subsequently "Egyptianized." Raes proposed a third alternative to explain the presence of numerous Egyptian elements in E-BAS, namely, that there was no "original" Greek version.[48] Rather, the liturgy arose in Egypt, and some of the uniquely Egyptian elements were later excised to form Byz-BAS—a position that accords quite well with Engberding's

44. For a full citation, see above, note 29. Capelle's essay considers verbal parallels between ES-BAS and Byz- BAS (particularly in the post-Sanctus section) and the writings of Basil, concluding, like Engberding, that Byz-BAS's namesake was also its redactor. See Capelle, "Les Liturgies 'Basiliennes' et Saint Basile," in Doresse and Lanne, *Un témoin archaïque*, 45–74. Capelle's remarks in the preface of Doresse and Lanne's edition suggest, however, that Basil may have used something like ES-BAS to ground his redaction—implying (unlike Engberding) that Basil may have been familiar with some form of E-BAS (see I-II; cf. 74).

45. See Doresse and Lanne, *Un témoin archaïque*, 12–33.

46. See A. Raes, "L'authenticité de la liturgie Byzantine de Saint Basile," *Revue des Études Byzantines* 16 (1958): 158–61.

47. See A. Raes, "Un nouveau document de la Liturgie de S. Basile," *Orientalia Christiana Periodica* 26 (1960): 401–11, especially 402–4.

48. Ibid., 404–5.

hypothesis about the formation of the prayer from an *Urgestalt* plus "ägyptisches Heimatgut."

W.E. Pitt (1961)

Working in Central Africa, W. E. Pitt did not have access to either the recently published critical edition of Doresse and Lanne or even to Engberding's study.[49] Suspecting that the material after the epiclesis in BAS may have originally belonged to a separate prayer, Pitt compared this material in Byz-BAS to other Eucharistic prayers.[50] He suggested that BAS includes much material that could have developed from the same Antiochene anaphoral tradition represented by the East Syrian liturgy of Addai and Mari (and the references to anaphoral structure in the catecheses of Theodore of Mopsuestia) and that, furthermore, BAS also includes significant chunks of material borrowed directly from the Anaphora of St. James (with the resemblance between BAS and JAS being most pronounced in the epiclesis, institution narrative, and anamnesis).[51]

Boris Bobrinskoy (1969)

Boris Bobrinskoy extended Capelle's examination of similarities between BAS (specifically Byz-BAS) and the writings of Basil where Capelle had left off, treating the institution narrative, the epiclesis, and some of the intercessions. In addition to philological analysis, Bobrinskoy considered theological ideas and images found in BAS, drawing attention to the Trinitarian theology in the preface; Christology in the Sanctus, post-Sanctus, and institution narrative; pneumatology in the epiclesis, and ecclesiology in the intercessions.[52] His study offers further evidence supporting some connection between BAS (at least Byz-BAS) and Basil the Great.[53]

---

49. W. E. Pitt, "The Origin of the Anaphora of the Liturgy of St. Basil," *Journal of Ecclesiastical History* 12, no. 1 (1961): 2, note 3.

50. This suspicion that the material after the epiclesis may have once comprised an independent prayer was based on the heading εὐχή ("prayer") between the epiclesis and a prayer for the fruits of communion. See Pitt, "The Origin of the Anaphora," 1 and note 14 above.

51. Ibid., 2–3ff.

52. Boris Bobrinskoy, "Liturgie et ecclésiologie trinitaire de saint Basile," *Verbum Caro* 23 (1969): 1–32.

53. See Fenwick, *The Anaphoras of St. Basil and St. James*, 28: "Engberding, Capelle, and Bobrinskoy together present an impressive, and perhaps conclusive, case for believing that St Basil himself was the source of much of

Albert Houssiau (1970)

In 1970, Albert Houssiau once again focused attention specifically on E-BAS.[54] After offering an extensive commentary on the various anaphoral components, Houssiau notes that E-BAS seems largely untouched by the Christological and Trinitarian controversies of the fourth century. He also highlights its "epiphany theology" of Christ, whereby holiness is communicated to human beings by God through the Spirit, with this "sanctification" becoming manifest in the Eucharistic bread and wine. Houssiau concludes that "the Alexandrine anaphora of Basil puts us in possession of a liturgy going back beyond St. Basil's time; it came probably from the north of Syria or Cappadocia."[55] A prayer very similar to E-BAS likely comprised the "normal anaphora of the Church of Cappadocia in the fourth century"—a prayer that Basil expanded to create the longer Byz-BAS.[56]

Leonel L. Mitchell (1976)

Leonel Mitchell wrote an essay following the publication (in 1975) of "A Common Eucharistic Prayer" based largely on ES-BAS and composed by an ecumenical committee. Just before the article's conclusion, Mitchell turns briefly to the issue of E-BAS's origin. Based on its structure, he classifies E-BAS as a member of the Antiochene or West Syrian anaphoral family—and consequently of non-Egyptian origin.[57] At the same time, Mitchell sees E-BAS (or something very much like it) as an ancient form on which the other surviving recensions of BAS are based. This suggests a changing interpretation of the Basilian liturgies; E-BAS was no longer "seen as a combination of *Urgestalt* and

---

the material that distinguishes the anaphora of Ω-Basil from that of E-Basil." Fenwick does criticize Bobrinskoy, however, for making direct comparisons between E-BAS and Byz-BAS, without considering Syr-BAS and Arm-BAS.

54. Albert Houssiau, "The Alexandrine Anaphora of St. Basil," in *The New Liturgy: A Comprehensive Introduction to the New Liturgy as a Whole and to Its New Calendar, Order of Mass, Eucharistic Prayers, the Roman Canon, Prefaces, and the Sunday Lectionary*, ed. L. C. Sheppard (London: Darton, Longman & Todd, 1970), 228–43.

55. Ibid., 243.

56. Ibid., 229. The author does not attempt to explain why or how a prayer very similar to a fourth-century Cappadocian anaphora might have migrated to Egypt.

57. Mitchell, "The Alexandrian Anaphora of St. Basil of Caesarea," 204–5. (For a full citation of Mitchell's article, see note 6.)

ägyptisches Heimatgut, but instead stood as the best representation of *Urgestalt,* if not *Urgestalt* itself."[58]

John R. K. Fenwick

Another major study that touched on Basil appeared in 1992 with the publication of John R. K. Fenwick's monograph, *The Anaphoras of St. Basil and St. James: An Investigation into their Common Origin.*[59] Methodologically, Fenwick adopts aspects of Engberding's approach, extending the verbal analysis of the anaphora to parts of BAS that Engberding did not examine in his seminal study of 1931 (i.e., the institution narrative, anamnesis, epiclesis, intercessions, and doxology) and also comparing the longer and shorter versions of BAS with the Anaphora of James (henceforth JAS), to which BAS is clearly related at certain points. Furthermore, Fenwick juxtaposes verbal analysis with a structural approach that seeks "to identify the distribution and re-location of material within the anaphora" in hopes of discovering clues to the process of anaphoral development.[60] Based on his analysis, Fenwick attempted to reconstruct the text of Ω-BAS, a hypothetical form containing material "in excess of E-Basil which it is reasonable to assert that all three members of the Ω-group originally possessed."[61]

Fenwick's consideration of the intercessions is especially pertinent to this discussion, as it offers important clues to the relationship between the various versions of Ω-BAS. Fenwick reaches the conclusion that Syr-BAS most closely reflects the initial ordering of the intercessions in Ω-BAS (which in turn supposedly preserved the sequence of Ur-BAS). The intercessions of Arm-BAS and Byz-BAS, in contrast, reflect later redactions of Ω-BAS, which show "progressive stages of sequence alteration" resulting in three or four structurally different versions of the Basilian anaphora rather than only two (i.e., the "short"

---

58. Todd E. Johnson, "Recovering *Ägyptisches* Heimatgut: An Exercise in Liturgical Methodology," *Questions Liturgiques* 76 (1995): 186.

59. For a full citation, see note 1. Originally written as his doctoral dissertation, Fenwick's investigation was first published in abbreviated form as *Fourth Century Anaphoral Construction Techniques* (Bramcote, Notts.: Grove Books, 1986). Unless otherwise indicated, all subsequent references to Fenwick's work in the footnotes of this essay refer to the longer study (*Anaphoras*).

60. Fenwick, *The Anaphoras of St. Basil and St. James,* 62.

61. Ibid., 64.

[E-BAS] and "long" [derivatives of Ω-BAS]) forms.[62] Therefore, "the discovery of further stages of reworking challenges the idea of a single 'leap' from E-Basil to Ω-Basil and therefore re-opens the question as to at which stage the various pieces of Ω material in the earlier sections of the anaphora were inserted."[63]

Fenwick suggests that a common source, Ur-BAS serves as the foundation for not only the liturgies of the E-BAS and Ω-BAS groups but also for the Anaphora of JAS. Hence, neither JAS nor BAS is directly dependent on the other, as previous scholars proposed, but both represent independent reworking and expansion of a common source.[64] For practical purposes, Fenwick considers ES-BAS to roughly correspond to the hypothetical Ur-BAS, whereas the longer recensions derive from subsequent redaction of the Ur-text, possibly by Basil himself.[65]

Working half a century after Engberding, Fenwick had access to critical texts that were not available to Engberding, and thus he is able to nuance and continue the trajectory that Engberding began. Todd Johnson, however, has criticized Fenwick's work for downplaying the Egyptian aspects of E-BAS, particularly through eliminating references to Engberding's "*ägyptisches Heimatgut*" in his simplified schematic of the genealogical development of the Basilian anaphoras.[66] Regarding the project as a whole, Bryan Spinks wondered "whether too much reliance has been put on Syrian Basil, given that many Syrian anaphoras

---

62. See ibid., 298; and also Fenwick, "The Significance of Similarities in the Anaphoral Intercession Sequence in the Coptic Anaphora of St. Basil and Other Ancient Liturgies," *Studia Patristica* 18, no. 2 (1989): 355–62.

63. Fenwick, *The Anaphoras of St. Basil and St. James*, 298.

64. Ibid., 301. In Fenwick's estimation, about 80 percent of the text of Ur-BAS is also found in JAS.

65. Fenwick proposes that, given the right confluence of circumstances, Basil may have been the redactor not only of Ω-BAS but perhaps of Syr-BAS, Arm-BAS, and Byz-BAS as well. See Ibid., 298–301.

66. See Johnson, "Recovering *Ägyptisches* Heimatgut," 187–88; compare the charts in Engberding, *Das Eucharistische Hochgebet*, LXXXVII and Fenwick, *The Anaphoras of St. Basil and St. James*, 25. Furthermore, Johnson notes that to support his hypothesis of Basilian "authorship" even of E-BAS (via Basil's possible influence on the Cappadocian liturgy), Fenwick cites Raes' earlier conclusion (1958) that Basil penned both the long and short versions of the anaphora, omitting mention of Raes' revised opinion in 1960 (even though he often cites the latter work in other contexts). See Johnson, "Recovering *Ägyptisches* Heimatgut," 187.

have been influenced by Syrian James."[67] Gabriele Winkler, in turn, notes that a misreading of Engberding on the significance of Arm-Bas (I) has hampered Fenwick's study. Whereas Fenwick understands Engberding to claim that "on textual grounds the Syriac and Byzantine versions form a superior unit to the Old Armenian," Engberding actually declared quite the opposite, expressing a general preference for the Old Armenian.[68] The page reference Fenwick cites supports Winkler's position. Engberding wrote:

> Thus S[yr-BAS] and B[yz-BAS] go back to a common archetype (ψ), and only with this is A[rm-BAS] related to the same extent. Now which of the two related witnesses [i.e., Arm-Bas I or ψ] is better from a text-critical perspective? In general we can give preference to A[rm-BAS]. For:
> 1. ψ is closer to Holy Scripture. . . .
> 2. ψ shows, from the standpoint of the general history of the eucharistic prayer, the more developed form . . .
> 3. ψ changes several passages for the sake of linguistic euphony . . .
> 4. Finally we may observe the additions in ψ . . . as secondary.[69]

Consequently, a great deficiency in Fenwick's work (according to Winkler) is his failure to treat Arm-BAS with the respect it deserves. While Fenwick's study moves the discussion of BAS's evolution forward and sheds light on the process of anaphoral development more generally, the points of critique raised above serve to illustrate the

67. Bryan D. Spinks, review of *The Anaphoras of St. Basil and St. James*, by John R. K. Fenwick, *The Journal of Theological Studies* 44, no. 2 (1993): 714.

68. See Fenwick, *The Anaphoras of St. Basil and St. James*, 25; and Gabriele Winkler, review of *The Anaphoras of St. Basil and St. James*, by John R. K. Fenwick, *Oriens Christianus* 78 (1994): 271–72. Winkler has recently revisited the question of the relationship between BAS and JAS in her current analysis of several themes across the extant versions of these anaphoras. (I received this information from NAAL colleagues.)

69. "Also S[yr-BAS] und B[yz-BAS] gehen auf einen gemeinsamen Archetypus (ψ) zurück; und erst mit diesem ist A[rm-BAS] in gleichem Grade verwandt. Wer von den beiden Bruderzeugen [i.e. Arm-Bas I or ψ] ist nun der textkritisch bessere? Im allgemeinen dürfen wir A[rm-BAS] den Vorzug geben. Denn 1. ψ steht der Hl. Schrift näher . . . . 2. ψ weist unter dem Gesichtspunkte der allgemeinen Geschichte des eucharistischen Hochgebetes die entwickeltere Gestalt auf . . . 3. ψ ändert einige Stellen des sprachlichen Wohllautes wegen . . .4. Endlich dürfen wir die Überschüsse in ψ . . . als sekundär betrachten." Engberding, *Das Eucharistische Hochgebet*, LXXI–LXXII.

complexity of the interrelationships among the various versions of BAS and the many questions that remain unresolved.

Todd Johnson (1995)

Todd Johnson surveyed twentieth-century scholarship regarding the origin of E-BAS and concluded that the "shadow of Proclus' testimony" had not been entirely banished from comparative liturgiological study.[70] He identifies three *a priori* assumptions that may have compelled scholars to favor certain possibilities while dismissing other equally legitimate explanations. First, despite the lack of historical evidence, many still attempt to connect Basil the Great not only to Byz-BAS but also to E-BAS. Second, the idea that an anaphora from elsewhere was brought to Egypt and "Egyptianized" has led to much speculation about how and when "Egyptian" elements may have been incorporated into the anaphora. Third, the idea that early anaphoras were relatively homogenous has led to multiple attempts to create a Greek retroversion of the text.[71] Having pointed out these pitfalls, Johnson undertakes his own analysis of the text of ES-BAS, minus these presuppositions. He suggests that E-BAS may have had an original Egyptian "core" consisting of the post-Sanctus, epiclesis, and doxology—and compares the older text of ES-BAS with other forms of E-BAS to build his case.[72] Johnson's conclusion resembles Engberding's: "an indigenous Egyptian prayer was combined with a 'second prayer' [perhaps another Egyptian prayer] to form Egyptian Basil."[73]

Achim Budde critiqued Johnson's methodological experiment, claiming that Johnson's proposal of linear development from E-BAS to Byz-BAS is too simplistic.[74] The transition from the post-Sanctus to the institution narrative is not as jarring as Johnson and others have claimed (insisting thereby that the institution narrative must be a

70. Johnson, "Recovering *Ägyptisches* Heimatgut," 183. (For a full reference to this article, see note 58.)

71. Ibid., 188–89.

72. See ibid., 193ff.

73. Ibid., 197–98; quote from 197.

74. See ibid., 198; and Achim Budde, "Wie findet man "Ägyptisches Heimatgut"?: Der Ägyptische Ursprung der Basileios-Anaphora in der Diskussion," in *Comparative Liturgy Fifty Years after Anton Baumstark (1872–1948)*, Orientalia Christiana Analecta 265, ed. Robert F. Taft and Gabriele Winkler (Rome: Pontificio Istituto Orientale, 2001), 674–76.

later addition to the prayer)—nor is it necessarily *typically* Egyptian.[75] Similar arguments can be made regarding many of the other "Egyptian" elements Johnson ascribes to E-BAS.[76] In terms of method, Johnson passes too quickly over Engberding's "family tree" of relationships among the Basilan anaphoras—and it is only within this context that Engberding's *"ägyptisches Heimatgut"* can be properly understood as elements that distinguished the forms of E-BAS from those deriving from the other major stem (Ω).[77] If one presumes *any* one form of BAS as the "standard" (e.g., Byz-BAS), one will be able to detect *"Heimatgut"* (be it Armenian, Syrian, or Egyptian) in the other three forms.[78]

D. Richard Stuckwisch (1997)

D. Richard Stuckwisch turns to a historical-theological approach (rather than philological or structural) to consider the relation of E-BAS and Ω-BAS. He suggests that perhaps Gregory Thaumaturgus of Pontus (a.k.a. Gregory the Illuminator) brought a liturgy to Neo-Caesarea in the late third or early fourth century—quite likely a *Palestinian* liturgy that he learned during his time of catechesis under Origen of *Alexandria*. This liturgy could have provided the *liturgical* foundation for what became E-BAS.[79] The redaction of Ω-BAS, likely made by Basil himself in the wake of fourth-century Trinitarian debates, made a primarily *theological* contribution to the development of BAS.[80]

RECENT DEVELOPMENTS: GABRIELE WINKLER AND ACHIM BUDDE

Gabriele Winkler (2005)

Winkler's recent studies of the Basilian anaphoras, especially her tome *Die Basilius-Anaphora*, have challenged the hitherto prevailing

---

75. See Budde, "Ägyptisches Heimatgut," 676–79.

76. Johnson, drawing upon the prior work of Raes and Fenwick, concludes that Egyptian features can be found not only in the post-Sanctus, epiclesis, and doxology of ES-BAS, but also in the institution narrative and the anamnesis (these latter sections possibly originating in another Egyptian prayer). See "Recovering *Ägyptisches* Heimatgut," 193.

77. See Budde, "Ägyptisches Heimatgut," 684ff.

78. Ibid., 687.

79. Stuckwisch, "The Basilian Anaphoras," 122. (For a full reference to Stuckwisch's article, see above, note 3.)

80. See ibid., 129–30.

consensus that ES-BAS represents the oldest extant textual witness of BAS. A long-standing interest in the Syrian and Greek *Formelgut* intertwined with the Armenian tradition and Athanase Renoux's French translation of the earlier Armenian redaction of BAS (1970) motivated Winkler to reconsider the relationship of the various Basilian anaphoras.[81] While Winkler does not claim that the extant Armenian versions are older than E-BAS, she does make the more measured assertion that E-BAS does not *consistently* reflect the oldest traditional layer. Rather, in some places the longer versions of Ω-BAS (especially aspects of the Armenian versions) more faithfully convey information about the oldest form of the text (the hypothetical "*Urtext*"). Furthermore, the Armenian recensions often (although not always) provide glimpses of Syrian traditions lurking in the textual hinterland of BAS—traditions that are most prominent in the versions of Arm-BAS but that are not entirely absent from E-BAS. This suggests a more complicated pattern of development than has usually been supposed, with Syrian traditions playing an important role.[82]

Winkler considers the first Armenian redaction, Arm-BAS I (and, to a lesser extent, Arm-BAS II) as the most significant representatives of Ω.[83] Building on Engberding's suggestion that the Old Armenian readings should generally be given preference among the Ω-recensions, Winkler expands on Engberding's conclusions. For example, while Engberding saw the line of development from Ur-BAS to Arm-BAS II as an indirect one, mediated through Byz-BAS, Winkler detects primitive terminology and grammatical forms in both Arm-BAS I and Arm-BAS II that suggest an early shared source standing behind both Armenian versions.[84] Winkler's research leads her to propose that a Syrian source lies behind both versions of Arm-BAS; hence the

---

81. See Winkler, *Die Basilius-Anaphora*, VI–VII and 2, 8–9. (Cf. note 23 for a full citation of this work.) For Renoux's translation, see A. Renoux, "L'anaphore arménienne de Saint Grégoire l'Illuminateur," in *Eucharisties d'Orient et d'Occident*, vol. 2, ed. B. Botte et al. (Paris: Les Éditions du Cerf, 1970), 83–108.

82. See Winkler, *Die Basilius-Anaphora*, 20; and also Gabriele Winkler, "The Christology of the Anaphora of Basil in its Various Redactions, with Some Remarks Concerning the Authorship of Basil," in *The Place of Christ in Liturgical Prayer: Trinity, Christology, and Liturgical Theology*, ed. Bryan D. Spinks (Collegeville, MN: Liturgical Press, 2008), 112–26, especially the "implications" on 125–26.

83. See, e.g., Winkler, *Die Basilius-Anaphora*, 861.

84. Ibid., 14.

aboriginal redaction of Ω may have occurred not in Syria itself but in Cappadocia.[85] This move also has drastic implications regarding the original language; if the Ω-recensions emerged first in Syria, the initial revisions would presumably not have been done in Greek. Hence the Byzantine recension, often seen as the paradigmatic example of a Eucharistic prayer with a high degree of Christological and Trinitarian development, may at its heart be a translation of a Syriac text.[86] This in turn would necessitate a reassessment of the conclusions of comparative liturgical scholarship about the prevailing direction of liturgical influence more generally.

Winkler's investigation of the Anaphora of Basil is divided into two large blocks. First, working from the various manuscripts and editions of Arm-BAS I and Arm-BAS II, including fragments, Winkler offers a critical text of each of the two versions of Arm-BAS, accompanied by a German translation. The remaining two-thirds of the work consists of a "comparative liturgical commentary" based on painstaking philological analysis of the texts, which draws on not only the Armenian recensions but also the Syrian and Byzantine versions of BAS, the various versions of E-BAS, and other pertinent source material, particularly from the creedal and baptismal traditions, in an attempt to clarify the developmental process underlying *all* the versions of BAS.[87] Winkler finds that BAS seems to be set out in several textual blocks with diverging themes, which are not only of different provenance but also reflect younger and older strata.[88] A consideration of several aspects of the anaphora in light of Winkler's analysis will serve to offer an overview of her conclusions.[89]

---

85. Ibid., 20.

86. See Achim Budde, "Typisch Syrisch? Anmerkungen zur Signifikanz liturgischer Parallelen: Der Ursprung der Basilius-Anaphora in der Diskussion," *Jahrbuch für Antike und Christentum* 45 (2002): 52. For a fuller discussion of the Christology of BAS, see Winkler, "The Christology of the Anaphora of Basil."

87. See Winkler, *Die Basilius-Anaphora*, 38.

88. Ibid., 862.

89. For a condensed presentation of Winkler's conclusions in English, see Gabriele Winkler, "On the Formation of the Armenian Anaphoras: A Completely Revised and Updated Overview," *Studi sull'Oriente Cristiano* 11, no. 2 (2007): 97–130, especially 105–18. (As its title suggests, this article is a revised version of Winkler's earlier essay, "On the Formation of the Armenian Anaphoras: A Preliminary Overview," published in *Worship Traditions in*

The Entrance and the Pre-Sanctus
(Oratio ante Sanctus or "Oratio Theologica")

Winkler detects an underlying unity in the anaphora from the *sursum corda* (or *sursum mentes*) to the angelic cries of "Holy" in the Sanctus.[90] The original focus of this section was likely centered around the various manifestations of angelic *praise* and worship; however, the received texts of Arm-BAS also contain initial references to the *oblatio*, suggesting that themes of *thanksgiving* (εὐχαριστεῖν) were subsequently interpolated into the initial portions of the anaphora in light of changing views about the function of this opening section as an entrance to the entire anaphora (rather than an introduction to the heavenly liturgy).[91] In both Arm-BAS I and E-BAS, the diaconal calls to look attentively point to the coming Sanctus as the revelation of the heavenly liturgy before the eyes of all assembled; consequently, the Sanctus must have formed an integral part of the *Ur-anaphora*.[92]

The words of praise used in the opening section (sung first by the angels, then appropriated also by human beings, as the post-Sanctus makes clear) were formed by impressions about the core of the heavenly liturgy sung by the highest ranks of angels that find their roots, ultimately, in Jewish conceptions of worship.[93] Winkler proposes that the original version of BAS contained references to angel *pairs* (rather than triads, which represent a secondary expansion of the tradition), with the cherubim-seraphim pair still occupying a prominent place in the surviving versions of BAS. This ordering (first cherubim, then seraphim) in the transition to the Sanctus and the angelic praise vocabulary are significant and probably ultimately derived from the Syrian traditions surrounding the Sanctus/Qedušša as the high point of angelic worship.[94] The same sequence (cherubim-seraphim) is found in the Anaphora of the Apostles (repre-

---

Armenia and the Neighboring Christian East, ed. Roberta R. Ervine (Crestwood, NY: St. Vladimir's Seminary Press and St. Nersess Armenian Seminary, 2006), 59–91. Unless otherwise indicated, subsequent citations to "Armenian Anaphoras" in this essay refer to the more recent article of 2007.)

90. See Winkler, *Die Basilius-Anaphora*, 862–63 and 344–45.

91. Ibid., 344.

92. Ibid., 346.

93. Ibid., 862.

94. See ibid., 498ff. for Winkler's speculation about the development of the "angel traditions" in the various forms of BAS, especially 498–99 and 509–11. In this case, she believes that Arm-BAS II preserves a more ancient layer of tradition regarding angels than either Arm-BAS I or E-BAS (see 509–11).

sented by Addai and Mari) as well as in other East Syrian sources. In the vision of Isaiah 6:2-3, it is the seraphim that cry "Holy!" and in the vision of Ezekiel (especially 3:12) the cherubim (*Ḥayyot*) sing "Blessed." Addai and Mari (as well as Arm-BAS I) lack a Benedictus; however, Winkler proposes that the apparently "missing" Benedictus is alluded to in the initial words of praise in the post-Sanctus. This is why in the pre-Sanctus, the cherubim (who sing "Blessed") are mentioned before the seraphim, who at that point are about to sing "Holy."[95] As God was adored with the call of "holy" at the Sanctus, similar language of praise is found before the epiclesis in the Ω-redactions.[96]

Winkler detects additional Syrian features in the pre-Sanctus. The reference to the "Lord of all" is found in many East-Syrian sources—including baptismal and Eucharistic texts, as well as texts pertaining to the Liturgy of the Hours. The phrase likely entered the liturgies through the influence of the Syriac creed. Another typically Syrian feature in the pre-Sanctus of Arm-BAS is the reference to the angels flapping their wings in connection with the beginning of the Sanctus—apparently a midrashic interpretation that crept into the liturgy through Syrian influence. For example, references to the angels flapping their wings occur in the East Syrian anaphoras of Nestorius and of Theodore of Mopsuestia, while the Egyptian versions of Basil that contain the pre-Sanctus section lack this reference.[97]

In E-BAS, themes of the heavenly liturgy and the sense of the entrance through the Sanctus forming a unit are much less developed. Whereas in the Armenian versions human participation in the anaphora represents an imitation by the people of the angelic liturgy, E-BAS entirely lacks words of praise placed on the lips of human beings after the Sanctus. On the other hand, the beginning of the corresponding unit in Arm-BAS I features the verb "glorify" (δοξάζειν). Arm-BAS I, with only one verb, corresponds not only to the earliest Syrian tradition but also to the Jewish tradition about the angels in the Book of Enoch.[98]

The Post-Sanctus (Oratio post Sanctus or "Oratio Christologica")

When the saving deeds of Christ are recounted in the post-Sanctus of BAS, the Armenian version tends to reflect statements from the

---

95. See Winkler, "Armenian Anaphoras," 114–15.
96. Winkler, *Die Basilius-Anaphora*, 863.
97. Winkler, "Armenian Anaphoras," 115–16.
98. Winkler, *Die Basilius-Anaphora*, 878–79.

Nicene Creed while the Egyptian versions tend to reflect a creed in a later stage of development, specifically the Nicene-Constantinopolitan Creed.[99] Contrary to Engberding's thesis that the shorter Egyptian form of BAS is closer to the Ur-form of the anaphora, Winkler observes that sometimes the longer forms of BAS appear to preserve older layers of the Basilian anaphoral tradition than E-BAS does. This is particularly apparent in the heavily-reworked statement about the incarnation in the various versions of BAS. In the Armenian (and Byzantine) versions, the reference to the Holy Spirit is absent (as it is in the Nicene Creed). All the Egyptian versions (and the Syriac version), on the other hand, include mention of the Holy Spirit. Likewise, the Armenian statement on the resurrection limits itself to a repetition of the Nicene reference to Jesus' resurrection "on the third day" (ἀναστάντα τῇ τρίτῃ ἡμέρᾳ) in the *Oratio post Sanctus*; the Egyptian versions add the phrase "from the dead" (ἐκ νεκρῶν in EG-BAS) here as well as in the anamnesis. The addition of "from the dead" is witnessed for the first time in the fourth formula of the creed from the Antiochene Synod of 341. This synod may also be the source of some other unique creedal features in the Armenian and Syriac forms of the anaphora, including the neologisms used in these texts to describe the incarnation: "'he became em-*bodied*' in the Armenian versions (which was not coined before the fifth century) and 'he was en*fleshed*' in the Syriac witness (stemming from the sixth century)."[100] Another distinctive feature of Arm-BAS is the notion that Jesus descended to hell *with his body*, a passage with parallels in the writings of Ephrem the Syrian.[101]

The *Formelgut* of the Antiochene synods, particularly the synod of 341 (which occurred in the context of the Arian controversy) contributed to early Armenian creedal formulas but also influenced the Christological doctrine in *all* the important recensions of BAS, particularly the Ω redactions. The features of the Antiochene synods probably entered the anaphora through Syrian mediation. This *Formelgut* is incor-

99. See ibid., 690–91; and "Armenian Anaphoras," 111.

100. Winkler, "The Christology of the Anaphora of Basil," 118–19 (italics hers); cf. Winkler, *Die Basilius-Anaphora*, 650–56, 666–67, and 691. Winkler suspects that this is not representative of the original form of Ur-BAS, which perhaps contained references to "becoming Man" or echoed Syrian clothing metaphors in claiming that Christ "clothed himself in flesh."

101. Winkler, *Die Basilius-Anaphora*, 681–86; and "Armenian Anaphoras," 117.

porated to a much lesser extent in the versions of E-BAS, but Winkler cautions against assuming for this reason that E-BAS is necessarily older.[102]

The So-Called "Institution Narrative"

Winkler speculates that the increasing significance of the "institution narrative" likely contributed to considerable reworking of BAS. As mentioned above, its presence likely led to the adaptation of the pre-Sanctus to incorporate ideas of εὐχαριστεῖν from the beginning, as would befit an anaphora. (This, however, led to the obfuscation of the once-clear connection between the entrance and the Sanctus of the angels.) Already in Arm-BAS I and ES-BAS, the words over the bread feature the verb pair "bless" and "sanctify" (εὐλογῆσαι-ἁγιάσαι), which has parallels in the Syrian tradition primarily with the epiclesis (cf. Byz-BAS and Arm-BAS II).[103] Consequently, Winkler proposes that the presence of this verb pair in E-BAS represents a secondary reworking of BAS that occurred under the influence of the epiclesis after the insertion of an institution narrative into the anaphora.[104] Winkler suggests that the "so-called institution narrative" originally served primarily a historical or narrative function in BAS rather than an explicitly consecratory role.[105]

The Epiclesis

A closely related issue is whether the *epiclesis* of BAS was originally conceived as an explicit "consecration" of the gifts. Winkler thinks that it was not; rather, the core of the epiclesis in Ur-BAS was likely limited to a request that the Holy Spirit "come" (ἐλθέ).[106] It is Arm-BAS II that retains the more primitive East Syrian tradition of asking the Holy Spirit to "come."[107] This request for the coming of the Holy

---

102. See the summary in Winkler, *Die Basilius-Anaphora*, 866–70, especially the chart on 868–69.

103. Ibid., 719–20. In some later versions of BAS, the verbs "bless" and "sanctify" over the bread are replaced by "give thanks" (εὐχαριστεῖν), making the "bread" and "cup" words parallel one another.

104. Ibid., 865–66, 880.

105. Ibid., 865.

106. Ibid., 829.

107. I.e., the Spirit is asked to "come" as opposed to the presumably later development of requesting that the Holy Spirit be "sent." Arm-BAS I, which

Spirit stands in contrast to the verb "send" (which is, in Winkler's estimation, more typical of West-Syrian and Greek anaphoras) or to the "sanctify" and "show" characteristic of the Egyptian tradition. All extant versions of BAS ask that the Holy Spirit might act on both the gathered people and on the gifts that have been set forth in order to "sanctify" (ἀγιάσαι) them. Most of the Ω versions bundle the request for the "coming" of the Holy Spirit with the verb pair "bless" and "sanctify" (εὐλογῆσαι-ἀγιάσαι).

The Intercessions

The anaphoral intercessions in Arm-BAS I have a different sequence from the Egyptian versions. In the Armenian text, the commemoration of the dead (represented by the mention of several categories of the deceased) flows directly out of the epiclesis; after remembering the dead, the intercessions continue with the commemoration of the living.[108] All the Egyptian reactions, however, seem to alter the sequence deliberately. In the versions of E-BAS, there is a clear break between the epiclesis and the intercessions (which begin with a new sentence). Furthermore, there is a vestige of a reference to the saints in the Egyptian versions that is cut off such that the intercessions can "begin" with a commemoration of the living followed by remembrance of the dead.[109]

Winkler traces this distinction to differing creedal traditions, particularly confessions of faith made in a baptismal context. Early Syriac creedal statements speak of the Lord coming again to judge the *dead and the living*, in that order. Likewise, the first Armenian recension of Basil begins with a commemoration of the dead "that we may find mercy on the day of the appearance of your right judgment with all the saints which from eternity were pleasing to your Godhead: the fathers, patriarchs, prophets . . . and all the souls of those who have died" and only after interceding for the dead do the intercessions for the living begin.[110] In all other known creeds, the Lord comes to judge the "living and the dead," which is the sequence found in other

---

is generally considered to be the earlier version of Arm-BAS, asks God at this point to "send" the Spirit, suggesting that it has undergone secondary modification in this instance.

108. Winkler, *Die Basilius-Anaphora*, 854ff.; and "Armenian Anaphoras," 112.
109. Winkler, *Die Basilius-Anaphora*, 858.
110. Winkler, "Armenian Anaphoras," 112–13; quote from 112.

anaphoras, including the Egyptian versions of BAS. Winkler notes that the concept of being "pleasing" (εὐδοκία) to God occurs in some form at the beginning of the epiclesis as well as at its conclusion (in the transition to the intercessions) in all forms of BAS. This suggests a clear connection of the epiclesis (and, by extension, the intercessions for the dead and the living) to the baptismal context; God declared that he was "well pleased" with Jesus at his baptism in the Jordan—a status in which Christians can share through their own baptism.[111]

Thus, Winkler sees herself standing in the line of Baumstark and Engberding when, prescinding from the obviously later additions of the Ω-redactions (which largely amount to Scriptural and doctrinal interpolations), she asks whether we can still claim that E-BAS is necessarily older if we are *not* considering the text as a whole. If one looks at the "original" layer of the Ω-versions, in particular Arm-BAS I (which Winkler repeatedly claims is the most ancient representative of this traditional strand), the pattern that emerges is somewhat different. It seems that it is not always the Egyptian version that preserves the more original forms.[112]

Critique of Winkler

Impressive in both size and scope, Winkler's comprehensive study of the anaphora of Basil in its various recensions presents many compelling conclusions regarding the possible origin of and interrelationships among the Basilian anaphoras. Her approach suggests that the comparative liturgical scholar undertaking a study of BAS needs to consider not only the available extant texts, but also evidence of various redactional layers within a particular text whose origin and dating may not be consistent with that of the text as a whole. Furthermore, as noted above, Winkler's study disputes not only the prior consensus that E-BAS is *invariably* the oldest surviving version of the text but also prevailing theories about the spread of liturgical influence from one region to another. Henceforth, thanks to Winkler's admirable contribution to Basilian liturgical scholarship, Arm-BAS (and Syr-BAS) must be viewed as influential witnesses to the developmental history of BAS as a whole. Her conclusions, however, have not gone entirely unchallenged.

---

111. Winkler, *Die Basilius-Anaphora*, 857–58.
112. Winkler, "Armenian Anaphoras," 108, 110.

In an essay titled "Typisch Syrisch? Anmerkungen zur Signifikanz liturgischer Parallelen," Achim Budde launches a substantial critique of Winkler's numerous "Syrian parallels."[113] Although he lauds Winkler's impressive philological undertaking, he does question whether the circumstantial evidence Winkler amasses necessarily compels one to conclude that at least the redaction Ω, if not the Ur-form itself, has a Syrian *origin* (which comprises an essential facet of Winkler's argument that the Armenian redactions are the oldest and most important representatives of Ω). Winkler may indeed have found significant parallels between the Armenian and Syrian tradition, but to cement Winkler's argument, it needs to be demonstrated that the majority of the evidence she amasses (1) certainly belongs to the Ω redaction and (2) clearly originated in a certain region and language.[114] In a number of instances, Budde believes that decisive testimony in this regard is lacking.

The first instance Budde considers involves Winkler's argument for Syrian influence on the anamnesis of Arm-BAS. A partial citation of the Armenian version of the anaphora transmitted in the history of Pseudo-Faustus of Byzantium contains a variant reading of a passage in the anamnesis that reflects on the relationship of the Father and the Son. Whereas the liturgical texts of Arm-BAS draw on Hebrews 1:2ff. and Philippians 2:6 to describe the nature of their relationship, the variant reading in Pseudo-Faustus uses non-Scriptural language. Based on Baumstark's laws, Winkler presumes that the variant reading is earlier, and cites *Formelgut* from "Syrian-influenced" Armenian baptismal confessions to make her case.[115]

Budde contends, however, that it is not certain that Pseudo-Faustus' reading actually belongs to Ω. The citation is hardly a "loose paraphrase" of the biblical text but rather a dogmatically-laden reconstruc-

---

113. For a full citation, see above, note 86. Writing in 2002, Budde is responding not to Winkler's *Die Basilius-Anaphora* (2005), but rather to a presentation Winkler delivered at a conference in 1998. Winkler's remarks on this occasion were later published as "Zur Erforschung orientalischer Anaphoren in liturgievergleichender Sicht II: Das Formelgut der Oratio Post Sanctus und Anamnese sowie Interzessionen und die Taufbekentnisse," in Taft and Winkler, *Comparative Liturgy Fifty Years after Anton Baumstark*, 407–93. The examples given in this article, to which Budde responds, however, are also developed at much greater length in *Die Basilius-Anaphora*.

114. Budde, "Typisch Syrisch?" 52.

115. Cf. Winkler, *Die Basilius-Anaphora*, 610–30.

tion. Furthermore, while Faustus' reading is older than the surviving liturgical manuscripts of Arm-BAS, the genre in which the citation occurs (i.e., the explanation of a miracle in a literary account) casts doubt on whether the internal agreement between this citation and Armenian baptismal confessions implies anything about the *liturgical* use of Arm-BAS in the fifth century. Finally, these parallels do not depend on a geographic origin of the text in Syria (or in the Syriac language), nor do they seem to touch the larger redaction-layer of Ω; consequently, there is a lack of "Syrian" corroborating evidence.[116]

According to Budde, Winkler also relies on some arguments from silence. For example, in the anamnesis she notes that both Byz-BAS and E-BAS contain *Darbringungsaussage:* "We offer you your own from your own . . . " (τὰ σὰ ἐκ τῶν σῶν σοὶ προσφέροντες in Byz-BAS). Syr-BAS and Arm-BAS, however, do not contain this phrase, and, based on this silence, Winkler builds a case that Ω contained no *Darbringungsaussage*, which in turn suggests a probable Syrian origin of Ω (since a number of other West Syrian anaphoras likewise lack an offering formula).[117] While it may be true that the *Darbringungsaussage* were lacking in Ω, Winkler is not entitled to posit, based on silence alone, a Syrian *origin* for Ω.[118]

In third set of observations, Budde explores the ways in which Winkler draws attention to terminological correspondence between elements of BAS, particularly Arm-BAS, and other Syrian anaphoras. Questions can be raised, Budde notes, about the significance of some of these comparisons. For example, Winkler postulates that the word "to suffer" (*Leiden*) was a central feature of the Syrian anamnesis, which through the influence of *Formelgut* from the Antiochene synod of 341 migrated to the versions of Arm-BAS.[119] Nevertheless, even Winkler herself can cite Syrian anamneses that do not contain references to Christ's suffering, and similar references to suffering are found in Greek texts from the same period—which leads one to wonder how "typically Syrian" such references actually were.[120] A similar situation exists regarding Winkler's citation of the word "come" in the epiclesis as a distinctively Syrian feature. While the word is present in Syriac

---

116. See Budde, "Typisch Syrisch?" 54–56.
117. See Winkler, *Die Basilius-Anaphora*, 723–41.
118. Budde, "Typisch Syrisch?" 56–57.
119. See Winkler, *Die Basilius-Anaphora*, 741ff.
120. Budde, "Typisch Syrisch?" 57.

anaphoras and in the description of the anaphora given in the cate-chetical homilies of Theodore of Mopsuestia, it can hardly be classified as a uniquely *Syrian* liturgical use. "Come" was known in Greek in the region of Antioch in the fourth century, and the influence could just as easily have entered the Basilian anaphoral tradition through Greek influence as through Syriac.[121]

Finally, Budde considers Winkler's discussion of the sequence of the intercessions, specifically the arrangement whereby the dead are com-memorated first, followed by the living. While Winkler wants to posit from the sequence (dead-living) in the Armenian recensions that the in-tercessions in Ω would have followed the same order, due to a conscious patterning after early Syrian baptismal confessions, Budde believes that the justification for this assertion falters on several points. First, Winkler does not offer a convincing argument to explain why the struc-ture of anaphoral intercessions should be patterned after a baptismal confession of faith. Furthermore, the only example Winkler cites of the "typical" East Syrian arrangement dead-living in the anaphoral interces-sions is the Anaphora of Addai and Mari. Winkler also refers, however to the lost *Urtext* of Addai and Mari—which, according to Engberding's reconstruction, did not originally contain a *memento* for the living and consequently could not have had the dead-living "arrangement" of the intercessions.[122] The fact that a later redactor could "disrupt" the prayer for the dead by inserting a prayer for the living in the middle further suggests that creating or maintaining a "dead-living" sequence was not the operative structuring principle in the redactor's mind.[123] The other East Syrian anaphoras, all of which remember the living before the dead, do not lend any further support to the idea that the dead-living sequence functioned as a "typically" Syrian feature of the anaphoral in-tercessions, especially when Syr-BAS contains the inverse order.

Budde insists that it is necessary to distinguish between the influ-ences on the Basilian-Anaphora and their provenance. When features in an anaphora seem to show Syrian influence, Winkler is not always careful, he claims, about pointing to the wider context of these fea-tures in *each* language and tradition, which might militate against a

121. Ibid., 57–58.
122. Ibid., 58; cf. H. Engberding, "Zum anaphorischen Fürbittgebet der ost-syrische Liturgie der Apostel Addaj und Mar(j)," *Oriens Christianus* 41 (1957): 108.
123. Budde, "Typisch Syrisch?" 59.

conclusion of Syrian *origin*.[124] Further study regarding whether the initial reworking of Ω was carried out in Syriac or in Greek might help to clarify the question of origins. While no evidence has been marshaled thus far to suggest Syriac linguistic influences on Byz-BAS, Sebastian Brock has suggested that at least one edition of Syr-BAS might have been based, at least in part, on a Greek model: "at least parts of it are a translation from Greek, and the vocabulary used suggests that the present Syriac can't be earlier than the 7th century."[125] Winkler does not often pause to consider what might have influenced the Syrian witnesses. Furthermore, she typically presents the Syrian evidence as "very early"—something that cannot necessarily be justified in all cases, especially given the uncertain dating of the text in many of the pertinent manuscripts.[126]

Achim Budde (2004)

Achim Budde's doctoral dissertation (published in 2004 under the title *Die ägyptische Basilios-Anaphora: Text—Kommentar—Geschichte*) represents another substantial body of work on the Basilian anaphoras. Budde focuses his research on the Egyptian versions of Basil, specifically the Greek, Sahidic, and Bohairic versions. Since Engberding's pioneering study, new texts of E-BAS have been discovered and previously known texts have become more available for critical study. This situation begged for a continuation of the work Engberding began on the Egyptian texts, which combined Engberding's primarily philological approach with a concern for the various theological layers evident in the texts as well as a historical approach to their practical implementation.[127] Budde's goal was to produce a *comparative* (as op-

124. Ibid., 60.

125. Sebastian Brock to John Fenwick, 9 October 1983; cited in Fenwick, *The Anaphoras of St. Basil and St. James*, 54.

126. Winkler responded to Budde's assessment with an essay of her own, titled "Zur Signifikanz eines kürzlich erschienenen Aufsatzes zur Basilius-Anaphora," *Studi sull'Oriente Cristiano* 8 (2004): 23–25. She deems his assessment "clever" and a reflection of Budde's considerable analytical skill; however, Budde's critique falters since it does not adequately acknowledge the *status quaestionis* regarding the connections between the Syrian and Armenian sources of BAS. See Winkler, *Die Basilius-Anaphora*, 30.

127. See Achim Budde, *Die ägyptische Basilios-Anaphora: Text—Kommentar— Geschichte*, Jerusalemer Theologisches Forum, Band 7 (Münster: Aschendorff , 2004), 13.

posed to *critical*) edition of the various strands of the E-BAS tradition; consequently, Budde opted not to reconstruct the supposed Egyptian *Urtext*, preferring instead to let information about the history and development of the various versions of E-BAS emerge from the extant texts themselves.[128] Budde ends by questioning the very existence of an Ur*text* and the value of resorting to hypothetical prior textual forms in scholarly attempts to decipher BAS's evolutionary history.

Budde's monograph is divided into three major sections. The first section considers the texts of E-BAS. Budde begins with a review of scholarship and an overview of his methodology, outlining five methodological principles that he intends to follow.[129] First, he seeks insofar as possible to establish an "absolute" (instead of merely relative) arrangement of the manuscript evidence. Second, he chooses to make his divisions on "liturgical" rather than literary grounds in cases where a choice between the two approaches must be made.[130] Third, he seeks a detailed comparison of texts in preference to a text-critical approach focused on establishing the single "best" reading for a particular tradition. Fourth, he seeks to preserve the unique "physiognomy" of the various manuscripts, believing deviations from the perceived "original form" and even mistakes to be potentially revelatory about the significance of the actual liturgical use of these texts. Fifth and finally, he seeks to explain rather than "erase" the history of E-BAS's development—a history in which older forms are likely to be found coexisting alongside newer ones. After outlining this methodology, Budde provides a comparative edition of EG-BAS, ES-BAS, and EB-BAS in parallel columns, along with a German translation.

The second major section of Budde's study, amounting to nearly half of the book, is a commentary on the text of BAS in which each section of the Egyptian anaphora is analyzed line-by-line, sometimes word-by-word (philologically, but also theologically and historically). His analysis, as one reviewer put it "allows Budde to suggest how the

---

128. Ibid., 63 and 35.

129. Ibid., 57–63.

130. Budde adopts this strategy because copyists of liturgical works, in contrast to literary ones, are not necessarily compelled to preserve all the details of a received manuscript (whether its author is known or unknown) by reproducing the text exactly; rather, it is natural for subsequent users of a liturgical tradition to transmit a version of the "original" text that is compatible with the current practices of their own communities.

text was expanded and changed in translation, but also establishes the Egyptian 'flavour' of this anaphora."[131] This commentary highlights some peculiarities found in the Egyptian versions of the texts that may have bearing on the origins and lines of influence not only of the Egyptian versions of the anaphora but also on the development of the Basilian anaphoral family as a whole. Some of these features will be discussed further below.

The third and final section of Budde's study, titled "Geschichte," attempts to outline a plausible course of the historical development that eventually yielded the extant Egyptian textual incarnations of BAS. Based on observations raised during the course of his analysis of the various texts of ES-BAS, EG-BAS, and EB-BAS, Budde posits the process of BAS's evolution as a series of "Improvisationsschemata." (These could well have originated through oral improvisation rather than from the deliberate reworking of a textual model.[132]) Budde proposes that the Basilian anaphoral tradition is ultimately not native to Egypt but most likely arose somewhere in the area between Jerusalem and Byzantium, whence it was subsequently dispersed to other regions.[133] Given the differences between the versions of E-BAS and the forms belonging to the Ω-BAS family of texts, a form of BAS must have reached Egypt at a fairly early stage of the anaphora's development. While exploring how the anaphora might have undergone further transformations in Egypt, Budde also attends to various factors that converged in the fourth century (and thereafter) to favor a transition from orally-transmitted version(s) of Eucharistic prayers to written form(s)—as well as the impact such changes would have had on Eucharistic praying.[134] This historical section also addresses the issue of

131. Bryan D. Spinks, review of *Die ägyptische Basilios-Anaphora: Text—Kommentar—Geschichte*, by Achim Budde, *Journal of Theological Studies* 57, no. 1 (2006): 303.

132. This point has implications not only for explaining some of the variation between the forms of E-BAS, but also for accounting for the differences between E-BAS and other forms of BAS and for the similarities between E-BAS and other anaphoras (such as the Anaphora of James and the Anaphora of Nestorius).

133. See Budde, *Basilios-Anaphora*, 550–51.

134. Such factors included the great expansion of Christianity in the fourth century, the increasing importance of theological precision in prayer formulas due to concerns about doctrinal orthodoxy, and changing expectations about the liturgical role of the bishop as presider of the Eucharistic prayer. See ibid.,

Basilian attribution. In light of his comparative analysis and the historical evidence, Budde proposes that the attribution of the anaphora to Basil may have been a euchological "Marketing-Konzept" that arose even before the two main lines of BAS diverged;[135] however, Budde does not rule out the possibility that Basil of Caesarea may have played some small role in shaping the text of the prayer.

Commentary on the Text of E-BAS

As mentioned above, the bulk of Budde's study consists of a commentary on the Egyptian forms of BAS. Since his conclusions regarding the different sections of the anaphora help to illumine the possible relationship not only among the various versions of E-BAS but also among E-BAS and other forms of BAS, it would be beneficial to examine them at greater length. For instance, the opening dialogue of the prayer seems to belong to a relatively stable textual tradition characteristic of anaphoras in general (as opposed to specific regional concerns). Whereas the Greek texts of E-BAS occasionally reflect Byzantine influence in their syntax and vocabulary, the Coptic versions (i.e., ES-BAS and EB-BAS) show more affinity with earlier Egyptian customs and/or the Syrian tradition, even in phrases that are also typical of comparable Greek anaphoras.[136] The Coptic versions also exhibit a greater tendency toward standardization of the text and toward smoothing the transition between the opening dialogue and the beginning of the prayer itself.

In E-BAS, the praise of creation that leads up to the Sanctus is filled with vague biblical references (rather than direct quotations) and seems to be largely unaffected by the theological concerns of the fourth century; hence the text seems to be the product of a biblically-formed milieu rather than a conscious literary adaptation of Scriptural material.[137] In this portion of the anaphora, E-BAS displays little connection with the three other versions designated "Ω" by Engberding (i.e., Arm-BAS, Byz-BAS, and Syr-BAS). Whereas the reference to creation in E-BAS is relatively brief, the Ω-versions only mention creation

553–59; and Allan Bouley, *From Freedom to Formula: The Evolution of the Eucharistic Prayer from Oral Improvisation to Written Texts* (Washington, DC: Catholic University of America Press, 1981).

135. Budde, *Basilios-Anaphora*, 570.

136. Ibid., 239.

137. Ibid., 268.

in passing before launching into praise and thanksgiving for God's saving action in history. Here E-BAS may well be, as Engberding speculated, the "product of Egyptian soil." There is no indication that the redactors of E-BAS and the other recensions were relying on an earlier shared tradition, textual or otherwise. Budde proposes that this opening section may represent an attempt to craft a new introduction for the Sanctus, based on Egyptian models, for a prayer with "Antiochene" rather than "Egyptian" structure.[138] Since the Sanctus of BAS does not serve as immediate preparation for the epiclesis (cf., e.g., the Anaphora of Mark), perhaps the compiler or redactor opted to cast the themes of earthly and heavenly realities (praise of creation and Sanctus) as a general "introduction" to the prayer.[139]

Parallels have been recognized between the narration of salvation history presented in BAS and the comparable sections of the Anaphora of James and the Anaphora of Nestorius. Budde suggests that BAS integrates various elements from multiple schemata recounting the major events of salvation history—perhaps based in part on the deliberate use of textual models by BAS's compiler(s) and redactors, but possibly just as much or more relying on verbal conventions that were the common property of many communities through their dissemination in creeds and other expressions of faith used in liturgical contexts.[140] Linguistically, nearly every formulation present in the text of E-BAS is already widespread by the fourth century, with some phrases being common to many creeds. If these phrases can be said to reflect regional customs, the area surrounding Antioch would be most heavily represented, with lesser connections to the regions of Asia Minor and Palestine.[141]

The connections between E-BAS and Ω-BAS are obvious; as Engberding observed, the longer Ω versions seem to represent, in general, an expansion and theological development of the concepts expressed

---

138. Note, however, Stuckwisch's caveat above (p. 238) about regarding BAS as an anaphora of the "Antiochene" form. This designation may have more to say about the shape of the prayer than its geographical origins.

139. Budde, *Basilios-Anaphora*, 271–72. In making this connection, Budde credits A. Gerhards, who made similar observations about the Anaphora of Gregory.

140. Ibid., 310.

141. Ibid., 316.

in the shorter E-BAS.[142] Whereas Engberding presumed the existence of an *Urtext* to explain the divergence of the two major strands of BAS at this point, however, Budde seeks to explore the possibility of literary dependence between the various forms of BAS (and other anaphoral texts).[143] Budde seeks to test his theory by surveying (1) the terms common to E-BAS, JAS, and Nestorius; (2) terms common to E-BAS and Ω-BAS that are not found in JAS and/or Nestorius; and (3) points at which E-BAS, JAS, and Nestorius agree but differ from Ω-BAS. Based on this analysis, Budde concludes that the bulk of the commonalities between E-BAS and Ω-BAS in this section of the anaphora are also found in other texts; thus the mere existence of verbal similarities is not in itself sufficient to demonstrate a relationship of redactional dependence between the various versions of BAS. There are, however, several instances of correspondence between E-BAS and Ω-BAS that are *not* shared by the other texts Budde considered—which suggest that there is a specific relationship between E-BAS and Ω-BAS, both of which clearly derive from the same prayer tradition. Considering the relationship between E-BAS and Byz-BAS more closely, Budde notes that nowhere does the verbal correspondence extend beyond three or four words in succession—which leads him to wonder whether the arrangement of commonalities is due to direct literary reworking or to a looser adaptation of elements from a common tradition.[144]

Budde characterizes the role of the institution narrative in BAS as "the anamnetically-realized foundation for the current fulfillment of the mystery, which is specifically prayed for in the epiclesis" that follows it.[145] Its focus is not on the significance—much less consecratory effect—of Jesus' interpretive words over the bread and cup; rather, what is emphasized is that it was *Christ himself* who "eucharistized" and sanctified the Eucharistic gifts of bread and wine through praise and thanksgiving. The text of the institution narrative in E-BAS is highly standardized, reflected particularly in the parallelism between the words concerning the bread and the cup. Nevertheless, there are

---

142. There are several instances in which aspects of E-BAS's narration of salvation history are not included in Ω-BAS. For the most part, however, Ω-BAS contains a parallel in such instances that could be considered as a theological expansion of the "omitted" concept. See ibid., 319.

143. See ibid., 316–17.

144. For a summary of Budde's conclusions on this point, see ibid., 318–19.

145. Ibid., 376.

a few indications, particularly when the oldest manuscript of ES-BAS is considered, that the institution narrative of E-BAS may be more closely related to the native Egyptian Anaphora of Cyril than to a Byzantine or Syrian model. While the two Coptic versions of E-BAS are clearly closely related to each other, there are also a few minor instances in which EB-BAS agrees with EG-BAS over and against ES-BAS, which makes it unlikely that the institution narrative of EB-BAS constitutes a direct translation of that of ES-BAS.[146]

Turning to the anamnesis and epiclesis, the questions of relationship and interdependence of the various versions of E-BAS become still more complicated. The elements in these sections of the prayer have parallels not only in the other recensions of BAS, but also in East Syrian anaphoras and the writings of Theodore of Mopsuestia, the Palestinian tradition, and West Syrian anaphoras (most notably JAS)—not to mention some close points of correspondence in Alexandrian liturgies. Some features of E-BAS are widespread by the late fourth century; a few others tend to be shared by many anaphoras of the "Antiochene" type (e.g., the verb "to remember"—as opposed to "announce" and other variants more typical of the Alexandrian tradition—and the tendency to refer to the "passion" of Christ in this context, rather than to his "death" as in the Alexandrian anaphoras).[147] Syrian and/or Byzantine influence on this section of the anaphora is possible. It is interesting to note that, in comparison to the institution narrative, the anamnesis-epiclesis sections of the various versions of E-BAS seem to be much less standardized. In particular, the Bohairic version seems to have followed a different trajectory of development from ES-BAS and EG-BAS, as evidenced not only by some differences in the formulation of the epiclesis but above all by a more precise understanding of the transformation requested, framed in terms of actualizing what was commemorated in the epiclesis (which in turn implies a more deliberate connection between these two sections of the anaphora than is articulated in the other versions).[148]

In terms of the intercessions, Engberding identified an issue that has yet to be adequately explained, namely: Why do the intercessions in Byz-BAS appear in a completely different order than those of E-BAS? And what significance does this have for the common history

146. See ibid., 374–75.
147. Ibid., 424–25.
148. Ibid., 430.

of the various forms of the Basilan anaphora? Whereas Engberding approached the issue in terms of reconstructing the order of the
intercessions in the supposed *Urtext*, Budde, who expresses doubts
throughout the course of his commentary about the need to posit
the existence of such an *Urtext*, seeks to fundamentally reconsider
Engberding's treatment of the intercessions. He adopts two criteria
at the outset: (1) the decision to examine only those intercessions that
are specific to the Basilian anaphoras (since intercessions that are
also common to other sources are less meaningful in this regard)—a
tactic Engberding employed as well—and (2) the hypothesis that any
intercessions already present in an *Urtext* ought to be well attested in
all branches of the manuscript tradition. With these criteria in hand,
Budde reconsiders all the passages that Engberding judged to be part
of an *Urtext*, using evidence from additional manuscripts that were
not available when Engberding conducted his research.[149] Budde
notes that, in terms of the intercessions, the features common to all
forms of BAS are (a) not very numerous, (b) variously arranged, and
(c) either too weak to provide a basis for making judgments about
related texts or also represented, in some form, in other texts.[150] Whatever the literary dependence (or lack thereof) between the intercessions in E-BAS and Ω-BAS, the specific ordering of the intercessions
in E-BAS could have been inspired by similar associations among the
intercessions in other prayers of the Coptic liturgical tradition.[151] Similarly, Budde considers E-BAS's concluding doxology to be characteristic of the native Coptic tradition rather than of external influence
from elsewhere.[152]

Critique of Budde

Budde performs a valuable service in highlighting the similarities
and differences among the various versions of the Egyptian recension
of the Anaphora of Basil. In addition, he also explores the possible connections between E-BAS, Byz-BAS, Syr-BAS, and Arm-BAS, probing
theological and liturgical parallels in addition to literary ones. Perhaps
one of Budde's more provocative moves is his subtle but repeated
questioning of whether one needs to posit the existence of a lost *Urtext*

149. Ibid., 527.
150. Ibid., 529.
151. Ibid., 534.
152. See ibid., 539–40.

to explain the common threads binding the various representatives of the Basilian anaphoral family. Budde contends that liturgical manuscripts should be compared with each other rather than "corrected" against a standard edition. Each manuscript is important in its own right, inclusive of variants and even mistakes, for the insight it can provide into the liturgical situation of a particular place and time and into the developmental history of a set of related liturgical texts. As Gerard Rouwhorst has noted, "This implies a fundamental criticism of the methods used by most scholars who are particularly concerned with the reconstruction of 'Urtexte' of the rituals."[153]

Nevertheless, Budde's effort to produce an "'édition comparée' statt 'édition critique'"[154] has both advantages and disadvantages when carried to its logical conclusion. Certainly a comparative edition of extant texts could prove more useful for reconstructing actual liturgical practice than piecing together a hypothetical "original" text that could hinder and misguide future researchers just as easily as it could help them. Yet, unless the number of manuscripts involved is very small, a comparative edition based on select representatives from the major subgroups of manuscripts would likely be more practical (and intelligible).[155] "Moreover, liturgical scholars will be best served with editions in which all too obvious mistakes have been corrected and implausible and idiosyncratic variants have been relegated to the critical apparatus."[156]

The sorts of compromises involved in preparing a comparative edition are evident in Budde's edition of the Egyptian versions of BAS. In this edition, Budde draws on a large number of manuscripts—twelve in Greek, ten in Sahidic, and twenty-eight in Bohairic. Selected texts from each language group—without modification—are presented in three parallel columns, with a German translation in a fourth column. The Greek and Sahidic versions of E-BAS feature the text of the oldest available manuscript in each language group. The Bohairic text is drawn from a Euchologion published for the Coptic Orthodox Church in 1902, and this is the version of the text represented by the German

---

153. Gerard Rouwhorst, review of *Die ägyptische Basilios-Anaphora: Text—Kommentar—Geschichte,* by Achim Budde, *Vigiliae Christianae* 62 (2008): 310.

154. Budde, *Basilios-Anaphora,* 63.

155. See Rouwhorst, 310–11.

156. Ibid., 311.

translation.[157] Such an arrangement effectively limits a full appreciation of the comparative textual work Budde has undertaken to those who are not only well-versed in the major Coptic dialects but also patient enough to sort through the additional information supplied by the supporting material. For, "in order to get insight into, for instance, the 7th century Sahidic version, one does not only have to be able to read Sahidic, but also to first study the critical apparatus and the commentary. German translations of each of the three versions . . . would have been of great help to the liturgical scholars who are not specialists in Coptic and are not interested in things such as the development of the orthography of Sahidic and Bohairic."[158] While Budde's work is certainly a substantial scholarly achievement, the highly unusual way in which he presents his data makes it somewhat challenging to use his book as a tool in the work of comparative liturgical scholarship.

Regarding the commentary on the text of E-BAS, Budde's preference for tracing the *Egyptian* traditional strands in E-BAS may lead him to overlook important contributions from other redactional layers (the Armenian, Byzantine, and Syrian); Gabriele Winkler, not surprisingly, is particularly critical of his relative neglect of the possible influences of the Syrian and Armenian forms of BAS on E-BAS.[159] A potentially glaring omission in this regard is that Budde devotes very little attention to the Old Armenian recension (Arm-BAS I). Bryan Spinks has observed this deficiency as well: "What is curious is the lack of extended discussion of [Arm-BAS I]. . . . This anaphora seems to be a form of Basil which is even earlier than the Egyptian, perhaps the inspiration for [the Armenian Anaphoras of] Cyril and Isaac, and predates Basil himself."[160] While Budde does attend to "Syrian" elements preserved in the text of E-BAS and explores how they might have traveled to

157. See the chart in Budde, *Basilios-Anaphora*, 140, for a list of the manuscripts used in the comparative edition of the text.

158. Rouwhorst, review of *Die ägyptische Basilios-Anaphora*, 311.

159. Gabriele Winkler, review of *Die ägyptische Basilios-Anaphora: Text—Kommentar—Geschichte*, by Achim Budde, *Orientalia Christiana Periodica* 72, no. 1 (2006): 248. Had Winkler's monograph (*Die Basilius-Anaphora,* 2005) been available as Budde was writing his dissertation, presumably he would have taken the conclusions demonstrated through Winkler's own work into account.

160. Spinks, review of *Die ägyptische Basilios-Anaphora*, 304. Spinks' surprise on this point is due to the fact that "Budde notes that Armenian Cyril and Isaac are close to the Basiline, and argues that they were influenced by Cappadocia where Basil lived" (ibid.).

Egypt along with a text of BAS,[161] critique on this point is not without merit. For example, when considering the connection between E-BAS and Ω-BAS, Budde tends to focus on Byz-BAS as the primary representative of Ω-BAS while devoting comparatively little attention to Syr-BAS in its own right and even less to Arm-BAS.

Finally, although Budde's thorough comparative study is a rich source of information for those interested in the specific content and interrelationship among the various textual witnesses of E-BAS, he may not have escaped entirely the temptation to posit an *Urtext* standing behind the extant versions, despite his claims to the contrary. Winkler contends that his inclusion of so many variant readings and technical expansions in an effort to examine the possible *liturgical* usages of the various texts of E-BAS compromises intelligibility at times, effectively resulting in the construction of a hypothetical text that could have served as a liturgical formulary in no real place or time.[162] On a related matter, while Budde's hypothesis of oral improvisation playing a part in the development of the textual tradition of BAS is intriguing, it also runs the risk of serving as a "black hole" of sorts in which unresolved issues can be deposited. Thus, while Budde provides helpful texts of several versions of E-BAS, his commentary and historical analysis nonetheless leave many questions for future research.

THE STATE OF THE QUESTION AND DIRECTIONS FOR FUTURE RESEARCH

Various versions of the Basilian anaphoras have been prayed by churches in the East, particularly the Coptic Orthodox Church and churches of the Byzantine Rite, for many centuries. The liturgical revisions of the twentieth century introduced prayers based on the Basilian anaphoras to the liturgical books of a number of Western churches. For example, BAS has assumed a place, in modified form, in the Missal of Pope Paul VI in 1969 (as Eucharistic Prayer IV), in the *Book of Common Prayer* of the Episcopal Church in the United States of America in 1979 (as Prayer D), in *The Service for the Lord's Day* of the Presbyterian Church (United States) in 1984 (as Great Prayer of Thanksgiving E—now F in the *Book of Common Worship* [1993]), and in the Church of England's *Common Worship* in 2000 (as Prayer F). In

---

161. See, e.g., Budde, *Basilios-Anaphora*, 578ff. (in the "History" section).
162. Winkler, review of *Die ägyptische Basilios-Anaphora*, 247–48.

terms of liturgical scholarship, however, the definitive "book" that sorts out all the uncertainties regarding the history of the Basilian anaphoras and the relationship of the many forms of the prayer to each other remains unfinished.

After nearly a century of liturgical scholarship following the groundbreaking publication of Engberding in 1931, scholars in recent years have proposed corrections or modifications to Engberding's methodology (e.g., Fenwick, Budde); called for the radical reconsideration of Engberding's paradigm of the relationship among E-BAS, Arm-BAS, Byz-BAS, and Syr-BAS (as Winkler has done recently with her call to reassess the importance of the Syrian and Armenian evidence); and even questioned the existence of an *Urtext* (Budde). Winkler's very significant study has raised interesting questions and pointed to avenues for further investigation. Such further investigation will be focused, undoubtedly, toward establishing definitively her implicit suggestion that the *Urtext* of BAS is ultimately of Syrian provenance. Likewise, Budde's recent monograph has focused renewed attention on the uniquely Egyptian characteristics of E-BAS but nonetheless cannot explain what significance this might have regarding either the anaphora's ultimate origin or its (possible) connection to Basil.

Future studies that attempt to determine more precisely the dating of the various manuscript and textual traditions of the Basilian family may further the quest to outline the process of textual development of the respective forms of BAS. Meanwhile, the labors of both Winkler and Budde have borne much good fruit and greatly advanced the state of Basilian anaphoral scholarship. The past decade has seen tantalizing new questions arise alongside perennial problems, leaving plenty of fertile ground for future scholarly exploration of the Basilian anaphoral tradition.

Michael Zheltov

XI. The Moment of Eucharistic Consecration in Byzantine Thought

I. THE EPICLESIS—A RULE OF FAITH?

The problem of the epiclesis, its meaning, and its importance—or, alternatively, expendability—for the consecration of bread and wine during a Eucharistic prayer has long been a highly polemical issue.[1] Despite their differences, scholars and theologians have often taken for granted that it was the Byzantine Church that always believed in a consecratory power of the epiclesis. Indeed, from the fourth century on (i.e., from the very starting point of the development of the Byzantine liturgy), the Byzantine Eucharistic prayers contained explicit epicleses with strong consecratory statements.

In this article I will demonstrate, however, that, while the Byzantines undoubtedly were very concerned about the epiclesis recited during their Eucharistic liturgy,[2] its mere existence did not always signify the importance it is ascribed in late- and post-Byzantine theological literature. For the Byzantines often pointed to some other elements of the rite as "consecratory," and were in nowise strangers to the idea of a Eucharistic consecration independent of an epiclesis.

---

1. Very useful overviews of the history of the debates and of the problem in general can be found in: Sévérien Salaville, "Épiclèse eucharistique," in *Dictionnaire de théologie catholique*, vol. 5, part 1a (Paris: Letouzey et Ané, 1924), 194–300; Cyprian Kern, *The Eucharist* [original title in Russian: архимандрит Киприан, Евхаристия] (Paris: YMCA-Press, 1947), 245–72; Παντελεήμον (Ῥοδόπουλος), μητροπολίτης Ὁ *καθαγιασμὸς τῶν δώρων τῆς θείας Εὐχαριστίας* (Λειτουργικὰ Βλατάδων 3; Thessaloniki, 2000²); John McKenna, *The Eucharistic Epiclesis: A Detailed History from the Patristics to the Modern Era*, 2nd ed. (Chicago: Hildenbrand Books, 2009), 70ff.

2. And because of this Byzantine concern I will start my article with a brief discussion of the relevant liturgical texts themselves, i.e., of the epicleses of the Byzantine liturgies of St. Basil the Great (BAS) and St. John Chrysostom (CHR), but without any intention to trace their origins.

II. THE EPICLESIS

II. 1. The Origins of the Epiclesis: A Brief Overview

The origins of the epiclesis are obscure and much debated. The earliest extant Eucharistic prayers from the *Didache* contain no explicit epicletic petition[3] (though some scholars identify the acclamation "Maranatha" from Did. 10.6 with a proto-epiclesis[4]). In pre-Nicaean Christian liturgical usage the words ἐπικαλεῖν / ἐπικαλεῖσθαι and ἐπίκλησις, as has been demonstrated,[5] referred more to "naming/applying the name" than to "calling forth in prayer."[6] It is, therefore, tempting to suggest that the epiclesis in

---

3. The literature on the *Didache* and its Eucharistic prayers is extensive; I would suggest to start reading with Kurt Niederwimmer, *Die Didache*, Kommentar zu den Apostolischen Vätern 1 (Göttingen: Vandenhoeck & Ruprecht, 1993²); Jonathan A. Draper, ed., *The Didache in Modern Research*, Arbeiten zur Geschichte des Antiken Judentums und des Urchristentums 37 (Leiden: Brill, 1996); Willy Rordorf and André Tuilier, *La Doctrine des Douze Apôtres (Didachè): Introduction, Texte Critique, Traduction, Notes, Appendice, Annexe et Index*, Sources Chrétiennes 248 (Paris: Les Éditions du Cerf, 1998); Huub van de Sandt and David Flusser, *The Didache: Its Jewish Sources and Its Place in Early Judaism and Christianity* (Assen: Fortress Press, 2002).

4. See Rudolf Stählin, "Der Herr ist Geist," in *Kosmos und Ekklesia: Festschrift für Wilhelm Stählin zu seinem siebzigsten Geburtstag*, ed. Heinz Dietrich Wendland (Kassel: J. Stauda-Verlag, 1953), 40–54; Karl Bernhard Ritter, "Bemerkungen zur eucharistischen Epiklese," in ibid., 163–73; John A. T. Robinson, "Traces of a Liturgical Sequence in 1 Corinthians 16:20-24," *Journal of Theological Studies* 4 (1953): 38–41. See a criticism of this view in Palle Dinesen, "Die Epiklese im Rahmen altkirchlicher Liturgien: Eine studie über die eucharistische Epiklese," in *Studia Theologica: Nordic Journal of Theology* 16 (1962): 42–107.

5. See R. Hugh Connolly, "On the Meaning of 'Epiclesis,'" *Downside Review* (January 1923): 28–43, written in reply to John Walton Tyrer, *The Eucharistic Epiclesis* (Liverpool: Longmans, Green, 1917); R. Hugh Connolly, "The Meaning of ἐπίκλησις: A Reply," *Journal of Theological Studies* 25 (1924): 337–64, written in reply to John Walton Tyrer, "The Meaning of ἐπίκλησις," ibid., 139–50. The two latter articles present a very detailed list of the contexts of the usage of ἐπικαλεῖν / ἐπικαλεῖσθαι and ἐπίκλησις in early Christianity. See also Odo Casel, "Zur Epiklese," *Jahrbuch für Liturgiewissenschaft* 3 (1923): 100–2; and idem, "Neue Beiträge zur Epiklese-Frage," *Jahrbuch für Liturgiewissenschaft* 4 (1924): 169–78; and Johannes Betz, *Die Eucharistie in der Zeit der griechischen Väter*, Bd. I/1 (Freiburg: Herder, 1955), 320–42.

6. It is noteworthy that in the Byzantine Eucharistic liturgies of BAS and CHR the verb ἐπικαλεῖσθαι is used in both senses. In the ekphonesis before the

its later sense of "a call to God/Spirit/Logos to come and show/
sanctify the bread and wine" is a result of the development of the
early epicletic "naming the divine Name" formulae. This possibility comes to light when one compares Origen's commentary on 1
Corinthians 7:5, where he describes the Eucharistic bread as the one
"over which the Name of God and of Christ and of the Holy Spirit
has been invoked" (FragmCor 34),[7] with a baptismal and a Eucharistic prayer from *Acta Thomae*:

> Come, holy name of the Messiah; come, power of grace, which is from
> on high; come, perfect mercy; come, exalted gift; come, sharer of the
> blessing; come, revealer of hidden mysteries; come, mother of the
> seven houses, whose rest was in the eighth house; come, messenger of
> reconciliation; and communicate with the minds of these youths; come,
> Spirit of holiness. (§ 27)[8]

> Come, gift of the Exalted, come perfect mercy; come, holy Spirit;
> come, revealer of the mysteries of the chosen among the prophets;
> come, proclaimer by his Apostles of the combats of our victorious
> Athlete; come treasure of majesty; come beloved of the mercy of the
> Most High; come, (you) silent (one), revealer of the mysteries of the
> Exalted; come, utterer of hidden things, and shewer [*sic*] of the works
> of our God; come, Giver of life in secret, and manifest in your deeds;
> come, giver of joy and rest to all who cleave to you; come, power of
> the Father and wisdom of the Son, for you are one in all; come, and
> communicate with us in this Eucharist which we celebrate and in the

---

Our Father it has the sense of "naming": "And make us worthy, Master, with
confidence and without fear of condemnation, to dare call You [ἐπικαλεῖσθαι],
the heavenly God, *Father*," while in the prayers of the clergy before the Great
Entrance (i.e., in the so-called "prayers of the faithful," though the actual
prayer of the laity is a litany read simultaneously with these) and after it (after
the Great Entrance—only in CHR, before—in both BAS and CHR) it has the
sense of "calling forth."

7. Greek text in Claude Jenkins, "Origen on I Corinthians, [part] III," *Journal
of Theological Studies* 9 (1908): 502. On Origen as a witness to the Eucharistic
theology and practice of his time see Harald Buchinger, "Early Eucharist in
Transition? A Fresh Look at Origen," in *Jewish and Christian Liturgy and Worship:
New Insights into Its History and Interaction*, ed. Albert Gerhards and Clemens
Leonhard (Leiden: Brill, 2007), 207–27, and the literature indicated there.

8. ET from Albertus Frederik Johannes Klijn, *The Acts of Thomas*, 2nd ed.
(Leiden: Brill, 2003), 77.

offering which we offer, and in the commemoration which we make. (§ 50)[9]

In an article published in 1949 Friedrich Nötscher attempted to explain the "mechanism" of the consecration via invoking the divine Name: as in the Bible, naming something by a person's name results in this person's taking possession of this thing.[10] Indeed, the notion of God "accepting" the gifts (in this or that way), sanctifying them in return, is well known in both the Christian East and the West. In the Roman Canon, for example, the idea is explicitly mentioned not even once.

Still, one should also remember that in the biblical tradition revealing the Name of God meant revealing God himself and that in earliest Christian thought the divine Name theology was closely related to Christology.[11] This could be the key to understanding the use of naming formulae in early Christian worship and also give a viable expla-

---

9. ET from ibid., 125. See Heinz Kruse, "Zwei Geist-Epiklesen der syrischen Thomasakten," *Oriens Christianus* 69 (1985): 33–53; Reinhard Meßner, "Zur Eucharistie in den Thomasakten: Zugleich ein Beitrag zur Frühgeschichte der eucharistischen Epilkese," in *Crossroad of Cultures: Studies in Liturgy and Patristics in Honor of Gabriele Winkler*, ed. Robert F. Taft, Orientalia Christiana Analecta 260 (Roma: Pontificio Istituto Orientale, 2000), 493–513. Cf. also the anaphora of the East Syrian liturgy of Theodore of Mopsuestia: "And we beseech you, O my Lord, and supplicate you, and worship you, and petition you, that your worshipful Godhead and your mercifulness may be well-pleased, O my Lord, and there may come upon us and upon this oblation the grace of the Holy Spirit. May He dwell and rest upon this bread and upon this cup, and may He bless, consecrate, and seal them in the Name of the Father, and of the Son, and of the Holy Spirit. By the power of your Name may this bread become the holy body of our Lord Jesus Christ, and this cup the precious blood of our Lord Jesus Christ" (ET by M. J. Birnie, from *Takhsa d'Kahaneh d'Adta d'Madinkha—Priestly Liturgical Manual of the Church of the East* [s.l., s.a.]).

10. Friedrich Nötscher, "Epiklese in biblischer Beleuchtung," *Biblica* 30 (1949): 401–4.

11. See Jarl E. Fossum, "Jewish-Christian Christology and Jewish Mysticism," *Vigilae Christianae* 37 (1983): 260–87; idem, *The Name of God and the Angel of the Lord: Samaritan and Jewish Concepts of Intermediation and the Origin of Gnosticism*, WUNT 1/36 (Tübingen: Mohr Siebeck, 1985); Charles Gieschen, *Angelomorphic Christology: Antecedents and Early Evidence* (Leiden: Brill, 1998); idem, "The Divine Name in Ante-Nicene Christology," *Vigilae Christianae* 57 (2003): 115–58.

nation for the fact that in some anaphoras God is asked "to manifest" or "to show," rather than "to convert" or "to make," the offered gifts the Body and Blood of Christ:[12] if *the* Name is Christ himself, then the application of the Name to the gifts should result in a manifestation of Christ in them.[13] The best known anaphora with such word usage is the anaphora of Basil (in its various versions), which in its epiclesis has the verb "to show" (ἀναδείκνυμι). Another interesting example is the anaphora from the Barcelona papyrus, the oldest extant manuscript of a Christian Eucharistic prayer, where for the same purpose the verb σωματοποιέω is used, meaning (among other things) "to make more solid, to depict, to represent [in art]."[14]

Another source for the epiclesis could be a petition for the unity of the Church, much accented already in the Eucharistic prayers of the *Didache* and presumably originating in the Jewish grace after meals.[15]

12. See Joseph Höller, *Die Epiklese der griechisch-orientalischen Liturgien* (Wien: Mayer & Company, 1912), 110–34; Erik Peterson, "Die Bedeutung von ΑΝΑΔΕΙΚΝΥΜΙ in den griechischen Liturgien," in *Festgabe für Adolf Deismann zum 60. Geburtstag* (Tübingen: Mohr Siebeck, 1927), 320–26; E. G. Cuthbert F. Atchley, *On the Epiclesis of the Eucharistic Liturgy and in the Consecration of the Font*, Alcuin Club Collections 31 (Oxford: Oxford University Press, 1935), 114–15; Martin Jugie, "De epiclesi Eucharistica secundum Basilium Magnum," *Acta Academiae Velehradensis* 19 (1948): 202–7; Séverien Salaville, "ΑΝΑΔΕΙΚΝΥΝΑΙ, ΑΠΟΦΑΝΕΙΝ: Note de lexicologie à propos de textes eucharistiques," in *Mémorial Louis Petit: Mélanges d'historie et d'archéologie byzantines* (Bucarest: Institut Français d'études byzantines, 1948), 413–22.

13. And this could intimate the idea of the Logos-epiclesis, which I will not discuss further. See McKenna, *The Eucharistic Epiclesis*, 107–9; Maxwell E. Johnson, *The Prayers of Sarapion of Thmuis: A Literary, Liturgical and Theological Analysis*, Orientalia Christiana Analecta 249 (Roma: Pontificio Istituto Orientale, 1995), 233–53; Robert F. Taft, "From Logos to Spirit: On the Early History of the Epiclesis," in *Gratias Agamus. Studien zum eucharistischen Hochgebet: Für Balthasar Fischer*, ed. Andreas Heinz and Heinrich Rennings (Freiburg e. a.: Herder, 1992), 489–502.

14. See my critical edition of this anaphora, Michael Zheltov, "The Anaphora and Thanksgiving Prayer from the Barcelona Papyrus: An Underestimated Testimony to the History of the Anaphora in the Fourth Century," *Vigiliae Christianae* 62 (2008): 467–504. I am unable to accept Paul Bradshaw's conclusions on this anaphora appearing elsewhere in this collection (pp. 129–38), and I hope soon to be able to respond in detail.

15. See Jules Souben "Le canon primitive de la messe," *Les Questions ecclésiastiques* 1 (1909): 326; Paul Cagin, *L'Anaphore apostolique et ses témoins* (Paris:

While in the Jewish prayer God is asked to gather his people in a concrete place—in the land of Israel—in the Christian perspective this petition was modified to an appeal to unite the Church in the Holy Spirit. Later this idea could have been transformed into a petition for sanctifying the congregation and, further on, to a Spirit-epiclesis.

Yet another possible explanation for the origins of the epiclesis could be sought in a petition concerning the unworthiness of the celebrant and the clergy and/or the worshiping community. It is precisely in this sense that Johannes de Turrecremata—the key Latin theologian at the Council of Florence—understood the epiclesis, i.e., as a prayer only and exclusively concerning the unworthiness of the celebrants (he realized that a consecratory interpretation of an epiclesis following the words of institution, as in the Byzantine anaphoras, would shed doubt on the consecratory power of Christ's words).[16] The same view can also be found in a number of works of subsequent Catholic authors, though there were also many criticisms of it by Anglican, Protestant, and some Catholic writers, and in the twentieth century the Catholic perspective has substantially shifted.[17] Despite the confessional coloring of this "unworthiness" idea, Ivan Karabinov, an outstanding Russian liturgical scholar of the early twentieth century, explained the origins of the epiclesis in the same way.[18]

The latter of the abovementioned hypotheses concerning the origins of the epiclesis actually seems to me to be the least likely. In this article, however, I intend neither to evaluate various theories on the ori-

Lethielleux, 1919), 234–36; Fernand Cabrol, "Épiclèse," in *Dictionnaire de théologie catholique*, vol. 5, part 1a (Paris: Letouzey et Ané, 1924), 142–84, here 174; Louis Bouyer, *L'Eucharistie: Théologie et spiritualité de la prière eucharistique* (Paris: Les Éditions du Cerf, 1966), 176–84, 301–3; McKenna, *The Eucharistic Epiclesis*, 117–19.

16. See Éphrem Boularand, "L'épiclèse au concile de Florence," *Bulletin de littérature ecclésiastique* 60 (1959): 241–73.

17. See a review of the problem: Robert F. Taft, "Ecumenical Scholarship and the Catholic-Orthodox Epiclesis Dispute," *Ostkirchliche Studien* 45 (1996): 201–26.

18. It is unfortunate that his book *The Eucharistic Prayer (or Anaphora): An Historical-Liturgical Investigation* [original title in Russian: Карабинов И. А. Евхаристическая молитва (анафора): Опыт историко-литургического исследования] (Saint-Petersburg, 1908), which contains many remarkable insights, remains largely unknown to Western scholars. This liturgical scholar died a martyr's death, having been killed by the Communists in 1937 solely because he was a professor at a Spiritual Academy.

gins of the epiclesis nor to enumerate them all. I shall rather turn my attention to the epicleses of the Byzantine anaphoras themselves.

II. 2. The Epiclesis of Classic Byzantine Anaphoras

The epiclesis of Basil (hereafter BAS) reads as follows (I have numbered the logical blocks to facilitate reference):

> Therefore, Master all-holy,
> <I.> we also, your sinful and unworthy servants, who have been held worthy to minister at your holy altar, not for our righteousness, for we have done nothing good upon earth, but for your mercies and compassions which you have poured out richly upon us, with confidence approach your holy altar.
> <II.> And having set forth the representations (ἀντίτυπα) of the holy Body and Blood of Your Christ,
> <III.> we pray and beseech You, O holy of holies, in the good pleasure of Your bounty, that Your [all-]Holy Spirit may come upon us and upon these gifts set forth, and bless them and sanctify and show (ἀναδεῖξαι) this bread the precious Body of our Lord and God Jesus Christ, [Amen,] and this cup the precious Blood of our Lord and God and Savior Jesus Christ, [Amen,] which was shed for the life of the world, [and salvation – Amen, amen, amen,]
> <IV.> and unite with one another all of us who partake of the one bread and the cup into communion with the one Holy Spirit;
> <V.> and make none of us to partake of the holy Body and Blood of Your Christ for judgment or for condemnation, but that we may find mercy and grace with all the saints who have been well-pleasing to You . . .[19]

It is extraordinary that the compiler of this anaphora was able to interweave nearly all of the abovementioned contexts of epicletic prayer into one text. Here we have: I. and V. Prayers concerning the unworthiness of the celebrants and the partakers; II. A petition for the acceptance by God of the gifts that have been brought forth; III. An appeal to God the Father for the Holy Spirit to come, and an expression of the

19. ET from: Ronald C. D. Jasper, Geoffrey J. Cuming, *Prayers of the Eucharist: Early and Reformed*, 3rd ed. (Collegeville, MN: Pueblo, 1990), 119–20 (with some corrections of mine). Greek text in Frank Edward Brightman, *Liturgies Eastern and Western*, vol. 1: *Eastern Liturgies* (Oxford: Clarendon Press, 1896), 329–30 and 405–6; Michael Orlov, *The Liturgy of St. Basil the Great* [original title in Russian: Орлов М., прот. Литургия св. Василия Великого] (Saint Petersburg, 1909), 200–210.

concept that by his coming the Holy Spirit will "show" the bread and wine to be the Body and Blood of Christ; IV. A prayer for the unity of the Church.

Compared with the epiclesis of BAS, the epiclesis of St. John Chrysostom (hereafter CHR) does not contain any of these ideas, except a mention of the offering.[20] In its petition for the sanctification of the gifts it follows a different—and more simple—scheme: God the Father is asked (1) *to send* down his Holy Spirit on "us" and the gifts and (2) *to make* bread and wine the Body and Blood, converting them with his Holy Spirit, (3) *so that they would be to the benefit* of the communicants:

> We offer You also this reasonable and bloodless service,
> and we pray and beseech and entreat You, send down Your Holy Spirit on us and on these gifts set forth;
> and make [ποίησον] this bread the precious Body of Your Christ itself, [converting (μεταβαλών) it by Your Holy Spirit, Amen,] and that which is in this cup the precious Blood of Your Christ itself, [Amen,] converting (μεταβαλών) it by Your Holy Spirit, [Amen, amen, amen,]
> so that they may become to those who partake for vigilance of soul, [for forgiveness of sins,] for communion of [Your] Holy Spirit, for the fullness of the Kingdom of Heaven, for boldness toward You, [and] not for judgement or condemnation.[21]

The terminology of this epiclesis is more direct than that of BAS ("make" and "convert" instead of "sanctify" and "show"), and the theology is less balanced—here we have the Father sending the Holy

20. On the offering motive in CHR, see Robert F. Taft, "Reconstituting the Oblation of the Chrysostom Anaphora: An Exercise in Comparative Liturgy," *Orientalia Christiana Periodica* 59 (1993): 387–402; idem, "Some Structural Problems in the Syriac Anaphora of the Twelve Apostles I," *ARAM* 5 (1993): 505–20; idem, "Understanding the Byzantine Anaphoral Oblation," in *Rule of Prayer, Rule of Faith: Essays in Honor of Aidan Kavanagh, OSB*, ed. Nathan Mitchell and John Baldovin (Collegeville, MN: Pueblo, 1996), 32–55; the latter article discusses both CHR and BAS.

21. ET from Jasper and Cuming, *Prayers of the Eucharist*, 133 (with some corrections of mine). Greek text in Brightman, *Liturgies Eastern and Western*, 329–30 and 386–37; Stefano Parenti and Elena Velkovska, *L'Eucologio Barberini gr. 336*, Bibliotheca "Ephemerides Liturgicae," "Subsidia" 80, 2nd ed. (Roma: CLV—Edizione Liturgiche, 2000), 78.

Spirit and converting the gifts himself, using the Holy Spirit in some unspecified way, while in BAS it is the Holy Spirit who is coming and sanctifying the gifts on his own.

As has been convincingly shown, the wording of the anaphora of the Jerusalem liturgy of James (JAS) is closely related to that of the Constantinopolitan BAS.[22] The epiclesis of the Greek JAS[23] reads as follows:

Have mercy on us, [Lord,] God the Father, almighty; [have mercy on us, God, our Saviour. Have mercy on us, O God, according to Your great mercy,]
and send out upon us and upon these [holy] gifts set before You Your [all-]Holy Spirit,
   the Lord and giver of life, Who shares the throne and the kingdom with You, God the Father and Your [only-begotten] Son, consubstantial and coeternal, Who spoke in the Law and the prophets and in Your New Testament, Who descended in the likeness of a dove upon our Lord Jesus Christ in the river Jordan [and remained upon Him,] Who descended upon Your holy apostles in the likeness of fiery tongues [in the Upper Room of the holy and glorious Zion on the day of the holy Pentecost; send down, Master, Your all-Holy Spirit Himself upon us and upon these holy gifts set before You,]
that He may descend upon them, [and by His holy and good and glorious coming may sanctify them,] and make (ποιήσῃ) this bread the holy Body of Christ, [Amen,] and this cup the precious Blood of Christ, [Amen,]
that they may become to all who partake of them [for forgiveness of sins and for eternal life,] for sanctification of souls and bodies, for bringing forth good works, for strengthening Your holy, [catholic and apostolic] Church, which You founded on the rock of faith, that the gates of hell should not prevail against it, rescuing it from every heresy, and from the stumbling-blocks of those who work lawlessness,

22. See John R. K. Fenwick, *The Anaphoras of St. Basil and St. James: An Investigation into Their Common Origin*, Orientalia Christiana Analecta 240 (Roma, 1992); see also John V. Witvliet, "The Anaphora of St. James," in *Essays on Early Eastern Eucharistic Prayers*, ed. Paul F. Bradshaw (Collegeville, MN: Pueblo, 1997): 152–72.

23. On this epiclesis see Andrè Tarby, *La prière eucharistique de l'Église de Jérusalem*, Théologie Historique 17 (Paris: Beauchesne, 1972), 152–82; Bryan D. Spinks, "The Consecratory Epiclesis in the Anaphora of St. James," *Studia Liturgica* 11 (1976): 19–38; Fenwick, *The Anaphoras*, 167–91.

[and from the enemies who rose and rise up,] until the consummation of age, [Amen.][24]

One can note that behind the loquacity of this text there stands the simple scheme: (1) *send down* the Spirit; (2) *make* bread and wine the Body and Blood; (3) *that they may be beneficial* in various ways. In following this scheme the epiclesis of the Greek JAS (the Syriac JAS being different in this point) is closer to the tradition reflected in CHR than to the one we find in BAS. On the other hand, the theology of the Greek JAS is more balanced than that of CHR in regard to the role of the Holy Spirit: in the Greek JAS it is the Holy Spirit who actually sanctifies (as in BAS), and he is not treated as some sort of instrument used in the process of sanctification (as in CHR).

II. 3. The Epiclesis in the Byzantine Theological Tradition
    The cited text of the Greek JAS is a late form of the liturgy presumably being interpreted by the author of the *Mystagogical Catecheses*,[25] a very famous text, much used by the Byzantine theologians, ascribed by tradition to Cyril of Jerusalem. The text reads:

> Then, having sanctified ourselves with these spiritual hymns,
> we beseech God, the lover of man, to send forth the Holy Spirit upon the (gifts) set before Him,
> that He may make (ποιήσῃ) the bread the Body of Christ, and the wine the Blood of Christ;
> for everything that the Holy Spirit has touched, has been sanctified and converted (μεταβέβληται). (Cat. 5, § 7)[26]

---

24. ET from Jasper and Cuming, *Prayers of the Eucharist*, 93. Greek text in Brightman, *Liturgies Eastern and Western*, 53–54; B.-Ch. Mercier, *La liturgie se Saint Jacques: édition critique du texte grec avec traduction latine*, Patrologia Orientalis XXVI, fasc. 2, No. 126 (Paris: Brepols, 1946), 204 [90]–206 [92].

25. See Emmanuel Joseph Cutrone, "Cyril's Mystagogical Catecheses and the Evolution of the Jerusalem Anaphora," *Orientalia Christiana* 44 (1978): 52–64; Kent J. Burreson, "The Anaphora of the Mystagogical Catecheses of Cyril of Jerusalem," in Bradshaw *Essays on Early Eastern Eucharistic Prayers*, 131–51.

26. ET from Jasper and Cuming, *Prayers of the Eucharist*, 85–86. Greek text in Cyrille de Jerusalem, *Catéchèses Mystagogiques*, introd., texte critique et notes de Auguste Piédagnel, trad. de Pierre Paris, Sources Chrétiennes 126 (Paris: Les Éditions du Cerf, 1966), 154.

Since the author of this text is clearly basing his words on a liturgical prayer, he is, in essence, reflecting an earlier form of what would become the epiclesis of JAS.[27] The cited piece is by no means an elaborate theology of consecration; it is simply a summary of the euchological text presented to the newly baptized. With time, though, these words were to become the quintessence of the Orthodox view on the theology of consecration.

But this was not to happen soon. The first Byzantine author after the *Mystagogical Catecheses* to choose this line of argument, that bread and wine become Body and Blood exactly when—and because—the priest invokes the Holy Spirit, asking "to make" and/or "to convert" the bread and wine, was Nicephorus, Patriarch of Constantinople († 828). He writes:

> These [gifts] are supernaturally converted (μεταβάλλεται) to the Body and Blood of Christ because of the celebrant's invocation (ἐπικλήσει τοῦ ἱερεύοντος), through the descent of the Holy Spirit. For this is what is exactly said in the priestly prayer. And [after this] we do not consider them [i.e., bread/wine and Body/Blood] to be two [different] things, but believe that they become one and the same. So, even if they [the gifts] are somewhere called representatives (ἀντίτυπα), this name is applied to them not after, but before consecration. (Antirrhet. II)[28]

The last sentence of this text betrays Nicephorus' dependence on John Damascene; I will return to this below. Another author of the same period[29]—and, like Nicephorus, an opponent of the heresy of the Iconoclasts—namely, Theodorus Abu-Qurrah († 820), writes:

> The priest places bread and then wine unto the holy altar, and, when he makes a supplication with the holy invocation (δεόμενος ἐπικλήσει ἁγίᾳ), the Holy Spirit comes, and descends on the [gifts] that are set forth, and by the fire of His Divinity, converts (μεταβάλλει) the bread and the wine into the Body and Blood of Christ. (Dial. cum Sar.)[30]

27. And, as we see, his witness corresponds to the Greek JAS and not the Syriac (which has in its epiclesis "to show" instead of "to make," etc.).

28. Greek text in PG 100, 336; ET is mine.

29. A description of the moment of consecration from yet another document of roughly the same time, *Historia Ecclesiastica*, will be discussed below (see the section on the words of insitution).

30. Greek text in PG 97, 1553; ET is mine.

The same reasoning as in Nicephorus appears in the *Protheoria* of Nicholas and Theodor of Andida, composed between AD 1055 and 1063 or 1085 and 1095:[31]

> After reciting the prayer [of anamnesis] the bishop points at the holy [gifts], saying: *And make this bread the precious Body of our Lord and God and Saviour Jesus Christ itself, and that which is in this cup the precious Blood of Your Christ itself, converting [them] by Your Holy Spirit.* And we know and believe that [bread and wine] are converted, according to what is said in the epiclesis (ὡς ἡ ἐπίκλησις ἔχει). But Basil the Great instead of *converting by Your Holy Spirit* gives *which was shed for the life of the world.* Yet there is no contradiction between the two [BAS and CHR]. . . . After the manifestation (ἀνάδειξιν) of the Divine Gifts the prayer continues. (§ 27)[32]

This text has been thereafter "cut and pasted" into another Byzantine liturgical commentary, falsely attributed to Sophronius of Jerusalem.[33]

An emergence of this line of argumentation—namely, that the gifts are made Body and Blood just because and exactly when the prayer says so—in ninth- through eleventh-century Byzantine texts must have had something to do with the process of the replacement of BAS, as the primary Eucharistic rite of the Constantinopolitan Church, with CHR.[34] As was shown above, BAS contains neither an explicit petition to "make" the gifts the Body and Blood, nor a petition that the gifts be

31. On this commentary see René Bornert, *Les commentaires byzantins de la Divine Liturgie du VIIᵉ au XVᵉ siècle*, Archives de l'Orient chrétien 9 (Paris: Institut Français d'études byzantines, 1966), 181–206; Jean Darrouzès, "Nicolas d'Andida et les azymes," *Revue des études byzantines* 32 (1974): 199–203.

32. Greek text in PG 140, 452–53; ET is mine.

33. See Bornert, *Les commentaires*, 210–11. The Greek text of Pseudo-Sophronius' commentary has been edited by Angelo Mai (= PG 87γ, 3981–4001), but from an incomplete manuscript, lacking about a half of the whole commentary. An edition of the full text is now in preparation by a student of mine, Alexey Cherkasov.

34. On this process see Stefano Parenti, "La 'vittoria' nella Chiesa di Constantinopoli della Liturgia di Crisostomo sulla Liturgia di Basilio," in *Comparative Liturgy Fifty Years after Anton Bumstark: Acts of the International Congress*, ed. Robert F. Taft and Gabriele Winkler, Orientalia Christiana Analecta 265 (Roma: Pontificio Istituto Orientale, 2001), 907–28.

"changed" (μεταβαλών).[35] The process of the replacement of BAS with CHR also took place in the ninth (or the ninth to tenth) century. This was probably a part of a complex reaction of the Orthodox party to the theology of the Iconoclasts (with which BAS, unlike CHR, could be more easily harmonized).[36] In any case, the authors of the *Protheoria* were clearly aware of the difference between BAS and CHR in relation to the epiclesis, despite their claim that it is not substantial. And when they call the consecration an ἀνάδειξις, this betrays their intention to reconcile BAS with CHR.

The opinion of the authors of the *Protheoria*, however, cannot be considered to be the general position of the Byzantine Church under the Komnenoi and even later. Almost until the end of Byzantium there was a persistent belief that the consecration takes place at the moment of the precommunion elevation, i.e., after the Eucharistic prayer (see below). The logic of Eucharistic consecration at the moment of the corresponding petition of the Eucharistic prayer (i.e., at the moment of the epiclesis) will reach its bloom only at the very end of Byzantium, in the fourteenth and fifteenth centuries, when Byzantine theologians, being reproached by the Latins, had to give an Orthodox answer to the Latin idea of consecration by the words of institution.

The best, and, as it seems, the first, of these answers was given by Nicholas Cabasilas († after 1392), who studied the problem of the

---

35. In the course of time the words Μεταβαλὼν τῷ Πνεύματί σου τῷ Ἁγίῳ from CHR began to be sporadically added to BAS. This addition, despite its incompatibility with the Greek syntax and the sense of the phrase, became the norm from the fifteenth century on, first among the Greeks and then, under their influence, among the Russians, Georgians, and the other Orthodox nations. But after the rigid criticisms of this addition by Nicodemus Hagioreta (Pedalion, commentary on canon 19 of the Council of Laodicea) the Greeks gradually removed these words from their editions of BAS. The Russians, among others, still have them; see Nicholas Desnov, "Some More Words in the Well-Known Greek-Russian Differences with Regard to the Liturgies of Sts. Basil the Great and John Chrysostom" [original title in Russian: *Деснов Н., прот.* Еще несколько слов об известных расхождениях между русскими и греками в литургиях святителей Василия Великого и Иоанна Златоуста], *Богословские труды* 31 (1992): 86–96.

36. See Stefanos Alexopoulos, "The Influence of Iconoclasm on Liturgy: A Case Study," in *Worship Traditions in Armenia and the Neighbouring Christian East*, ed. Roberta R. Ervine, AVANT Series 3 (Crestwood, NY: St. Vladimir's Seminary Press, 2006), 127–37.

epiclesis at length.[37] Much has been written about this, and I will not repeat it here.[38] I would just mention that Cabasilas, defending the consecrative power of the epiclesis, is at the same time holding the words of institution in no less regard:

> The priest recites the story of that august Last Supper . . . repeating those words [of Christ,] the celebrant prostrates himself and prays, while applying to the offerings these words of the Only-Begotten, our Saviour, that they may, after having received His most Holy and all-powerful Spirit, be transformed (μεταβληθῆναι)—the bread into His holy Body, the wine into His precious and sacred Blood. (Expl. Div. lit. 27)[39]

According to Cabasilas, the consecration is, therefore, impossible without both the words of institution and the epiclesis, the latter being interpreted as the only possible way of "applying" the former to bread and wine.

Besides trying to combine the beliefs in the consecratory power of the words of institution and in the epiclesis, Nicholas Cabasilas was also at pains to demonstrate that not only on a theological but also on a ritual level the Latin and the Byzantine Eucharists were substantially the same. In chapter 30 of his commentary he identifies the prayer "Supplices te rogamus" of the Roman Canon as the epiclesis

37. See § 27-32 of his Commentary on the Divine Liturgy: Nicholas Cabasilas, *Explication de la Divine liturgie*, trad. et notes de S. Salaville, texte grec par R. Bornert, J. Gouillard, et P. Périchon, Sources Chrétiennes 4bis (Paris: Les Éditions du Cerf, 1967), 172–206.

38. See Markus Biedermann, "Die Lehre von der Eucharistie bei Nikolaos Kabasilas," *Ostkirchliche Studien* 3 (1954): 29–41; Bornert, *Les commentaires byzantins*, 233–37; Gouillard's article in Nicholas Cabasilas, *Explication*, 31–36; McKenna, *The Eucharistic Epiclesis*, 76–78; Lambert Mellis, *Die eucharistische Epiklese in den Werken des Nikolaos Kabasilas und des Symeon von Thessaloniki (Doktoraldissertation)* (Roma: Pontificia Università Lateranense, 1977), 148–96; Παντελεήμον ('Ροδόπουλος), *Ὁ καθάγιασμος* . . . , 50–59; Costel Habelea, "Die Erklärung der Göttlichen Liturgie nach Nikolaos Kabasilas," *Ostkirchliche Studien* 51 (2002): 249–93, here 276–83.

39. ET from Nicholas Cabasilas, *A Commentary on the Divine Liturgy*, trans. J. M. Hussey and P. A. McNulty, with an introd. by R. M. French, 5th ed. (Crestwood, NY: St. Vladimir's Seminary Press, 2002), 69–70. Greek text in Nicholas Cabasilas, *Explication*, 172–74.

of the Latin Mass.[40] Actually, this choice seems a bit odd; why did he not choose the "Quam oblationem" instead, since it contains a more explicit consecratory petition?[41] First of all, Cabasilas' choice was due to the plain fact that "Supplices te rogamus" comes *after* the words of institution and "Quam oblationem" is read *before* them. Then, Cabasilas supplies a theological interpretation, arguing that if in the "Supplices te rogamus" a priest prays for the intervention of an angel, who should transfer the gifts onto the heavenly altar, this necessarily means that they are still unconsecrated—since this does not belong to an angel, to offer the heavenly sacrifice (although angels can offer the Church some help when still preparing the sacrifice).[42] Finally (and quite probably), his choice could have something to do with the ritual that was performed during the "Supplices te rogamus." Since the Carolingian times a practice had begun to spread whereby a priest would bless the bread and the wine respectively while mentioning these elements in the course of the "Supplices te rogamus"; by the fourteenth century this practice became ubiquitous.[43] The Byzantines, in their turn, were used to their practice of a priest blessing the gifts during the epiclesis; this is prescribed already in the earliest extant manuscript of CHR, *Vatican Barberini gr.* 336.[44] By Cabasilas' times, or probably earlier, this blessing came to be understood as a substantial part of the consecration itself. Thus, Theodore Meliteniotes († 1393), Cabasilas' contemporary, writes that at the moment of consecration the priest lends God "his tongue *and his hand*."[45] Cabasilas could have equated the blessing of the Byzantine epiclesis with the blessing of the

40. See Nicholas Cabasilas, *Explication*, 190–98.

41. Characteristically, the Catholic authors who sought an epiclesis in their Mass pointed exactly at the "Quam oblationem"; see Salaville, "Épiclèse," 273–74.

42. It is quite clear that Cabasilas was unaware that the Latin commentators of the Mass, beginning with Ivo of Chartres († 1116; cf.: PL 162, 557), often identified the "angel" in "Supplices te rogamus" with Christ himself. See Bernard Botte, "L'ange du sacrifice et l'épiclèse de la messe romaine au Moyen Age," *Recherches de théologie ancienne et médiévale* 1 (1929): 285–308. See also Taft, "Ecumenical Scholarship," 213.

43. See Johannes Brinktrine, *Die heilige Messe*, 2nd ed. (Paderborn: Schöningh, 1934), 299.

44. Cf. Parenti and Velkovska, *L'Eucologio*, 78. BAS in this manuscript lacks its epiclesis.

45. See PG 149, 957.

Latin "Supplices te rogamus." He mentions neither, though. So, if my assumption is true, this ritualistic logic is only implied by Cabasilas.

It was Symeon of Thessalonica († 1429) who explicitly accented—and not just once—the role of a priestly blessing in the Eucharistic consecration. He writes:

> We firmly believe that bread and wine become the Body and Blood of Christ on the grounds of the priestly prayers, and this is fulfilled with the sign of the cross and the invocation (τῇ ἐπικλήσει) of the Holy Spirit—so that the Master's words, namely, "Take, eat," and "Drink ye all of it," and "Do ye this in commemoration of Me," which once were entrusted to the apostles and the heirs of their grace, [now] can be enacted through the prayers. That's why the priest, having addressed the Father and hymned the [deeds] of the oeconomia, begins with crying out the divine verbs of Christ, and [thus confirms] that He Himself instituted this, and [then says:] "Because of this we offer You [*i.e.*, the Father] these [gifts] on behalf of everything, in accordance with His [*i.e.*, the Son's] commandment, and we beseech You, [so that] You will send Your Spirit onto me [*sic*] and onto the gifts set forth. And make them His Body and Blood, as He declared, converting [them] with Your Holy Spirit." And while the priest pronounces [the last sentence,] he makes the sign [of the cross.] And after he made the sign [of the cross] three times, the priest believes that the bread and the cup are the Body and Blood [of Christ] themselves. . . . In order to explain all this more clearly, I will emphasize [the fact,] that the priest does not bless the gifts, when he is saying: "Take, eat" and "Drink ye all of it." (Exp. de div. templ. 88)[46]

In the same chapter Symeon criticizes those who think that particular words are alone sufficient for the sacrament to happen. He strongly emphasizes that since all the sacraments are performed by the special grace of the Holy Spirit, which lives only in the bishops and priests, a priestly prayer and a blessing are necessary for this grace to be enacted. The words of institution are "from the beginning the foundation (θεμέλιος) of the sacred rite,"[47] and "the sacred words, which were pronounced by the Saviour Himself when He celebrated [the first Eucharist],"[48] but seemingly they do not have an active role in the

46. Greek text PG 155, 736–37; ET is mine.
47. Exp. de div. templ. 88. Greek text PG 155, 737; ET is mine.
48. Ibid., 86. Elsewhere Symeon calls them "the sacred words, which were pronounced by the Saviour Himself when He celebrated [the first Eucharist]"

subsequent Eucharistic consecrations. Therefore, Symeon's theology of the epiclesis[49] differs significantly from that of Cabasilas.

Honestly, Symeon's reasoning concerning the necessity of the epiclesis is not that convincing: for instance, it is unclear why the divine grace of the priesthood should act through the epiclesis and not through the words of institution, or why the manual act of blessing with a hand is so extremely important. But Symeon was obviously more concerned about defending the liturgical practice of his Church, than about conducting a proper theological dispute.

Such a dispute did, nonetheless, occur at the Council of Florence in 1439. The question of the epiclesis was posed in a discussion between Pope Eugene IV (and his theologian, Johannes de Turrecremata) and the Greek party, consisting of metropolitans Isidore of Kiev, Bessarion of Nicaea, Dorotheus of Trebizond, and Dorotheus of Mitylene. At first the Greek hierarchs stuck with Cabasilas' line of argumentation, without mentioning him by name. They compared the Byzantine epiclesis with "Supplices te rogamus" of the Roman Canon, like he did, and stated that the epiclesis is an actualization of the power of the words of institution. Isidore of Kiev called the words of institution a seed that becomes a fruit through the epiclesis: "Dominicae voces habent operationem ut semina, quia sine semine non potest effici fructus."[50] But this was not enough for the Latins, and they made the Greek metropolitans confess that consecration is achieved through the words of institution only.[51] Looking back from our time it is quite obvious that this happened not because of any particular solidity of the Latin argument but because the Byzantine theological training of the time could not withstand the sophisticated terminology and logic techniques of the Scholastics.

The capitulation of the four leading metropolitans was unacceptable for another key figure of the Council, Mark Eugenikos, metropolitan of Ephesus, who did not take part in the dispute itself. Instead he wrote a brief treatise titled "That Not Only as a Result of Recitation

---

(Exp. de div. templ. 86); Greek text PG 155, 732; ET is mine.

49. See Bornert, *Les commentaires byzantins*, 258–59; Mellis, *Die eucharistische Epiklese*, 230–47; Παντελεήμων (Ῥοδόπουλος) Ὁ καθάγιασμος, 45–49; Ἐ. Σκούμπυυ, Λατινικές καινοτομίες στήν περί ἁγίς Τριάδος καί ἱερῶν μυστηριῶν διδασκαλία τοῦ Συμεών Θεσσαλονίκης (Athens, 2003), 77–89.

50. Joannes Dominicus Mansi, *Sacrosanctum Conciliorum nova et amplissima collectio*, Supplementum ad Tomum XXXI, 2nd ed. (Paris, 1901), 1687.

51. See Salaville, "Épiclèse," 197–99; Boularand, "L'épiclèse."

of the Words of the Lord the Divine Gifts are Sanctified, but Because of a Prayer [Read] after These [Words] and of a Blessing of a Priest, by the Power of the Holy Spirit."[52] Here Mark is giving a synthesis of liturgical texts,[53] citations from John Chrysostom and *Corpus Areopagiticum*, and the reasonings of Nicholas Cabasilas and Symeon of Thessalonica. He recognizes that the words of institution "put in the [gifts—*or* the prayers] which are being celebrated the sanctifying power (τὴν ἁγιαστικὴν δύναμιν ἐνιᾶσι τοῖς τελουμένοις)," but states that it is the epiclesis that "fits [these words to bread and wine] and completes the [gifts] set forth, and makes them the Body and Blood of the Lord."[54] This is the line of thought of Cabasilas. Then, having confirmed the importance of the words of institution and the need for the epiclesis and (NB!) a priestly blessing, Mark confronts the Latins with a critical observation. He notices that when a Latin priest consumes his personal host and drinks the whole cup alone, this contradicts the words "Take . . ." and "Drink ye all . . .," which the Latins claim to be so important. In general, he does not hesitate to show his hostility to Latin liturgical practice, and in this respect his position differs from Cabasilas' approach significantly.[55]

After the council it was the position of Mark Eugenikos—and not that of the metropolitans who entered into the union with Rome—that became the rule of the Orthodox faith. Still, the problem of the epiclesis persisted. Even Georgios Scholarios (who later become a monk, and thereafter the patriarch of Constantinople, taking the name Gennadios), a close friend and a follower of Mark Eugenikos, while supporting Mark's line of rejecting the union with the Latins, took a purely Latin position in the question of Eucharistic consecration. In fact, he plainly

52. Greek text in Louis Petit, *Documents relatifs au Concile de Florence, II: Œuvres anticonciliaires de Marc d'Éphèse*, Patrologia Orientalis XVII, fasc. 2, No. 83 (Paris: Brepols, 1923), 426 [288]–434 [296]. See a review of this work in Παντελεήμον ('Ροδόπουλος), Ὁ *καθάγιασμος* . . . , 40–44.

53. It is noteworthy that Mark is the first author who calls BAS and CHR an abbreviation of JAS (he has no doubt as to the purely apostolic origin of JAS and the liturgy of the eighth book of the "Apostolic Constitutions"); cf. Petit, *Documents*, 428 [290]. About a century later Constantine Paleocappa will produce a long-lasting forgery out of this idea, ascribing it to Proclus of Constantinople (see François J. Leroy, "Proclus, 'De traditione divinae Missae': un faux de C. Paleocappa," *Orientalia Christiana Periodica* 28 (1962): 288–99).

54. Petit, *Document.*, 430 [292].

55. Ibid., 433 [295]–434 [296].

stated in his homily, "On the Sacramental Body of Our Lord Jesus Christ," and in the treatise "What is Needed for [a Celebration of the] Sacrament of the Eucharist," that the consecration is accomplished by the proclamation of the words of institution.[56] The epiclesis, according to Scholarios, is merely a way to express the priest's "intention" to commemorate the Last Supper and to confess that it is God and not a man who is actually performing the sacrament.[57]

It is only in the course of the seventeenth century that the Orthodox dogma of the epiclesis was finally formulated and officially proclaimed[58]—but this story exceeds the scope of my essay. Still, I should note that in most of the official Orthodox documents of the modern era the epiclesis is mentioned along with the blessing of a priest. Therefore, it is somewhat inaccurate to say that the Orthodox Church officially believes in the epiclesis as the "form" of the Eucharist. *Officially,* she believes in the epiclesis *and* the blessing of a priestly hand, and that the words of institution should also be present in the Eucharistic prayer.

III. THE WORDS OF INSTITUTION

III. 1. Fourth- through Eighth-Century Eastern Christian Writers

The collision between the Scholastic and the Late Byzantine theologies concerning the epiclesis reveals an important difference in their

---

56. Georges (Gennade) Scholarios, *Œuvres complètes*, ed. L. Petit, X. A. Sidéridès, M. Jugie, 1 (Paris: Maison de la bonne presse, 1928), 124; ibid., 4 (1935), 309.

57. See Martin Jugie, "La forme de l'Eucharistie d'après Georges Scholarios," *Échos d'Orient* 33 (1934): 289–97. A new study on Scholarios' Eucharistic theology is currently being prepared by Michael Bernatsky.

58. See Martin Jugie, *Theologia dogmatica christianorum orientalium ab Ecclesia catholica dissidentium* 3 (Paris: Sumptibus Letouzey et Ané, 1930), 288–301; Gerhard Podskalsky, *Griechische Theologie in der Zeit der Türkenherrschaft (1453– 1821): Die Orthodoxie im Spannungsfeld der nachreformatorischen Konfessionen des Westens* (München: C.H. Beck'sche Verlagsbuchhandlung, 1988); Παντελεήμον (Ῥοδόπουλος), *Ὁ καθαγιασμός*, 34–39; Michael Bernatsky, "Orthodox Eucharistic Theology in the 16–18th Centuries" [original title in Russian: *Бернацкий М. М. Православное богословие Евхаристии в XVI–XVII вв.*], in *Православная энциклопедия* 17 (Moscow: ЦНЦ "Православная энциклопедия," 2008), 638–54 (a part of the huge article "Eucharist" from the *Orthodox Encyclopedia*, currently being published in Moscow).

approaches to the Eucharistic prayer as a whole. Whereas the Latins insisted on consecration by the words of institution only, many of the Byzantines, while defending the epiclesis as the moment of consecration, still considered the words of institution extremely important. This was not so just by accident or because of an imitation of the Latin theology. The belief in the consecratory power of the words of institution had its own story in the Christian East.

Among the Greek fathers of the fourth century it is Gregory of Nyssa († about 394) who states that in the Eucharist

> the bread, as says the apostle, "is sanctified by the Word of God and prayer" . . . it is at once changed into the Body by means of the Word, as the Word itself said, "This is My Body." (Or. catech. 37. 105-7)[59]

But while contending that the Eucharistic transformation happens "at once," Gregory does not explain at which moment exactly. It could be that this happens at the words of institution, since Gregory is talking about them, but it could be at some other moment as well. Likewise, in another of his writings he says that

> bread . . . is at first common bread, but when the sacramental action consecrates it, it is called, and becomes, the Body of Christ. So with the sacramental oil; so with the wine: though before the benediction they are of little value, each of them, after the sanctification bestowed by the Spirit, has its several operation. (Or. de Bapt. Christ.)[60]

Is this, again, a description of a Spirit-epiclesis, or just a statement that it is the Holy Spirit who is operative in the Eucharist? This operation could occur through the epiclesis, but this can also be through the words of institution, etc. Therefore, while Gregory of Nyssa obviously holds in high regard both the words of institution and the operative power of the Holy Spirit, his witness is ambiguous.[61]

---

59. Greek text in James Herbert Srawley, *The Catechetical Oration of Gregory of Nyssa* (Cambridge: Cambridge University Press, 1903), 149–51. ET from Philip Schaff and Henry Wace, eds., *A Select Library of Nicene and Post-Nicene Fathers of the Christian Church: Second Series*, 5 (Edinburgh: T&T Clark, 1893), 163–64.

60. Greek text in PG 46, 581; ET from Schaff e. a., NPNF, second series, vol. 5, 175.

61. See Andrew Kirillov, *The Dogmatic Teaching on the Sacrament of the Eucharist in the Works of Two Catechizators of the Fourth Century, Saints Cyril of*

The same ambiguity is found in the works of John Chrysostom († 407). One of his sayings eventually became the most cited in the polemics over the epiclesis. It is referred to in the works of John Damascene, Michael Glykas (who limits his reasoning with this quote—Cap. theol. 84 ad Joannic. monach.), Nicholas Cabasilas, Symeon of Thessalonica, Mark Eugenikos, documents of the Florentine Council, etc. It reads as follows:

> It is not man who causes what is present to become the Body and Blood of Christ, but Christ Himself Who was crucified for us. The priest is the representative when he pronounces those words, but the power and the grace are those of the Lord. "This is My Body," He says. This word changes the things that lie before us; and as that sentence "increase and multiply," once spoken, extends through all time and gives to our nature the power to reproduce itself; even so that saying "This is My Body," once uttered, does at every altar in the Churches from that time to the present day, and even till Christ's coming, make the sacrifice complete. (De prodit. Jud. 1. 6)[62]

Based on this quote, the Latins pointed out over and over again that, according to Chrysostom, the consecration happens when the words of institution are recited. But elsewhere Chrysostom himself depicts the liturgy in this way:

> The priest stands before an altar, raising his hands to heaven, calling the Holy Spirit to come and touch the [gifts] set forth. . . . And when the Spirit gives the grace, when He descends, when He touches the gifts which are set forth . . . then you can see the Lamb, already slain and prepared. (De coemet. et de cruc. 3)[63]

This citation, along with the proper text of CHR, rendered the references of the Latins to Chrysostom pointless in the eyes of the Orthodox.[64]

Jerusalem and Gregory of Nyssa [original title in Russian: Кириллов А. А. Догматическое учение о таинстве Евхаристии в творениях двух катехизаторов IV века, святых Кирилла Иерусалимского и Григория Нисского] (Novocherkassk, 1898); Betz, *Die Eucharistie*, Bd. I/1, 97ff.

62. Greek text in PG 49, 380; ET from McKenna, *The Eucharistic Epiclesis*, 54.
63. Greek text in PG 49, 398; ET is mine.
64. See further Andrew Kirillov, "The Dogmatic Teaching on the Sacrament of the Eucharist in the Works of St. John Chrysostom" [original title in Russian:

Among the Easterners it was the leading Syrian theologians who unambiguously proclaimed that the consecration is accomplished through the words of institution and happens exactly at their recitation. Thus, Severus of Antioch († 521) writes:

> It is not the offerer himself who, as by his own power and virtue, changes the bread into Christ's Body, and the cup of blessing into Christ's Blood, but the God-befitting and efficacious power of the words which Christ, Who instituted the mystery, commanded to be pronounced over the things that are offered. The priest who stands before the altar, since he fulfills a mere ministerial function, pronouncing His words as in the person of Christ, and carrying back the rite that is being performed to the time at which He began the sacrifice for His apostles, says over the bread, "This is My Body which is given for you: do this in remembrance of Me;" while over the cup again he pronounces the words, "This cup is the New Covenant in My Blood, which is shed for you." Accordingly it is Christ Who still even now offers, and the power of His divine words perfects the things that are provided so that they may become His Body and Blood. (Letters III. 3)[65]

In another place he confirms his position, saying that "Christ completes it [the Eucharistic sacrifice] through the words uttered by the offerer"—and this did not prevent him from adding that "[Christ] changes the bread into Flesh and cup into Blood, by the power, inspiration, and grace of His Spirit."[66] James of Edessa († 708) and John of Dara (ninth century) held the same views.[67] From this evidence I can conclude that for the authors of that period it was absolutely normal

---

Кириллов А. А. Догматическое учение о таинстве Евхаристи в творениях св. Иоанна Златоуста], *Христианское чтение* 1 and 3 (1896): 26–52 and 545–72; August Nägle, *Die Eucharistielehre des heiligen Johannes Chrysostomus des Doctor Eucharistiae,* Straßburger theologische Studien 3, Heft 4-5 (Freiburg im Breisgau: Herder, 1900); Anne-Marie Malingrey, "L'eucharistie dans l'oeuvre de saint Jean Chrysostome," *Parole et Pain* 52 (1972): 338–45; Frans van de Paverd, "Anaphoral Intercessions, Epiclesis and Communion-rites in John Chrysostom," *Orientalia Christiana Periodica* 49 (1983): 303–39.

65. English text taken from Ernest Walter Brooks, *The Sixth Book of the Select Letters of Severus, Patriarch of Antioch, in the Syriac Version of Athanasius of Nisibis,* vol. 2 (London: Williams & Norgate, 1904), 238 (the Syriac text in ibid., vol. 1, 269).

66. Ibid., vol. 2, 234–35 (the Syriac text in ibid., vol. 1, 265).

67. See Sévérien Salaville, "La consécration eucharistique d'après quelques auteurs grecs et syriens," *Échos d'Orient* 13 (1910): 321–24.

to talk about the operative power of the Spirit in the Eucharist and to use (as the Monophysites did and still do) an explicit epiclesis in the liturgical rite—but at the same time to profess the consecrative power of precisely the words of institution.

Therefore, when John Damascene († about 740) develops the argumentation quoted below, this does not necessarily mean that here we have the same reasoning as will be later developed by Nicholas Cabasilas (where the power of the "omnipotent" command contained in the words of institution is declared to be actualized only through a Eucharistic epiclesis):

> If God the Word of His own will became man and the pure and undefiled blood of the holy and ever-virginal One made His flesh without the aid of seed, can He not then make the bread His body and the wine and water His blood? He said in the beginning, "Let the earth bring forth grass," and even until this present day, when the rain comes it brings forth its proper fruits, urged on and strengthened by the divine command. God said, "This is My Body," and "This is My Blood," and "This do ye in remembrance of Me." And so it is at His omnipotent command until He comes: for it was in this sense that He said until He comes: and the overshadowing power of the Holy Spirit becomes through the invocation (διὰ τῆς ἐπικλήσεως) the rain to this new tillage. For just as God made all that He made by the energy of the Holy Spirit, so also now the energy of the Spirit performs those things that are supernatural and which it is not possible to comprehend unless by faith alone. "How shall this be," said the holy Virgin, "seeing I know not a man?" And the archangel Gabriel answered her: "The Holy Spirit shall come upon thee, and the power of the Highest shall overshadow thee." And now you ask, how the bread became Christ's Body and the wine and water Christ's Blood. And I say unto thee, "The Holy Spirit is present and does those things which surpass reason and thought." (De fide Orth. 86 [IV. 13])[68]

Crucial for reading the text in the way of Cabasilas would be understanding the word ἐπίκλησις in the sense of a *terminus technicus* for the certain part of an anaphora. But there is no assurance that this word

---

68. Greek text in Bonifatius Kotter, ed., *Die Schriften des Johannes von Damaskos* 2, Patristische Texte und Studien 12 (Berlin: De Gruyter, 1972), 193–94; ET by Stewart Dingwall Fordyce Salmond from Schaff and Wace, *A Select Library of Nicene and Post-Nicene Fathers* 9 (New York: Charles Scribner's Sons, 1899), 82–83 (second pagination).

should be understood this way here; it could still mean the Eucharistic prayer in general—or even have the sense of "naming." This is true despite the fact that the late- and post-Byzantine Orthodox theologians, naturally, understood ἐπίκλησις exactly as an appeal for the Holy Spirit to come and therefore used this quote from Damascene as an unambiguous testimony to their position.

The general idea of the "Exact Exposition of the Orthodox Faith" of John Damascene seemingly was an attempt to harmonize the patristic sayings concerning various topics of Christian belief, and to organize them into a system, thus producing a synthetic picture of Orthodoxy itself. This is certainly true in regard to chapter 86 of the "Exact Exposition," which is dedicated to the Eucharist, and a fragment of which I have quoted already. The sources that Damascene is trying to combine in this chapter include the anaphoras of JAS and BAS, *Corpus Areopagiticum*, famous passages from Gregory of Nazianzen, Gregory of Nyssa, and John Chrysostom. In particular, the already quoted text of Damascene is a harmonization of some sayings of the latter two authors. The most characteristic feature of John Damascene's Eucharistic theology was exactly this talent of combining and harmonizing—and by no means any specific inventions of his own.[69]

III. 2. The Problem of ἀντίτυπα

Among the other pieces Damascene used to create his mosaic of patristic theology were the works of Anastasius Sinaita († after 701). It was this dependency that left the idea of consecration through the words of institution no chance in Byzantine theology. In a passage concerning the usage of the word ἀντίτυπα from the already-quoted chapter, Damascene writes:

> If some persons called the bread and the wine antitypes (τὰ ἀντίτυπα) of the Body and Blood of the Lord, as did the divinely inspired Basil, they said so not after the consecration but before the consecration, so calling the offering itself (αὐτὴν τὴν προσφοράν). (De fide Orth. 86 [IV. 13])[70]

69. Therefore, I would not agree with Nicholas Armitage, "The Eucharistic Theology of the 'Exact Exposition of the Orthodox Faith' of Saint John Damascene," *Ostkirchliche Studien* 44 (1995): 292–308.

70. Greek text in Kotter, *Die Schriften* 2, 197; ET by Stewart Dingwall Fordyce Salmond from Schaff and Wace, *A Select Library of Nicene and Post-Nicene Fathers* 9, 84 (second pagination).

The word ἀντίτυπα as a designation of the holy gifts has been quite traditional in the early Church.[71] It is used with no qualms in the so-called *Apostolic Tradition*; in the Syriac *Didascalia*; in the writings of Irenaeus of Lyon, Cyril of Jerusalem, Gregory of Nazianzen, and Eustathius of Antioch; and in the *Corpus Macarianum*. But beginning with the sixth century it becomes undesirable. The last author to "lawfully" use it is Eutychius of Constantinople († 582), while already in the Greek *Apophthegmata Patrum* (compiled in the last decades of fifth or the first decades of sixth century) there is given a story, the moral of which is to prohibit an application of this word to the holy gifts.[72] It is unclear which specific schism or heresy the author of this story was targeting. Leslie MacCoull suggests[73] that it could be the followers of Julian of Halicarnassus, but it is unlikely, since Anastasius Sinaita witnesses that the Julianites (whom he calls the Gaianites) agreed with him in a refusal to apply the term to the holy gifts. It is more probable that this had something to do with a reaction to Nestorian Eucharistic theology, but I will not discuss this further here.

Be that as it may, Anastasius Sinaita placed rejection of symbolic language in application to the Eucharist in general,[74] and of the word ἀντίτυπα in particular, into the foundations of his Christology (see his *Viae Dux* 23. 1[75]). John of Damascus, in his turn, was relying on Anastasius. He had, therefore, to reconcile Anastasius' rejection of the word with the text of the anaphora of BAS where this word is plainly

71. See D. A. Wilmart, "Transfigurare," *Bulletin d'ancienne littérature et d'archéologie chrétiennes* 1 (1911): 282–92; Kenneth John Woollcombe, "Le sens de 'type' chez les Pères," *La Vie Spirituelle: Supplementa* 4 (1951): 84–100; Betz, *Die Eucharistie* Bd. I/1, 223–26; Taft, "Understanding the Byzantine Anaphoral Oblation," 48–55.

72. PG. 65. Col. 156–60.

73. See her "John Philoponus, 'On the Pasch' (CPG, N 7267): The Egyptian Eucharist in the Sixth Century and the Armenian Connection," *Jahrbuch der österreichischen Byzantinistik* 49 (1999): 2–12.

74. It is noteworthy that in the last book (which remained unpublished for a long time) of *Hexaemeron*, ascribed to Anastasius Sinaita, there is, on the contrary, a strongly symbolic understanding of the Eucharist (see Anastasius of Sinai, *Hexaemeron*, ed. and trans. Clement A. Kuehn and John D. Baggarly, Orientalia Christiana Analecta 278 [Roma: Pontificio Istituto Orientale, 2007], 474–78); this alone casts serious doubts on Anastasius' authorship of this treatise.

75. Greek text in Karl-Heinz Uthemann, ed., *Anastasii Sinaitae* Viae Dux, Corpus Christianorum: Series Graeca 8 (Turnhout: Brepols, 1981), 307–8.

used.[76] He solved the problem by claiming that the word is actually acceptable—but only as a designation of the unconsecrated bread and wine. And since this word is used in BAS *after* the words of institution, Damascene's solution eliminated for these words an opportunity to be understood as consecratory.

It could have happened that Damascene's judgment concerning ἀντίτυπα would not be the last. Indeed, he himself did not consider the above conclusion to be the only possibility, giving in the end of the same chapter 86 another explanation of this term, this time clearly applied to the already consecrated gifts.[77] But eventually it was the first of the two explanations of Damascene that became the undisputed and exclusive one in the Greek East. This happened very soon, in the course of polemics over the Eucharistic theology of the Iconoclasts. This latter theology, which in Damascene's time had not yet been developed (at least, he shows no acquaintance with it), was proclaimed already in 754, at the iconoclastic Council of Hieria.[78] The Iconoclasts were very much concerned with the iconic and symbolic notion of the Eucharist. Besides other matters, they considered the presence of ἀντίτυπα in the text of BAS to be a strong argument in their favor.[79] On the other hand, John Damascene was a famous polemicist against early Iconoclasm, and his judgment concerning ἀντίτυπα gave the Iconodules a key to interpret BAS in an anti-iconoclastic way.

As a result, the cited passage of John Damascene was read at the Seventh Ecumenical Council of 787,[80] and thereafter repeated by Nicephorus, a leader of the anti-iconoclastic party and Patriarch of Constantinople.[81] Events surrounding the Iconoclasm controversy

76. See Martin Jugie, "L'épiclèse et le mot antitype de la messe de saint Basile," *Échos d'Orient* 9 (1906): 193–98.

77. Kotter, *Die Schriften* 2, 198: Ἀντίτυπα δὲ τῶν μελλόντων λέγονται οὐχ ὡς μὴ ὄντα ἀληθῶς σῶμα καὶ αἷμα Χριστοῦ, ἀλλ' ὅτι νῦν μὲν δι' αὐτῶν μετέχομεν τῆς Χριστοῦ Θεότητος.

78. See Stephen Gero, "The Eucharistic Doctrine of the Byzantine Iconoclasts and Its Sources," *Byzantinische Zeitschrift* 68 (1975): 4–22.

79. And, as has been noted above, the possibility of conforming BAS to the iconoclastic views on the Eucharist was a possible reason for the "victory" of CHR over BAS right after the victory of the Iconodules (see Alexopoulos, "The Influence").

80. Mansi, *Sacrosanctum* 13 (1767), 265.

81. See the passage that I have already quoted in the section on the epiclesis.

became for the Byzantines a strong inoculation against the use of any symbolic language in relation to the already consecrated Eucharistic gifts. Therefore the Damascene's passage concerning the use of ἀντίτυπα in BAS was to be quoted unceasingly. One can find it in a number of Byzantine authors, including Euthymius Zigabenus,[82] Theodore Meliteniotes,[83] Symeon of Thessalonica,[84] and Mark Eugenikos.[85] And since in the light of this interpretation no one can claim the words of institution to be sufficient for the consecration, the Byzantines accordingly did not consider them to be consecratory.[86]

III. 3. Traces of an Understanding of the Words of Institution as Consecratory in the Orthodox Liturgical Practice

Before completely dying out in Byzantine theology, however, the idea of consecration by the words of institution seems to have infiltrated no less than the most popular Byzantine liturgical commentary, the *Historia Ecclesiastica* of Pseudo-Germanus of Constantinople. Here is the description of the moment of consecration from this commentary:

> The priest expounds on the unbegotten God, that is the God and Father, the womb [which is] before the morning star, which bore the Son before the ages, as it is written: "Out of the womb before the morning star have I begotten you." [It is God] Whom [the priest] asks to accomplish the mystery of His Son—that is, that the bread and wine be changed into the very Body and Blood of Christ and God—so that it might be fulfilled that "Today I have begotten You." Then (ὅθεν) the Holy Spirit, invisibly present by the good will of the Father and volition of the Son, demonstrates the divine operation and, by the hand of the priest, testifies, and seals (ἐπισφραγίζει), and completes the holy gifts set forth into the Body and Blood of Christ and our Lord, Who

82. See PG 129, 665.
83. See PG 149, 952.
84. See PG 155, 737.
85. See Petit, *Documents*, 430 [292].
86. Jugie tried to show that the belief in the consecratory power of the words of institution was quite common among the Byzantines even after Damascene (see Jugie, *Theologia dogmatica* 3, 277–84), but his confidence in this is based solely on his interpretations of the texts he quotes, while actually none of these texts contends that during an ordinary Byzantine liturgy (i.e., not at the Last Supper or in apostolic times) the gifts are consecrated exactly through the words of institution.

says: "For their sake I sanctify Myself, that they also may be sanctified," so that "He who eats My flesh and drinks My blood abides in
Me and I in him."[87]

At a first glance this is just a traditional Eastern description of a Spirit-
epiclesis. But the author of the commentary immediately continues:

> Thus (ὅθεν) becoming eye-witnesses of the divine mysteries, partakers
> of eternal life, and sharers in divine nature, let us glorify the great, and
> immeasurable, and unsearchable mystery of the oeconomia of the Son
> of God. Therefore (ὅθεν), glorifying, let us cry: "We praise You"—the
> God and Father, "We bless You"—the Son and Word—"We give thanks
> to You"—the Holy Spirit—"O Lord our God"—the Trinity in a Monad
> and the Monad in a Trinity, consubstantial and undivided.

This is really striking: the acclamation "We praise You, we bless You,
we thank You, O Lord, and we pray to You our God" comes in the
Byzantine anaphora after the *words of institution* and *not* after the epiclesis, and, since the author interprets it as a glorification *after* the consecration, he apparently hints that the consecration is accomplished
through the words of institution.[88]

This accent on the operation of the Holy Spirit in the Eucharist together with a confidence in the consecratory power of the words of institution closely resembles the Eucharistic theology of Severus of Antioch
and the Syrian authors. This fact, along with the presence of some Palestinian features in the commentary,[89] points at some Oriental influence on
Byzantine Eucharistic theology, reflected in the *Historia Ecclesiastica.*[90]

Yet there could be another explanation. The words "We praise You,
we bless You, we thank You, O Lord, and we pray to You our God"

---

87. Greek text in Frank Edward Brightman, "The *Historia Mystagogica* and
the Other Greek Commentaries on the Byzantine Liturgy," *Journal of Theological Studies* 9 (1908): 248–67 and 387–97, here 395. ET (with some corrections
of mine) from Paul Meyendorff, *St. Germanus of Constantinople: On the Divine
Liturgy* (Crestwood, NY: St. Vladimir's Seminary Press, 1984), 97–99.

88. See Martin Jugie, "De sensu epicleseos iuxta Germanum Constantinop-
olitanum," *Časopis katolického duchovenstva*, Slavorum 2, 3, 4 (1908): 385–91.

89. These have been already noted by Nikolay Krasnoseltzev; see his work "On
the Ancient Liturgical Commentaries" [original title in Russian: Красносельцев
Н. Ф. О древних литургических толкованиях] (Odessa, 1984), 227.

90. I owe this idea to Alexey Pentkovsky.

are actually sung by the choir simultaneously with the recitation of the epiclesis by the priest, and the author of *Historia Ecclesiastica* could have placed these words after his description of the consecration because they were sung not *after,* but *at the same time* as it. But this is actually quite odd as well (especially in comparison with the other Eastern rites)—that in Byzantine usage the words of institution are chanted aloud and the people answer "Amen" after them,[91] while the epiclesis is read in a low voice and its "Amens" are pronounced only by a deacon.[92] And since even the oldest extant manuscript of CHR, *Vatican Barberini gr.* 336, cannot be taken as a genuine witness to the pre-iconoclastic practice (because this manuscript, dated to the late eighth century, already contains a prayer, ascribed to Germanus of Constantinople,[93] and some features of the rites here could be a sort of reply to Iconoclasm[94]), this usage could have originated at roughly the same time as the *Historia Ecclesiastica* and could reflect the same possible influence.

Another influence, this time unquestionable, resulted in the appearance in the Byzantine rite of a ritual of elevating the *discos* (paten) and the chalice during the *ekphonesis* "Offering You your own" after the words of institution and before the epiclesis. This ritual is an imitation of the Latin elevation of the host and the chalice, performed after the priest has pronounced the words of institution. It was instituted in the West in order to give the Catholic believers a chance to participate

91. Besides these "Amens," people also sing "Amen" after the final doxology of the anaphoras of BAS and CHR: "And grant that with one voice and one heart we may glorify and praise Your most honored and majestic Name, of the Father and the Son and the Holy Spirit, now and forever and to the ages of ages—Amen." This doxology, by the way, is not only an ending of the whole prayer (and, therefore, the "Amen" after it is referred to the anaphora as a whole, cf.: 1 Cor 14:16) but also the "epiclesis" in the early Christian sense of "naming the Name" (see above).

92. The current practice of some Orthodox parishes, especially in the West, for the people to say solemnly, "Amen," "Amen," "Amen, amen, amen," at the epiclesis, is a pure innovation, which has nothing to do with the Byzantine tradition.

93. See Parenti and Velkovska, *L'Eucologio*, 240.

94. Cf. Marie-France Auzépy, "Les Isauriens et l'espace sacré: l'église et les reliques," in *Le sacré et son inscription dans l'espace à Byzance et en Occident,* sous la dir. de M. Kaplan, Byzantina Sorbonensia 18 (Paris: Presses de la Sorbonne, 2001), 13–24.

in the sacrament with their eyes.[95] In the Orthodox milieu this ritual emerged in early seventeenth-century Ukraine. The rubrics of the printed Ukrainian *Leitourgika* of this time[96] have undergone some re-working. In particular, the revised rubrics instructed the priest to point at the bread and the wine during the words of institution, holding his fingers in a blessing gesture (or just to bless the gifts at this moment), and to elevate the discos and the chalice thereafter (i.e., precisely during the ekphonesis "Offering You your own"). This was a clear sign of a strong influence of Catholic theology, including the belief in the consecration through the words of institution. In 1655 these "crypto-Catholic" Ukrainian rubrics found their place in the revised Moscow edition of the *Leitourgikon*. The editions of 1656, 1657 (the first), 1657 (the second), 1658 (the first), 1658 (the second), 1667, 1668, 1676, and 1684, as well as the 1677 edition of the *Archieratikon*, also contain them.[97] The obvious contradiction between the views held by the Ukrainian editions and the late- and post-Byzantine Greek theological thinking concerning the moment of consecration resulted in a controversy, which emerged in Moscow in the last third of the seventeenth century and which ended only in 1690, when an official refutation of the belief in the consecratory power of the words of institution was promulgated.[98] In the 1699 Moscow edition of the *Leitourgikon* the

95. See Godefridus J. C. Snoek, *Medieval Piety from Relics to the Eucharist* (Leiden: Brill, 1995), 54–60.

96. Namely, the editions: Stryatin 1604, and Kiev 1620, 1629, etc.

97. See Alexey Dmitrievsky, *The Correction of the Liturgical Books in the Times of Patriarch Nikon and His Successors* [original title in Russian: Дмитриевский А. А. Исправление книг при патриархе Никоне и последующих патриархах / Подготовка текста и публикация А. Г. Кравецкого] (Moscow: Языки славянской культуры, 2004).

98. See Gregory Mirkovich, *Concerning the Time of Transubstantiation of the Holy Gifts: Polemics which Took Place in Moscow in the Second Half of the Seventeenth Century* [original title in Russian: Миркович Г. Г. О времени пресуществления Св. Даров: Спор, бывший в Москве во второй половине XVII века (Опыт исторического исследования)] (Vil'no, 1886); Alexander Prozorovskij, *Sil'vestr Medvedev: His Life and Activities* [original title in Russian: Прозоровский А. А. Сильвестр Медведев: Его жизнь и деятельность (опыт церковно-исторического иследования)] (Moscow, 1896); Michael Smentzovsky, *The Brothers Lichud* [original title in Russian: Сменцовский М. Н. Братья Лиухды: Опыт иследования из истории церковного просвещения и церковной жизни конца XVII и начала XVIII века] (Saint Petersburg, 1899).

appropriate rubrics were reworked, and the prescription to bless the bread and the wine during the words of institution was omitted.[99] Still, the ritual of pointing at the bread and the wine during the words of institution (without holding the fingers in a specific gesture) remained—as did the ritual elevation after their recitation, which is now performed by Orthodox everywhere, including Greece, Georgia, etc., although its original meaning is totally forgotten.

IV. THE ELEVATION

IV. 1. The Evidence

One might ask: since in Byzantine thought the interpretation of the epiclesis as *the* moment of consecration began to be more or less clearly formulated after Iconoclasm, achieving its final form only in the fourteenth and fifteenth centuries, and the belief in the consecratory power of the words of institution alone has never felt itself at home in Byzantium, were the Byzantines—till the late-Byzantine epoch—ever concerned about the precise moment of the Eucharistic consecration? The answer is that they actually were, though their particular choices of this moment may seem unusual for the modern reader. A number of sources witness that quite often the Byzantines associated the consecration with the elevation of the Eucharistic bread at the ekphonesis "Τὰ ἅγια τοῖς ἁγίοις" ("The holy [things] to the holy"). This ekphonesis is an ancient call to communion,[100] so that such association withdraws the consecration—or, rather, its final accomplishment—from the anaphora entirely.

It is due to the peculiarity of this idea that modern scholars and theologians failed to notice it altogether, though it is attested in a number of sources. It was Robert Taft who was the first to draw scholarly attention to this idea, showing that it is widely attested in the *Lives* of the Byzantine saints, where one can find the following topos: a saint is celebrating the Divine Liturgy, and when he is going to elevate the

99. In the Russian *Archieratikon* the instruction to bless the bread and the wine during the words of insitution—an action performed by no one since the 1690s—remained untouched for three centuries, finally being omitted only in the 2009 (!) Moscow edition.

100. See Miguel Arranz, "Le 'sancta sanctis' dans la tradition liturgique des églises," *Archiv für Liturgiewissenschaft* 15 (1973): 31–67; Robert F. Taft, *The Precommunion Rites: A History of the Liturgy of St. John Chrysostom*, vol. 5, Orientalia Christiana Analecta 261 (Roma: Pontificio Istituto Orientale, 2000), 231–40.

Eucharistic bread and/or proclaim "Τὰ ἅγια τοῖς ἁγίοις" the Holy Spirit comes and sanctifies the gifts. Taft lists the following *Lives* containing this topos: the *Life of St. Theodore of Sykeon* (probably written by his disciple George of Sykeon sometime after 641), the *Life of St. Stephen the Sabaite* (written by his disciple Leontius after 794), Symeon Metaphrastes' *Life of St. John Chrysostom* (written at the end of the tenth century), and the *Life of St. Bartholomew of Simeri* (written in the 3rd quarter).[101] To this list I would add yet another two instances of the same story: a miracle of St. Nicholas of Myra, known as the *Praxis de tributo*, composed sometime between the fifth and the tenth centuries,[102] and the *Life of St. Sergius of Radonezh* (written by his disciple Epiphanius the Wise in 1417–1418).[103]

At the same time, from hagiographic sources one cannot expect the precision of official dogmatic formulae. But a belief in the consecratory significance of the moment of elevation can also be found at the highest levels. *Response 9* of Constantinopolitan patriarch Nicholas III Kyrdanites Grammaticus (1084–1111) states:

---

101. Taft, *The Precommunion*, 211, 214, 227–28. Strictly speaking, the first of these, the *Life of St. Theodore of Sykeon*, does not witness that the descent of the Holy Spirit takes place at the moment of elevation. Described here is not the consecration itself, but a Eucharistic miracle, when the Holy bread began to jump on the discos, "showing clearly that the sacrifice of the celebrant was acceptable" (§ 126; ibid., 214), and elsewhere in this *Life* the descent of the Holy Spirit onto the gifts is explicitly linked to the Eucharistic prayer (§ 80).

102. BHG 1351. Publication: Gustav Anrich, *Hagios Nikolaos: Der heilige Nikolaos in der griechischen Kirche. Texte und Untersuchungen* 1 (Leipzig-Berlin: B. G. Teubner, 1913), 98–110. See also my article titled "The Liturgical Data Contained in the *Praxis de Tributo* of Saint Nicholas of Myra" [original title in Russian: Желтов М. С. Литургические данные, содержащиеся в "Деянии о подати" (Praxis de tributo) святителя Николая Чудотворца (к вопросу о возможной датировке)], in *Правило веры и образ кротости . . . Образ святителя Николая, архиепископа Мирликийского, в византийской и славянской агиографии, гимнографии и иконографии.* А. В. Бугаевский, ред. (Moscow, 2004), 111–24.

103. In § 31 here it is said that during a liturgy celebrated by the saint his disciple Simon saw the divine flames around the altar, which entered the chalice "when the saint was going to partake of it." Cf. also the eighth- to ninth-century *In vitam s. Basilii* of Ps.-Amphilochius [François Combéfis, *SS. Patrum Amphilochii Iconensis, Methodii Patarensis, et Andreae Cretensis opera omnia* (Paris, 1644), 176].

It is fitting to elevate only one prosphora, as everyone does, when the "One [is] holy, one Lord, Jesus Christ," is proclaimed. The rest [of the gifts] set out [on the altar] are blessed by the descent of the Holy Spirit, which *we believe* happens at this time.[104]

Commenting on this text, Taft calls the belief in the consecration through elevation "seemingly unorthodox."[105] This is true—but only from the post-Byzantine perspective. For it would be a mere projection of our own post-Byzantine mindset to evaluate the genuine Byzantine sources on the grounds of later confessional definitions. Since the seventh and eighth centuries this belief was embraced by the Byzantines, and it is witnessed not only in the hagiography and the rubrical casuistry concerning the actual performance of the Eucharistic elevation[106] (the quoted passage from *Response 9* of Nicholas III Kyrdanites Grammaticus belongs to this category of texts), but in the Byzantine liturgical commentaries as well.

When Taft wrote that "the classical Byzantine commentators are blissfully unaware of the problems in Eucharistic pneumatology raised by Nicholas III's views,"[107] he was not entirely accurate—unless the criterion of a differentiation between the "classical" and the "non-classical" Byzantine commentaries would be the presence of them in the well-known study by René Bornert.[108] For Bornert has ignored a whole family of the Byzantine and then Slavonic liturgical commentaries, which could be characterized by two distinct features: they follow a popular form of a dialogue, and their overall plot is built around a vision of angels taking a direct part in the liturgical celebration. The latter motif betrays a quite traditional nature of these commentaries, because the idea of the angelic concelebration is so ancient that it is firmly established in the official liturgical prayers themselves—cf. the Byzantine prayer of the Little Entrance or the Roman prayer "Supplices te rogamus." But in the Byzantine and Slavonic commentaries I have mentioned this motif is developed into a whole story.

104. Greek text and ET in Taft, *The Precommunion*, 219.
105. Ibid., 227.
106. As we already saw, in the Byzantine era there was only one elevation during the liturgy, that is, the one at the ekphonesis "Τὰ ἅγια τοῖς ἁγίοις." The other elevation of the modern liturgy "according to the Byzantine rite," the one during the anaphora, has nothing to do with Byzantine practice.
107. Ibid., 229.
108. Bornert, *Les commentaires byzantins.*

The first of these is a commentary in the form of a dialogue between Jesus and a certain John (either Chrysostom or the Theologian). The dialogue touches on a number of ethical and ritual themes, including the celebration of the Divine Liturgy, and it is literally connected to the apocryphal Apocalypse of St. John. Because of this François Nau, the first editor of this text, called it "The Second Greek Apocryphal Apocalypse of St. John."[109] Nau's edition was made on the basis of the sixteenth-century manuscript *Paris gr.* 947. In the BHG another manuscript from the same century is indicated;[110] among the new Sinai finds there is yet another manuscript with this text, the eighth- to ninth-century МГ 66.[111] The text is probably to be dated with the period of the controversy over Iconoclasm, i.e., between the 720s and AD 843.[112] The moment of elevation in this commentary is described as follows:

> When a priest elevates[113] the bread, and says: "Τὰ ἅγια τοῖς ἁγίοις," then the Holy Spirit descends upon them [i.e., the bread and the cup— or the bread and the priest?]. (§ 39)[114]

This is exactly what we have in the *Lives* mentioned above.

Another commentary is a fictional dialogue between Gregory of Nazianzen and the "holy fathers." It is extremely important for the history of theological thought among the Slavs, forming the core of the most popular Old-Russian liturgical commentary, *The Liturgy Interpreted* (Толковая служба),[115] and having influenced a number of other

---

109. François Nau, "Une deuxième apocalypse apocryphe grecque de Saint Jean," *Revue biblique* 11, no. 2 (1914): 209–21. Nau's Greek text is reproduced in John M. Court, *The Book of Revelation and the Johannine Apocalyptic Tradition,* Journal for the Study of the New Testament Supplement Series 190 (Sheffield: Academic Press, 2000), 67–103. Court also offers an ET with his comments but the translation is often erroneous and the comments pointless.

110. See BHG 922i.

111. Τα Νέα ευρήματα του Σινά (Athens, 1998), 153.

112. See Alice Whealy, "The Apocryphal Apocalypse of John: A Byzantine Apocalypse from the Early Islamic Period," *Journal of Theological Studies* 53 (2002): 533–40.

113. *Paris gr.* 947: νήψει instead of ὕψει.

114. Greek text in Nau, "Une deuxième apocalypse," 220; ET is mine.

115. See Nikolay Krasnoseltzev, "*The Liturgy Interpreted* and Other Compositions Related to the Liturgical Interpretation in Old Rus' before the Eighteenth Century" [original title in Russian: *Красносельцев Н. Ф.* Толковая служба и

Slavonic Eucharistic stories and tractates[116] as well as post-Byzantine Orthodox iconography. The Greek original of this commentary was considered unknown; I have prepared an edition of it according to a twelfth-century manuscript, *Paris Coisl. gr.* 296. Here Gregory is depicted describing in every detail the angelic participation in the liturgy. In particular, during the anaphora the angels brought a Child to the altar. But it was only at the moment of the elevation when Gregory

> saw the angels with the knives, and they slaughtered the Child, and His blood poured out to the holy chalice, and they cut the body in pieces and put it above the bread, and the bread became the Body, and the chalice the Blood of our Lord Jesus Christ. (Fol. 67r)

Here we have quite a different story, in comparison with the previous one. Instead of a descent of the Holy Spirit the cup is being filled with blood, and the bread turns into a body because of a physical contact. This story is a continuation of the tradition of seeing the Child during the Eucharist and communicating in His flesh, present already in the *Apophthegmata Patrum* (see above) and later in a similar tale attributed to Gregory Decapolites.[117] Various combinations of the commentary of Pseudo-Gregory of Nazianzen, the account from the *Apophthegmata Patrum*, the tale of Gregory Decapolites, and even some Western accounts of the Eucharistic miracles[118]—including the history of the Holy Grail—generated quite a variety of apocryphal stories (partly known under the name of Ephrem the Syrian), preserved in many Slavonic manuscripts of the post-Byzantine period.[119]

другие сочинения, относящиеся к обьяснению богослужения в древней Руси до XVIII века: Библиографический обзор], *Православный собеседник* 5 (1878): 3–43.

116. See Nikolay Tunizky, "Ancient Tales about the Miraculous Appearance of Christ the Child in the Eucharist" [original title in Russian: *Туницкий Н. Л. Древние сказания о чудесном явлении Младенца-Христа в Евхаристии*], *Богословский вестник* 2, no. 5 (1907): 201–29.

117. Greek text PG 100, 1199–1212; ET in Daniel J. Sahas, "What an Infidel Saw that a Faithful Did Not: Gregory Dekapolites (d. 842) and Islam," *Greek Orthoodox Theological Review* 31 (1986): 47–67.

118. On this theme see Peter Browe, *Die eucharistischen Wunder des Mittelalters* (Breslau: Müller & Seiffert, 1938); Snoek, *Meideval Piety*, 309–44.

119. See Alexander Yatzimirsky, "Concerning the History of the Apocryphs and Legends in South Slavonic Literature, IX: Stories about the Eucharistic Miracle" [original title in Russian: *Яцимирский А. И.* К истории апокрифов и

The notion of Christ coming from heaven into the midst of the Eucharistic celebration and residing in the holy gifts finds its parallel in the prayer Πρόσχες Κύριε,[120] which is read during the Byzantine Divine Liturgy before the elevation and the ekphonesis "Τὰ ἅγια τοῖς ἁγίοις," and in the early sources is placed between them. It reads as follows:[121]

> Lord Jesus Christ our God . . . come to sanctify us, you who are seated on high with the Father, and yet are invisibly present here with us.[122]

Therefore, there could be some connection between the prayer and the notion of Christ coming and entering the bread and the wine right after its reading.

On the other hand, I am quite certain that it was exactly the understanding of the elevation as *the* moment of consecration that resulted in surrounding this rite, from the thirteenth century on, with the prayers and hymns directed to the Holy Spirit, among them the Pentecost sticheron "Βασιλεῦ οὐράνιε,"[123] the troparion of the Third hour "Κύριε, ὁ τὸ πανάγιόν σου Πνεῦμα,"[124] etc.[125] There is no doubt that it was for the same reason that the elevation was prefixed with a rubric, instructing the priest to make three bows (and sometimes to incense the

---

легенд в южнослав. письменности IX в.: Сказания о евхаристическом чуде], Известия Отделения русского языка и словесности Императорской Академии наук 15 (1910): 1–25, and the literature indicated there.

120. Cf. Gabriele Winkler, "Anmerkungen zu einer neuen Untersuchung von R. F. Taft über die auf den Kommunion-Empfang vorbereitenden Ritus," *Oriens Christianus* 86 (2002): 171–91, here 176–80.

121. Taft, *The Precommunion*, 225–26. Taft also points out that some sources instruct the priest to extend his arms while saying the prayer (ibid., 208).

122. Greek text and ET in ibid., 201.

123. Cf. Alexey Dmitrievsky, *A Description of the Liturgical Manuscripts* [original title in Russian: Дмитриевский А. А. Описание литургических рукописей, хранящихся в библиотеках Православного Востока] 2 (Kiev, 1901) 158, 174–75, 828.

124. Cf. ibid., 175; Jacques Goar, Εὐχολόγιον, 2nd ed. (Venice, 1730), 89.

125. See Taft, *The Precommunion*, 248–56. It should be noted that Taft does not link these developments, despite his observation concerning the pneumatological character of some of them (ibid., 254) with the understanding of the elevation as consecratory.

298

gifts),[126] and the bishop to put on his omophorion.[127] Some manuscripts even direct the celebrant to make a single or triple sign of the cross over (or with) the Holy bread,[128] thus resembling the triple blessing at the epiclesis, discussed above.[129] Finally, the strongly pneumatological character of the formulas accompanying the manual acts, which follow the elevation—the commixture and the rite of zeon[130]—is, in my view, an outcome of understanding the elevation as the moment of the descent of the Holy Spirit onto the bread and the wine.

IV. 2. A Possible Explanation

What could be the rationale for this understanding? In my view, this idea originated in a plain interpretation of the elevation as not only an invitation to communion but also the final accord of the "consecratory" part of the Liturgy of the Faithful. Being final, it should be decisive.[131] And while being the conclusion of the "consecratory" part of the liturgy, it is at the same time the opening of the "communion" part of the liturgy. It is with the elevation that the breaking of the Eucharistic bread begins, and it is no accident that in the Acts of the Apostles and in a few other earliest Christian sources the expression "the breaking of bread" seems to be the *terminus technicus* for designating the Eucharist as a whole.[132] The words of institution themselves were said when Christ was *giving* the bread and cup to his disciples. Therefore, the elevation should be interpreted as the turning point in the liturgical action, and this explains the meaning it acquired in Byzantium from the eighth century on.

126. Ibid., 258–59.

127. Ibid., 209.

128. Ibid., 347.

129. Three preliminary bows and putting on the omophorion also have their parallel in the Byzantine manner of the celebrant's preparation to recite the epiclesis (cf. Παναγιότης Τρεμπέλας, Αἱ τρεῖς Λειτουργίαι κατὰ τοὺς ἐν Ἀθήαις κώδικας [Athens, 1935], 113–14).

130. See Taft, *The Precommunion*, 381–502.

131. Yet, other explanations could also be suggested: the Byzantines could have heard some mystical overtones in the ekphonesis "Τὰ ἅγια τοῖς ἁγίοις," or felt the need for the bread to be "shown" to the Father (cf. the anaphora of BAS: "He [Jesus] took the bread in His holy and undefiled hands and showed it to You, the God and Father"; Jasper and Cuming, *Prayers of the Eucharist*, 119), but these are less likely.

132. Cf. Theodor Schermann "'Das Brotbrechen' im Urchristentum," *Biblische Zeitschrift* 8 (1910): 33–52, 162–83.

The text of the Byzantine Divine Liturgy itself gives a hint that even after the epiclesis there is some need in the consecration. At the end of the anaphora of BAS there is the following petition:

> Remember, Lord, also my unworthiness, according to the multitude of Your mercies: forgive my every offence, willing and unwilling; and do not keep back, on account of my sins, the grace of Your Holy Spirit from the gifts set forth.[133]

This petition is also present in a number of manuscripts of the anaphora of CHR.[134] The post-Byzantine commentators interpret this petition as pertaining solely to the question of a worthy/unworthy communion, but, still, on the grounds of the text as it reads (i.e., without turning to the extrinsic theological constructions) such interpretation is not that obvious.

The incompleteness of the anaphora seems to be once again intimated by a petition from the post-anaphoral litany, where a deacon calls the people to pray "for the precious gifts,"

> that our loving God who has received them at His holy, heavenly, and spiritual altar as an offering of spiritual fragrance, may in return send upon us divine grace and the gift of the Holy Spirit.

This petition resembles the "Supplices te rogamus" so much that it is even intriguing that Nicholas Cabasilas did not compare them with each other. But as Cabasilas finds the "Supplices te rogamus" to be a legitimate replacement of the Eastern epiclesis, so, in a more general sense, a petition to God to accept the gifts, giving his grace in return (sometimes called "an ascending epiclesis"), undoubtedly has a consecratory coloring. And in the quoted fragment of the post-anaphoral Byzantine litany we have precisely such a petition.[135]

Nevertheless, it was none other than Nicholas Cabasilas who left the elevation with no consecratory value, interpreting it together with the ekphonesis "Τὰ ἅγια τοῖς ἁγίοις" as a mere invitation to communion.[136]

---

133. ET from Jasper and Cuming, *Prayers of the Eucharist*, 122 (with some corrections of mine). Greek text in Brightman, *Liturgies Eastern and Western*, 336 and 409; Orlov, *The Liturgy of St. Basil*, 246–48.

134. Cf. Τρεμπέλας, *Αἱ τρεῖς Λειτουργίαι*, 124.

135. Cf. Winkler, "Anmerkungen," 179–80.

136. Nicholas Cabasilas, *Explication*, 222.

Undoubtedly, the elevation lost its former relevance because of the polemics with the Latins by the fourteenth century. Symbolic of this was the transposition of the troparion of the Third hour from the moment of elevation (or the priestly communion that follows the elevation), where it had once entered the Eucharistic liturgy, to the moment of epiclesis.[137]

Still, liturgical practice and popular piety, as often happens, retained some traces of the earlier understanding even after the theological reasoning has undergone major changes. The hymns directed to the Holy Spirit, surrounding the elevation, are attested in the manuscripts till the sixteenth century (i.e., till the beginnings of the era of printed liturgical books), and the formulae accompanying the manual acts that follow the breaking of the Holy bread remain strongly pneumatological until our own day. The elevation is also still preceded by three bows, which are indicated in all standard editions of the *Leitourgikon*.[138] Finally, the notion of consecration via elevation, forgotten in reference to the Eucharist itself, has survived in a secondary rite of the Elevation of the Panaghia, and in the Greek custom of elevating the *antidoron* (to be distributed at the end of the liturgy) after the epiclesis.[139]

V. THE PRESANCTIFIED LITURGY

Another trace of an earlier belief in consecration via elevation is the rubrical legislation concerning the elevation of multiple Lambs, including a prohibition to elevate the commemorative particles.[140] In *Response 9* of patriarch Nicholas III Kyrdanites Grammaticus quoted above, as well as in some other similar explanations,[141] it is stated that

137. Cf. Τρεμπέλας, *Αἱ τρεῖς Λειτουργίαι*, 113. In the course of the nineteenth and twentieth centuries the Greeks have abandoned the practice of reciting this troparion before the epiclesis, but in Russian usage it is still said there, despite much criticism; see Desnov, "Some More Words."

138. Cf. Τρεμπέλας, *Αἱ τρεῖς Λειτουργίαι*, 129–30. To this one could add the custom for laity to make a full prostration after the ekphonesis "Τὰ ἅγια τοῖς ἁγίοις," which is observed in some places; but this prostration is prescribed nowhere and seems to be a late development.

139. On this rite, see John J. Yiannias, "The Elevation of the Panaghia," *Dumbarton Oaks Papers* 26 (1972): 226–36.

140. Such a prohibition is made, for example, by Symeon of Thessalonica; see Steven Hawkes-Teeples, *The Praise of God in the Twilight of the Empire: The Divine Liturgy in the Commentaries of Symeon of Thessalonika († 1429)*, unpublished doctoral dissertation (Roma: Pontificio Istituto Orientale, 1997), 231.

141. See Taft, *The Precommunion*, 216–25.

if there is more than one Lamb, the elevation should be performed with only one of them. In contrast to this, in late- and post-Byzantine usage, all the Lambs, if there are several, are elevated. Such a situation occurs at a Sunday Divine Liturgy in preparation for a Presanctified Liturgy to be celebrated the coming week.

The Presanctified Liturgy is the Byzantine Lenten liturgy, during which the wine is consecrated through an immersion of the consecrated Lamb into the chalice.[142] As the eleventh-century Constantinopolitan patriarch Michael Kerularios wrote, during the Presanctified Liturgy

> the preconsecrated and perfected Holy bread is dropped into the mystical cup, and in this way the wine therein is changed (μεταβάλλεται) and believed to have been changed (πιστεύεται μεταβάλλεται) into the Holy blood of the Lord.[143]

Based on this and the other witnesses, Ivan Karabinov has shown at length that this was the proper belief of the Byzantine Church, while from the seventeenth century the Russian Church refused, under Catholic influence, to believe in the consecration of the chalice during the Presanctified Liturgy.[144] The current Greek and Russian usages still differ on this point.

Further discussion of this rite would extend the scope of my article. I should only mention that the Byzantine Presanctified Liturgy is an example of the Eucharistic consecration *without* an epiclesis. This is especially clear if we compare it with the Syrian Presanctified rites.[145] In

142. See a recent study of the Byzantine Presanctified Liturgy by Stefanos Alexopoulos, *The Presanctified Liturgy in the Byzantine Rite: A Comparative Analysis of its Origins, Evolution, and Structural Components*, Liturgia condenda 21 (Leuven: Peeters, 2009).

143. Greek text and ET in ibid., 259.

144. See his article "The Holy Chalice of the Presanctified Liturgy" [original title in Russian: Карабинов И. А. Святая Чаша на литургии Преждеосвяще нных Даров], *Христианское чтение* 6 (1915): 737–53; 7–8 (1915): 953–64. Karabinov's conclusions were reproduced in an article by Nikolay Uspensky, which was thereafter translated into English and is usually cited by Western authors, while the genuine study of Karabinov remains regrettably unknown.

145. See Humphrey William Codrington, "The Syrian Liturgies of the Presanctified," *Journal of Theological Studies* 4 (1903): 69–82; 5 (1904): 369–77 and 535–45.

these rites there is a separate prayer to be read over the chalice, while in Byzantine usage the chalice is consecrated with no prayer, solely through putting the Lamb into it.

Another interesting detail is a rubric forbidding the elevation of the Presanctified Lamb during this liturgy, which seems to be a trace of the belief in the consecratory power of the elevation itself.[146]

VI. THE PROTHESIS

Finally, one should not forget the prothesis—a separate rite of "preparing" the Gifts, celebrated before the beginning of the Byzantine Eucharist proper.[147] A consecratory value—of some kind—for this rite is doubtless, and sometimes this has led Orthodox writers to conclude that the bread and the wine become the Body and Blood of Christ already at this point.[148] There are at least two instances of an explicit statement that the Gifts are consecrated at the prothesis. One is from the unedited *Story of an Unworthy Priest* (BHG 1277a),[149] where an angel is said to come and sanctify the Gifts after the protagonist of the story pronounced the prayer of the prothesis, and another is contained in the famous Russian *Life of Archpriest Avvakum*.[150] As the second testimony is dated to the seventeenth century, and the first also seems to be a post-Byzantine composition, both are insufficient for asserting

146. See Alexopoulos, *The Presanctified*, 248–52. Mikhail Bernatsky is currently working on an extensive article on this.

147. On this rite, see: Sergey Muretov, *A Historical Study of the Rite of the Prothesis . . .* [original title in Russian: Муретов С. Д. Исторический обзор чинопоследования проскомидии до «Устава литургии» Константинопольского Патриарха Филофея: Опыт историко-литургического исследования] (Moscow, 1895); Marco Mandalà, *La protesi della liturgia nel rito bizantino-greco* (Grottaferrata: Scuola tipografica italo-orientale S. Nilo, 1935).

148. This could also make sense because of a widespread popularity of symbolic explanations of the Divine liturgy, where its different parts are treated as visual depictions of certain moments of Christ's life; the idea of presence of Christ from the very beginning of the liturgy could give this depiction a more realistic meaning.

149. An edition is being prepared by Dmitry Afinoguenov.

150. *The Life of Archpriest Avvakum by Himself, and His Other Compositions*, ed. Nikolay Gudziy e. a. [original title in Russian: Житие протопопа Аввакума, им самим написанное, и другие его сочинения] (Moscow: Goslitizdat, 1960), 66–67.

that the Byzantines also knew the idea of a complete consecration of the Gifts already at the prothesis.[151]

It seems, however, that this idea had something to do with the late- and post-Byzantine custom—much criticized by the Catholics but defended by Nicholas Cabasilas, Symeon of Thessalonica, and others—for the faithful to make a full prostration during the Great Entrance, when the prepared bread and wine are transferred to the altar before the anaphora.[152] Byzantine theologians experienced difficulties trying to give this practice a suitable explanation. Symeon of Thessalonica even invented a theory that though the Gifts are consecrated only at the epiclesis, they already cease to be the ordinary bread and wine and become the ἀντίτυπα of the Body and Blood of Christ at the prothesis,[153] befitting adoration.[154] And it is no mere accident that in a number of Greek manuscripts of the Divine liturgy of St. John Chrysostom,[155] as well as St. Mark and Egyptian Basil,[156] and Slavonic manuscripts of Byzantine Basil,[157] the customary prayer of the prothesis

151. There is, however, an interesting place in the writings of St. Maximus the Confessor (7th c.), where he mentions "the Body and Blood of the Lord at the prothesis (ἐν τῇ προθέσει)" (Maximi Confessoris Opera. Quaestiones et dubia, Jose H. Declerck, ed., Corpus Christianorum: Series Graeca 10 (Turnhout: Brepols, 1982), 10, but it is unclear, whether the Greek word πρόθεσις here should mean the rite of the prothesis strictly speaking, or the Eucharistic rite as a whole. Cf. Robert F. Taft, The Great Entrance: A History of the Transfer of Gifts and other Preanaphoral Rites of the Liturgy of St. John Chrysostom Orientalia Christiana Analecta 200 (Roma: Pontificio Istituto Orientale, 1975), 45. In the coming forty-third issue of the Russian theological periodical, Богословские труды, a short article of Alexey Dunaev concerning the problems of interpretation of this question-and-answer of St. Maximus should appear.

152. See Taft, The Great Entrance, 213–14.

153. That's how the story of the term ἀντίτυπα in the Byzantine Eucharistic theology ended (see above, III. 2).

154. PG 155, 728–29.

155. See André Jacob, Histoire du formulaire grec de la liturgie de saint Jean Chrysostome (unpublished doctoral dissertation: Université de Louvain, 1968), 74–85.

156. See Oswald Hugh Edward Burmester, "An Offertory-Consecratory Prayer in the Greek and Coptic Liturgy of Saint Mark," Bulletin de la Société d'archéologie copte, 17 (1963–64), 23–33.

157. See Michael Zheltov, "The Rite of the Divine Liturgy in the Oldest (11–14th cc.) Slavonic Sluzhebniki (Leitourgika)" [original title in Russian: Желтов Михаил, диак. Чин Божественной литургии в древнейших (XI–XIV

is replaced by another one, which is in fact nothing but the epiclesis of an Egyptian anaphora.[158]

The prayer of the prothesis was always said by the priest, but all the manual acts of this rite—i.e., cutting off the Lamb, etc.—were initially performed by the deacon. (This is logical, since preparation of Eucharistic bread and wine had been the task of the deacons since Apostolic times). But at the turn of the eleventh and twelfth centuries these manual acts were taken from the deacon and began to be performed by the priest. And, in spite of a possible prosaic explanation of this change,[159] it is clear that a consecratory value given by the Byzantines to the prothesis, together with their special attention to the different manual acts of the Eucharistic celebration, should once have turned the manipulations with the bread and wine at the prothesis into highly sacral and purely priestly actions.

VII. CONCLUSION

By way of conclusion, I would repeat the statement I made at the beginning of this essay: with respect to a "moment" of the Eucharistic consecration, the Byzantines by no means limited themselves to the epiclesis. But the most distinct feature of their approach seems to be not their preference for one set of words over another but their reverence toward the manual acts of the Eucharistic celebration—be it the priestly blessing, the elevation, or the immersion of the Lamb into the chalice. However strange this attitude may seem, there is some logic behind it. It stresses the unity of the liturgical text and the ritual action, and, in the case of the elevation, the importance of experiencing the whole Divine Liturgy in its entirety—the gifts are not "complete" until they are needed for communion. Such a perception of the liturgy reveals its holistic and integral character and does not allow its reduction to

---

вв.) славянских Служебниках], *Богословские труды* 41 (2007), 272–359, here 292–98.

158. See Jacob, *Histoire du formulaire grec*, 82–84.

159. The deacons of St. Sophia of Constantinople often held more important positions than the priests and showed up at the service later than them; see Michael Bernatsky, Michael Zheltov, "Questions and Answers of Elias, Metropolitan of Crete . . ." [original title in Russian: *Бернацкий М. М., Желтов Михаил, диак.* Вопросоответы митрополита Илии Критского: Свидетельство об особенностях совершения Божественной литургии в нач. XII века], *Вестник ПСТГУ. I: Богословие, философия* 14 (2005): 23–53.

the recitation of a "sacramental formula." Moreover, this approach also has important consequences for Christian anthropology—it stresses that not only the rational and spiritual aspects of human nature can participate in the divine mystery, but that sometimes even the bodily actions are of ultimate importance. For the Eucharist itself is, in the end, the sacrament of "real food" and of "real drink" (John 6:55), and not just of word and prayer.[160]

160. I would like to express my deepest gratitude to Rev. Prof. Robert Taft and Sr. Dr. Vassa Larin for their invaluable help in improving the English language of my text.

Albertus G. A. Horsting

XII. Transfiguration of Flesh:
Literary and Theological Connections between
Martyrdom Accounts and Eucharistic Prayers

In his account of the great evil the Christians had caused to the Roman world, Julian condemns Christianity for loving the dead more than the living and for having turned the world into a cemetery: "You keep adding many corpses newly dead to the corpses of long ago. . . . You have filled the whole world with tombs and sepulchers."[1] His criticism is only a hyperbolic expression of a nearly universal pagan disgust at the Christian practice, ancient even then, of preserving and drawing near to the bodies of those who had fallen asleep in the Lord.

Early Christian communities, east and west, behaved in a way that breached one of the most important social and topographical distinctions of the ancient world. Christians would dig up, dismember, kiss, and venerate the remains of their beloved dead. What is more, they would bring them from the cities of the dead and place them in the midst of the living. In all this, they demonstrated their belief that the martyrs had power to bless and curse through their continued earthly presence and through their intimate friendship with God.[2] Those who approached the remains of the faithful dead with a pure heart could expect blessing and grace. Those who approached unworthily were told to fear the judgment and condemnation of the saint. Jerome is afraid even of coming close if he is harboring an impure or angry thought: "I do not dare to enter the shrines of the martyrs. I quake

---

1. πολλοὺς ἐπεισάγοντες τῷ πάλαι νεκρῷ τοὺς προσφάτους νεκρούς. . . . πάντα ἐπληρώσατε τάφων καὶ μνημάτων. *Contra Galilaeos* 235c. All translations from primary sources are the author's own.

2. P. R. L. Brown, *The Cult of the Saints: Its Rise and Function in Latin Christianity*, Haskell Lectures on History of Religions, New Series, 2 (Chicago: University of Chicago Press, 1981), 6.

with my whole body and soul."[3] Among the saints, the martyrs were singled out for special attention and love.[4]

In the first few centuries of our era, we can trace a growing certainty that the bodies of the martyrs are to be venerated and even feared and that these same bodies are capable of conveying grace to those who abide by them. In this essay I wish to argue that literary descriptions of the sanctified flesh of the martyrs contain linguistic and theological echoes of the Eucharistic liturgy. The stories of martyrdom, therefore, make use of Eucharistic liturgical language to describe the martyr's self-oblation.[5] Though many have noticed the connections between the language of the Eucharist and that of the martyr's sacrifice, I know of no investigation that deals in particular with one important consequence of this allusion: the martyr's body, like the Eucharistic host, becomes transfigured during the confession and passion. The martyr becomes the priest who offers his very body in the manner of the Eucharistic sacrifice.

HISTORY OF MARTYRDOM AND ITS REPRESENTATION IN EARLY CHRISTIAN LITERATURE

The history of the rise of Christianity in the ancient world cannot be told apart from the history of the Church's persecution and her self-reflection on the nature of this persecution. Jesus' willing self-sacrifice

---

3. Quando iratus fuero, et aliquid mali in meo animo cogitavero: et me nocturnum phantasma deluserit, basilicas martyrum intrare non audeo; ita totus et corpore et animo contremisco. *Contra Vigilantium* 12.

4. This is especially true in the period before the rise of monasticism and the peace of the Church. After the end of persecution, it is the ascetic who becomes the most perfect model of the Christian life. This transformation of the ideal of the martyr to that of the ascetic is reflected in a transference of the language of martyrdom to the spiritual warfare waged by the monk in the desert: "In Egypt, despite the immense and lasting veneration for the martyrs, and the vogue enjoyed even by the African *Acta Perpetuae*, the Church of the martyrs failed. Once the majority of the monks had rallied to Athanasius, Christianity in Egypt became the Christianity of the martyr's substitute, his 'brother' and sometimes his rival, the ascetic" (W. H. C. Frend, *Martyrdom and Persecution in the Early Church: A Study of a Conflict from the Maccabees to Donatus* [Oxford: Basil Blackwell, 1965], 541).

5. Or, perhaps in a more controversial formulation, the Eucharistic liturgies make use of the language of martyrdom. Tracing the direction of influence in such circumstances is nearly an impossibility. The best one can do is point to a certain convergence of language and theme in the two genres.

is the intellectual and spiritual center of this new strand of Second Temple Judaism. Throughout the writings of the New Testament, there is an expectation that suffering and tribulation await those who follow Jesus. Even in this earliest stratum of Christian theology, one finds reflections on the nature, purpose, and value of suffering. It is notable that Luke describes Stephen, later called the protomartyr, as being full of grace and having a face "like the face of an angel" (Acts 6:15). While he is being stoned, he prays for his persecutors and receives a vision of God's glory in heaven. At the moment of his death, the veil that separates this present age from the eschaton is rent. Precisely in his act of innocent self-oblation, Stephen becomes a sign of the resurrection of the dead and the outpouring of grace that was expected to come in the Last Days.

Likewise, Paul argues for an intimate connection between his personal sufferings and those of Christ on the cross. The Christian is "granted" the "privilege" of suffering alongside Christ (Phil 1:29-30). Paul rejoices that he is "being poured out as a libation over the sacrifice and the offering" of the faith of the Philippian Church (2:17-18). The writer of the letter to the Colossians writes that he is now "rejoicing in [his] sufferings for [their] sake, and in [his] flesh [he is] completing what is lacking in Christ's afflictions for the sake of his body, that is, the church" (Col 1:24). The suffering of the Christian, already in the New Testament, is not a brute fact but an act that has meaning and perhaps even a redemptive, expiatory value.

That the earliest writings of the Church should already evince such a notion of the propitiatory sacrifice of the innocent should not be a matter of surprise. The Judaism from which Christianity emerged already had a developed notion of the martyr and the value of the death of the innocent man or woman. W. H. C. Frend provocatively makes this claim:

> Without Maccabees and without Daniel a Christian theology of martyrdom would scarcely have been thinkable. Without the apocalyptic of the Palestinian Essenes, it could hardly have sustained the necessary fanaticism to overcome the universal hostility of the Roman Empire. Without the Dispersion, and in particular, the Alexandria interpretation and allegorization of this apocalyptic, the ultimate reconciliation of Church and Empire would have been impossible.[6]

6. Frend, *Martyrdom and Persecution*, 65.

In the story of the martyrdoms of Eleazar, the seven brothers, and their mother, the dependence of the early Church on the theological framework of Second Temple Judaism can most clearly been seen. Fourth Maccabees, considered by some to be either a homily or a sort of funeral oration read during the anniversary of the martyrdoms,[7] provides Christian readers ample material for reflection. It becomes the text *par excellence* for discussions of martyrdom and its ends. The conceit of the work is that of an extended disquisition on the virtue of reason and its power to master the passions. Eleazar, the old priest, is compared to a young athlete who does battle in the arena against his foe, Antiochus (7:13-14). In this way, his struggle is the vindication of the philosophical way and proof of the possibility of continence.

And yet, there is more to Eleazar's suffering than just perseverance. As he dies, he prays:

> You know, O God, that though I might have saved myself, I am dying
> in burning torments for the sake of the law. Be merciful to your people,
> and let our punishment [or justice] suffice for them.

> σὺ οἶσθα, θεέ, παρόν μοι σῴζεσθαι βασάνοις καυστικαῖς ἀποθνήσκω διὰ
> τὸν νόμον. ἵλεως γενοῦ τῷ ἔθνει σου ἀρκεσθεὶς τῇ ἡμετέρᾳ ὑπὲρ αὐτῶν
> δίκῃ. (6:27-28)

His great concern not to eat defiling flesh is, of course, not to transgress God's law, but it also comes out of his refusal to meet his ancestors in a state of impurity (5:37). His own purity is essential if his self-sacrifice is to be efficacious: "Make my blood their purification, and take my soul as a ransom for theirs" (καθάρσιον αὐτῶν ποίησον τὸ ἐμὸν αἷμα καὶ ἀντίψυχον αὐτῶν λαβὲ τὴν ἐμὴν ψυχήν [6:29]).[8] The glorification of the martyr is even clearer in the martyrdom of the seven brothers and their mother. In the narrator's encomium to them, he speaks of the family almost as if they were Hellenistic kings and

---

7. J. W. van Henten, *The Maccabean Martyrs as Saviours of the Jewish People: A Study of 2 and 4 Maccabees*, Supplements to the Journal for the Study of Judaism, 57 (Leiden: Brill, 1997), 104-5.

8. ἀντίψυχον, here translated "ransom," is a rare word twice used in 4 Macc. It occurs four times in Ignatius' epistles, where some have argued it indicates Ignatius' knowledge and appropriation of the work. See especially O. Perler, "Das vierte Makkabäerbuch, Ignatius von Antiochien und die ältesten Märtyrerberichte," *Rivista di archeologia cristiana* 25 (1949): 47–72.

queens who are translated into the celestial realms after their deaths. The mother, like a moon in the sky, beholds God in heaven while her sons surround her like the stars (17:5-6). Having undergone this apotheosis, they are installed in the heavenly court. From there, they act as agents of God's mercy and wrath. The narrator assures us that their sacrifice is the cause of Antiochus' eternal punishment, and of the purification of the homeland. Likewise, their sufferings act as a

> ransom for the sin of the people. And through the blood of those pious ones and the atonement of their death, divine providence preserved Israel that previously had been mistreated.

> ἀντίψυχον γεγονότας τῆς τοῦ ἔθνους ἁμαρτίας. καὶ διὰ τοῦ αἵματος τῶν εὐσεβῶν ἐκείνων καὶ τοῦ ἱλαστηρίου τοῦ θανάτου αὐτῶν ἡ θεία πρόνοια τὸν Ἰσραηλ προκακωθέντα διέσωσεν. (17:21-22)

The martyrs, in the purity of their self-sacrifice, have effected both the condemnation of their foe and the salvation of their people.

Even in the earliest periods of its history, Christian martyrdom was a locus for theological reflection, always being drawn toward two different perspectives, both of which are evident in the story of the Maccabean martyrs. One view regards the innocent sufferer primarily as a witness and example, while the other sees him as an expiatory sacrifice. In either case, martyrdom is always a meaning-laden event, and "because martyrs bore the name of Christ, they were themselves like letters meant to be read by the community and the world."[9]

One can see the struggle to discover the content of the martyrial "letter" in numerous writings of the early Church. What happens when the martyr undergoes sufferings that appear to imitate those of his Savior? Is the martyr a hero, a great exemplar who demonstrates the pinnacle of the Christian ethic, but who does not otherwise accomplish redemption and the forgiveness of sins for others? One thinks especially of the Alexandrian theological tradition and Clement's horror at voluntary martyrdom. For him, and to an even greater extent for his Gnostic opponents such as Heracleon, Christians should do what is in their power to avoid martyrdom.[10] When and if it comes, the mar-

---

9. R. D. Young, *In Procession before the World: Martyrdom as Public Liturgy in Early Christianity*, Pére Marquette Lecture in Theology, 2001 (Milwaukee, WI: Marquette University Press, 2001), 10.

10. Clement, *Stromateis* 4.8ff.

tyr's death is a culminating act, "the climax of a life already directed solely by the love towards God."[11] In this way, the martyr is a personal witness to the truth and to what has already taken place through rigorous ascetical and philosophical training. It is the ultimate challenge, the great arena of faith, but there is no notion that this endurance of savage violence is somehow redemptive for the one undergoing it or for others.

On the other hand, there was an even stronger current in the thought of the early Church that saw the martyr's death as a sacrifice pleasing to God, which could turn away his wrath and gain his favor. It is especially in this perspective where one can observe the use of Eucharistic imagery. Stephen prays for the forgiveness of those who persecute him, and because he is "full of grace," because he has already entered the heavenly court, his prayer is fulfilled by the conversion of Saul.

Because of her steadfastness under great suffering, Perpetua is worthy to receive a consolatory vision in which she participates in a meal that seems to resemble the Eucharistic liturgies of her day (4.1-10). Moreover, God heeds her intercessions for the salvation of her brother Dinocrates, who had died in sin at a young age (7.1-10; 8.1-4). She has become a conduit of grace, and her sacrifice is a redemptive one. She is proof that the "one and ever the same Holy Spirit is working, even now" (*unum et eundem semper Spiritum Sanctum usque adhuc operari testificentur* [21.11]). This is further emphasized by the numerous allusions that compare her to the woman who would tread on the serpent's head (*calcavi illi caput et ascendi* [4.7]).

Among the writings of the first three centuries, the connection between martyrdom and sacrifice (and especially the Eucharistic sacrifice) is perhaps clearest in the writings of Ignatius of Antioch. In his admonitory letter to the Roman congregation, whom he will soon meet on his way to his execution, he pleads that they do nothing to prevent his martyrdom:

> Only grant that I may be poured out as a libation to God, while the altar is still ready. . . . Let me be food for the beasts, through whom one may attain to God. I am the grain of God, and I am ground by the beasts' teeth so that I may be shown to be pure bread. . . . Beseech Christ for my sake so that through these instruments I may be found to be a sacrifice to God.

11. Frend, *Martyrdom and Persecution*, 355.

πλέον μοι μὴ παράσχησθε τοῦ σπονδισθῆναι θεῷ, ὡς ἔτι θυσιαστήριον
ἕτοιμόν ἐστιν . . . . ἄφετέ με θηρίων εἶναι βοράν, δι᾽ ὧν ἔστιν θεοῦ
ἐπιτυχεῖν. σῖτός εἰμι θεοῦ καὶ δι᾽ ὀδόντων θηρίων ἀλήθομαι, ἵνα καθαρὸς
ἄρτος εὑρεθῶ. . . . λιτανεύσατε τὸν Χριστὸν ὑπὲρ ἐμοῦ, ἵνα διὰ τῶν
ὀργάνων τούτων θεῷ θυσία εὑρεθῶ. (2.2–4.2)[12]

His very self is the sacrifice offered for the churches, paradoxically a
sacrifice that will be consumed not by those for whom it is made, but
by those who torment him. The beasts he speaks of are of course those
of the arena, but Ignatius also uses the term to refer to his guards. Just
as he bids the churches to gather around the Eucharist, he wishes to be
consumed by his persecutors, for in being so consumed he becomes
Christ to them.[13] His personal salvation, his "attaining to God," is connected to properly carrying out the sacrifice of martyrdom. His sufferings, therefore, are a repetition and a fulfillment of Christ's own passion.

SANCTIFIED BODIES

Moving now from a more general account of the persecution of the
Church, we will consider two martyrdoms in particular that illustrate
what Robin Darling Young has called the "public liturgy" of martyrdom.[14] The accounts of the martyrdoms of Polycarp and Pionius, separated by about one hundred years, reflect the change and continuity of
Eucharistic language in martyrdom accounts. Both martyrdoms took
place in Smyrna, and the narrator of Pionius' account is particularly
at pains to make the similarities between Pionius' passion and that of
Polycarp clear:

> On the second day of the sixth month, it being a great Sabbath, on the
> birthday of the blessed martyr Polycarp, during the perseuction of
> Decius, there were arrrested the Presbyter Pionius. . . . Now Pionius
> saw on the day before Polycarp's birthday that they were to be seized
> on that day.

12. The long and middle recensions of the text further emphasize the Eucharistic quality of his death and his body by adding θεοῦ and τοῦ Χριστοῦ,
respectively, after καθαρὸς ἄρτος.

13. See Frederick C. Klawiter, "The Eucharist and Sacramental Realism in
the Thought of St Ignatius of Antioch," *Studia Liturgica* 37, no. 2 (2007): 129–63,
for further discussion of the connections in Ignatius' thought between Eucharist and martyrdom.

14. Young, *In Procession before the World*, 23.

Μηνὸς ἕκτου δευτέρα ἐνισταμένου σαββάτου μεγάλου, ἐν τῇ γενεθλίῳ ἡμέρᾳ τοῦ μακαρίου μάρτυρος Πολυκάρπου, ὄντος τοῦ διωγμοῦ τοῦ κατὰ Δέκιον, συνελήφθησαν Πιόνιος πρεσβύτερος. . . . ὁ οὖν Πιόνιος πρὸ μιᾶς ἡμέρας τῶν Πολυκάρπου γενεθλίων εἶδεν ὅτι δεῖ ταύτῃ τῇ ἡμέρᾳ αὐτοὺς συλληφθῆναι. (2.1)

Pionius and Polycarp, therefore, are two examples of a continuous tradition of reflection on the nature of martyrdom stemming from the regions of western Anatolia. In both documents, one can observe the connections seen in the thought of Ignatius reaching their full flowering: if the martyr is a priest sacrificing his own body in the manner of a Eucharistic celebration, then his body must become "Eucharistized."

The *Martyrdom of Polycarp* is of an uncertain date. Though Evarestus, the narrator, tells us that he was martyred on 22 (or perhaps 23) February, the year is uncertain. Dates from 155 to 160 have received the most support from recent scholarship, and perhaps greater accuracy than this is not warranted.[15] The document is preserved as a letter from the Church of Smyrna to the Church of Philomelium, a form that was to be copied many times in the long history of the genre. Polycarp's life before his martyrdom is also of note for understanding the nature of Roman persecution, for Polycarp had lived in relative peace within the city for eighty-six years. He appears to have been a man of means who owned both a city and country home as well as some slaves. There is little indication of a Church under constant persecution, and indeed there is little evidence that the Church of Smyrna continued to suffer grievously after these persecutions. This sudden outbreak of violence may have resulted from a particularly terrible plague that broke out around 165.[16]

After a brief introduction to the state of affairs, Evarestus describes the way in which Polycarp was discovered by his pursuers. He asks for an hour to pray (8.1). Of note is the way in which his prayer alludes to the language of Eucharistic litanies, including a prayer for the universal Church. Then in the first of many reminiscences of Jesus' last days, the guards lead Polycarp into the city on a donkey on a

15. M. W. Holmes, "The *Martyrdom of Polycarp* and the New Testament Passion Narrative," in *Trajectories through the New Testament and the Apostolic Fathers*, ed. A. F. Gregory and C. M. Tuckett (Oxford: Oxford University Press, 2005), 301.

16. Frend, *Martyrdom and Persecution*, 269.

great Sabbath.[17] After an extended series of attempts to have Polycarp recant, the authorities finally determine to execute him by burning. It is precisely at this moment, after his good confession of Christ, as he is being led to the slaughter, that the Eucharistic language reaches its climax:

Looking up to heaven, he said:

O Lord God almighty, Father of your beloved and blessed child Jesus Christ, through whom we have received knowledge of you, O God of the angels, the powers, and of all creation, and of all the family of the just who live before you:

I bless you because you have deemed me worthy of this day and this hour, to have a share among the number of the martyrs in the cup of your Christ, for the resurrection to eternal life of both the soul and the body in the incorruptibility of the Holy Spirit. May I be received this day among them before you as a rich and acceptable sacrifice, as you, the God of truth who cannot deceive, have prepared, revealed, and fulfilled beforehand.

Hence I praise you, I bless you, I glorify you above all things, through the eternal and celestial high priest, Jesus Christ, your beloved child, through whom be glory to you with him and the Holy Spirit now and for all ages to come. Amen.

ἀναβλέψας εἰς τὸν οὐρανὸν εἶπεν·

Κύριε ὁ θεὸς ὁ παντοκράτωρ, ὁ τοῦ ἀγαπητοῦ καὶ εὐλογητοῦ παιδός σου Ἰησοῦ Χριστοῦ πατήρ, δι᾿ οὗ τὴν περὶ σοῦ ἐπίγνωσιν εἰλήφαμεν, ὁ θεὸς ἀγγέλων καὶ δυνάμεων καὶ πάσης τῆς κτίσεως παντός τε τοῦ γένους τῶν δικαίων, οἳ ζῶσιν ἐνώπιόν σου,

εὐλογῶ σε ὅτι ἠξίωσάς με τῆς ἡμέρας καὶ ὥρας ταύτης τοῦ λαβεῖν μέρος ἐν ἀριθμῷ τῶν μαρτύρων, ἐν τῷ ποτηρίῳ τοῦ Χριστοῦ σου εἰς ἀνάστασιν ζωῆς αἰωνίου ψυχῆς τε καὶ σώματος ἐν ἀφθαρσίᾳ πνεύματος ἁγίου, ἐν οἷς προσδεχθείην ἐνώπιόν σου σήμερον ἐν θυσίᾳ πίονι καὶ προσδεκτῇ, καθὼς προητοίμασας καὶ προεφανέρωσας καὶ ἐπλήρωσας ὁ ἀψευδὴς καὶ ἀληθινὸς θεός.

---

17. For a discussion of these many connections see especially Holmes, "The *Martyrdom of Polycarp*."

διὰ τοῦτο καὶ περὶ πάντων σὲ αἰνῶ, σὲ εὐλογῶ, σὲ δοξάζω διὰ του αἰωνίου καὶ ἐπουρανίου ἀρχιερέως Ἰησοῦ Χριστοῦ ἀγαπητοῦ σου παιδός, δι᾽ οὗ σοὶ σὺν αὐτῷ καὶ πνεύματι ἁγίῳ δόξα καὶ νῦν καὶ εἰς τοὺς μέλλοντας αἰῶνας. ἀμήν (14.1-3)

This is of course not an anaphora in the strict sense of the word. Though certain vigorous attempts have been made to connect this prayer to an "apostolic" form of the Eucharistic prayer, it seems clear that the most that can be said is that it reflects the deep structures of the euchology of Asia Minor at the end of the second century.[18] Of particular note is Polycarp's use of the title *child* to describe Christ, a common formula of the second century also found in numerous sources such as *Didache* 9 and 10 and *1 Clement* 9. This title can also be seen in *Apostolic Tradition*, which like this prayer both begins and concludes with a reference to the "beloved child" of the Father (ἀγαπητὸς παῖς, *dilectus puer*).[19]

Polycarp begins with an invocation of God, giving thanks for creation, knowledge, and the gift of God's beloved child. He then blesses God for making him worthy to be counted among the martyrs.[20] At the climax of this pseudo-Eucharistic liturgy, he asks that the Lord accept his offering as a "rich and acceptable sacrifice," but of course it is

18. P. Cagin, *L'Anaphore apostolique et ses témoins* (Paris: Lethielleux, 1919). On attempts to demonstrate the connection between Polycarp's prayer and the larger phenomenon of a "second-century pattern of anaphoral prayer" associated especially with western Anatolia, see D. Tripp, "The Prayer of St. Polycarp and the Development of Anaphoral Prayer," *Ephemerides Liturgicae* 104 (1990). Mazza also notes a similarity to the Coptic fragment of the anaphora of Basil, in E. Mazza, *The Origins of the Eucharistic Prayer*, trans. R. Lane (Collegeville, MN: Liturgical Press, 1995), 154–56.

19. There are numerous other, minor connections between Polycarp's prayer and that of *Apostolic Tradition*. Tripp takes this as another piece of circumstantial evidence for the Anatolian provenance of *Apostolic Tradition*, which he sees as an elaboration of the anaphoral form seen in Polycarp, Irenaeus, Justin, and others with the addition of other elements such as the institution narrative (Tripp, "The Prayer of St. Polycarp," 119–23). Of course, since Polycarp's prayer is not an anaphora *sensu stricto*, but merely a prayer that uses anaphoral imagery, perhaps such exact comparisons of elements are not justified.

20. Again one is reminded of *Apostolic Tradition*: "giving you thanks because you have held us worthy to stand before you and minister to you" (*gratias tibi agentes, quia nos dignos habuisti adstare coram te et tibi ministrare* [21]).

his very own body and his sufferings that compose the offering (14.2). Polycarp's own body and sacrifice has replaced that of the Eucharist, for he has become holy through his pure confession. In this prayer we can see how deeply the habits and forms of Eucharistic prayer have become entwined with the language of martyrdom. Polycarp, or at least his narrator, has no difficulty in appropriating the language of the Eucharist for this novel purpose.

Once Polycarp concludes his prayer and the fires envelop him, the narrator seeks to describe the transformation that has taken place during Polycarp's prayer:

> For the fire, like a ship's sail filled by the wind, formed into the shape of a vault and surrounded the martyr's body with a wall. And he was within it not as burning flesh but rather as bread being baked, or like gold and silver being proved in a furnace. And from it we smelled such a delightful fragrance as though it were redolent of incense or some other costly perfume.

> τὸ γὰρ πῦρ καμάρας εἶδος ποιῆσαν ὥσπερ ὀθόνη πλοίου ὑπὸ πνεύματος πληρουμένη, κύκλῳ περιετείχισεν τὸ σῶμα τοῦ μάρτυρος. καὶ ἦν μεσον οὐχ ὡς σὰρξ καιομένη ἀλλ᾽ ὡς ἄρτος ὀπτώμενος ἢ ὡς χρυσὸς καὶ ἄργυρος ἐν καμίνῳ πυρούμενος. καὶ γὰρ εὐωδαίς τοσαύτης ἀντελαβόμεθα ὡς λιβανωτοῦ πνέοντος ἢ ἄλλου τινὸς τῶν τιμίων ἀρωμάτων. (15.2)

The allusion to the Eucharist, i.e., the smell of baking bread, is coupled with that of a refining fire, which eliminates the dross and leaves behind only the precious metal. Polycarp's flesh is not consumed and it certainly does not burn. Rather, all that veiled its glory has been removed, and the flames, like those that enveloped the bodies of the Maccabean martyrs, reveal the true nature of Polycarp's body: it has become a host, a vehicle of grace to those around him. The narrator insists that Polycarp's body is πυρουμένη and not καιομένη, that the flames have not burned him but rather have been infused into him. He has consumed the fires that tried to consume him.

Indeed, the entire arena has been transformed and reconfigured into a church. The flames that envelop his body "formed into the shape of a vault and surrounded the martyr's body with a wall" (15). In addition to sensing the odor of baking bread, the witnesses report smelling incense burning. Not only has Polycarp offered up his own flesh in a Eucharistic ritual, but God provides the entire liturgical context, establishing an altar, a church, incense, and even a celestial voice to participate in the liturgy.

The result of the martyrdom is the creation of a holy and powerful object treasured by the Church of Smyrna. This result is apparent to the Christians and to the "jealous and envious Evil One" who:

> saw to it that not even his dear body should be taken away by us, even though many desired to do this and to commune with his dear and holy flesh.

> ὁ δὲ ἀντίζηλος καὶ βάσκανος καὶ πονηρός . . . ἐπετήδευσεν ὡς μηδὲ τὸ σωμάτιον αὐτοῦ ὑφ᾿ ἡμῶν ληφθῆναι, καίπερ πολλῶν ἐπιθυμούντων τοῦτο ποιῆσαι καὶ κοινωνῆσαι τῷ ἁγίῳ αὐτοῦ σαρκίῳ. (17.1)[21]

They do not merely wish to possess Polycarp's bones, but, in the language that would later be used to describe the reception of the Eucharistic host, they desire to "commune with his dear and holy flesh" (17.1). To make the junction between the two forms of sacrifice complete, the Smyrneans gather around his tomb to celebrate the Eucharistic liturgy, for his bones have become "more precious to [them] than precious stones and finer than gold" (τιμιώτερα λίθων πολυτελῶν καὶ δοκιμώτερα ὑπὲρ χρυσίον [18.2]). They commune with his flesh even as they commune with the body and blood of the Lord. The conflation of the two sacrifices, of the two offerings of flesh, is complete.

The *Martyrdom of Pionius the Presbyter and His Companions* survives as an episode in Eusebius' *Historia ecclesiastica*, who dates it to the middle of the third century around the times of the Decian Persecution (249–251). Herbert A. Musurillo says that it is "written in a moving style which probably reflects the homiletic genre of the period, full of scriptural quotations."[22] Its high degree of artistry may make it a problematic document for historical reconstruction, but the more it reflects the imaginative processes of the time the better it serves the aims of

---

21. Note the use of the two diminutives σωμάτιον and σαρκίον. These dimunitives are meant to indicate the intimacy of the Smyrneans with Polycarp's remains. The first is often translated "poor body," which misses the point that there is nothing poor or pitiful about his remains. Rather, Polycarp has conquered death and is "now crowned with the garland of immortality and the winner of an incontestable prize" (17.1).

22. Herbert Anthony Musurillo, *The Acts of the Christian Martyrs*, Early Christian Texts (Oxford: Clarendon Press, 1972), xxvii.

this discussion.[23] In this document the belief of the terrible holiness of the self-immolated body is clearly identifiable.

The martyrdom is a long one, with numerous interrogations and episodes of torture. These events serve to demonstrate the malicious folly of Roman and Jewish ways and the indefatigable perseverance of the saints. Pionius seeks to demonstrate the folly of the Jews and pagans of Smyrna by refuting them from their own works. He, like Polycarp before him, undergoes a number of trials that the narrator compares to Christ's sufferings. Like Polycarp, he also prophesies his martyrdom. No context is given for why the outbreak of violence takes place.

Before Pionius and his associates are arrested, we find them celebrating the Eucharist in the form of "sacred bread with water" (3.1). Once in prison, he delivers an extended homily to his prisoners in which he explains the eschatological nature of their sufferings. Numerous interrogations with different officials in various locations follow, during which Pionius demonstrates his resolve to give a true confession. Having remained steadfast, he is led back to the prison. The narrator then says, "Some remarked of Pionius: 'He has always looked so pale, but now look how ruddy his complexion is!'" (καί ἔλεγόν τινες περὶ Πιονίου· πῶς ἀεὶ χλωρὸς ὢν νῦν πυρρὸν ἔχει τὸ πρόσωπον [10.1]). The word πυρρὸς, derived from πῦρ, is notable since it is not normally used to describe a flushed or ruddy face. Its use here may be a foreshadowing of the flames he will endure. Already then, at the moment of his confession, Pionius has undergone some form of transformation.

Finally, Pionius' day arrives. The proconsul grows tired of the extended dialogue and in his exhaustion asks Pionius why he hastens to his death. His response, "not toward death, but toward life" (τί σπεύδεις ἐπὶ τὸν θάνατον; ἀπεκρίνατο· οὐκ ἐπὶ τὸν θάνατον ἀλλ᾽ ἐπὶ τὴν ζωήν [20.5]), seals his fate. He has uttered the proper confession of the living God, and so he is led to the amphitheater. There, in the arena of his self-immolation, Pionius undergoes something like an antivesting ritual, where he willingly removes his clothing, complete with an attendant to help him: "hastily he went to the amphitheater because of the zeal of his faith, and he willingly disrobed as the prison-keeper stood by" (ἀπελθόντος δὲ αὐτοῦ μετὰ σπουδῆς εἰς τὸ στάδιον

23. Though quite notably Louis Robert has argued for its value in reconstructing the topography and institutions of Smyrna in the third century. See Louis Robert, ed., with the assistance of G. W. Bowersock and C. P. Jones, *Le martyre de Pionios, prêtre de Smyrne* (Washington, DC: Dumbarton Oaks, 1994).

διὰ τὸ πρόθυμον τῆς πίστεως καὶ ἐπιστάντος τοῦ κομενταρησίου ἑκὼν ἀπεδύσατο [21.1]). In her first vision, Perpetua similarly enters the arena shrouded and unaware of the transformation that has already taken place, for she has become man-like in preparation for her contest (*Passio Perpetuae* 10.7). Pionius finally realizes that something has happened to his body, perhaps seeing for the first time what the crowds had already understood:

> Then realizing the holiness and dignity of his body, he was filled with great joy; and looking up to heaven he gave thanks to God who had preserved him so; then he stretched himself out on the wood and handed himself over to the soldier to hammer in the nails. . . . he said: "I am hurrying that I may awake all the more quickly, manifesting the resurrection from the dead."

> εἶτα κατανοήσας τὸ ἁγνὸν καὶ εὐσχημον τοῦ σώματος ἑαυτοῦ πολλῆς ἐπλήσθη χαρᾶς, ἀναβλέψας δὲ εἰς τὸν οὐρανὸν καὶ εὐχαριστήσας τῷ τοιοῦτον αὐτὸν διατηρήσαντι θεῷ ἥπλωσεν ἑδυτὸν ἐπὶ τὸν ξύλου καὶ παρέδωκε τῷ στρατιώτῃ πεῖραι τοὺς ἥλους. . . . εἶπεν· διὰ τοῦτο σπεύδω ἵνα θᾶττον ἐγερθῶ, δηλῶν τὴν ἐκ νεκρῶν ἀνάστασιν. (21.2-4)

One must note the similarities to Polycarp's prayer.[24] Besides the explicit mention of Polycarp earlier in the martyrdom, here Pionius begins his prayer at the same moment in the martyrdom as Polycarp did. He begins with what must now have been the paradigmatic gesture of the innocent sufferer: looking up to heaven. The Eucharistic connections are even more explicit, and the narrator calls his prayer an act of *Eucharistia*.

As Pionius' veil is removed, he recognizes that something took place during his confession: his body, like that of the Eucharistic host, has somehow become transfigured and filled with light. After a biting response to the executioner's offer to remove the nails that had been driven into his hands, he says, "I am hurrying that I may awake all the more quickly, manifesting the resurrection from the dead" (21.4). Once again, we can see a connection to the anaphora of *Apostolic Tradition*:

> we render thanks to you God, through your beloved child Jesus Christ . . . who when he was being handed over to voluntary suffering, that

---

24. On the more general dependence of the *Martyrdom of Pionius* on that of Polycarp, see J. den Boeft and J. N. Bremmer, "Notiunculae Martyrologicae III," *Vigiliae Christianae* 39, no. 2 (1985): 115.

he might destroy death and break the bonds of the devil, and tread down hell and illuminate the righteous, and fix a limit and manifest the resurrection.

gratias tibi referimus, Deus, per dilectum puerum tuum Iesum Christum . . . qui cumque traderetur voluntariae passioni, ut mortem solvat et vincula diaboli dirumpat, et infernum calcet et iustos illuminet, et terminum figat et resurrectionem manifestet. (PE 81)[25]

Δηλόω is an excellent candidate for a *Vorlage* of *manifestare*. Also notable is that both instances of "manifesting the resurrection" occur within the context of a victory over death by a voluntary death (Polycarp: παρέδωκε; *Apostolic Tradition*: *traderetur*). Especially if this part of the *Apostolic Tradition* is from an older strand, questions about the direction of influence become very difficult to answer. The most that can be said is that both prayers participate in the Eucharistic language of Asia Minor. In both cases, the act of self-oblation leads to the destruction of death and the manifestation of life.

Pionius' self-discovery does not remain hidden from those around him. After the fires burn out, the witnesses discover that his body, like that of Polycarp's, was not burned but refined:

Indeed his crown was made manifest through his body. For after the fire had been extinguished, those of us who were present saw his body like that of an athlete in full array at the height of his powers. His ears were not distorted; his hair lay in order on the surface of his head; and his beard was full as though with the first blossom of hair. His face shone once again—wondrous grace!—so that the Christians were all the more confirmed in the faith, and the terrified and conscience-filled unbelievers returned full of fear.

ἐσημάνθη δὲ αὐτοῦ ὁ στέφανος καὶ διὰ τοῦ σώματος. μετὰ γὰρ τὸ κατασβεσθῆναι τὸ πῦρ τοιοῦτον αὐτὸν εἴδομεν οἱ παραγενόμενοι ὁποῖόν

25. P. Bradshaw, M. E. Johnson, and L. E. Phillips, trans., *The Apostolic Tradition: A Commentary*, Hermeneia (Minneapolis, MN: Fortress Press, 2002). The editors note that the text under discussion may come from one of the more ancient layers of the prayer. They also suggest Irenaeus as a useful comparandum: "Our Lord by his passion destroyed death , and dispersed error, and put an end to corruption, and destroyed ignorance, while he manifested life and revealed truth, and bestowed the gift of incorruption" (*Adversus Haereses* 2. 20. 3); "he manifested the resurrection" (*Demonstration* 38). Ibid., 47.

τε τὸ σῶμα ἀκμάζοντος ἀθλητοῦ κεκοσμημένου. καὶ γὰρ τὰ ὦτα αὐτοῦ
‹οὐ› μυλλὰ ἐγένοντο καὶ αἱ τρίχες ἐν χρῷ τῆς κεφαλῆς προσεκάθηντο,
τὸ δὲ γένειον αὐτοῦ ὡς ἰούλοις ἐπανθοῦσιν ἐκεκόσμητο. ἐπέλαμπε δὲ
καὶ τὸ πρόσωπον αὐτοῦ πάλιν, χάρις θαυμαστή, ὥστε τοὺς Χριστιανοὺς
στηριχθῆναι μᾶλλον τῇ πίστει, τοὺς δὲ ἀπίστους πτοηθέντας καὶ τὸ
συνειδὸς ἔχοντας πεφοβημένον κατελθεῖν. (22.2-4)

If anything, his body seems more glorious, stronger, and youthful than
it did before his sufferings. The mention of his corpse's youthful appearance is particularly striking, since he is portrayed as the leader
of the community and is compared to the elderly Polycarp at the beginning of the narrative. This also recalls the description of Eleazar's
body, which becomes youthful after his suffering (4 Macc 7:13-14). The
earlier play with the meaning of πυρρός now becomes clear: Pionius
has drawn the flames into himself, and his face now "shines."

The saints come to his remains in order to strengthen their faith;
the unbelievers fear to draw near. His body, like the flame it passed
through, is now warmth to the pure and punishing fire to the impure.
Cyprian, a contemporary of Pionius, describes the power of the Eucharistic species in similar terms: "There was a woman who with
impure hands tried to open the locket in which she was keeping Our
Lord's holy body, but fire flared up from it and she was too terrified to
touch it."[26] For Cyprian, the Eucharist not only effected a communion
between Lord and recipient, it was also a talisman with apotropaic
powers. The saint who kept the host with him could repel demons
and treacherous men.[27] In the same way would the bodies of the martyrs be transferred to basilicas and shrines, where they could provide
a similar sort of patronage by driving out the demons and bringing
heaven down to earth.

CONCLUSION

The literary connections that accounts of martyrdom made between
the Eucharistic sacrifice and that of the martyr were a cause of much
reflection. One of the earliest and most explicit treatises dedicated to
the topic is Origen's letter to Ambrose and Prototectus in which he

26. *De lapsis* 26. Cited in N. Mitchell, *Cult and Controversy: The Worship of the
Eucharist outside Mass*, Studies in the Reformed Rites of the Catholic Church, 4
(New York: Pueblo, 1982), 13.
    27. Ibid., 15.

encourages them to pursue martyrdom. Although Origen does not describe the martyr's body as such, he provides us with language to describe what happens during the martyr's confession and suffering. Origen's *Exhortation to Martyrdom* is conceived of as a book to prepare Christians to perform properly the public liturgy of self-oblation. Its arrangement of biblical texts and brief maxims could serve as a sort of textbook of impassibility, of philosophical resolve. By repetition and memorization, the would-be martyr develops the inner stability he would need in the moment of trial.[28] We see, therefore, behind this work a mind engaged with understanding the relationship between the sacrificial realities of the Eucharist and that of the martyr's death. Origen's answer is compelling since it finds the ground for the analogy in the twofold process of proclamation and action, of word and deed, which is found in every liturgical moment.

Origen argues that once the Christian has come before the authorities, he has no choice about whether he will sacrifice. The only questions that remain unanswered are what and to whom he will offer sacrifice. If the martyr fails to render a true confession and

> if he should deny that there is one God and his Christ and confess demons or fortunes, let him know that by preparing "a table for demons" and by filling "a cup for Fortune" (Is. 65. 11; Prov. 9. 2) he forsakes the Lord and forgets his holy mountain in yielding to these disgraces.[29]

> εἰ δέ τις . . . ἀρνήσαιτο μὲν τὸ εἶναι ἕνα θεὸν καὶ τὸν Χριστὸν αὐτοῦ ὁμολογῆσαι δέ δαιμόνια ἢ τύχας, ἴστω ὁ τοιοῦτος ἑτοιμάζων "τῷ δαιμονίῳ τράπεζαν" καὶ πληρῶν "τῇ τύχῃ κέρασμα" ἐγκαταλιπὼν κύριον καὶ ἐπιλανθανόμενος τοῦ ὄρους τοῦ ἁγίου αὐτοῦ τούτοις τοῖς ἐλέγχοις ὑποκεισόμενος. (40)

Cyprian expresses a similar notion: "poor fellow, why bring any other offering or victim for the sacrifice? You yourself are the offering and the victim come to the altar."[30] Whether or not the would-be martyr actually performs an act of sacrifice, for Origen he has already sacrificed through his improper confession.

---

28. Young, *In Procession before the World*, 14.

29. R. A. Greer, trans., *Origen: An Exhortation to Martyrdom, Prayer, and Selected Works*, Classics of Western Spirituality (New York: Paulist Press, 1979).

30. *De lapsis* 8, Cyprian, *The Lapsed: The Unity of the Catholic Church*, trans. M. Bévenot, Ancient Christian Writers, 25 (Westminster: Newman Press, 1957).

We see, therefore, that for Origen it is the content and manner of the confession that make the sacrifice of the martyr either pure or impure. To say "any word foreign to our confession" is to "defile ourselves" and to defile "the measure of our confession" by "mixing into it something foreign" (11). The martyr offers up himself and his testimony to God as a sacrifice. If he fails to utter the proper words, that is, if he does not properly perform the liturgy of martyrdom, then the ritual action becomes invalid. Conversely, "who else is the blameless priest offering a blameless sacrifice than the person who holds fast to his confession and fulfills every requirement the account of martyrdom demands?" (30). The martyr's confession is the sanctifying prayer that renders his body holy, inviolate, and beautiful. It is the confession that confects the martyrial sacrament, for through it his words become the words of Christ.

With such a logic thoroughly in place already in the middle of the third century, can it be any surprise that we find the martyrs participating in the liturgy of the Church in various ways? First and most obviously, the bodies of the martyrs, dismembered so that they may touch more people, find their way into the churches. Especially by the fourth century, the traffic in martyrs' relics becomes one of the most important ways bishops assert their authority and proclaim the continuity of the Constantinian Church with the Church of the Martyrs. When the relics of Saints Gervasius and Protasius were discovered in 385, Ambrose moved the remains from the shrine in which they had been discovered into his new basilica within two days. As Brown notes, "by this move, Gervasius and Protasius were inseparably linked to the communal liturgy."[31] Or, in other words, the transfigured bodies of Gervasius and Protasius, now residing below the altar, were inseparably linked to the Eucharist confected above them. The two spheres of sacrifice and offering now overlap in space as well as in the mind.

Finally, we must note the interpolation of lists of martyrs into prayers of the Church, perhaps most obviously in the Roman Canon. In both the *Communicantes* and the *Nobis quoque* we find extended lists of martyrs, mostly local, inserted into the middle of the Eucharistic prayer, forming bookends of sorts around the consecration. Though there have been numerous studies about the formation of the list of

---

31. Brown, *Cult of the Saints*, 37.

the saints and their changes over time,[32] there remains perhaps the more fundamental question of why one would wish to include a particular list of martyrs within the anaphora. Since the martyrs had already been associated with the Eucharistic sacrifice, and indeed since their bodies had already been translated to the space below the altar, it is altogether reasonable that the Eucharistic sacrifice should seek to associate itself with that of the martyrs.

32. E.g., V. L. Kennedy, *The Saints of the Canon of the Mass*, 2nd ed., Studi di antichità cristiana, 14 (Vatican City: Pontificio Istituto di Archeologia Cristiana, 1963). For the commemoration of the dead in the liturgy of St. John Chrysostom see R. F. Taft, *The Diptychs*, Orientalia Christiana Analecta, 238 (Rome: Pontificium Institutum Studiorum Orientalium, 1991).

Neil J. Roy

XIII. The Mother of God, the Forerunner, and the Saints of the Roman Canon: A Euchological *Deësis*[1]

The anaphora known as the Roman Canon (Eucharistic Prayer I) constitutes one of the most precious treasures of the Latin church's patrimony of liturgical prayer, a gem so highly prized by the church herself that when, in the 1960s, liturgists and other specialists approached Paul VI for permission to update and reform the Canon, the Pope altogether forbade any tampering with the prayer. Instead, Cipriano Vagaggini was allowed to compile an alternative to the Roman Canon that might be used, for instance, on weekdays.[2] This new prayer, in effect, was supposed to express the euchological ideals

---

1. The author gratefully acknowledges the kind assistance of the following scholars in preparing the manuscript of this essay for publication: Maxwell E. Johnson of the University of Notre Dame, who carefully reviewed the text and made valuable suggestions; Robert Randolf Coleman of the University of Notre Dame, who furnished important details concerning the frescoes at Torcello and Cellini's *Last Judgment* in S. Cecilia in Trastevere, as well as insight into Michelangelo's *Last Judgment*; and finally Édouard Jeauneau, Canon of Chartres Cathedral and Senior Fellow of the Pontifical Institute of Mediaeval Studies, Toronto, whose golden jubilee of priestly ordination in 1997 initiated the conversation that led to this paper. Any errors of course are the responsibility of the author. An earlier version of this essay appeared as "The Roman Canon: Deësis in Euchological Form" in *Benedict XVI and the Sacred Liturgy*, ed. Neil J. Roy and Janet E. Rutherford (Dublin: Four Courts, 2010).

2. See Cipriano Vagaggini, *Il canone della messa e la riforma liturgica* (Torino-Leumann: Elle di Ci, 1966); English translation: *The Canon of the Mass and Liturgical Reform*, trans. Peter Coughlan (Staten Island, NY: Alba House, 1967), 24: "the purpose of this book is above all a practical one, namely to examine objectively the virtues and defects of the Roman canon; to see if these defects can be corrected; to suggest in conclusion a second canon, and one alternative canon to accompany it."

and theological views of several scholars who were fast becoming "the liturgical establishment." Vagaggini's anaphora, known today as Eucharistic Prayer III, is used far more frequently than the Roman Canon, which it was intended to improve.

This essay has little to do with the new Eucharistic prayers formulated over roughly the last forty years. Nor do these remarks concern the early anaphora of *The Apostolic Tradition*, attributed by Bernard Botte and others to Hippolytus of Rome but the authorship of which has come under increasing scrutiny.[3] This essay addresses only the Roman Canon as it has developed and come down to us over the course of at least seventeen centuries and, in particular, the two lists of saints that occur in it before and after the narrative of institution and anamnesis. The first list occurs in the *Communicantes* prayer ("In union with the whole Church"); the second list appears in the prayer beginning with the words *Nobis quoque peccatoribus* ("For ourselves, too, we ask"). This paper contends that the two groups of saints, led in the first instance by the Blessed Virgin Mary and in the second by St. John the Baptist, constitute a *Deësis* in euchological form, by which these saints are presented in an intercessory role on either side of Christ made present on the altar in the institution.

THE ROMAN CANON

The earliest extant evidence of the Roman Canon dates to between 380 and 390, when St. Ambrose of Milan (c. 339–397) analyzed it for his newly baptized Christians in the series of mystagogical lectures titled *De sacramentis*.[4] The Eucharistic Prayer, in the version presented by Ambrose, begins with a primitive form of the epicletic *Quam oblationem* and concludes with another epicletic prayer, the *Supplices te rogamus*. In Ambrose's day, it seems, the canon that has come to be associated most closely with the see of Rome did not include what are now known as the prayers of intercession. These intercessory prayers

---

3. See Paul Bradshaw, Maxwell E. Johnson, and Edward Phillips, *The Apostolic Tradition: A Commentary*, ed. Harold W. Attridge (Minneapolis, MN: Fortress, 2002).

4. Ambrose of Milan, *De sacramentis*, IV.5.21–6.26, *De sacramentis = Über die Sakramente. De mysteriis = Über die Mysterien*, ed. Josef Schmitz, Fontes Christiani 3 (Freiburg/Breisgau and New York: Herder, 1990), 148–52; *Des sacrements; Des mystères: Explication du symbole*, ed. Bernard Botte, 2nd ed., 3rd reprint, Sources Chrétiennes 25 bis (Paris: Cerf, 2007).

for the hierarchy, for the rest of the church on earth, and for the dead found their way into the Roman Canon by the fifth century.[5]

The intercessions in the Roman Canon are divided into two groups on either side of the narrative of institution and anamnesis (see figure 1 at the end of this chapter). The *Memento Domine* of the living, a prayer for the hierarchy and the other members of the church militant, precedes the consecratory petition over the gifts and the narrative of institution itself, whereas the *Memento etiam Domine* of the dead comes after the tripartite core of the anaphora, namely, the institution narrative, the anamnesis (memorial), and the epicletic petition for grace and blessing. Immediately following the *Memento* of the living, the *Communicantes* refers to the communion that the church militant on earth enjoys with the church triumphant in heaven. Not only do the faithful on earth share communion with the saints now in glory; we also venerate them as they plead for us with the Son of God:

> Communicantes,
> et memoriam venerantes,
> in primis gloriosae semper Virginis Mariae,
> Genetricis Dei et Domini nostri Iesu Christi:
> sed et beati Ioseph, eiusdem Virginis Sponsi,
> et beatorum Apostolorum ac Martyrum tuorum,
> Petri et Pauli, Andreae,
> Iacobi, Ioannis,
> Thomae, Iacobi, Philippi,
> Bartholomaei, Matthaei, Simonis et Thaddaei:
> Lini, Cleti, Clementis, Xisti,
> Cornelii, Cypriani,
> Laurentii, Chrysogoni,
> Ioannis et Pauli,
> Cosmae et Damiani
> et omnium sanctorum; quorum meritis precibusque concedas,
> Ut in omnibus protectionis tuae muniamur auxilio.[6]

5. See Joseph Andreas Jungmann, *Missarum sollemnia: Eine genetische Erklärung der Römischen Messe* (Vienna: Herder, 1948), 1:70–71; *Mass of the Roman Rite: Its Origins and Development (Missarum sollemnia)* (New York: Benziger Brothers, 1955), 1:54–55.

6. *Missale Romanum ex decreto sacrosancti oecumenici concilii Vaticani II instauratum auctoritate Pauli PP. VI promulgatum, editio typica* (Vatican City: Vatican Polyglot Press, 1970), 448 (henceforth MR 1970); *Missale Romanum ex decreto sacrosancti oecumenici concilii Vaticani II instauratum auctoritate Pauli PP. VI*

First in order of prominence comes Mary, the glorious ever-virgin Mother of God. Since 1962, the canon has included immediately after Mary her chaste spouse, St. Joseph.[7] There follows a list of twenty-four saints: twelve apostles, including St. Paul but not St. Matthias, and twelve male martyrs, corresponding to the number of elders mentioned in the Apocalypse or book of Revelation.[8] The twelve martyrs who follow the apostles include five popes or bishops of Rome; one bishop from abroad (Cyprian of Carthage, linked by bonds of friendship and correspondence with Cornelius); the Roman deacon Lawrence, who followed Pope Sixtus II (†7 August 258) to martyrdom a few days later (10 August 258); the cleric and catechist Chrysogonus; and finally, four laymen, who actually constitute two sets of brothers—John and Paul, associated if only by name with a *domus ecclesiae* on the Coelian Hill, and the eastern physicians Cosmas and Damian, under whose patronage a church in the Roman forum was dedicated in the sixth century.[9]

Joseph Jungmann proposed Pope Gregory I (reigned 590–604) as the redactor of the final list of twenty-four saints in the *Communicantes*.[10]

---

promulgatum Ioannis Pauli PP. II cura recognitum, editio typica tertia (Vatican City: Libreria Editrice Vaticana, 2002), section 85, p. 572 (henceforth MR 2002). The liturgical books of the post–Vatican II reform benefit from the presentation of prayers *per cola et commata* thereby clarifying the sense of the text and, in the case of the saints of the *Communicantes* and the *Nobis quoque*, enabling the reader to intuit all the more easily the dynamic underlying the various groupings and subgroupings. For the *Communicantes* in the various important editions of the Roman Missal printed before the reform of 1970, see *Missalis Romani editio princeps Mediolani anno 1474 prelis mandata*, ed. Anthony Ward and Cuthbert Johnson, Bibliotheca Ephemerides Liturgicae Supplementa 3 (Rome: CLV Liturgiche Edizioni, 1996), section 1009, p. 179 (henceforth MR 1474); *Missale Romanum, editio princeps (1570)*, anastatic edition with introduction and appendix by Manlio Sodi and Achille Maria Triacca, Monumenta Liturgica Concilii Tridentini 2 (Vatican City: Libreria Editrice Vaticana, 1998), section 1510, p. 342 (henceforth MR 1570); *Missale Romanum anno 1962 promulgatum*, ed. Cuthbert Johnson and Anthony Ward, Bibliotheca Ephemerides Liturgicae, Supplementa 2 (Rome: CLV Edizioni Liturgicae, 1994), section 1090, p. 302.

7. See *Decretum de S. Ioseph nomine Canoni Missae inserendo*, 13 November 1962, AAS 54 (1962): 873. The insertion of St. Joseph's name in the canon of the Mass took effect on 8 December 1962.

8. Rev 4:4, 10; 5:5, 6, 8, 11, 14; 7:11, 13; 11:16; 14:3; 19:4.

9. For a detailed overview of these, see figure 2: Saints of the Roman Canon.

10. Jungmann, *Missarum sollemnia*, 2:214; *Mass of the Roman Rite*, 2:175.

Cipriano Vagaggini generally supports this claim, concluding that "since the time of Gregory the Great it [the canon] has undergone no further changes of any real importance."[11] Other churches in both east and west employed their own lists of saints in their respective Eucharistic prayers.[12] It therefore comes as no surprise either to liturgical scholars or hagiologists to find variant lists of saints, including any number of local saints, in manuscripts copied beyond Rome. What remains noteworthy, though, is that both lists of saints, fixed at last in late antique or early medieval Rome, reflect a significant hierarchical arrangement and a sacred numerology at work in their particular groups and subgroups: the *Communicantes* with its twenty-four elders comprising twelve apostles and twelve male martyrs who personify the visible hierarchy of the church militant from popes to bishops to lower clergy to laymen; and the *Nobis quoque* with its twice seven martyrs, male and female, the five virgins bringing up the rather eschatological train.

Immediately after the oblique, epicletic petition *Supplices te rogamus*,[13] comes the *Memento etiam* prayer for the dead. Next, the *Nobis quoque peccatoribus* petitions the Lord to grant to us sinners some share in the fellowship (*societas*) of the saints, mentioning by name St.

---

11. Vagaggini, *The Canon of the Mass and Liturgical Reform*, 84.

12. See for example the earliest Roman Mass Book, the Gelasian Sacramentary, which includes the Parisian protomartyrs Dionysius (Denis), Rusticus, and Eleutherius, as well as the Gallic confessors Hilary and Martin; the doctors Augustine, Gregory, and Jerome; and even the father of western monasticism, Benedict. See the facsimile copy of the Gelasian Sacramentary thought to have been copied at Chelles around 750: *Sacramentarium gelasianum e codice Vaticano Reginensi latino 316 vertente anno sacro MCMLXXV iussu Pauli PP. VI phototypice editum*. Codices e Vaticanis Selecti 38 (Vatican City: Bibliotheca Apostolica Vaticana, 1975), fols. 180v–181r; also the edited version: *The Gelasian Scaramentary: Liber sacramentorum Romanae ecclesiae*, ed. H. A. Wilson (Oxford: Clarendon, 1894), 234. Ambrose appears in some but not all of the manuscripts of the Gelasian Sacramentary. He does not figure, for example, in Vatican City: BAV, Vat. Reg. lat. 316, just cited. For other lists of saints in Eucharistic prayers, see the anaphora of St. Basil as given in Vagaggini, *The Canon of the Mass and Liturgical Reform*, 57.

13. "the consecratory part of the epiclesis occurs before the institution (in the *Quam oblationem* at least), although there is no explicit mention of the Holy Spirit, as is fairly often the case in the history of the epiclesis; the request for a fruitful communion comes after it (*Supplices . . . iube . . . ut quotquot*)" (Vagaggini, *The Canon of the Mass and Liturgical Reform*, 92).

John the Baptist, the Precursor of the Lord, and a list of fourteen martyrs: seven males and seven females:

> Nobis quoque peccatoribus famulis tuis,
> de multitudine miserationum tuarum sperantibus,
> partem aliquam et societatem donare digneris
> cum tuis sanctis Apostolis et Martyribus:
> cum Ioanne, Stephano,
> Matthia, Barnaba,
> Ignatio, Alexandro,
> Marcellino, Petro,
> Felicitate, Perpetua,
> Agatha, Lucia,
> Agnete, Caecilia, Anastasia
> et omnibus Sanctis tuis:
> intra quorum nos consortium,
> non aestimator meriti, sed veniae,
> quaesumus, largitor admitte.[14]

Several questions arise at once: What are we to make of these two lists? How are we to understand their significance? It is worth noting that the Roman Canon remains unique among other anaphorae in dividing the saints invoked into two distinct groups: one mentioned before, the other mentioned after the central action of the Eucharistic prayer. Can we discern any logic either in their specific internal arrangement or in their positions as distinct groups in relation to each other and to the principal action of the canon? Reference to Christian art may afford us considerable insight into the significance underlying the arrangement of the saints within the canon of the Mass. Certainly the division of the two main groups of saints corresponds to an iconographic commonplace in both western and eastern Christian art called the *Deësis* or *Deisis*, which is worthwhile exploring in detail.

This essay, as mentioned at the outset, maintains that the arrangement of the lists of saints in the Roman Canon constitutes a *Deësis* in euchological form. In other words, as the canon unfolds, the celebrant mentions the living members of the church (the hierarchy, those present, those for whom the Eucharistic sacrifice is offered, and those who offer it), recalling the communion shared with the Blessed Virgin Mary

---

14. MR 1970, section 98, p. 454; MR 2002, section 96, p. 578; MR 1474, section 1020, p. 180; MR 1570, section 1525, p. 345; MR 1962, section 1110, p. 310.

and the first list of saints, whose memory the church venerates and on whose merits and intercession the earthly church hopes by God's grace to be aided and strengthened. Then Christ, through the consecratory petition and words of institution, takes his place at the very center of the Eucharistic prayer. After the anamnesis and post-institutional epiclesis, the celebrant then prays for the dead, imploring immediately thereafter some share for the communicants in the fellowship (*partem aliquam et societatem*) of the holy apostles and martyrs led by John the Baptist. The final prayer before the doxology petitions Christ, as the Judge of merit, to dispense forgiveness rather than the justice due to sinners and to admit us to fellowship (*consortium*) with these saints.

Just as in Christian iconography the *Deësis* presents the typical grouping of the Blessed Virgin Mary as Mother of God and St. John the Baptist as Forerunner of the Lord, interceding on either side of Christ in majesty, so too the Roman Canon presents Mary and John the Baptist on either side of the Lord who became the central focus via the narrative of institution. The saints who follow Mary and those who follow John the Baptist express two elements or dimensions of the church: the hierarchic and the charismatic. By reviewing in closer detail the saints listed in the *Communicantes* and the *Nobis quoque*, this essay will consider the significance of their specific arrangement and point to several implications of this *Deësis* in euchological form.

THE *DEËSIS* IN CHRISTIAN ART

The Greek word δέησις (*deësis*) means supplication, entreaty, petition, or intercession. The imperial court of Byzantium maintained an official who presented to the emperor petitions on behalf of those making requests or seeking favors. Since the nineteenth century, art historians have applied the term to a particular kind of composition: the Mother of God and St. John the Baptist standing on either side of Christ in majesty. The earliest reference to such an image occurs in *The Miracles of Cyrus and John*, attributed to Sophronius, bishop of Jerusalem (634–639).[15] The figures of Mary and of the Forerunner

---

15. See Ken Parry, "Deesis," *The Blackwell Dictionary of Eastern Christianity*, ed. Ken Parry, David J. Melling, Demetrius Brady, Sidney H. Griffith, and John F. Healey (Oxford, UK, and Malden, MA: Blackwell, 1999), 158–59; also John Rupert Martin, "Deesis," *Dictionary of the Middle Ages*, ed. Joseph R. Strayer (New York: Scribner, 1982–1989), 4:131. The earliest description of an icon of the *Deësis*, attributed to Sophronius, follows: "Au centre, elle représantait en couleurs

333

sometimes present to Christ a scroll inscribed ostensibly with a petition. In this regard, they resemble the petitioner of the imperial court. Otherwise, the Blessed Virgin and the Forerunner of the Lord usually approach Christ with hands extended in supplication. A *Deësis* occasionally will depict two other saints in the act of petitioning the Lord, but the usual format presents the Virgin Mary and St. John the Baptist entreating Christ in majesty.

The figural arrangement of the *Deësis* is closely related theologically and artistically to themes of the Last Judgment. The motif of Christ in glory flanked by the Mother of God on his right and the Precursor on his left appears in monumental art and also in private, votive art, as, for example, on sepulchers, in triptychs made for devotional use, and in manuscript prayer books. Examples of the *Deësis* in extant monumental art include the early-eleventh-century relief in the south aisle of St. Mark's Cathedral, Venice; the mid-eleventh-century mosaic of the *Last Judgment* in the Cathedral of Torcello; the twelfth-century mosaic in the north gallery of Hagia Sophia, Iznik, Turkey; the tympanum and archivolts of the central portal, south transept of Chartres Cathedral executed ca. 1215–1220; Pietro Cavallini's fresco of the *Last Judgment* (c. 1293) on the interior of the west wall of the church of St. Cecilia in Trastevere, but since the eighteenth century in severe disrepair; the upper panels of Jan van Eyck's interior of the altarpiece completed in 1432 and erected in the Cathedral of St. Bavo, Ghent, Belgium. In the thirteenth-century apsidal mosaic of the *Deësis* in the cathedral of Pisa, John the Evangelist replaces the Baptist.

Modern western treatments of the typical *Deësis* arrangement with Mary and John the Baptist interceding on either side of Christ in majesty include the fresco of the *Dispute of the Blessed Sacrament* (1509) by Raffaello Sanzio da Urbino (Raphael) in the Sala della Segnatura of the Apostolic Palace, Vatican City, and the undated *Paradise* by Carlo Saraceni (1579–1620) now in the Metropolitan Museum of Art, New York.

---

le Seigneur Christ. À la gauche du Christ, il y avait Notre Dame Marie Mère de Dieu, toujours Vierge, et, à sa droite, Jean, Baptiste et Précurseur du Sauveur lui-même, lui qui dans la matrice l'a annoncé par ses tressaillements (en effet, même s'il avait parlé, comme il y était enfermé, on ne l'aurait pas entendu). Il y avait aussi une parti du chœur glorieux des apôtres, des prophètes et la troupe des martyrs" (Miracle no. 36, Sophronius of Jerusalem, *Miracles des saints Cyr et Jean* [BHG I:477-479], trans. with notes by Jean Gascou [Paris: De Boccard, 2006], 26, p. 134). It is unclear when the first images of the *Deësis* first appeared.

Even Michelangelo's *Last Judgment* (1536–1541), which dominates the renowned Sistine Chapel of the Vatican, presents a kind of *Deësis*, although in this case the Virgin and the Baptist do not flank Christ but come first in a spiraling movement that emanates from Christ the *Sol iustitiae*.[16] A western example of a *Deësis* in devotional, votive art appears in Jacques Legrand's Gothic *Livre des Bonnes Meurs*, completed around 1435 in Brittany, possibly by the Master of Marguerite d'Orléans.[17]

THE *DEËSIS* IN CHRISTIAN DOCTRINE

Sergei Bulgakov (1871–1944), perhaps the most profound Orthodox systematic theologian of the twentieth century,[18] explains the importance of the theological underpinnings of the *Deësis*:

> We do not know when or where the icon of the *Deisis* appeared, but the fact is that it was very widespread in the Church. It clearly has an enormous dogmatic significance for what can be called a unified Mariology and Johannology. "Deisis" means prayer. On the icon the Savior is represented in royal or high-priestly garments, in His power and glory, sitting on a throne and with the Mother of God and the Forerunner standing before Him with hands raised in prayer. What are they praying for? Not for the forgiveness of their sins, for they do not have any. Nor, in general, for themselves. Those who are in a glorified state have nothing to ask for, for they have everything. It only remains for them to praise and to give thanks, like the angels. Therefore, they pray not for themselves but for the world and for the human race. In standing before the throne of God and showing great audacity in their prayer, they are first in the Church, the greatest representatives of the human race. . . .
>
> But the *Deisis* implies something even more significant. Here it is a question not of a prayer among the prayers of other saints and with them, but of a certain primacy of presence, a leading of the entire

16. The title comes from Mal 4:2. Michelangelo's *Last Judgment* presents a heliocentric movement of all creation, in the sense that all revolves around Christ the Word, the Alpha and the Omega.

17. Princeton University Library, Garrett 130, folio 25r. It is not entirely clear that the female figure on Christ's right (viewer's left) is the Blessed Virgin Mary since she is unveiled and clothed in a reddish mantle. The figure may be Mary Magdalene.

18. See Boris Jakim, "Translator's Introduction," Sergei (Sergius) Bulgakov, *The Friend of the Bridegroom: On the Orthodox Veneration of the Forerunner* (Grand Rapids, MI, and Cambridge, UK: Eerdmans, 2003), viii.

Church in prayer. And this concerns the presence not only of the Mother of God and not only of the Forerunner but of the two *together*. This is not only a presence together in prayer but a union in Christ and through Christ in the fullness of the whole prayer of the Church. It is a kind of high-priesthood in the Church, a presence before Christ's throne in prayer, a liturgy celebrated in the name of the whole Church.[19]

The usual position of the icon or triptych panels of the *Deësis* in eastern liturgy is in the third row of the iconostasis, above the icon of the *Last Supper*. According to Bulgakov and his sources, the name *Deësis* may have been applied to this sacred representation of Christ flanked by his Mother and his Forerunner because "below this icon, the prayer ended with the Greek word *Deisis* (prayer), and those who did not know Greek took this to be the name of the icon."[20] In any case, it remains a convenient term for this figural grouping and will continue to be used throughout this essay, despite its late usage.

THE SAINTS OF THE *COMMUNICANTES*

The hierarchical arrangement of the saints of the *Communicantes* is well-known, thanks to Joseph Andreas Jungmann[21] and Vincent Lorne Kennedy.[22] The ever-virgin Mother of God leads the twelve apostles and twelve martyrs. The inclusion of St. Joseph immediately after the Blessed Virgin constitutes an embolism of Marian devotion; it reflects likewise an increase in devotion to the spouse of the Mother of God particularly since the nineteenth century.[23] The twelve apostles occur

19. Bulgakov, *The Friend of the Bridegroom*, 143.

20. Ibid., 143, n. 4. Bulgakov is sketchy in his citation of the source of this proposal. Without reference to the author and title of the article or even to the editors and bibliographical particulars of the work cited, he attributes this notion to *The Orthodox Theological Encyclopedia*, vol. 4, 975–76.

21. Jungmann, *Missarum sollemnia; The Mass of the Roman Rite*, 2:172–73.

22. Vincent Lorne Kennedy, *The Saints of the Canon of the Mass*, 2nd rev. ed., Studi di Antichità Cristiana 14 (Vatican City: Pontificio Istituto di Archeologia Cristiana, 1963), passim.

23. In 1870, Pope Pius IX declared St. Joseph the patron saint of the universal church. See Sacred Congregation for Rites, Decree *Quemadmodum*, 8 December 1870, *Acta Sanctae Sedis* (ASS) 6 (1871): 193–94; Pius IX, Brief (*litterae apostolicae*) *Inclytum*, 7 July 1871, ASS 6 (1871): 324–27; Consistorial Decree *Novum caeleste praesidium*, 6 May 1872, ASS 6 (1871): 591–92. The papal adoption of the cultus of St. Joseph reached its zenith when John XXIII inserted the name of St.

in the following order: first, the princes of the apostles, Peter and Paul, followed by Peter's brother Andrew the Protoclete (*Protoklétos*) or "first-called." Then come the sons of Zebedee: James the Greater and John the Evangelist, who, with Peter, constituted the "pillars" of the early church (Gal 2:9). After these major apostles, there follow, in the order of their feasts on the liturgical calendar, the minor apostles: Thomas (21 December until 1969), James and Philip (1 [until the institution in 1956 of the feast of St. Joseph the Worker], 10 [1956–1969], 3 May [since 1970]), Bartholomew (24 August), Matthew (21 September), Simon and Jude (28 October). Then follow the successors of St. Peter in the see of Rome: Linus, Cletus, Clement, Sixtus, Cornelius. The order is chronological except for Cornelius (✝ 253), who has been placed after his successor Sixtus (✝ 258) in order to be juxtaposed with his North African correspondent and counterpart Cyprian, bishop of Carthage. Of the remaining six martyrs, the two clerics Lawrence and Chrysogonus precede the laymen John and Paul, and Cosmas and Damian.

The *Communicantes* follows the *Memento* of the living, which mentions by name ecclesial and civil authorities (popes, bishops, emperors, kings) and then, more generally, all those gathered about the altar ready to offer the Eucharistic sacrifice. The saints of the *Communicantes*, headed by Mary, model and mother of the church, express the church's hierarchical nature. The twelve apostles precede five successors of Peter in the see of Rome (Linus, Cletus, Clement, Sixtus, Cornelius) and one bishop or successor of the apostles (Cyprian of Carthage). The Roman deacon Lawrence and the cleric Chrysogonus precede two sets of laymen: John and Paul ostensibly from Rome, and Cosmas and Damian from the east. Most of the saints mentioned in the *Communicantes*, as with those of the *Nobis quoque*, have some association with a church, a catacomb, or a shrine in Rome.[24] Cyprian (✝ 258), although without a church in Rome dedicated in his honor, nevertheless suffered martyrdom a few years after Cornelius (✝ 253); Rome commemorated him liturgically as early as the fourth century.[25]

Joseph into the Roman Canon. For an Orthodox view of the western eclipse of the cultus of St. John the Baptist by that of St Joseph, see Sergei Bulgakov, "St John the Forerunner and St Joseph the Betrothed," excursus 3, *The Friend of the Bridegroom*, 177–88.

24. See Kennedy, *The Saints of the Canon of the Mass*, passim.

25. See Jungmann, *Missarum sollemnia*, 2:212–13; *Mass of the Roman Rite*, 2:174.

The *Nobis quoque*, with its list of saints, follows at once upon the *Memento* of the dead. After interceding for those members of the church "who have gone before us marked with the sign of faith," the prayer beseeches God to afford members of the worshiping congregation some share in the communion of the saints in glory, in other words, to grant them admission to the blessed society of John the Baptist, Stephen, Matthias, Barnabas, Ignatius, Alexander, Marcellinus, Peter, Felicity, Perpetua, Agatha, Lucy, Agnes, Cecilia, Anastasia, and all the saints. Coming as they do after the epiclesis over the faithful and immediately after the *Memento* of the dead, these figures suggest the pneumatological and eschatological dimensions of the Eucharist. The number seven is associated throughout Scripture with the Holy Spirit.[26] The figures themselves generally have some association with the Holy Spirit.

John the Baptist stands as the last and greatest of the prophets of the Old Testament and the Forerunner of the Lord. The prophets received a pneumatological unction or anointing with the Holy Spirit that enabled them to bear witness to the coming Messiah. At the Baptism of the Lord in the Jordan, Jesus brings to a close John's baptism of repentance. The Theophany on the bank of the Jordan, recorded by each of the four evangelists,[27] manifests to Israel the triune God. It also reveals God the Father anointing Jesus as the Christ ("the Anointed One") with the Holy Spirit. This Spirit of prophecy comes upon Jesus, driving him into the desert where he overcomes the temptations of the evil spirit and undertakes his messianic role "in the power of the Spirit."[28]

Bulgakov affords further insight into the role of John the Baptist in the *Deësis* or intercession before the divine majesty:

> The Forerunner's participation in this prayer, attesting to his elevated place and his nearness to God's throne, merges with the work of mercy of the Mother of God. Together with Her, he is the Church in which lives the Holy Spirit, interceding before the Father and the judging Word with ineffable sighs. And although the judgment is the Son's, its

26. From Genesis, where the Spirit of God breathed over the waters on the first of the seven days of creation, to the Apocalypse of John, where the number seven (churches, candelabra, seals, etc.) continues to figure throughout the account of the seer. The seven gifts of the Holy Spirit (wisdom, understanding, counsel, fortitude, knowledge, piety, and the fear of the Lord) figure in Isa 11:2-3.

27. See Matt 3:13-17; Mark 1:9-11; Luke 3:21-22; John 1:31-34; Acts 10:38.

28. Luke 4:14; see also 4:1, 18-21.

final accomplishment is the work of the entire Holy Trinity, including the Holy Spirit, who, after the dread sundering, restores the world and heals its wounds.

Why does the Forerunner occupy this position of intercession alongside the Mother of God? For even the angels gaze with fear and trembling upon what takes place here and are only obedient agents; whereas, by his prayer of intercession the Forerunner opposes the condemnation, as it were; he desires to soften the decree of the righteous judge and to replace it with mercy. The Forerunner occupies this position because he is not only an angel but also a human being. And it is as a *human being* that he, like the Mother of God, intercedes for forgiveness.[29]

Directly after the Baptist comes the first of fourteen martyrs, Stephen, who in Acts 7:60 entreated the Lord Jesus to have mercy upon his persecutors. The Acts of the Apostles describes the protomartyr Stephen as "filled with the Holy Spirit."[30] Acts 1:15-26 recounts how the Holy Spirit chooses Matthias to replace Judas Iscariot after the demise of the latter. In Acts 13:1-4, the Holy Spirit directs that Barnabas and Saul be set apart for the evangelization of the Gentiles; consequently, the prophets and teachers lay hands upon the two missionary companions thereby sending them out as apostles with the power of the Holy Spirit. Ignatius is reckoned by tradition to have succeeded Peter in the see of Antioch, where, according to Acts 11:26, the disciples of Jesus first became known by the name "Christians." In the absence of any cultus of Ignatius in Rome until the late Middle Ages, Kennedy suggests that it is owing to his correspondence with the church of Rome that Ignatius was accorded the privilege of a place among the saints listed in the Roman Canon.[31] Of all the saints in the *Nobis quoque*, the most challenging to identify with certainty is Alexander. Whether he is the martyr of the Via Nomentana, later identified with Pope Alexander I and venerated on 3 May, or perhaps another Alexander drawn from several other groups of martyrs, remains a

---

29. Bulgakov, *The Friend of the Bridegroom*, 144–45.

30. Acts 6:5; 7:55 (RSV); Stephen is described also as "full of grace and power" (Acts 6:8). After his prophetic speech bearing witness to the divinity of Jesus Christ (Acts 7:1-53), Stephen suffers martyrdom by stoning (Acts 7:59-60).

31. See Kennedy, *The Saints of the Canon of the Mass*, 157.

matter of conjecture.[32] Kennedy rejects the notion that this Alexander is Pope Alexander I on the grounds that, as a pope or bishop of Rome, he would have preceded Ignatius of Antioch, since the order of the saints is "strictly hierarchical";[33] and, furthermore, no evidence confirms that Alexander I died as a martyr. A counterargument might suggest that Ignatius in fact succeeded Peter in the see of Antioch, whereas Alexander I was one of Peter's successors in the see of Rome. Nevertheless, it remains unclear exactly which Alexander is intended in the *Nobis quoque*. It is sufficient, however, that Alexander enjoyed some cultus in the local church of Rome. The priest Marcellinus and the exorcist Peter are linked to the eponymous house of the church (*domus ecclesiae*) on the Via Labicana.[34] Peter's role as an exorcist may well have earned him admission to this list of saints of distinctly pneumatic significance.

As for the list of seven female martyrs, the Roman matron Felicity, once identified with the mother of the Seven Brothers martyred under Marcus Aurelius and commemorated on 10 July,[35] and her North African counterpart Perpetua precede the five virgin martyrs: Agatha from Catania and Lucy from Sicily, then the Romans Agnes, Cecilia, and Anastasia. These parallel the five wise virgins of the eschatological parable in Matthew 25:1-14, who go out with lighted lamps to meet their Lord. Given the hierarchical structure of the lists of saints in the Roman Canon, it may strike the reader as unusual that the virgins of the *Nobis quoque* should follow, rather than precede, the matrons. Perhaps the arrangement presents one of the paradoxes presented by Christ in the gospel that the last shall be first and the first, last.[36] It may well serve as a strategic allusion to the Lamb of God, soon to be fractured after the Eucharistic prayer. After all, it is the vocation of the virgins to follow the Lamb wherever he goes.[37] At any rate, the list of saints in the *Nobis quoque* is led by the virgin John and concluded by the five wise virgins Agatha, Lucy, Agnes, Cecilia, and Anastasia.

---

32. See ibid., 158–65.

33. Ibid., 163.

34. Ibid., 165–68.

35. See ibid., 170–75.

36. See Matt 19:30; 20:16; Mark 9:34; 10:31, 44; Luke 13:30.

37. See Rev 14:4-5. "Hi sunt qui cum mulieribus non sunt coinquinati, virgines enim sunt: hi sequuntur Agnum quocumque ierit. Hi empti sunt ex hominibus, primitiae Deo et Agno, et in ore eorum non est inventum mendacium; sine macula enim sunt ante thronum Dei."

Like the Roman Canon, eastern anaphorae too mention the Mother of God and St. John the Baptist, but invariably after the narrative of institution and the epiclesis.[38] In this regard, Eucharistic Prayers II, III, and IV, included since 1970 in the Roman Missal, also contain references to the communion of saints, although only the Blessed Virgin Mary is consistently mentioned by name in each of them. Eucharistic Prayer III, composed as we have seen by Vagaggini, furnishes an opportunity to insert the saint of the day or a patron saint; it likewise makes explicit reference to the constant intercession of Mary and the saints on which the church on earth continues to rely for help.[39] Eucharistic Prayer II, based ostensibly upon the anaphora proposed as a sample prayer in *The Apostolic Tradition*, avoids any mention of the intercession of Mary and the saints; it refers instead to the communion of saints and their praise of God in the life eternal.[40] Eucharistic Prayer IV, based on eastern models, includes a mention of Mary, the apostles, and the saints immediately after the prayer for the dead, but this prayer omits any reference to their intercessory power.[41]

38. See for example the Greek Alexandrine anaphora of St. Basil given in Vagaggini, *The Canon of the Mass and Liturgical Reform*, 57: "Especially be mindful of our most holy, most glorious, immaculate, most blessed Lady, Mother of God and ever-virgin Mary; of your holy and glorious prophet John the Baptist, precursor and martyr: of our most holy father St Mark, apostle and evangelist, of our holy father Basil, the wonderworker: of Saint N. whose memory we celebrate today, and of all your choir of saints. By their prayers and intercession have mercy on us and save us for the sake of your holy name which is invoked upon us."

39. "Ipse nos tibi perficiat munus aeternum, ut cum electis tuis haereditatem consequi valeamus, in primis cum beatissima Virgine, Dei Genetrice, Maria, cum beatis Apostolis tuis et gloriosis Martyribus (cum Sancto N., Sancto diei vel patrono) et omnibus Sanctis quorum intercessione perpetuo apud te confidimus adiuvari" (Eucharistic Prayer III, MR 2002, section 113, p. 588).

40. "Omnium nostrum, quaesumus, miserere, ut cum beata Dei Genetrice Virgine Maria, beatis Apostolis et omnibus Sanctis, qui tibi a saeculo placuerunt, aeternae vitae mereamur esse consortes, et te laudemus et glorificemus per Filium tuum Iesum Christum" (Eucharistic Prayer II, MR 2002, section 105, p. 583).

41. "Nobis omnibus, filiis tuis, clemens Pater, concede, ut caelestem hereditatem consequi valeamus cum beata Virgine, Dei Genetrice, Maria, cum Apostolis et Sanctis tuis in regno tuo, ubi cum universa creatura, a corruptione peccati

The Mass of the Roman Rite involves a split epiclesis, the Holy Spirit being invoked first upon the offerings that will be converted into the Eucharistic Body and Blood of the Lord, then upon the congregation for a fruitful reception of Communion. Split likewise on either side of the liturgical action within the canon are, beforehand, intercessions for the living and the invocation of the saints led by the Mother of God, and, afterward, the prayer for the dead and the invocation of the second list of saints led by St. John the Baptist. The slight asymmetry of the numbers (the Virgin Mary + St. Joseph + twenty-four elders in the *Communicantes*; St. John the Baptist + seven male martyrs + seven female martyrs in the *Nobis quoque*) reflects the dynamics of each group: the first being the more hierarchical, institutional, and magisterial, the other being the more pneumatic, prophetic, and eschatological. The apostles and elders of the *Communicantes* may sit as judges over the new Israel (the church militant); the Baptist and his charismatic cohort implore the mercy of God upon those now beyond the realm of earthly choices.

As is clear from figure 1, there remains, despite the difference in the number of saints in each list, a distinct symmetry in the Roman Canon. Pius Parsch described it in 1936 as "a series of concentric circles."[42] It may strike the reader as odd, then, to find Vagaggini so emphatic in his criticism of the arrangement of intercessions in the canon as one of its ten "defects":

> In the anaphoras of other traditions the prayers of intercession are grouped together. They may be before the beginning of the canon, when the gifts are placed on the altar—as happens in the Gallican liturgies—or, as at Alexandria, within the canon before the Sanctus. Or again, they may be placed within the canon, but after the prayer for a fruitful communion (Antioch tradition) or after the anamnesis (Edessa). The Roman Church prays for the Church in general and for the hierarchy before the institution (*in primis quae tibi offerimus*); for those present offering the Mass (the first *Memento* and normally the *Hanc igitur* too, though this was once a prayer inserted only for special intentions. (It remains so today in certain circumstances, as at Easter and Pentecost.) After the institution there are further prayers for the

---

et mortis liberate, te glorificemus per Christum Dominum nostrum, per quem mundo bona cuncta largiris" (Eucharistic Prayer IV, section 122, p. 596).

42. Pius Parsch, *The Liturgy of the Mass*, trans. Frederic C. Eckhoff (St. Louis, MO, and London, UK: Herder, 1936, 1942), 194–95; see the diagram titled "The Concentric Structure" on p. 196.

dead (the second *Memento*) and for the ministers (*Nobis quoque*). Such a distribution is hardly a model of simplicity and clarity. It is as though the worst possible solution had been chosen: as if the choice had been made deliberately to split up the connection of ideas and so ruin the unity of this great prayer.[43]

This is a harsh judgment, particularly in view of the fact that it fails to take into account the beauty of a symmetry laden with theological significance. Splaying the saints on either side of the institutional narrative actually heightens the order inherent in the Roman Canon, and draws attention to the incarnational dimension of Christ's presence in the Eucharist. As Bulgakov points out:

> The *Deisis*, showing the presence of the Forerunner and of the Mother of God before Christ, fully reveals the mystery of the Incarnation. It is the icon of the Incarnation, for the latter was accomplished through the Mother of God, who gave Christ Her flesh, which became for Him a living temple, as well as through the Forerunner, who baptized Christ, thus accomplishing His anointment through the descent of the Holy Spirit on His human nature (cf. 1 Tim 3:16). Both the Most Pure Mother of God and the Forerunner manifest in themselves the fullness of the Theophany, not only of Church but of the entire Holy Trinity, for the Father's love reposes upon the Son in the Holy Spirit.[44]

How apposite, then, that as the Roman Canon unfolds, the Mother of God emerges with her train of saints representative of the church as the mystical Body of Christ arrayed in hierarchic order. It is fitting that she who preceded Christ in time as the morning star (Sir 50:6) or as the dawn heralding the Sun of Justice (Mal 4:2) should precede him in that prayer whereby he is made present again upon earth, albeit now under the sacramental veils of bread and wine.

After the narrative of institution and anamnesis, bookended by the split epicleses, comes John the Baptist with his train of saints distinguished by their rapport with the Holy Spirit. It is worth recalling here that when the Holy Spirit first came upon the Virgin Mary by a pneumatic overshadowing in Luke 1:35, she became the Mother of the incarnate Son of God. Likewise when the Spirit came upon Mary a second time, at Pentecost, she became the mother of the mystical body

43. Vagaggini, *The Canon of the Mass and Liturgical Reform*, 95–96.
44. Bulgakov, *The Friend of the Bridegroom*, 141.

of Christ.[45] Next, the Spirit comes upon the offerings as the celebrant pronounces the words of institution. The Spirit, called down from the Father in the *Quam oblationem*, makes fruitful the narrative of institution as uttered by the priestly (episcopal or presbyteral) celebrant. After the anamnesis or memorial, the Spirit is invoked upon the congregation. Then John the Baptist, the friend of the Bridegroom and witness to his messianic anointing with the Holy Spirit on the banks of the Jordan, emerges as if to escort, with his train of martyrs and virgins, the Lamb to the consummation of his wedding feast at Holy Communion. The Roman Canon, then, introduces in marvelous order the Bride, the Bridegroom, and the Friend of the Bridegroom who will welcome all those invited to the Mystical Supper, the Lamb's high feast.

IMPLICATIONS FOR FURTHER CONSIDERATION

It is a pity, given the considerable freedom accorded artists in the western church, that the *Deësis* as presented euchologically in the Roman Canon has not inspired them to depict this particular throng around the Lamb upon his altar-throne. The fact that for centuries the Roman Canon was uttered in silence may account for this. Nevertheless, one might have expected a priest, a bishop, or a pope at some point in history to have commissioned an artist to portray in a fresco, a mosaic, or a mural the saints of the canon of the Mass. After all, such a subject would surely have made a worthy point of reference for the devotion if not of the faithful then at least of the clergy of the Roman Rite, who would have pronounced these names each day over the course of the earthly exercise of their priestly office. Now that the practice of reciting the Eucharistic prayer audibly has become widespread, it may be hoped that at least where the Roman Canon is used with some frequency, and where all the saints are included in the lists of both the *Communicantes* and *Nobis quoque*, perhaps some artist may find the inspiration to produce, or a donor the desire to commission a depiction of the saints of this exquisite anaphora for display either in a church or at least in a missal. Even a holy card would make a good beginning. At any rate, a revival of interest in the Roman Canon as a prayer may lead to such a venture.[46]

---

45. See Acts 1:14; 2:1-4. It was precisely to underscore Mary's motherhood of the church that Pope John Paul II opened the Marian Year of 1987–1988 on Pentecost Day 1987 and closed it on Assumption Day, 15 August 1988.

46. For a recent appreciation of this beautiful prayer, with its complete lists of saints, see Lawrence S. Cunningham, "The Roman Canon and Catholicity: A

Against modern criticisms that the lists of saints in the Roman Canon are too long, involve too many historical difficulties concerning the lives of some of the saints mentioned, and offer only limited representations of Christian holiness,[47] it may be argued that such an arrangement, once endorsed if not actually compiled by a liturgical thinker of the eminence of Gregory the Great, deserves to be preserved in its integrity if only for the sake of some future generation that yet may come to appreciate the subtle truths and layers of beauty contained therein. Some room should be left for mysterious allusions that escape the comprehension of latter-day rationalists all too eager to discard that which may not be fully clear at once. Above all, the principle ought to be kept in mind that, over the course of history, distinct liturgical rites are formative of distinct liturgical groups. Each generation that claims to belong to a given tradition has a responsibility to receive that tradition, be formed by it, and to transmit it faithfully to the next generation. It takes a remarkable degree of confidence to decide that, after some fifteen hundred years of daily use, a long-cherished prayer has come due for major alterations, or is simply obsolete.

Worship (*cultus*) finds broad expression in culture (*cultura*). Joseph Ratzinger, in his capacity as a theologian who seeks to mine the significance underlying the great *depositum fidei* committed to the church in trust, has underscored time and again the correspondence between the church's faith and the expression of that faith in liturgy and art. He explains in *The Spirit of the Liturgy*, for example, how over the centuries the church has expressed in various styles and manners her belief in the paschal mystery through art and architecture. "Art," he maintains, "is always characterized by the unity of creation, Christology, and eschatology."[48] This threefold unity is abundantly evident in the *Deësis* present in the euchology of the Roman canon. "Art," Ratzinger continues, "is still ordered to the mystery that becomes present in the liturgy, it is still oriented to the heavenly liturgy." This is sufficient reason for teachers of the liturgy and participants in the sacred rites to esteem and cherish this liturgical *Deësis*. They do well, moreover, to encourage

---

Meditation," *Church* (Spring 2006), 5–10. Cunningham deplores the omission of the majority of saints on the relatively rare occasions that the Roman Canon is recited at all.

47. See Vagaggini, *The Canon of the Mass and Liturgical Reform*, 106.

48. Joseph Ratzinger, *The Spirit of the Liturgy*, trans. John Saward (San Francisco: Ignatius, 2000), 125.

also its artistic representation in various media so as to elucidate and confirm the meaning underlying its liturgical expression.

Ratzinger himself actually points out the importance of returning to an embrace of the incarnational dimension of the Christian faith by expressing the truths we profess and the liturgical mysteries we celebrate in a meaningful iconography:

> The Church in the West does not need to disown the specific path she has followed since about the thirteenth century. But she must achieve a real reception of the Seventh Ecumenical Council, Nicaea II (AD 787), which [against the heresy of the Iconoclasts] affirmed the fundamental importance and theological status of the image in the Church.

The saints of the Roman Canon, headed by the Blessed Virgin Mary and by St. John the Baptist, exemplify the church in glory interceding for the church on earth and for the whole world. They remind us that, according to the Constitution on the Sacred Liturgy,

> In the liturgy on earth, we are sharing by anticipation in the heavenly one, celebrated in the holy city, Jerusalem, the goal towards which we strive as pilgrims, where Christ is, seated at God's right hand, he who is the minister of the saints and of the true tabernacle. We are singing the hymn of God's glory with all the troops of the heavenly army. In lovingly remembering the saints in our liturgy, we are hoping in some way to share in what they now enjoy, and to become their companions. We are waiting for our savior, our lord Jesus Christ, until he, our life, appears, and we appear with him in glory.[49]

As the Roman Canon is prayed it is comforting to be surrounded by that great "cloud of witnesses" (Heb 21:1) who intercede on our behalf and who long to welcome us into the fullness of that kingdom prepared from the foundation of the world.[50]

---

49. Second Vatican Council, Constitution on the Sacred Liturgy (*Sacrosanctum Concilium*), 8 in *Decrees of the Ecumenical Councils*, ed. Norman P. Tanner (London and Washington, DC, 1990); vol. 2: Trent–Vatican II, *Sacrosanctum concilium*, 823.

50. See Matt 25:34.

Figure 1: Prayers of the Roman Canon

1	Intercessions for the Living 2	Invocation of the Saints 3	4	Epiclesis (I) 5	Institution Narrative and Consecration 6	Anamnesis 7	Offering 8	Epiclesis (II) 9	Intercessions for the Dead 10	Invocation of the Saints 11	12
Te Igitur	In primis quae tibi offerimus	Communicantes et memoriam venerantes	Hanc igitur	Quam oblationem	Qui pridie	Unde et memores	Supra quae	Supplices te rogamus	Memento etiam Domine	Nobis quoque	Per quem
We come to you Father	We offer them for your holy Catholic Church	In union with the whole Church we honour Mary the ever Mother of Jesus Christ our Lord and God	Lord accept this offering from your whole family	Bless and approve our offering	On the night He was betrayed	Father calling to mind	Look with favour upon these offerings	Almighty God, we pray that your angel may take this sacrifice	Remember, Lord, those who have gone before us marked with the sign of faith	For ourselves, too, we ask some share in the fellowship of your apostles and martyrs	Through Him you give us all these gifts

Figure 2: Saints of the Roman Canon

#	Saint	Title	Dates	Location	Relics	Feast MR62	Feast MR70	Historic Feast	Other	EHL	BHL Sp 86	Source
Saints of the Communicantes												
Apostles - major												
	BVM	gloriosa semper-Virgo, Genetrix Dei et Domini nostri Iesu Christi eiusdem Virginis Sponsus				1-Jan			15-Aug	5334-4'4	5333m-412d	Mt 1-2; Lk 1-2; Jn 2, 19
	Joseph		Saec. I	Palestine		19-Mar				s.n.	4452m	Mt 1-2; Lk 2
1	Peter	Princeps ap. / Vicarius Christi	64	Rome	Rome	29-Jun		22-Feb	1-Aug	6644-8E	6644-87m	Jn 1:40-42; 21:15-19; Mt 16:18
2	Paul	Doctor gentium	68	Rome	Rome	29/30 June		25-Jan		6569-83	6568s-82s	Acts 7:58; 8:1; 9:1-30
3	Andrew	Protocletos	saec. I	Patros/Achaia	Greece	30-Nov				428-42	4271-42c	Mt 4:18-20; Jn 1:35-42
4	James	apostle	saec. I	Jerusalem?	Compostella	25-Jul				4056-85	4056-83g	Mt 4:20-22; 20:20-23
5	John	apostle & evangelist	100-110	Ephesus	Ephesus	27-Dec				4316-28	4316-28f	Jn 13:23-25; 21:19-24
Apostles - minor												
6	Thomas	apostle (Didymus)	saec. I	Persia / India	Ortona (1258)	21-Dec	3-Jul			8136-49	8136-49d	Jn 14:5-7; 20:24-29
7	James	apostle	60-62	Jerusalem	Rome	1-May	3-May	25-Mar	11-May	4086-99	4086-99b	
8	Philip	apostle	c. 80	Hierapolis	Rome	1-May	3-May			6813-18	6813-18b	Jn 1:43-48; 14:8-14
9	Bartholomew	apostle (Nathaniel)	saec. I	Armenia/India	Benevento/Rome	24-Aug				1001-14	1001-14e	Jn 1:45-51
10	Matthew	apostle & evangelist	saec. I	Ethiopia	Salerno	21-Sep				5689-94	5690-94e	Mt 9:9-13; Mk 2:14-17; Lk 5:27-32
11	Simon	apostle (Zealot)	107	Persia	Persia	28-Oct				7749-54	7749-53d	
12	Jude Thaddeus	apostle	saec. I	Palestine	Rome	28-Oct				7749-54	7749-53d	
Popes and Bishops												
13	Linus	pope	Nero: 79	Rome	Rome	23-Sep				s.n. post 4935	s.n. post 4935	*Liber pontificalis* 1.121
14	Cletus	pope	saec. I	Rome	Rome	26-Apr				s.n. post 1868	s.n. post 1863	*Liber pontificalis* 1.222
15	Clement	pope	saec. I/101	Rome/Orient	Rome	23-Nov				1848-57	1847m-57e	
16	Sixtus (II)	pope	258	Rome	Rome	6-Aug	7-Aug			7800-12	7801-12e	
17	Cornelius	pope	253	Rome	Rome	16-Sep				1958-66	1958-66	
18	Cyprian	bishop	258	Carthage	Carthage	16-Sep				2037-46	2037-46d	
Ministers and Laity												
19	Lawrence	deacon	258	Rome	Rome	10-Aug				4752-89	4752-87f	
20	Chrysogonus	teacher, cleric?	303	Aquileia	Rome	24-Nov				1795-97	1795-96	
21	John	lay	361-3	Rome?	Rome	26-Jun				3236-44	3236-44	listed with Gallicanus
22	Paul	lay	361-3	Rome?	Rome	26-Jun				3236-44	3236-44	listed with Gallicanus
23	Cosmas	lay	303	Aegea, Cilicia	Constantinople	27-Sep	26-Sep			1967-79	1967-79	
24	Damian	lay	303	Aegea, Cilicia	Constantinople	27-Sep	26-Sep			1967-79	1967-79	
Saints of the Nobis quoque												
Male Martyrs												
1	John Baptist	praecursor Domini	saec. I	Palestine	Rome [S. Sylvester]	29 Aug		3-Aug		4290-4315	4289m-315e	Lk 1:5-24; Mk 6:17-29
2	Stephen	protomartyr	saec. I	Jerusalem	Rome	26-Dec				7848-95	7848c-91	Acts 6:8-10; 7:54-59
3	Matthias	apostle	saec. I	-	Rome?	24-Feb	14-May			5695-5719	5695-719m	Acts 1:15-26
4	Barnabas	apostle	saec. I	Cyprus	Cyprus	11-Jun				983-90	984-88b	Acts 11:21-26; 13:1-3
	Ignatius	bishop	Trajan 107	Antioch/Rome	Antioch	1-Feb	17-Oct			4255-63	4255-261d	
5	Alexander	presbyter? pope?	?	Rome	Rome	27/28-Feb	3-May					
6	Marcellinus	presbyter	299	Rome	Rome	2-Jun				5230-33	5230-31	
7	Peter	exorcist	299	Rome	Rome	2-Jun				5230-33	5230-31	
Matron Martyrs												
8	Felicity	Roman matron	150	Rome	Rome	23-Nov		10-Jul		2853-55	2853-55d	
9	Perpetua	N. African matron	203	Carthage	Carthage	6-Mar	7-Mar			6633-36	6633-35	
Virgin Martyrs												
10	Agatha	virgin	251	Catania	Catania	5-Feb				133-40	133-40	
11	Lucy	virgin	304	Syracuse	Venice	13-Dec				4992-5007	4992-5000	
12	Agnes	virgin	313?	Rome	Rome	21-Jan		28-Jan (II)		156-67	156-67c	
13	Cecilia	virgin	230?	Rome	Rome	22-Nov				1495-1500	1495-99c	
14	Anastasia	virgin	303	Palmaria	Rome	25-Dec				400-03	400-01f	

Nathaniel Marx

XIV. The Revision of the Prefaces in the Missal of Paul VI

A TREASURY OF PREFACES

In a series of recent essays, Lauren Pristas critically evaluates the revision of the orations of the Roman Missal that took place as part of the reform of the Roman liturgy prompted by the Second Vatican Council.[1] Noting that "the revisers did a huge amount of work in a relatively short span of time and, as one of them put it, 'material failures' cannot be lacking," Pristas calls upon liturgical scholars to assume the "duty of carefully reviewing and evaluating specific revision decisions made by those charged with carrying out that reform."[2] Following her own analysis of the orations as revised in the postconciliar Missal of Paul VI, Pristas raises a troubling possibility: "It may be the case that nearly all the texts of our missal reflect the strengths and weaknesses, the insights and biases, the achievements and limitations of but one age, our own."[3] Consequently, while "we owe those who labored to produce the new texts a debt of gratitude," it is nonetheless

---

1. See Lauren Pristas, "The Orations of the Vatican II Missal: Policies for Revision," *Communio* 30 (Winter 2003): 621–53; Pristas, "Theological Principles that Guided the Redaction of the Roman Missal (1970)," *The Thomist* 67 (2003): 157–95; Pristas, "The Collects at Sunday Mass: An Examination of the Revisions of Vatican II," *Nova et Vetera* 3, no. 1 (Winter 2005): 5–38; Pristas, "The Pre– and Post–Vatican II Collects of the Dominican Doctors of the Church," *New Blackfriars* 86, no. 1006 (November 2005): 604–21; and Pristas, "The Post–Vatican II Revision of the Lenten Collects," in *Ever Directed Towards the Lord: The Love of God in the Liturgy of the Eucharist Past, Present, and Hoped For*, ed. Uwe Michael Lang (London and New York: T&T Clark, 2007), 62–89.

2. Pristas, "The Pre– and Post–Vatican II Collects," 604. Pristas cites Antoine Dumas, "Les orasions du nouveau Missel," *Questions Liturgiques* 25 (1971): 263–70 passim, at 270. An English translation of this entire article is provided in Pristas, "Orations of the Vatican II Missal," 629–39.

3. Pristas, "Theological Principles," 197.

necessary that "the work of the reformers in all its various particulars be made subject to serious scholarly and ecclesiastical reappraisal."[4]

The present essay undertakes a small piece of the scholarly task by appraising a different part of the revised Missal, namely, the collection of variable prefaces provided for use with Eucharistic Prayer I (the Roman Canon) and Eucharistic Prayer III.[5] Interestingly, the work of revising the prefaces was carried out by the very same group of scholars responsible for the revised orations that Pristas finds problematic. There is reason from the outset for thinking, however, that the revision of the prefaces has been rather successful. In the letter to bishops accompanying his July 2007 *motu proprio*, *Summorum Pontificum*, Pope Benedict XVI suggests that the "ordinary form" of celebrating the Mass according to the Missal of Paul VI and the "extraordinary form" using the earlier 1962 *Missale Romanum* can be "mutually enriching." Yet he offers only two examples, both of which are an "enrichment" of the pre–Vatican II Missal with material from the revised Missal. "New Saints and some of the new Prefaces can and should be inserted in the old Missal."[6] The desire to commemorate saints that had not been canonized in 1962 is self-explanatory, but why should the revised prefaces deserve special attention in this context?

The explanation that this essay offers is threefold. First, the post–Vatican II revision of the prefaces responded to one of the most keenly felt deficiencies of the former Missal. The dramatic increase in the number of prefaces from sixteen in the former missal to eighty-one in the first typical edition of the Missal of Paul VI suggests one aspect of the perceived need, but much more can be said about the kind of

4. Ibid.; Pristas, "Orations of the Vatican II Missal," 653.

5. While Eucharistic Prayer II has its own "fixed" preface—unlike Prayers I and III—this preface may be swapped for one of the variable prefaces if the presider so chooses. In this way it is more akin to Prayers I and III than to Prayer IV, whose preface is always fixed. The preface for Prayer II is also available as a Common Preface for weekday use in Prayers I and III. See Anthony Ward and Cuthbert Johnson, eds., *The Prefaces of the Roman Missal: A Source Compendium with Concordance and Indices* (Rome: Tipografia Poliglotta Vaticana, 1989), 289–94; Annibale Bugnini, *The Reform of the Liturgy 1948–1975*, trans. Matthew J. O'Connell (Collegeville, MN: Liturgical Press, 1990), 455–58.

6. "Letter of Pope Benedict XVI Accompanying the Apostolic Letter *Summorum Pontificum*," unofficial English translation published in United States Conference of Catholic Bishops Committee on the Liturgy *Newsletter*, vol. 43 (May/June 2007): 20–23, at 22.

expansion that was desired. Second, the revision followed principles of liturgical reform that were, on the whole, historically, theologically, and pastorally sound (see SC 23).[7] Third, the revision implemented these principles successfully, with the result that the Roman Missal now possesses a thematically varied yet stylistically consistent treasury of prefaces that has become an indispensable font of Eucharistic theology for the community at prayer.

In order to demonstrate the first point of this explanation, it will be necessary not only to examine the history of the Roman preface but also to get a sense of how this history was being told around the time of the Second Vatican Council. From this sketch of the perceived need for reform, we can move to a discussion of our second point—the principles that the revisers felt would ameliorate the problems and add to the richness of the prefaces. Here it will help to focus on the individuals most responsible for the actual work of revising the prefaces. Of these individuals, the most important are Placide Bruylants, OSB, and Antoine Dumas, OSB, the two scholars who led the study group charged with revising the orations and prefaces of the Missal. Fortunately, both published articles about their work and about the principles that guided it. Examination of these articles will provide the basis for evaluating the degree to which the texts that made it into the Missal of Paul VI adhere to the principles that the redactors sought to follow. The evaluations offered here, both of individual prefaces and of the collection as a whole, should at least begin to demonstrate our third point that the revisers were largely successful in doing what they set out to accomplish. We will conclude with a necessarily preliminary comparison of the results of this study with those obtained by Pristas in her investigations into the revision of the orations of the Roman Missal.

THE PREFACE AS *EUCHARISTIA*

Any effort to trace the history of the Roman Eucharistic preface necessarily involves a judgment about what a "preface" is and is not. At the same time, of course, this judgment about the fundamental "character" of the preface can only be made in light of historical data. It is not surprising, therefore, to find liturgical scholars around the time

7. Second Vatican Council, Constitution on the Sacred Liturgy (*Sacrosanctum Concilium*), in Austin Flannery, ed., *Vatican Council II: The Basic Sixteen Documents* (Northport, NY: Costello Publishing Company, 1996).

of the Second Vatican Council attempting to answer both questions simultaneously. A good example of this is contained in an article by Louis Bouyer, "La préface et le Sanctus," published in *La Maison-Dieu* in 1966 while the work of revising the Missal was in full swing.[8] He begins with the Latin name given in the Roman Missal to the text in question: *praefatio*. "It seems likely that the term, in the ancient Roman books, maintains the sense of the Latin *praefari* which, in the classical language, was applied to the pronunciation in a loud voice by the pontiff of a consecratory prayer."[9] Bouyer is clearly in agreement with Joseph Jungmann, who had said some twelve years earlier at a Liturgical Week for priests that the rendering of *praefatio* as "preface" was "to say the least a misleading translation."[10] In his voluminous and highly influential study of the Mass, Jungmann had argued that "even as late as the turn of the eighth century the preface was still included in the conception of the canon."[11] In this context, *praefatio* must have referred to the whole of the "Great Prayer," spoken "before God and before the community of the faithful."[12] This would have meant that the presider's words between the introductory dialogue and the Sanctus were in a position to set the tone for the entire Eucharistic prayer from *within* the prayer itself. Bouyer agrees that it was only later, when the term *praefatio* was applied exclusively to this text, that it actually became "nothing more than a preface, in the banal sense of the word, an hors-d'oeuvre, and not the very source of all that was to follow."[13]

In the earlier context, then, what was the tone that the preface sets as it begins the "Great Prayer" of the church? In Jungmann's words, it offers "the only proper response to εὐαγγέλιον," namely, "εὐχαριστία."[14] If the Eucharistic prayer as a whole is a "thanksgiving," then the preface is thanksgiving *par excellence*.[15] Moreover,

8. Louis Bouyer, "La préface et le Sanctus," *La Maison-Dieu* 87 (1966): 97–110. All translations of this article are my own.

9. Ibid., 97.

10. Joseph A. Jungmann, *The Eucharistic Prayer: A Study of the Canon Missae*, trans. Robert L. Batley (Bath: Pitman Press, 1955), 7–8.

11. Joseph A. Jungmann, *The Mass of the Roman Rite (Missarum Sollemnia)*, trans. Francis A. Brunner, vol. 2 (New York: Benziger Brothers, 1955), 103.

12. Jungmann, *The Eucharistic Prayer*, 8.

13. Bouyer, "La préface et le Sanctus," 97.

14. Jungmann, *The Mass of the Roman Rite*, 115.

15. See also Cipriano Vagaggini, *The Canon of the Mass and Liturgical Reform*, trans. Peter Coughlan (New York: Alba House, 1967), 85.

Bouyer thinks that this claim about the fundamental character of the preface can be supported with historical evidence. "Our Roman preface, *by dint of its origins*, constitutes the properly Eucharistic part of the Eucharist, the thanksgiving in the full primitive sense of a confession, in praise, of the *mirabilia Dei*."[16] For Bouyer, the "origins" of the preface are to be found in Jewish prayer. His central argument is that "the most ancient Christian Eucharistic liturgies, such as that of Addai and Mari and that of the *Apostolic Tradition* . . . , are visibly modeled after the Jewish meal liturgy, and more precisely on the three *berakoth* accompanying the final cup."[17] Bouyer associates the three prayers of the *Birkat ha-Mazon*—which bless God for providing nourishment, thank God for delivering Israel into the Promised Land, and petition God for the restoration of Jerusalem—with Christian praise for creation, thanksgiving for redemption in Christ, and petition for eschatological fulfillment.[18] In the case of Addai and Mari, the three *berakoth* are reflected in the apparently tripartite structure of the prayer.[19] In the *Apostolic Tradition* the first and second *berakoth* have been reversed in order and "fused" into the text that stands between the introductory dialogue and the institution narrative.[20] Thus, Bouyer concludes that "our preface evidently corresponds" to this part of the *Apostolic Tradition* prayer and to the first two of the three *berakoth* in the *Birkat ha-Mazon*.[21]

Bouyer's appeal to the *Birkat ha-Mazon* to explain the ultimate origin of the Eucharistic preface has undoubtedly been influential. Eugène Moeller, in the introduction to his 1981 collection of Latin prefaces, essentially follows Bouyer in his exposition of the "Hebraic origin"

16. Bouyer, "La préface et le Sanctus," 101 (emphasis added).

17. Ibid., 101–2.

18. Ibid., 99. For texts of the *Birkat ha-Mazon*, see Anton Hänggi and Irmgard Pahl, eds., *Prex Eucharistica: Textus e Variis Liturgiis Antiquioribus Selecti*, 3rd ed., Spicilegium Friburgense 12 (Fribourg: Éditions Universitaires Fribourg Suisse, 1998), 8–12; Ronald C. D. Jasper and Geoffrey J. Cuming, eds., *Prayers of the Eucharist: Early and Reformed*, 3rd ed. (Collegeville, MN: Liturgical Press, 1987), 7–11.

19. See Hänggi and Pahl, *Prex Eucharistica*, 375–80; Jasper and Cuming, *Prayers of the Eucharist*, 41–44.

20. See Hänggi and Pahl, *Prex Eucharistica*, 80–81; Jasper and Cuming, *Prayers of the Eucharist*, 34–35.

21. Bouyer, "La préface et le Sanctus," 99.

of the preface.[22] Nevertheless, he is forced to add that more recent scholarship has challenged the smooth transposition of a Jewish *Birkat ha-Mazon* structure onto that of early Christian Eucharistic prayers. Thomas Talley, in particular, has argued that too much emphasis on the notion of *berakah* as "blessing" has obscured the "unmistakable priority" that early Christian Eucharistic language gives "to thanksgiving as over against benediction" as well as the connection of *Eucharistia* with "sacrifice," a notion that is absent in the *Birkat ha-Mazon*. Besides this, there are structural differences between Jewish and Christian prayers that require him to conclude that *"berakah* is not the same as *Eucharistia."*[23] Moeller admits that this is true, but he does not think that it precludes us from recognizing in the early Christian *Eucharistia* the influence of a "theme" from the Jewish *berakoth*, namely, the "confession of faith in praise" of God for creation and redemption. If this thematic content "found in the *berakoth* of the *Birkath-ha-mazon* . . . corresponds 'mutatis mutandis' to our Latin preface," then we can still say that the preface has its origins in the very earliest period of anaphoral development, when Jewish *berakah* and Christian *Eucharistia* were mutually influential, though not identical.[24]

Yet what historical reason can be offered for associating the "theme" of *Eucharistia* with a particular part of the textual structure of the Eucharistic prayer—the part that comes to be called the "preface" in the Latin West? For Bouyer and other scholars of his generation, this question calls for comparative study of early anaphoras, but the answer depends above all on analysis of the Eucharistic prayer contained in the fourth chapter of the *Apostolic Tradition* attributed to Hippolytus. As we have seen, Bouyer associates the initial pericope of this prayer both with the first two prayers of the *Birkat ha-Mazon* and with "our preface."[25] Appearing in the same issue of *La Maison-Dieu* as Bouyer's article is another by Bernard Botte titled "Tradition Apostolique et Canon Romain." Botte rejects any a priori postulation of "continuity between the anaphora of Hippolytus and the Roman Canon, as if the

22. Edmond (Eugène) Moeller, ed., *Corpus Praefationum: Étude Préliminaire*, Corpus Christianorum Series Latina 161 (Turnholt: Brepols, 1981), xii–xvii. All translations of Moeller's introduction are my own.

23. Thomas J. Talley, "From Berakah to Eucharistia: A Reopening Question," *Worship* 50 (1976): 115–36, at 128–29, 137.

24. Moeller, *Corpus Praefationum*, ix.

25. Bouyer, "La Préface et le Sanctus," 99.

latter had come out of the former by successive transformations."[26] Moreover, after attempting to pare down the Roman Canon to the form it possessed "around the end of the 4th century," Botte still finds that "for the general scheme as well as for details of the text, one turns up no indication of a dependence vis-à-vis the anaphora of Hippolytus," which he locates in Rome at "the beginning of the 3rd century."[27] Since more recent scholarship has challenged this date and place and shown it to be unlikely that this prayer was composed all at once,[28] there is even less reason now to think that the first section of the anaphora in *Apostolic Tradition* 4 is a "source" for the preface of the Roman Canon in the strict sense of structural or textual parentage.

Nevertheless, although "the *Apostolic Tradition* is not the key that opens all doors," it is in Botte's opinion "a model of Eucharistic prayer" whose "orthodoxy" and antiquity demand our attention.[29] The main reason for bringing this anaphora up in a discussion of the Roman preface is that it has in its first pericope following the dialogue precisely what the Roman Canon no longer possesses, namely, thanksgiving. Botte points out that "juridically, there was no longer any thanksgiving in the Canon" once Roman liturgical books took the *Te igitur* as the start of the Canon and treated the preface "as a simple preparation."[30] The revisers of the Missal could easily return the preface to its rightful place within the Canon, but this would not completely solve the problem since the thanks expressed would usually lack a proper object. Bouyer observes that "the common preface . . . despite its presence in the most ancient manuscripts of the Roman Canon, is only an empty frame" into which proper texts were evidently supposed to be inserted.[31] Yet for centuries, such "embolisms"

---

26. Bernard Botte, "Tradition Apostolique et Canon Romain," *La Maison-Dieu* 87 (1966): 52–61, at 54. All translations of this article are my own.

27. Ibid., 55–56. Botte accomplishes this reconstruction of the primitive Roman Canon primarily by referring to Ambrose's *De Sacramentis*.

28. See Paul Bradshaw, "Hippolytus Revisited: The Identity of the So-Called Apostolic Tradition," *Liturgy* 16 (2000): 9–10; Paul Bradshaw, Maxwell E. Johnson, and L. Edward Phillips, *Apostolic Tradition: A Commentary*, Hermeneia Commentary Series (Minneapolis: Fortress Press, 2002), 1–6, 13–15.

29. Botte, "Tradition Apostolique et Canon Romain," 57.

30. Ibid., 59. Jungmann describes this shift in Roman Mass books as beginning in the ninth century and being complete by the end of the Middle Ages. See below and Jungmann, *Mass of the Roman Rite*, 103–6.

31. Bouyer, "La préface et le Sanctus," 103.

did not exist for most weekdays or even for Sundays in Ordinary Time (though the use of the preface of the Trinity on these Sundays was prescribed in 1759).[32] Thus, God the Father was thanked through Christ the Lord, but the thanks were not offered "for" anything in particular; that is to say, no mention was made of any reasons for giving thanks. The prayer in *Apostolic Tradition* 4, by contrast, is quite clear about why thanks are being offered to God:

> We render thanks to you, O God, through your beloved child Jesus Christ, whom in the last times you sent to us as a savior and redeemer and angel of your will; who is your inseparable Word, through whom you made all things, and in whom you were well pleased. You sent him from heaven into a virgin's womb; and conceived in the womb, he was made flesh and was manifested as your Son, being born of the Holy Spirit and the Virgin. Fulfilling your will and gaining for you a holy people, he stretched out his hands when he should suffer, that he might release from suffering those who have believed in you.[33]

The contrast with the Roman Canon is heightened, moreover, when one views this prayer alongside other ancient anaphoras in which the "thanksgiving" is not "purely Christological" but also "evokes creation and the economy of the Old Testament as well as that of the New." Botte especially has in mind the Egyptian Anaphora of St. Basil here, but the principle applies to virtually any ancient anaphora that one cares to look at: "If we compare these anaphoras with the Roman Canon, what strikes us is that the thanksgiving is richer in content."[34] Scholars were coming to see that the Eucharistic prayer of the Roman Rite was strangely short on *Eucharistia*.

It is not surprising, then, to find these scholars looking to ancient anaphoras for help in returning a "Eucharistic" character to the Roman preface. Botte asks, "Couldn't one foresee for these days prefaces that are inspired by the ancient anaphoras and that give thanks for the economy of redemption celebrated in the Eucharist? It would be possible, for example, to make from the beginning of the anaphora of Hippolytus an embolism for a Roman preface."[35] In fact, Botte got his

32. Jungmann, *Mass of the Roman Rite*, 123.

33. Jasper and Cuming, *Prayers of the Eucharist*, 35. The translation is from the Latin version of the *Apostolic Tradition*.

34. Botte, "Tradition Apostolique et Canon Romain," 58–59.

35. Ibid., 59.

wish, as the first pericope of the prayer in *Apostolic Tradition* 4 became the model for the "fixed" preface of Eucharistic Prayer II.[36] It is important to note, however, that although the anaphora of *Apostolic Tradition* 4 was the favorite example of scholars who called for a more "Eucharistic" preface, it was certainly not the only example.[37] Indeed, Botte's closing remark is that scholars should not be "hypnotized" by this one prayer but should give equal attention to "oriental anaphoras."[38] Inasmuch as scholars found themselves "hypnotized" by the *Apostolic Tradition*, they were undoubtedly under the spell of mistaken conclusions about the "Roman" origin of this text, its antiquity, and the unity of its composition. None of this, however, affects their fundamental argument, which was that the action of giving thanks in the Roman Canon was deficient by comparison with virtually all traditions of Eucharistic praying, both ancient and contemporary. Moreover, their point is only reinforced if we accept Paul Bradshaw's suggestion that the most ancient core of the prayer we find in *Apostolic Tradition* 4 includes only "a substantial hymn of praise for redemption, a brief offering/thanksgiving formula . . . a short petition for the communicants . . . and a concluding doxology."[39] The only "substantial" part of this Eucharistic prayer—at least in terms of text on the page—is its opening section thanking and praising God for the work of redemption. That which seems most vital to this ancient anaphora is precisely that which was most lacking in the Roman Canon.

Still, why pin the blame for this deficiency and the hope for its remedy on the Roman preface? If the "empty frame" of the common preface was meant to be filled with "a confession, in praise, of the *mirabilia Dei*," then why did the Missal as it had been received possess so few preface embolisms? And what of the fifteen "proper prefaces" that were available—the prefaces of the Nativity, the Epiphany, and the Ascension; of Lent and Easter; of the Holy Cross, the Holy Spirit, the Trinity, and the Sacred Heart; of Christ the King, Mary, Joseph, and the Apostles; of the Chrism Mass and the Mass for the Deceased? Were these not sufficient expressions of praise and thanks? For liturgical

36. See n. 5.

37. See Bouyer, "La preface et le Sanctus," 104–6; Botte, "Tradition Apostolique et Canon Romain," 58–61; Bugnini, *Reform of the Liturgy*, 458–60.

38. Botte, "Tradition Apostolique et Canon Romain," 61.

39. Paul Bradshaw, *Eucharistic Origins* (Oxford: Oxford University Press, 2004), 135–36.

scholars working around the time of Vatican II, history provided a clear answer to these questions, and subsequent scholarship has confirmed their conclusions.[40]

In the first place, examination of the oldest extant Roman liturgical books shows that proper prefaces have not always been scarce. On the contrary, writes Cipriano Vagaggini in his influential 1966 study, *The Canon of the Mass and the Liturgical Reform*, "the Roman anaphora tradition is well known for the extraordinary richness of its prefaces, both in their number and in their quality."[41] Vagaggini joins Jungmann and Bouyer in offering as the oldest example of this "rich" tradition of prefaces the so-called Leonine or Verona Sacramentary—actually a collection of Roman Mass *libelli* assembled over the course of the sixth century.[42] This book, though "quite incomplete" in terms of its coverage of the liturgical year, has 267 prefaces—one for each Mass formulary.[43] The seventh-century *Gelasianum Vetus* has fifty-four prefaces, and the "Gallicanized" Gelasians of the eighth century have around two hundred.[44] These collections of prefaces demonstrate an important feature of Roman anaphoral prayer that was shared early on with the Mozarabic, Gallican, and Ambrosian traditions. Vagaggini explains, "In contrast to the East, it is customary throughout the West to vary the first part of the anaphora in accordance with the feast" so that "a particular aspect of the economy of salvation can be developed each time." In other words, a survey of the *mirabilia Dei* for which praise and thanks are offered is achieved through a *variable* preface. The "treasures" of euchological composition produced by this reliance on a variable preface supply the "*Eucharistia* par excellence" of the Roman eucharistic prayer. For Vagaggini, it would be "unthinkable" to es-

40. See, for example, the histories offered in Moeller, *Corpus Praefationum*, viii–xii, xix–xxii; Ward and Johnson, *Prefaces of the Roman Missal*, 10–12.

41. Vagaggini, *Canon of the Mass*, 86.

42. Ibid., 86–87; Jungmann, *Mass of the Roman Rite*, 118; Louis Bouyer, *Eucharist: Theology and Spirituality of the Eucharistic Prayer*, trans. Charles Underhill Quinn (Notre Dame, IN: University of Notre Dame Press, 1968), 362; see also Eric Palazzo, *A History of Liturgical Books from the Beginning to the Thirteenth Century*, trans. Madeleine Beaumont (Collegeville, MN: Liturgical Press, 1998), 38–42. It should be noted that although Vagaggini, Jungmann, and Bouyer still refer to this book as the "Leonine" Sacramentary, Bouyer, at least, points out the mistaken attribution (*Eucharist*, 360).

43. Jungmann, *Mass of the Roman Rite*, 118.

44. Ibid.; Bouyer, *Eucharist*, 362.

chew this feature of the Roman anaphoral tradition in any attempt at liturgical reform.[45]

Yet it is clear that past reforms *have* done away with a great deal of variability by drastically reducing the number of available prefaces, and it is essential to understand why this happened. Bouyer describes a recurring problem:

> Even at a very early date, we find in the Roman or Romano-Frankish books (as well as in the Gallican or Mozarabic books . . .) formulas which have little (or nothing) to do with the traditional Eucharist. Undoubtedly Jungmann was right in showing in the "confession" of the εὐχαριστία the response to the εὐαγγέλιον previously proclaimed. It might therefore have seemed normal to give each mass an echo in the preface of the particular theme underlined in the Gospel of the day within the great harmony of the Christian mystery. But even in many of the most successful compositions from this viewpoint, we note an inevitable tendency to retain only a secondary aspect of the mystery. And, only too often, the result was that the Eucharist turned into a moralizing didacticism.[46]

Although the variable preface allowed for "flexibility" in making the thanksgiving fit the particular occasion,[47] it also opened the door to less "Eucharistic" expressions including "more or less fanciful hagiography" and even outright diatribe.[48] Consequently, one observes throughout the history of the Roman preface a back-and-forth struggle between those who would rein in the worst abuses and those who would not be content with a meager selection of prefaces. Thus, the Gregorian Sacramentary imposed on much of the Christian West by Charlemagne contained a mere fourteen prefaces, but straightaway the Supplement to the *Hadrianum* increased the number of texts to a staggering 333.[49] "Towards the end of the tenth century," Bouyer notes, "the canonist Burchard of Worms attempted to reduce the authorized prefaces to nine, by producing a decretal attributed to Pelagius II (who died in 590), but which he most probably made up completely

---

45. Vagaggini, *Canon of the Mass*, 85–87.

46. Bouyer, *Eucharist*, 363–64.

47. Vagaggini, *Canon of the Mass*, 86.

48. Bouyer, *Eucharist*, 364.

49. Ward and Johnson, *Prefaces of the Roman Missal*, 11.

himself."[50] The addition of the preface of the Blessed Virgin Mary brought the authorized number up to ten and completed the collection of proper prefaces that would be included in the Missal of Pius V prepared after the Council of Trent. This number remained fixed for centuries, though all along there were churches "not content with this poverty" that would supplement this selection with other compositions, especially for important local feasts.[51] In the twentieth century, prefaces for St. Joseph (1919), the deceased (1919), Christ the King (1925), the Sacred Heart (1928), and the Chrism Mass (1955) were added to the Roman Missal.[52] Consequently, there were fifteen prefaces (sixteen including the common preface) officially in use on the eve of Vatican II.

In quality and in number, how well did these texts represent the Roman tradition of giving thanks for the *mirabilia Dei* through use of a variable preface? Placide Bruylants took it upon himself to write an answer to this question even as he was starting the work of revision. He first reviews the history of the Roman preface and identifies the kinds of "deviations" that have taken place. Examples abound of prefaces that are really prayers of supplication, anti-heretical definitions, hagiographies, or shallow catecheses. Such texts are not true to their "character" as expressions of "thanksgiving" in which "the Church evokes the astonishing memory of redemption."[53] Turning to the prefaces in the pre–Vatican II Missal, he finds that "the principal deviations that we have turned up in the history of the preface have unfortunately succeeded in slipping into the current Missal despite the extremely reduced number of texts that it has conserved."[54] The preface for Lent is a simplistic catechesis on the merits of fasting in which "one searches in vain for an allusion to the great Paschal mystery that the Church commemorates at this time of the liturgical year."[55] The preface of the Holy Trinity, repeated every Sunday during Ordinary Time, is a definition of the three "persons" in one "substance" that "occupies in the Sunday liturgy a place that, despite its doctrinal value,

---

50. Bouyer, *Eucharist*, 363.

51. Jungmann, *Mass of the Roman Rite*, 120–21.

52. Ward and Johnson, *Prefaces of the Roman Missal*, 11.

53. Placide Bruylants, "Les préfaces du Missel Romain," *La Maison-Dieu* 87 (1966): 111–33, at 114–16. All translations of this article are my own.

54. Ibid., 132.

55. Ibid., 122.

is manifestly exaggerated and risks engendering familiarity, even boredom, when the faithful hear it in the language of their country."[56] The prefaces for Christmas and Epiphany ignore the concrete "scriptural" portrayal of the Incarnation in favor of an overly "speculative or spiritual angle" on the mystery.[57] Finally, the preface of the Apostles, which opens with "supplication" and never goes beyond it, is "not a thanksgiving but quite simply an oration," a "prayer of request" that doesn't belong in the category of preface at all.[58] Indeed, the only texts that escape Bruylants's criticism are the Easter preface and the preface of the Blessed Virgin Mary.[59] In his view, therefore, the revision of the prefaces will necessarily possess a "double objective." While the "extremely reduced number" of texts makes "a renewal and an enrichment" of the treasury of prefaces "absolutely indispensable," it is also necessary to revise or remove those prefaces that "do not reflect, in all its purity, the authentic tradition of the Church."[60] Thus, the history of the preface brings Bruylants, along with the other scholars we have been discussing, back around to the fundamental "character" of the preface. The claim that *Eucharistia* is the "authentic" orientation of the preface is a statement about the history *and* the theology of the Eucharistic prayer.

PRINCIPLES FOR REVISION

To complete the revision of the Roman Missal and implement other reforms called for in the Second Vatican Council's Constitution on the Sacred Liturgy (SC 25, 50), Paul VI established in 1964 the *Consilium ad exsequendam Constitutionem de Sacra Liturgia*. While deliberative authority was vested in the "members" of the *Consilium* (nearly all of them bishops), the work of preparing revised liturgical texts was entrusted to expert "consultors" or *periti* who were divided into over thirty small study groups.[61] The study group or *coetus* charged with the task of revising the prayers (*orationes*) and prefaces was *coetus* 18bis. Its members were Placide Bruylants and André Rose of Belgium,

56. Ibid., 127.
57. Ibid., 116–17, 119–21.
58. Ibid., 115, 128–29.
59. Ibid., 124–25, 127–28.
60. Ibid., 132.
61. For details on the structure and working procedures of the *Consilium*, see Bugnini, *The Reform of the Liturgy*, 60–68.

Antoine Dumas of France, Giovanni Lucchesi of Italy, Walter Düring of Germany, Henry Ashworth of England, and Juan Antonio Gracía of Spain.[62] Bruylants, a Benedictine "known everywhere for two solid volumes on the prayers of the Missal," was the original "relator" of the group responsible for directing its efforts and reporting back to the *Consilium*.[63] Bruylants died of a heart attack in October 1966 (just a few days after making a major presentation of the group's initial work to the whole *Consilium*), and it fell to Dumas, also a Benedictine priest, to take over the leadership of the *coetus*.[64] Shortly after his death, Bruylants's article examining the prefaces of the pre–Vatican II Missal appeared in the same issue of *La Maison-Dieu* that contained Bouyer's article on the history of the preface and Botte's article on the *Apostolic Tradition*.[65] It provides considerable insight into how perceived problems with the collection of prefaces in the then-current Roman Missal shaped the principles that the redactors followed in their work. Dumas later published articles that set out these principles in even greater precision and provided some hints about the sources that figured in the texts eventually produced by his *coetus*.[66]

In the same way that it is impossible to make a clear distinction between the "character" of the Roman preface and its history, the principles followed in the revision of the prefaces cannot be simply divided into "historical," "theological," and "pastoral" categories. It will be more helpful to note how each of the various principles responds to these concerns. Since Dumas actually lists "criteria of the reform" and "principles of composition" in his two articles,[67] it might be appropriate to employ his headings, but they differ somewhat from one

62. Ibid., 397 n. 10, 944–52.

63. Ibid., 397.

64. Ibid., 157, 398. Pristas points out that the English translation of Bugnini's book incorrectly states that A. Rose became the relator upon Bruylants's death (see ibid., 397 n.10). The correct information appears in the Italian original: Annibale Bugnini, *La Riforma Liturgica* (1948–1975) (Rome: CVL Edizione Liturgiche, 1984), 393 n.10. See Pristas, "The Orations of the Vatican II Missal," 627 n.20.

65. See n. 52.

66. Antoine Dumas, "Les nouvelles préfaces du Missel Romain," *La Maison-Dieu* 94 (1968): 159–72; Dumas, "Les préfaces du nouveau Missel," *Ephemerides Liturgicae* 85 (1971): 16–28. All translations of these articles are my own.

67. Dumas, "Les nouvelles préfaces," 159–61; Dumas, "Les préfaces du nouveau Missel," 17–21.

article to the other. It seems best to organize the specific criteria that both Bruylants and Dumas describe under six general principles: (1) respecting the "Eucharistic" character of the preface, (2) maintaining a consistently "Roman" style and genre, (3) filling in the gaps while supplying a choice of texts, (4) conserving the best prefaces of the former Missal, (5) retrieving liturgical texts that have fallen into disuse, and (6) using non-liturgical sources to inspire new texts. Dumas points out that these principles of revision were "not fixed a priori, but inspired as much by the research of liturgists as by the requests of pastors and the faithful."[68]

Dumas reiterates the point that other liturgical scholars have been making all along: "The fundamental character of the preface is to be the opening of the Eucharistic prayer . . . It is therefore above all thanksgiving: its role is to proclaim the motives of the present Eucharist of the Church."[69] As we have seen, this is a claim about both the history and the theology of the Roman Eucharistic prayer. The point can also be expressed in terms of the pastoral "function" of the preface. Bruylants says, "The preface determines the attitude of the soul in which we are going to participate sacramentally in the sacrifice of Christ. This attitude is, without question, thanksgiving."[70] Anything that would obscure the fundamentally Eucharistic character of the preface must be ruled out. This includes supplication, hagiography, moral or doctrinal didacticism, speculation, and panegyric. More positively, whatever recalls "the mysteries of salvation and the *mirabilia Dei*" is the proper subject for a preface.[71] This is the most basic principle of the revision; all other criteria serve it as corollaries. It is what Dumas calls "the principle of truth": fidelity not only to the doctrines that concern the central mysteries of the faith, but also to the true character of the preface and of the Eucharist itself, in which these mysteries are expressed and "actualized."[72]

While the "function" of the preface is to determine an "attitude of the soul," Dumas points out that gratitude is not evoked as a diffuse

68. Dumas, "Les préfaces du nouveau Missel," 17.

69. Ibid.

70. Bruylants, "Les préfaces du Missel Romain," 115.

71. Ibid., 115–16; Dumas, "Les nouvelles préfaces," 160; Dumas, "Les préfaces du nouveau Missel," 18.

72. Dumas, "Les préfaces du nouveau Missel," 18; Bruylants, "Les préfaces du Missel Romain," 115.

feeling but as a focused response to "one fact or one aspect of the mystery commemorated in the celebration or in the history of salvation in general."[73] Here the "particular genius of Roman prayer" and especially of the variable preface is raised as another principle of revision. "The motivation for thanksgiving will not develop the whole of the mystery being celebrated, but will instead be like a flash thrown upon some important aspect of the feast or of the season, while the totality of the liturgical texts will furnish a more complete synthesis from other points of view." Without ever forgetting the central mystery being celebrated in the Eucharist, the preface can and should "expose with clarity, for the people of God, the proper theology of the season or of the feast."[74] Besides possessing the ability to make this connection between the Eucharist and the liturgical year, the Roman preface has the advantage of brevity. The pastoral importance of this feature should not be underestimated. "To be comprehensible and effective, the exposition of this fact or of this mystery [commemorated in the celebration] should be quite brief."[75] Still, it is possible to maintain "the precision and discretion of the Roman type" while achieving a "certain lyricism" exemplified by the "beautiful lapidary formulas" that the tradition has produced in the past. This lyricism should be "easily retrievable" in various vernacular translations, yet it must also be pleasingly sonorous in Latin and amenable to setting in chant, which is "the privileged mode of expression of the preface."[76] Thus, even when retrieving prefaces from non-Roman sources or when composing new texts, one must not "break with the unity of the Roman tradition, whose style possesses at once a sobriety and a density that provides the model for all liturgical prayer and a powerful safeguard against the chattiness that would serve as the vehicle for 'intentions' of every kind."[77]

Since the Roman preface spreads its survey of salvation history over the course of an entire liturgical year, it is crucial to "fill in the gaps" where seasonal and proper prefaces are lacking in the Missal. "By reason of the proper function of the preface and by fidelity to a healthy

73. Dumas, "Les nouvelles préfaces," 160.

74. Bruylants, "Les prefaces du Missel Romain," 118.

75. Dumas, "Les nouvelles préfaces," 160–61.

76. Dumas, "Les préfaces du nouveau Missel," 20; Bruylants, "Les préfaces du Missel Romain," 118.

77. Dumas, "Les nouvelles préfaces," 161.

liturgical tradition, it has been decided that each season, solemnity or important feast, as well as Masses celebrated on the occasion of various rites or sacraments (marriage, funerals, etc.), should be given a preface of its own."[78] At the same time, "the liturgical seasons (Advent, Christmas, Lent, Eastertide) demand a certain variety of prefaces, and more still Ordinary Time (*per annum*), which covers more than half the year."[79] While true to the Roman liturgical tradition, the concern for variety is raised first of all by pastoral considerations. In addition to providing a way for the entire economy of salvation to be portrayed in a series of short "flashes," variety "avoids the monotony caused by too frequent repetition."[80] The potential for monotony is also raised by the "immutability of the initial formula: *Vere dignum . . . aeterne Deus*, and of the ending of the preface, which, despite a certain elasticity . . . does not present a very great variety." Bruylants thinks it is "beyond doubt that, sung or read in living language, these stereotypical formulas risk quickly becoming a jingle, to which no one will pay attention any longer."[81] Thus, the revisers use a larger number of "protocols" and "eschatols" in the prefaces, and they also provide an appendix containing "a choice of various formulas, generally inspired by Mozarabic sources" that may be used in place of those supplied with the embolisms in the Missal.[82]

Although the shortcomings of many of the prefaces in the pre–Vatican II Missal are all too apparent to Bruylants and Dumas, these are nevertheless the first texts that they turn to in order to supply prefaces for the revised Missal. "It was not a question, indeed," says Dumas, "of demolishing in order to create systematically but, above all, of respecting the traditional texts of the Missal, each time that they were satisfactory and responded to their proper function. That is why we have conserved them, even while correcting or completing them where there was a place for it."[83] Thus, even texts that have been used continuously for centuries must conform to the "principle of truth"

78. Ibid., 160.

79. Dumas, "Les préfaces du nouveau Missel," 18.

80. Dumas, "Les nouvelles préfaces," 160; Dumas, "Les préfaces du nouveau Missel," 17.

81. Bruylants, "Les préfaces du Missel Romain," 119.

82. Dumas, "Les préfaces du nouveau Missel," 20. See Ward and Johnson, *Prefaces of the Roman Missal*, 535–46.

83. Dumas, "Les préfaces du nouveau Missel," 19.

with respect to their "proper function" as the opening of the Eucharistic prayer and to their fundamental "character" of thanksgiving.

When one must eventually turn to other liturgical sources in order to complete the work of "renewal and enrichment" of the corpus of prefaces, "one has at one's disposal an abundant and varied choice," for "the number of prefaces that the liturgical documents have transmitted to us exceeds by far the thousand mark." Bruylants adds, "Several among them are remarkable, and one can only be astonished that they have remained unused for so long."[84] On the other hand, says Dumas, "Experience proves more than abundantly that, in the spirit of liturgical reform, ancient texts that can be used as one finds them are very rare."[85] In the first place, if history shows us that the preface is the "lens" through which the entire Eucharistic action is viewed as *Eucharistia*, it also demonstrates that "this lens is not always found with equal clarity in all of the ancient sources."[86] One must select those texts that best exemplify the theological "principle of truth" that has been established. Moreover, since certain "pastoral" needs of the praying assembly differ in each age, one cannot simply lift texts from one of the ancient sacramentaries and drop them unmodified into the new Missal. Dumas explains, "It was necessary therefore that the chosen texts, carriers of a venerable tradition, be translatable into modern languages and adapted to contemporary mentality. That is why, if many ancient texts have been retained, very few, however, have been so in their entirety." In addition to "numerous cuts" and some "discrete corrections,"[87] the work of revising ancient texts for contemporary use often involves the use of "centonization," a process whereby one "assembles in a new composition the elements of value scattered and . . . sometimes drowned in otherwise banal compositions."[88]

In the case that the unavailability or "insufficiencies" of traditional liturgical texts present an obstacle to finding a preface required by "the needs of renewal and enrichment," the revisers are not without recourse to other material from the church's tradition. "Biblical citations, certain homilies of Saint Leo, sermons of Saint Augustine, and several passages from the Acts of Vatican II furnished expressions very well

84. Bruylants, "Les préfaces du Missel Romain," 132.
85. Dumas, "Les nouvelles préfaces," 161.
86. Bruylants, "Les préfaces du Missel Romain," 115.
87. Dumas, "Les préfaces du nouveau Missel," 19.
88. Bruylants, "Les préfaces du Missel Romain," 132.

adapted to the great realities celebrated in the course of the Liturgical Year: incarnation, redemption, church, Virgin Mary, etc."[89] Use of this non-liturgical material actually requires criteria and procedures analogous to those used to retrieve ancient prefaces and other prayers. "In this case also, it was necessary to proceed to an assimilation of texts under a form comprehensible by our contemporaries—without betraying in any way the message carried—and in a style of liturgical prayer, or more exactly of Eucharistic proclamation."[90] This precise "literary form," being "intermediate between prayer and hymn," is "specifically proper" to the preface, and it should serve to "incite the faithful, and of course the celebrant, to praise and joy."[91]

In his desire to see the praise and joy inspired by the confession of the *mirabilia Dei* "bloom fully in the communal enthusiasm of the *Sanctus*,"[92] Dumas clearly takes to heart the council's insistence that "in the restoration and development of the sacred liturgy the full and active participation by all the people is the paramount concern" (SC 14). Although theological and historical concerns shaped the principles that *coetus* 18bis sought to follow in the revision of the prefaces, the major motivating force behind their work is undoubtedly this "paramount concern" of the council, "which had defined the liturgical reform first of all as a response to pastoral needs."[93] The revised prefaces must be able to unify the faithful in an act of *Eucharistia* so that together they may join the angels in singing God's praises. Dumas does not, unfortunately, define the "contemporary mentality" to which the revised prefaces must be "comprehensible." Yet it would seem that this criterion involves a genuine attempt at pastoral sensitivity rather than a simplistic contrasting of "contemporary" with "medieval" or "ancient" ways of thinking and praying. The preface, after all, represents a *living* tradition of Eucharistic prayer: "Why does the People of God, *today, in this liturgical time, in such circumstances,* proclaim the wonders of its Lord and offer him in the Eucharist the sacrifice of Christ? That is for the preface to say, from the solemn opening of the Eucharistic prayer."[94]

89. Dumas, "Les préfaces du nouveau Missel," 19.
90. Ibid.
91. Dumas, "Les nouvelles préfaces," 160.
92. Dumas, "Les préfaces du nouveau Missel," 19.
93. Ibid.
94. Ibid., 17–18 (emphasis added).

RESULTS OF THE REVISION

A complete evaluation of the revised prefaces contained in the Missal of Paul VI would require analysis of each text with reference to the principles of reform that the revisers sought to follow. We can only make a start at this task here. Still, by selecting texts that represent how *coetus* 18bis worked with different kinds of sources, we can get a good initial sense of how these principles shaped the final product of their labors. Therefore, we will examine five examples: the revision of a preface from the pre–Vatican II Missal, the recovery of a preface from the Supplement to the *Hadrianum*, the centonization of two prefaces from the Verona Sacramentary to produce a single new text, the splitting of a preface from the Ambrosian *Sacramentarium Bergomense* to produce two new texts, and the composition of a new preface based on a sermon of Leo the Great. The sources are those identified in the first place by Dumas in his 1971 article that we have been examining.[95] More recently, Anthony Ward and Cuthbert Johnson have published an extensive source compendium for all the prefaces in the *editio typica altera* of the Missal of Paul VI.[96] All of the Latin texts are taken from this volume. The translations that I have prepared sacrifice optimal English phrasing and syntax in order to more closely represent structural and textual changes that have been made in the revision of the source material. Additionally, the eschatols have been left off, and generally only the ends of the protocols have been provided.

Our first example has already been discussed as a text in the pre–Vatican II Missal that Bruylants found particularly vexing: the preface of the Apostles.[97] Even though the former text displays so little "Eucharistic" character that Bruylants is inclined to deem it a simple oration, his study group needs to make very few changes in order to "restore" this character. By removing the first line, by turning the purpose clause (*ut . . .*) into a relative clause (*Qui . . .*), and by changing the subjunctive verbs *deseras* and *custodias* to the present indicative *deseris* and *custodis*, the petition for God's continuous protection is turned into grateful acknowledgment of the same. The "leaders" whom God has gathered to "preside" over the church are described as "vicars of your Son" rather than "vicars of your work"—a change that

---

95. Ibid., 21–27.
96. Full citation in n. 5.
97. See n. 57.

Former *Missale Romanum* Praefatio de Apostolis[98]	Missal of Paul VI Praefatio I de Apostolis
Vere dignum et iustum est, aequum et salutare,	*Vere dignum et iustum est, aequum et salutare,* *nos tibi semper et ubique gratias agere:* *Domine, sancte Pater, omnipotens aeterne Deus:*
Te, Domine, suppliciter exorare	
ut gregem tuum, Pastor aeternae, non deseras	Qui gregem tuum, Pastor aeterne, non deseris,
sed per beatos Apostolos tuos continua protectione custodias:	sed per beatos Apostolos continua protectione custodis,
Ut iisdem rectoribus gubernetur,	ut iisdem rectoribus gubernetur,
quos operis tui vicarios eidem contulisti praeesse pastores.	quos Filii tui vicarios eidem contulisti praeesse pastores.
Truly meet and just it is, right and salutary,	*Truly meet and just it is, right and salutary,* *that we always and everywhere give thanks:*
To humbly beg, Lord,	*Lord, holy Father, almighty eternal God:*
that you, the eternal Pastor, may not forsake your flock,	You are the eternal Pastor who does not forsake your flock,
but through your blessed Apostles watch over it with unceasing protection:	but through the blessed Apostles watches over it with unceasing protection,
So that it will be guided by those leaders	so that it is guided by those leaders
whom you gathered to preside over it as pastors and vicars of your work.	whom you gathered to preside over it as pastors and vicars of your Son.

is perhaps intended to evoke *Lumen Gentium*'s description of the office of bishop. As "successors to the apostles," bishops "take the place of Christ himself, teacher, shepherd, and priest, and act in his person" (LG 21, 24).[99] Otherwise, the revised text is nearly identical to the old. The prayer already possesses the "sobriety and density" typical of the best "Roman" style.[100] It fills the need for a preface that

98. Reprinted in Ward and Johnson, *Prefaces of the Roman Missal*, 436–37.

99. Second Vatican Council, Dogmatic Constitution on the Church (*Lumen Gentium*), in Flannery, *Vatican Council II*.

100. See n. 76.

can be used on the feast days of the apostles. There can be no justifiable reason for scrapping the text since it can be so easily "restored" to its proper Eucharistic function. This "restoration," however, is not of the archaeological kind, since the original *praefatio* in the Verona Sacramentary that Ward and Johnson identify as a "liturgical antecedent" is undeniably a petitionary prayer; the embolism begins with "*suppliciter exorantes.*"[101] Here, following the "principle of truth" requires one to say that even this very old text contains some "distortion" of the true Eucharistic character of the preface.

Our next example is the third of five proper prefaces provided in the Missal of Paul VI for the Sundays of Lent. Each of the five makes reference to the gospel reading heard on these Sundays during Year A in the revised lectionary cycle. According to Dumas, each has as its primary source a preface from the Supplement to the *Hadrianum.*[102]

Supplementum Anianense 1566: [Dom. II in Quadragesima] Feria Sexta[103]	Missal of Paul VI Dominica III Quadragesimae: Praefatio
. . . *per Christum Dominum nostrum.* Qui ad insinuandum humilitatis suae mysterium, fatigatus resedit ad puteum. Qui a muliere Samaritana aquae sibi petiit porrigi potum, qui in ea creaverat fidei donum. Et ita eius sitire dignatus est fidem, ut dum ab ea aquam peteret, in ea ignem divini amoris accenderet. Imploramus iatque tuam immensam clementiam,	. . . *per Christum Dominum nostrum.* Qui, dum aquae sibi petiit potum a Samaritana praeberi, iam in ea fidei donum ipse creaverat, et ita eius fidem sitire dignatus est, ut ignem in illa divini amoris accenderet.

101. Leo Cunibert Mohlberg, Leo Eizenhofer, Petrus Siffrin, eds., *Sacramentarium Veronense* (Rome, 1956), no. 376. Reprinted in Ward and Johnson, *Prefaces of the Roman Missal*, 437.

102. Dumas, "Les préfaces du nouveau Missel," 22–23; see also Ward and Johnson, *Prefaces of the Roman Missal*, 123–51.

103. "Supplementum Anianense" in Jean Deshusses, ed., *Le Sacramentaire Grégorien*, t. 1, (Fribourg, 1971), no. 1566. Reprinted in Ward and Johnson, *Prefaces of the Roman Missal*, 135–36.

ut contemplantes tenebrosam pro- funditatem vitiorum, et relinquentes noxiarum hydriam cupiditatum, et te qui fons vitae et origo bonitatis es semper sitiamus, et ieiuniorum nostrorum observa- tione tibi placeamus.	
. . . through Christ our Lord. Who, in order to insinuate the mys- tery of your humility, sat down by the well, having become tired. Who asked the Samaritan woman to extend a drink of water to him, having caused the gift of faith to grow in her. And in this way he saw fit to thirst for her faith, so that while he asked for water from her, in her he ignited the fire of divine love. Therefore we implore your great mercy, that regarding the dark depth of sins, and relinquishing the water-pot of harmful lusts, we may always thirst for you who are the font of life and source of goodness, and by our Lenten observance please you.	*. . . through Christ our Lord.* Who, while he asked the Samaritan woman to offer him a drink of water, had already caused the gift of faith to grow in her, and in this way saw fit to thirst for her faith, so that he might ignite in her the fire of divine love.

Here, the obvious problem that the revisers seem to have with the
source text is its length. This prayer may represent non-Roman influence in the *Supplementum.* Indeed, Ward and Johnson believe that
the "ultimate liturgical source" is a much longer preface in the *Liber
Mozarabicus Sacramentorum.*[104] Whatever the case may be, it is clear

104. Ward and Johnson, *Prefaces of the Roman Missal,* 136. See M. Férotin, ed.,
Liber Mozarabicus Sacramentorum (Paris, 1912), no. 358. Reprinted in Ward and

to the revisers that although a "forgotten text" is available to fill this very specific gap in the corpus of prefaces, it cannot be used "as is." The length of the text is not its only problem. Although it begins with a recollection of Christ's self-revelation to the Samaritan woman, the purpose of this is to provide the context for supplication of God's mercy. The revisers simply remove this petitionary half of the prayer. The remaining text is made even shorter by removing the first two lines and one from the middle of the prayer (*dum ab ea aquam peteret*), which, despite forming a nice parallel construction (*ab ea peteret . . . in ea accenderet*), is redundant. The remaining changes—mostly of word order—are probably made to facilitate proclamation, understanding, and translation of the text. The final result is that a "forgotten" preface, whose length, petitionary elements, and relatively florid style would make a simple "revival" problematic, is nonetheless made to serve.

Our third example involves the process of "centonization" described above. In order to create a preface for use on Sundays during Advent, what is seen to be "of value" in two prefaces from the Verona Sacramentary is extracted and recombined. The boldface type and italicized type indicate which parts of the revised preface have been drawn from which parts of the two source texts.

Sacramentarium Veronense 184: VIIII, VI. [Preces in Ascensa Domini] Item alia[105]	*Sacramentarium Veronense* 179: VIIII, IIII. [Preces in Ascensa Domini] Item alia[106]	Missal of Paul VI Praefatio I de Adventu
Vere dignum: in hac die, quo Iesus Christus Filius tuus, Dominus noster divini consummato fine mysterii **dispositionis antiquae munus explevit,**	*Vere dignum:* teque suppliciter exorare, ut mentibus nostris tua inspiratione concedas, quo redemptor noster conscendit adtolli: *ut secundo mediatoris adventu manifesto munere*	*. . . per Christum Dominum nostrum.* Qui, primo adventu in humilitate carnis assumptae, **dispositionis antiquae munus implevit, nobisque salutis perpetuae**

Johnson, *Prefaces of the Roman Missal*, 136–37.

105. Mohlberg et al., *Sacramentarium Veronense*, no. 184. Reprinted in Ward and Johnson, *Prefaces of the Roman Missal*, 58.

106. Mohlberg et al., *Sacramentarium Veronense*, no. 179. Reprinted in Ward and Johnson, *Prefaces of the Roman Missal*, 58.

ut scilicet et diabolum caelestis operis inimicum per hominem quem subiugaret elideret, **et humanum reduceret ad superna dona substantiae.**	*capiamus,* *quod nunc audemus spe- rare promissum:*	**tramitem reseravit:** *ut, cum secundo venerit in suae gloria maiestatis, manifesto demum munere capiamus,* *quod vigilantes nunc audemus exspectare promissum.*
Truly meet [etc.]: on this day in which your Son Jesus Christ, our Lord, having accomplished the end of the divine mystery, **satisfied his role in the ancient plan,** indeed, so that by heav- enly works he might drive out the devil through man, which the enemy had subjugated, **and lead humanity back to the supernal gifts of their nature.**	*Truly meet [etc.]:* and to beg you humbly, that you would grant our minds to be exalted by your inspiration, for which reason our re- deemer ascended: *so that at the second com- ing of the mediator we may clearly obtain by his office* *what we now dare to hope for as a promise.*	*. . . through Christ our Lord.* Who, at his first coming in the humility of as- sumed flesh, **fulfilled his role in the ancient plan and opened for us the path of perpetual salvation:** *so that when he comes the second time in the glory of his majesty we may at last clearly ob- tain by his office what we who are vigilant now dare to look for as a promise.*

Interestingly, both of the source prefaces are for Ascension, not Advent. The choice is fitting, however, since the Ascension opens the historical season of waiting for the Lord's second advent, as *Veronense* 179
indicates. The first half of that prayer is a petition, so it is not surprising that the revisers leave it behind. They look instead to *Veronense* 184
for a connection to Christ's first advent. The emphasis in this prayer
is on Christ's "role" or "office" (*munus*) in God's "plan" (*dispositio*) for
humanity's redemption, but the addition of a line by the revisers links
the plan and the office to the incarnation. The word *munus* seems to be
the thread that connects the two sources and highlights Christ's role
as the mediator of God's plan and promise to redeem fallen humanity.
The decision to significantly alter the final phrase of *Veronense* 184 so
that the restoration of human "substance" or "nature" (*substantia*) is replaced by a more general reference to "salvation" is interesting. It may
represent an instance of adaptation to a "contemporary mentality"

that has difficulty appropriating a term like *substantia*, steeped as it is in ancient and medieval philosophy. Since the goal of centonization is not simply to retrieve an old text in its original form but to piece together a new prayer that meets the needs of the present-day church, there seems to be no reason to rule out a decision like this one. This work of hybridizing old texts, grafting a few new phrases onto them, and pruning where necessary ultimately produces a healthy preface that is the outgrowth of a living tradition of Roman Eucharistic prayer.

In our fourth example, the revisers adopt a procedure opposite to the one we have just seen. A single funeral preface found only in the "Saint Mark Fragment" of the Ambrosian *Sacramentarium Bergomense* is split to provide two new prefaces for the deceased.

Sacramentarium Bergomense "Fragmentum Sancti Marci" 40: Missa in die despositionis tertii, septimi vel trigesimi[107]	Missal of Paul VI Praefatio IV de Defunctis	Missal of Paul VI Praefatio V de Defunctis
VD aeterne Deus. Cuius imperio nascimur, cuius arbitrio regimur, cuius mysterio redempti sumus, cuius etiam praecepto in terra, de qua sumpti sumus, praevaricationis lege dissolvimur, atque tuo nutu resurrectionis ad gloriam, pulvis ex homine in hominem reparatur.	*. . . omnipotens aeterne Deus:* Cuius imperio nascimur, cuius arbitrio regimur, cuius praecepto in terra, de qua sumpti sumus, peccati lege absolvimur. Et, qui per mortem Filii tui redempti sumus, ad ipsius resurrectionis gloriam tuo nutu excitamur.	*. . . omnipotens aeterne Deus:* Quia, etsi nostri est meriti quod perimus,

107. "Fragmentum Sancti Mauricii," in Angelo Paredi, ed., *Sacramentarium Bergomense* (Bergamo: Edizioni Monumenta Bergomensi, 1962), 367–78; and also in Basilio Rizzi, "Il Frammento di San Maurizio," *Ecclesia Orans* III (1986): 147–80, 225–62, no. 40. Reprinted in Ward and Johnson, *Prefaces of the Roman Missal*, 513–14, 517–18.

Nostri est, Domine, meriti quod perimus; tuae vero pietatis et gratiae quod morte consumpti, redivivo cinere perpetuam revocamur ad vitam.		tuae tamen est pietatis et gratiae quod, pro peccato morte consumpti, per Christi victoriam redempti, cum ipso revocamur ad vitam.
Truly meet [etc.] eternal God. By whose command we are born, by whose judgment we are ruled, by whose mystery we were redeemed, and by whose precept on the earth from which we were taken we have been released from the law of transgression. By your command of resurrection to glory, dust from man is renewed into man. It is worthy of us, Lord, that we perish; but of your faithfulness and grace that we, consumed by death, as ashes reused are recalled to everlasting life.	*. . . almighty eternal God:* By whose command we are born, by whose judgment we are ruled, by whose precept on the earth from which we were taken we have been released from the law of sin. We who have been redeemed through the death of your Son to the glory of his own resurrection are raised by your command.	*. . . almighty eternal God:* For although it is worthy of us that we perish, nevertheless it is worthy of your faithfulness and grace that we, consumed by death because of sin, are redeemed through Christ's victory, with whom we are recalled to life.

The two "sentences" of the original Ambrosian preface can be split quite easily into two prayers, each of which is a self-contained meditation on death and resurrection. The major change that the revisers make to both halves is to explicitly link the death and resurrection of the deceased Christian to the death and resurrection of Christ. This is a very appropriate reference to make, especially here at the beginning of the Eucharistic prayer. This does mean that the original preface's imagery of "dust renewed" and "ashes reused" is lost, but it seems an acceptable sacrifice of figurative language in favor of a confident confession of faith in Christ's resurrection. Perhaps this represents a concession to the "sobriety" of the Roman euchological tradition. It is noteworthy that concern for the "contemporary mentality" does not lead the revisers to water down the statement that humanity is "deserving of death," even here in the context of a funeral Mass. Still, it is emphasized in the revised preface that human beings merit death specifically as the "wages of sin" (Rom 6:23; NRSV).

Our final example is a "new composition" for use during the fifth week of Lent and in Masses commemorating the Passion of the Lord. It is inspired by a sermon of Leo the Great.

Leo Magnus, *Sermo* 59, 7[108]	Missal of Paul VI Praefatio I de Passione Domini
O admirabilis **potentia Crucis**, o **ineffabilis** gloria Passionis, in qua et tribunal Domini, et **iudicium mundi et potestas** est crucifixi. Traxisti enim, Domine, omnia ad te, et cum expandisses tota die manus tuas ad populum non credentem et contradicentem tibi, **confitendae maiestatis tuae sensum totus mundus accepit.**	. . . *omnipotens aeterne Deus:* Quia per Filii tui salutiferam passionem **totus mundus sensum confitendae tuae maiestatis accepit,** dum **ineffabili crucis potentia iudicium mundi et potestas** emicat **Crucifixi.**
O wonderful **power of the Cross**, O **indescribable** glory of the Passion, in which there is the tribunal of the Lord and **the judgment of the world and the authority of the crucified.** Thus, Lord, you drew all things to you, and when you had stretched out your hands the whole day to an unbelieving people speaking against you, **the whole world understood that your majesty must be confessed.**	. . . *almighty eternal God:* Because through the saving passion of your Son **the whole world has understood that your majesty must be confessed,** while by the **indescribable power of the cross** **the judgment of the world and the authority of the Crucified** breaks forth.

---

108. S. Leonis Magnis, *Opera Omnia*, vol. 1, ed. J.-P. Migne, *Patrologia Latina* 54 (Paris: J.-P. Migne, 1846), 341. Reprinted in Ward and Johnson, *Prefaces of the Roman Missal*, 152.

Leo's sermon is already a "confession of faith in praise" that goes to the very heart of the paschal mystery, so it seems an ideal text on which to base a Eucharistic preface. Still, while Leo addresses the "Cross" and the "Lord," it is necessary for a preface to address God the Father. Bruylants says, "The structure which, pastorally as well as ideologically, is most favorable to an exact understanding of the role of the preface in the great Eucharistic prayer seems to be that in which we address our thanksgiving directly to the Father, through Christ, and in unison with the praise of the angels."[109] Therefore, the revisers adopt the procedure of selecting a few phrases from the source text and reordering them to create a new composition. The "majesty" confessed of Christ in the sermon is attributed to God the Father in the preface, though it is still made manifest through the Son's passion. It is interesting that the revisers set aside the adjective *admirabilis* ("wonderful") in favor of the apophatic *ineffabilis* ("indescribable") to "describe" the cross, as if in explanation of this Roman prayer's economy of words. In the final line of the preface, the use of the verb *emicat* ("it leaps/dashes/bursts/shines out") in place of *est* ("it is") more vividly expresses the shock of God's self-revelation in the crucifixion.

These five examples help to show how the revisers were able to maintain a rigorously "Eucharistic" character and a decidedly "Roman" style for all the prefaces despite relying on a wide variety of source texts. The following table, which follows Ward and Johnson in the designation of "new compositions," summarizes the kinds of sources employed:

Source	Prefaces	Percent
Former *Missale Romanum*	14	17
Ancient / Medieval Liturgical Documents	50	62
New Compositions	17	21
Total	**81**	*100*

Preserving the prefaces of the former *Missale Romanum* was clearly a priority, their shortcomings notwithstanding. Of the fifteen proper prefaces in the pre–Vatican II Missal, nine were preserved unchanged,

109. Bruylants, "Les préfaces du Missel Romain," 118.

two were revised,[110] and three received a different eschatol.[111] Only the preface for the Chrism Mass was scrapped, and even it appears to have influenced the new text that replaced it.[112] The gaps in the corpus of prefaces were large enough, however, that "forgotten" texts from liturgical books that had not been used for centuries had to serve as sources for the majority of the revised prefaces. As we have seen, there was rarely a one-to-one relationship between a source text and a new preface. Editing, centonization, and addition of newly composed material usually played significant roles in the formation of a final text. Slightly more than one-fifth of the revised prefaces were "new compositions" in the sense that they display no readily identifiable textual relationship with a liturgical antecedent, though some ancient and medieval prefaces may have offered inspiration. More frequently, non-liturgical sources influenced the composition of these prefaces.

Working with these various sources, the revisers decisively expanded the corpus of prefaces, thus filling in the gaps and providing many more choices of texts. The following comparison of the two Missals illustrates this:

110. The prefaces of the Epiphany and of the Apostles. See Ward and Johnson, *Prefaces of the Roman Missal*, 88–92, 436–40.

111. The prefaces of Easter, of the Ascension, and of the Holy Spirit. See Ward and Johnson, *Prefaces of the Roman Missal*, 176–81, 209–14.

112. See Ward and Johnson, *Prefaces of the Roman Missal*, 166–75.

113. Includes the following (prefaces in italics also included in the former *Missale Romanum*): Passion II, Palm Sunday, *Chrism Mass*, Eucharist I (Holy Thursday).

114. Actually the preface of the Trinity. See above.

115. Recall that the "common preface" in the former *Missale Romanum* contained nothing other than a protocol (*Vere dignum et iustum est, aequum et salutare, nos tibi semper et ubique gratias agree: Domine, sancte Pater, omnipotens aeterne Deus: per Christum Dominum nostrum.*) and an eschatol (*Per quem maiestatem tuam laudant Angeli, adorant Dominationes, tremunt Potestates. Caeli caelorumque Virtutes, ac beata Seraphim, socia exsultatione concelebrant. Cum quibus et nostras voces ut admitti iubeas, deprecamur, supplici confessione dicentes: Sanctus*). There was no embolism specifying the reasons for giving thanks, as in each of the fifteen "proper prefaces" (see above, pp. 355ff.). The six "common prefaces" of the Missal of Paul VI, on the other hand, are not "common" in the former sense, as each possesses a proper embolism in addition to a protocol and eschatol.

116. Includes the following (prefaces in italics also included in the former *Missale Romanum*): Presentation, Annunciation, Transfiguration, *Holy Cross, Christ the King, Sacred Heart, Trinity, Holy Spirit I*, Holy Spirit II, Eucharist II.

Season, Feast, or Ritual Mass	Former *Missale Romanum*	Missal of Paul VI (*editio typica*)
Advent	0	2
Christmas/Epiphany	2	5
Lent	1	10
Holy Week[113]	1	4
Easter/Ascension/Pentecost	2	8
Sundays in Ordinary Time	(1)[114]	8
Common Prefaces	1[115]	6
Mysteries of the Lord[116]	5	10
Feasts of Mary	1	4
Saints	2	12
Church Dedication	0	2
Marriage/Religious Profession	0	4
Deceased	1	5
Christian Unity	0	1
Total	**16**	**81**

Advent and Ordinary Time appear as the most impoverished seasons of the liturgical year in the former Missal, though Lent and Easter don't make out much better. Besides remedying these deficiencies, the revised Missal provides many more prefaces for Saints' feasts and for Masses celebrated around church dedications, marriages, and funerals. One might be concerned that this sudden quintupling of the number of prefaces represents the kind of unhealthy bloating that seems to have plagued the medieval liturgical books. The expansion might also be perceived as license for bishops' conferences, dioceses, and even individual priests to try their hands at composing their own prefaces. Dumas, however, thinks that the opposite is more likely. "Perhaps the prefaces, so often misunderstood because they demand more effort, take on today a value even greater than in other times. Indeed, before yielding to the insatiable itch of creativity, one will see in studying their texts that they are able to respond, if they are well chosen, to whatever one desires in adapting to seasons, to feasts, and to circumstances."[117]

117. Dumas, "Les préfaces du nouveau Missel," 28.

CONCLUSION: A CITY OR A GARDEN?

As we noted at the outset, Lauren Pristas has evaluated the work of *coetus* 18bis with respect to the other major task assigned to the study group: the revision of the orations of the Missal.[118] After examining both the principles and the results of this revision, she concludes: "Those responsible for the revision of the Missal made extensive changes to the corpus of Sunday and Holy Day collects. The result is not the revival of either a Roman or a non-Roman Latin liturgical tradition that fell into disuse over the centuries, but something essentially new."[119]

This "essentially new" body of prayers is tainted both by "an uncritical archeologism" and by "Enlightenment preoccupations and presuppositions."[120] Pristas criticizes Dumas in particular, who "exhibits a rather cavalier approach to tradition for he deems it entirely fitting for the men of a particular age to sift through a treasury amassed over two thousand years and separate, according to the lights of their own times, the wheat from the chaff."[121] This abandonment of "the conservative nature of liturgical reform prior to Vatican II" has the negative result that "Catholics of today . . . have far less liturgical exposure to the wisdom of the past and the wondrous diversity of Catholic experience and tradition than did the Catholics of earlier generations."[122]

The present essay has not offered any analysis of the orations, but since Pristas suggests that her conclusions may apply to other texts of the revised Missal, it seems necessary to consider them in light of our study of the prefaces. In the first place, then, it is difficult to identify anything "cavalier" in the approach taken by Dumas and his study group to the revision of the prefaces. As we have seen, nearly all of the prefaces from the pre–Vatican II Missal were preserved intact. The changes that were made were done in accordance with a "principle of truth" that is demonstrably the possession of ages prior to our own. Departure from the "true" character of the preface as *Eucharistia* is judged a "deviation" not on account of what the revisers would like

118. See n. 1.
119. Pristas, "Collects at Sunday Mass," 35.
120. Pristas, "Orations of the Vatican II Missal," 650; Pristas, "Theological Principles," 197.
121. Pristas, "Orations of the Vatican II Missal," 652.
122. Ibid.; Pristas, "Theological Principles," 197.

the preface to be but because their theology of the Eucharistic prayer is well grounded in a comprehensive history of the Roman liturgical tradition. Moreover, the revisers do not appear to be operating under the illusion that simple retrieval of the "oldest" form of a preface is always desirable or even possible. Neither do they thoughtlessly excise all material that challenges the "contemporary mentality," such as the statement that human beings "merit death" for their sins. Finally, there is simply no question but that the admittedly far-reaching revision of the prefaces has greatly expanded Catholics' "liturgical exposure" to the "wisdom" and "diversity" of the Catholic tradition of Eucharistic prayer, not restricted it. As Benedict XVI indicates by suggesting that the revised prefaces be used even in celebrations according to the preconciliar Missal, the current treasury of prefaces is much richer than it was, thanks to the work of the revisers.

Metaphors other than that of "treasury" could be applied to the corpus of prefaces. Pristas likens the "euchological texts of the Roman Missal"—at least before the revision—"to a great old city built up over time" that needs occasional "repair" but not much new construction and certainly not a "new . . . architectural plan."[123] While there is much to be said for this historical preservationist approach to liturgical reform, it seems to focus on the monuments of the tradition more than on the people who have to live inside them. In the case of the prefaces, at least, it is clear that history has been much more fluid than a metaphor of buildings and structures suggests. Even during the long period when the number of authorized prefaces was severely restricted, local creativity could not be entirely suppressed. Moreover, texts that have been used for centuries take on new meanings and new functions even as their history grows longer. Perhaps the work of revising liturgical texts is more like tending a garden than preserving a city's architectural monuments. In addition to caring for the best plants, it is necessary to weed out unhealthy ones, transplant some to more appropriate locations, prune back undesirable growth, graft new vines onto older stock, and plant new seeds. None of these activities need change the fundamental "character" of the garden as one grown "over the course of centuries."[124] Yet just as the tree shall be known by its fruit, the "authentic" liturgical tradition shall be known by the fruit it yields to the praying community today. Thus, Dumas concludes that

123. Pristas, "Orations of the Vatican II Missal," 651–52.
124. Cf. ibid., 651.

the revised prefaces are "like a fortifying and substantial nourishment that the church has given us with as much wisdom as generosity. It is for us not to neglect them in favor of food more agreeable but of lesser worth."[125]

125. Dumas, "Les préfaces du nouveau Missel," 28.

Acknowledgments

Matthieu Smyth's essay, "The Anaphora of the So-called 'Apostolic Tradition' and the Roman Eucharistic Prayer," originally appeared in French as "L'anaphore de la prétendue 'Tradition Apostolique' et la prière eucharistique Romaine," *Revue des sciences religieuses* 81, 1 (2007): 95-118. It was translated expressly for this collection of essays by Michael S. Driscoll. A somewhat different version appeared in *Usus Antiquior*, 1, 1 (2010): 5–25.

An earlier version of Neil J. Roy's essay, "The Mother of God, the Forerunner, and the Saints of the Roman Canon: A Euchological *Deësis,*" appeared as "The Roman Canon: Deësis in Euchological Form, " in Neil J. Roy and Janet E. Rutherford, eds., *Benedict XVI and the Sacred Liturgy* (Dublin: Four Courts, 2010), 181–99.

The editor wishes to thank the following for their permission to reprint previously copyrighted material in this volume:

Liturgical Press for permission to reproduce Eucharistic Prayer texts in English Translation from R. C. D. Jasper and G. J. Cuming, *Prayers of the Eucharist: Early and Reformed*, 3rd ed. (Collegeville, MN: Liturgical Press, Pueblo, 1987).

Contributors

John Paul Abdelsayed, a Coptic Orthodox priest, is a PhD student in the history of Christianity and liturgical studies at the University of Notre Dame, Notre Dame, IN.

Paul F. Bradshaw, a priest of the Church of England, is professor of liturgical studies in the Department of Theology, University of Notre Dame, Notre Dame, IN.

Michael S. Driscoll, a Roman Catholic priest of the Diocese of Helena, MT, is associate professor of liturgical studies in the Department of Theology, University of Notre Dame, Notre Dame, IN.

Hans-Jürgen Feulner, Roman Catholic, holds the Chair in Liturgiewissenschaft at the University of Vienna.

Albertus G. A. Horsting, Roman Catholic, is a PhD candidate in the history of Christianity at the University of Notre Dame, Notre Dame, IN.

Maxwell E. Johnson, a pastor of the Evangelical Lutheran Church in America, is professor of liturgical studies in the Department of Theology, University of Notre Dame, Notre Dame, IN.

Nathaniel Marx, Roman Catholic, is a PhD candidate in liturgical studies at the University of Notre Dame, Notre Dame, IN.

Anne Vorhes McGowan, Roman Catholic, is a PhD candidate in liturgical studies at the University of Notre Dame, Notre Dame, IN.

Walter D. Ray, Eastern Orthodox, is assistant professor and political papers archivist at Southern Illinois University, Carbondale, IL.

Neil J. Roy, a Roman Catholic priest of the Diocese of Peterborough, Canada, is visiting assistant professor in the Department of Theology at the University of Notre Dame, IN.

Nicholas V. Russo, a Melkite Catholic, recently received his PhD in liturgical studies at the University of Notre Dame, under the direction of Maxwell E. Johnson. He is teaching part-time at the University of Scranton, PA.

Matthieu Smyth, Roman Catholic, teaches liturgical history in the Faculté de Théologie Catholique, Université Marc Bloch, Strasbourg.

Bryan D. Spinks, a priest of the Church of England, is professor of liturgical study at the Yale Divinity School and Yale Institute of Sacred Music, New Haven, CT.

Michael Zheltov, a priest of the Russian Orthodox Church, is head and professor, holding the chair of practical and liturgical theology, at Sts. Cyril and Methodius Postgraduate and Doctoral School of the Russian Orthodox Church, and is professor at the Moscow Spiritual Academy.

Index

Benedict XVI, Pope, 350, 381; *see also* Ratzinger, Joseph.

Benedictus (qui venit), 122, 130, 142, 144–45, 163–64, 167–72, 174–81, 184, 187, 199, 201–2, 207, 211, 242

Birkat ha-mazon, 48–49, 102, 104, 353–54

Bobrinskoy, Boris, 232, 233 n. 53

Book of the Bee, 64

Botte, Bernard, 37, 44–46, 58, 71 n. 4, 72 n. 7, 73 n. 10, 77 n. 17, 82 n. 29, 83 n. 31, 88 n. 51, 94 n. 60, 95–96, 102, 142 n. 20, 192 n. 9, 239 n. 81, 277 n. 42, 328, 354–56, 357 n. 37

Bouley, Allan, 32 n. 44, 253 n. 134

Bouyer, Louis, 37, 88 n. 51, 99, 114, 119, 122, 125–26, 268 n. 15, 352–55, 357 n. 37, 358–59, 360 n. 50

Bradshaw, Paul, vii–viii, x–xi, xv n. 14, 1, 3 nn. 5–6, 9 n. 15, 16 n. 25, 17 n. 28, 18 n. 29, 28 n. 26, 30 n. 30, 66, 71 n. 4, 73 n. 11, 77 n. 16, 86 n. 37, 89 n. 56, 102 n. 21, 133 n. 17, 136 n. 19, 142 nn. 17–18, 152 n. 62, 158 n. 92, 178 n. 39, 179 n. 24, 182, 183 n. 49, 186, 220 n. 3, 222 nn. 8–9, 223 n. 13, 271 n. 22, 272 n. 25, 321 n. 25, 328 n. 3, 355 n. 28, 357 n. 39

Brightman, F. E., 150 n. 34, 193 n. 16, 225 n. 20, 269 n. 19, 270 n. 21, 272 n. 24, 290 n. 87, 300 n. 133

British Museum Tablet, 101, 117–18, 121, 132, 135, 142, 158, 179

Brock, Sebastian, 38 n. 74, 40 n. 78, 49 n. 116, 50 nn. 118–19, 56 n. 140, 58 n. 147, 147, 150, 185 n. 53, 208 nn. 65 & 67, 209 n. 69, 250

Brown, Peter L., 307 n. 2, 324

Brown, Raymond E., 2 nn. 2–3

Bruylants, Placide, 351, 360–66, 368, 377

Budde, Achim, 199 n. 42, 221, 237–38, 240 n. 86, 247–55, 257–61

Bulgakov, Sergei (Sergius), 335–36, 337 n. 23, 338, 339 n. 29, 343

Burreson, Kent, 157, 272 n. 25

Byzantine, viii, xi–xiii, 22 n. 6, 34, 40 n. 79, 57 n. 114, 118, 123, 142–43, 151, 189–91, 194, 196–200, 205, 209, 219, 222 n. 9, 223 n. 14, 224–26, 236, 240, 243, 253, 256, 259–60, 263–306

Byzantium, 224, 252, 275, 293, 299, 333

C

Cabasilas, Nicholas, 275–80, 283, 285, 300, 304

canon missae, viii, x, xiii, 35, 61, 197, 352 n. 10; *see also* Roman Canon.

Canons of Hippolytus, 73, 136, 158

Capelle, Bernard, 227 n. 29, 230–32

Catergian, Jospeh, 192 n. 9, 193 nn. 13–16, 194 nn. 17–22, 195 nn. 24–25, 196–97, 199

Chaldean Catholic Church, viii–ix, 21, 23–24, 41, 60

Chrysostom, John, 30, 35–37, 57, 153–54, 186, 280, 283, 286, 296

    Anaphora/Liturgy of St., 34, 60, 66, 87, 89, 91–93, 95, 118, 149–50, 153, 194, 197, 205, 221 n. 5, 263 n. 2, 270, 304, 325 n. 32

Church of the East, *see* Assyrian Church of the East.

Clement of Alexandria, 156, 165, 311

Clement of Rome, 329, 337, 348

    First Letter of/1, 124 n. 59, 136–37, 148, 187, 316

Collomp, P., 101 n. 13

Connolly, R. H., 47, 49 n. 117, 51 n. 122, 54 n. 130, 56 n. 138, 72 n. 7, 94 n. 61, 264 n. 5

consecration, viii, xii–xiii, 22 n. 6, 30, 33, 36, 41–42, 61, 67, 85 n. 36, 96, 157, 166–67, 182–83, 188, 223 n. 13, 244, 263–306, 324

Macomber, William F., 42–43, 45, 47, 48 n. 110, 56–58, 142, 143 nn. 24 & 26

Malabar, 41–43

Malka, viii–ix, 24, 25 n. 10, 51, 63–70

Mark, Anaphora of St., x, 76 n. 14, 77, 81, 83, 92–93, 96, 99–127, 141, 146, 148–50, 154, 158, 163, 175, 179, 221, 254, 304

Mark, Gospel of, 14, 15–17, 28

Maronite, 45, 48, 167

martyr(s), martyrdom, xiii, 19, 44, 46, 64, 74–75, 105, 107 n. 29, 109, 116, 136, 148, 215–16, 268, 307–25, 329–34, 336–37, 342, 344, 348

Marx, Nathaniel, xiii–xiv, xvi, 349

Matthew, Gospel of, 6 n. 10, 9–10, 15, 17, 28, 132

Mazza, Enrico, ix–x, 34, 79 n. 22, 82 n. 29, 83 n. 32, 87 n. 48, 99–100, 102 n. 22, 103–5, 107, 109–10, 114–15, 117, 119, 125–26, 161, 316

McGowan, Andrew, 28 nn. 26–27

McGowan, Anne Vorhes, xii, 219

Meßner, Richard, 173 n. 31, 176–78, 184

Metaphrastes, Symeon, 294

miracles, Eucharistic, 249 n. 101, 294, 297

Missal of Pope Paul VI, vii, xiii, 349–82

Missale Gothicum (*Vat. Lat. Reg.* 317), 82, 84, 92, 112

Mitchell, Leonel L., 157, 221 n. 6, 233–34

monophysite(s), 66, 285

Mosul, 21–22, 48

Mozarabic, 101, 107–8, 111, 115–16, 121 n. 52, 123, 358–59, 365

Mystagogical Catecheses, 10, 137 n. 24, 140–51, 153, 159, 272, 273

mystery, ix, 32, 39, 44, 45, 47, 49, 54–55, 61, 63, 67, 70, 75, 81, 135, 154, 204, 213, 215, 255, 284, 289, 290, 306, 343, 345, 359–61, 364, 371, 373, 375, 377

N

Narsai, 49, 54 n. 130, 56, 60, 94

Nestorius, Anaphora of, 24, 38, 50, 53, 54 n. 130, 55, 59–60, 66, 242, 252 n. 132, 254, 255

Nicaea, First Council of, 38, 156

Nicaea, Second Council of, 346

Nicephorus, Patriarch of Constantinople, 273–74, 288

O

oblation, 9, 24, 39, 52, 79, 84–85, 86 n. 40, 90, 93, 135, 174, 185, 204, 213, 266 n. 9, 308–9, 321, 323

odor, 113, 123–24 n. 58, 151, 317; *see also* fragrance.

offering, 19, 30 n. 32, 36, 39, 44, 47, 56 n. 138, 58 n. 146, 68, 75, 78, 82 n. 29, 83, 85, 90, 92, 96, 103–9, 111–17, 120–26, 131, 133–34, 136, 138, 150, 151 nn. 60–61, 152, 156 n. 81, 164, 204, 212, 217, 223, 228, 233, 248, 266, 270, 286, 291–92, 300, 309, 316–17, 323–24, 342, 357

Origen, 10, 38, 132 n. 14, 143, 148 n. 46, 154–56, 159, 162–63, 165, 187–88, 238, 265 n. 7, 323–24

P

Parsch, Pius, 342

Paul, St., 1, 4, 12, 17, 18, 28, 36, 42, 51, 309, 330, 337, 348

Paul VI, Pope, 327, 361; *see also* Missal of Paul VI.

Paverd, F. van de, 284 n. 64

Perpetua, 187, 308 n. 4, 312, 320, 332, 338, 340, 348

Peter, St., 35, 52, 6–65, 74, 140, 337–40, 348

Philo of Alexandria, 78 n. 20
Pionius, 313–14, 318–22
Pitt, W.E., 223 n. 14, 232
pneumatological, 61, 84–85, 90, 298
   n. 125, 299, 301, 338
Polycarp, xiii, 136, 313, 314–22
postbaptismal anointing, 29, 60,
   76–77, 168
Post-sanctus, 40, 50, 89, 121–24, 131,
   138 n. 25, 140 n. 6, 151 n. 61, 164,
   173, 175, 179, 201–4, 208, 211,
   222–23, 226 n. 25, 227, 230, 231 n.
   44, 232, 237, 238 n. 76, 241–43
prebaptismal anointing, 60, 166–68,
   183
Preface, vii, xiii, 81–82, 96, 100, 105,
   107–10, 112–13, 117, 119–20, 144,
   148–49, 179, 221–22, 230, 232,
   349–82
Presanctified, 194, 197, 301–3
Pristas, Lauren, 349, 350–51, 362 n.
   64, 380, 381
prosphora, 172, 295
Protheoria, 274–75
prothesis, 303–5
Pseudo-Denys/Pseudo-Dionysius,
   141, 169
Pseudo-Faustus of Byzantium, 247
Pseudo-Gregory of Nazianzen, 297

Q
Qedushah, 119, 169–70, 172, 175, 180
Qedušša, 241
Qumran, 143
Qurbana, ix, 24, 25, 63

R
Raes, Alphonse, 28 n. 23, 38 n. 75,
   180 n. 45, 231–32, 235 n. 66, 238
   n. 76
Rahmani, I., 88 n. 49, 227 n. 27
Ratcliff, E. C., 43 n. 89, 48, 83 n. 33,
   84, 142, 162, 164, 179 n. 41

Ratzinger, Joseph, 345–64; see also
   Benedict XVI, Pope.
Ray, Walter D., x–xi, 99, 102 n. 21,
   103 n. 24, 104 n. 26, 117 n. 45, 152
   n. 62
rāzâ, 45, 63, 70; see also mystery.
Roca-Puig, R., 81 n. 25, 101 n. 19,
   102–3 n. 23, 129 n. 2
Roman Canon, viii, x, xiii, 8 n. 12, 30,
   33–35, 61, 74, 76–78, 80–81, 83–86,
   87 n. 46, 92–95, 99, 102–3, 105,
   108–10, 114–15, 117, 119–23, 125,
   266, 276, 279, 324–25, 327–48, 350,
   354–57
Rome, viii, x, 18, 29, 41, 66, 71–72, 74,
   76, 81, 86–87, 95, 99, 107, 110, 120
   n. 51, 123, 125–27, 158, 280, 328,
   330–31, 337, 339–40, 348, 355
Rouwhorst, Gerard, 258, 259 n. 158
Roy, Neil J., xiii, 327
Russo, Nicholas, viii–ix, 21, 142 n. 21,
   143 n. 26

S
sacrifice, viii, 8–9, 18–19, 24, 50, 53,
   74–75, 78, 82, 84–85, 90, 92–93, 96,
   104, 106, 108, 111–15, 120–26, 131,
   134, 148–52, 163–64, 184–86, 200,
   208, 210, 212, 215–18, 223, 277,
   283–84, 294 n. 101, 308–13, 315–18,
   322–25, 332, 337, 354, 363, 367–68,
   376
saints, xiii, 74–75, 109, 111, 115, 116,
   173, 215–18, 224 n. 15, 245, 269,
   293, 308, 319, 322, 324–25, 327–48,
   350, 379
   martyrs as, 308, 324–25, 331
sanctification, 78, 84, 135, 164, 172,
   174, 223, 270–72, 282
Sanctus, viii, x–xi, xiv, 39, 48, 68, 78,
   80, 91, 94–96, 101–2, 107, 119, 121–
   25, 129, 130, 133, 138 n. 25, 139,
   141–46, 148–49, 159, 161–88, 199,